AUTHENTIC MEXICAN

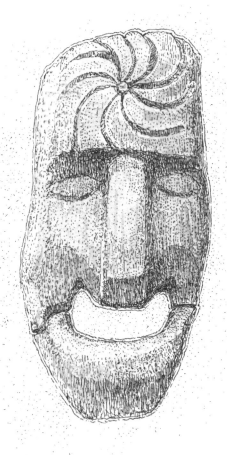

Cook's mask with hinged mouth

AUTHENTIC MEXICAN

Regional Cooking from the Heart of Mexico

Twentieth-Anniversary Edition

RICK BAYLESS
with
Deann Groen Bayless

Illustrations by John Sandford

Photographs by Christopher Hirsheimer

WILLIAM MORROW

An Imprint of HarperCollins Publishers

HarperCollins books may be purchased for educational, business, or
sales promotional use. For information please write: Special Markets
Department, HarperCollins Publishers, 10 East 53rd Street, New
York, NY 10022.

Twentieth-anniversary edition published by William Morrow in 2007.

Book design by Ginger Legato

Library of Congress Cataloging-in-Publication Data

Bayless, Rick
     Authentic Mexican.
     Bibliography: p.
     Includes index.
     1. Cookery, Mexican. I. Bayless, Deann Groen.
II. Title.
TX716.M4B29   1987   641.5972   86-12706

ISBN: 978-0-06-137326-8

09 10 11 RRD 10 9 8 7 6 5

*To the memory of Gladys Augusta Potter, my grandmother,
who taught me that you can bring a lot more than food
to the dinner table*

PREFACE TO THE TWENTIETH-ANNIVERSARY EDITION

In the mid-eighties, when my wife, Deann, and I were living in Mexico—traveling through every one of that country's thirty-one states, exploring age-old markets, working with local cooks to learn the dishes that had stood the test of time—I knew just what kind of cookbook was in the making. I was crafting firsthand reports of who was cooking what in Mexico, and exactly where they were doing it. I was amassing historical, geographical and social context for Mexico's regional cooking. And I was capturing vivid verbal snapshots of authentic ingredients and traditional techniques that seemed to be getting nudged out as more shoppers (yes, even in Mexico) opted for the less diverse packaged stuff at mega-stores like Aurrerá and Wal-Mart.

Clearly, I was writing a cookbook for Americans who would describe themselves as adventurous and dedicated cooks—definite fans of Mexican food. And I assumed (or at least hoped) that they had traveled (or hoped to travel) through Mexico, and had a hankering for the non-Americanized real thing. That didn't mean, however, that this motivated group wouldn't end up bewildered as they sorted through the great variety of Mexico's regional dishes and ingredients.

What those adventurous, dedicated souls needed, I resolved, was a cookbook that clearly explained the steps to traditional flavor within the context of both their American kitchens and the native kitchens of those who had created the traditions. Having lived for several years in Mexico after finishing an undergraduate degree in Spanish language and literature, followed by graduate studies in linguistics and anthropology, I was offering to become their guide and translator.

Little did I know how food and culture would evolve in the United States over the next twenty years. Hispanics, the majority of them Mexican, have become the fastest-growing immigrant group in North America. Which means two things: most non-Hispanic Americans don't have to travel south of the border to encounter a taste of real Mexico (there are "authentic" grocery stores and ma-and-pa restaurants catering to Mexicans popping up as fast as Starbucks), and once-rare ingredients like chipotle chiles, tomatillos and key limes are now available in American grocery stores. So easily available, in fact, that they've started taking on a new life in the American kitchen, flavoring everything from barbecue sauces to chutneys to salad dressings. *Dulce de leche* (aka *cajeta* in Mexico) has become one of the most popular Häagen-Dazs ice cream flavors. Salsa, as we've heard repeatedly from the news media, is outselling ketchup.

Regional Mexican ingredients are even available in fresher and more convenient forms. When I was writing *Authentic Mexican,* tinny-tasting canned tomatillos were all most Americans could find; now citrus-bright fresh tomatillos are our norm. Back then, cilantro was called "Chinese parsley," and those lustrous dark-green poblanos claimed almost no real estate in our country's produce departments. Smoky, spicy dried chipotle chiles used to be an American cook's dream; nowadays a quick search in practically any U.S. town will produce chipotles in a variety of forms: dried (both the tan and the red varieties), powdered, canned in *adobo,* even pickled. Cactus paddles, if you were lucky to stumble upon them twenty years ago, were slimy, pickly strips in a dusty jar; just yesterday I bought beautifully fresh paddles for grilling at my local natural-foods grocery. Recently, when I discovered that a national retailer had started canning roasted tomatoes—roasting tomatoes is a technique traditional Mexican cooks use to add sweetness and depth—I knew that traditional Mexican food had taken on a more expanded role in the American kitchen.

In short, the food of Mexico has started to shed its exotic, ethnic character and is moving right toward the mainstream. Even Mexican-American food (Tex-Mex, Cal-Mex, New-Mex or whatever regional variation seems appropriate) is evolving, trading in its cheese-covered heaviness for a fresher, lighter approach that characterizes much of the food that's eaten south of the border.

Yet all of this accessibility of ingredients and growing familiarity with Mexican cuisine hasn't eliminated the need for a good set of classic recipes. That's why I—like so many of you—continue to turn to *Authentic Mexican* for a really great tortilla soup or fresh corn-poblano chowder, for a soul-satisfying pork *tinga* or Yucatecan shrimp *a la vinagreta,* for street-style red chile enchiladas or that savory, fruity Oaxacan *mole* they call *manchamanteles.* The recipes I mined over many years from hundreds of Mexico's traditional cooks—and perfected in my American kitchen—have never let me down.

ACKNOWLEDGMENTS

A great number of people are responsible for the creation of this book: My mother and stepfather, Levita and Andy Anderson, and Deann's mother, Edith Groen, who provided generous support, both emotional and financial. The scores of Mexican cooks in markets, street stalls, small restaurants and homes, who shared both the details of their craft and a love for their specialties. Employees of the tourism offices all over Mexico, who went out of their way to supply information on local specialties and where to find them. The people running the gastronomical library at the offices of the Loredo restaurant group in Mexico City, who offered unlimited access to their collection of regional Mexican cookbooks. Cliff and Sue Small, who generously opened their Mexican home to us and introduced us to rural Mexican life. Carol Zylstra, Virginia Embrey and Maria Villalobos (and her mother), who shared their love for Mexican life, knowledge of little-known places and (in the case of Maria and her mother) delicious recipes. Fran and Jim Murray of Murray Western Foods in Los Angeles, who unflaggingly supported us through the years, and Peggy Playan, who was always encouraging and gracious in spite of our erratic consulting schedule. Craig Sumers and Brad Friedlander of Lopez y Gonzalez restaurant in Cleveland, who believed that regional Mexican dishes were not only very tasty but could attract an enthusiastic clientele. Many friends and family (especially Georgia and Dan Gooch, Floyd and Bonnie Groen, Paul and Macky Groen, Jewel and Bob Hoogstoel, Bill and Yvonne Lockwood, Jan and Dan Longone, Margot Michael, Nancy and Gary Oliver, Mary Jane and Steve Olsen, Pep and Ilene Peterson and Peg Tappe), who contributed valuable knowledge, encouragement and recipe-testing skills. LuAnn Bayless, my sister, who freely devoted a good portion of one summer to testing recipes with us, and Molly Finn, who tested recipes in New York. Maria Guarnaschelli, my editor, who saw value in my research and worked enthusiastically to give it a beautiful, easily usable form. Amy Edelman, my copy editor, who scrutinized all the details with amazing rigor, unearthing lost ingredients and taming wayward punctuation. Molly Friedrich, my hardworking agent, who gives sound advice. And finally, John Sandford, whose kindness and sensitivity have made him a treasured friend and whose brilliant illustrations lovingly celebrate regional cooking from the heart of Mexico. My respect and thanks to you all.

Twenty years later: Thank you to those who helped us realize the twentieth-anniversary edition: Christopher Hirsheimer for photos that so perfectly capture the heart of Mexico; Doe Coover for organizing the details; and Stephanie Fraser, David Sweeney and Michael Morrison from HarperCollins for seeing it to completion.

CONTENTS

INTRODUCTION

❖

Beans and dry goods, Guadalajara market

THE TWO WORLDS OF MEXICAN COOKING

My taste buds were trained on Mexican food. And it was real Mexican food to our family: hot tamales and tacos from a little drive-in wedged in between a greasy auto-repair yard and a hubcap seller, and El Charrito down on Paseo with its oozy cheese-and-onion enchiladas smothered with that delicious chile gravy. We knew it was authentic, assertive, almost wickedly good Mexican fare, and we knew there were few places to find it outside Oklahoma City.

In Austin at El Patio, we found the food tasty, as we did at Mi Tierra and at a few places on up through Dallas and Forth Worth. But in New Mexico, even the best-loved Mexican restaurants served dishes that, to my taste, were unexpectedly different. And when I made it to totally Mexican East Los Angeles some years later, I truthfully came across nothing with that familiar savor of home. I ate in the recommended family-run joints—the ones that reminded me of the tamale drive-in back home, and El Charrito and El Patio. Oh, the food was good, but not like the Mexican food that heritage had convinced me was the best.

There in East L.A., they claimed to serve the real food of Mexico . . . and *that* I found surprising.

I suppose it's that way with most folks who've learned the world's cuisines at their local eateries and loved them. Then they venture out; they set that first foot onto foreign soil, and their noses don't catch a whiff of anything expected. Menus filled with the best (even better-than-the-best) versions of dishes they'd learned at home never materialize. And they return home, a little more world-wise, to report with disappointment (and a little pride) that Mexican food down at Pablo's, say, is better than anything you can find in Mexico.

When I first saw Mexico and ate what it offered, I was too innocently captivated by foreign ways to afford myself that opinion. I lapped up what was put before me, was convinced I loved it, and, of course, felt it necessary to feign at least some understanding. But with time that wonderment wore off, and I began to see that I would have to either go back to the El Charrito I knew so well or figure out what these puzzlingly enticing dishes really were and why they weren't like anything at home.

I did both. And after a number of years shuffling between the two cultures, I have come to a simple answer: There have developed two independent systems of Mexican cooking. The first is from Mexico, and (with all due respect to what most of us eat and enjoy in this country) it is the substantial, wide-ranging cuisine that should be allowed its unadulterated, honest name: Mexican. The second system is the Mexican-American one, and, in its many regional varieties, can be just as delicious. But its range is limited, and to my mind it forms part of the broader system of North American (or at least Southwest North American) cookery.

Mexico's Mexican food has rarely been imported to the United States, except to a few well-insulated Mexican neighborhoods like the one in East Los Angeles and some on the South Side of Chicago. The Mexican-American style of cooking seems to win out most everywhere else that *paisanos* set up shop. Even in the small family restaurants, the inflexible health-department guidelines must be conformed to, the "general" customer's tastes accommodated. Progress, sadly, seems to be made most quickly by North Americanization.

What I've discovered, though, while teaching Mexico's Mexican cooking throughout the United States, is that most North Americans don't really even know well-prepared Mexican-American foods. Their unhappy experience is often limited to some mass-produced takeoff on the Southwest Traditional at a Chi Chi's or El Torito's or whatever the regional chain restaurant is called. And unfortunately, at the hands of such forces, Mexican-American food seems to have suffered unmercifully, to have become a near-laughable caricature created by groups of financially savvy businessmen-cum-restaurateurs who saw the profits in beans and rice and margaritas.

Mexico and the fare of its peoples is thoroughly different from all that, and most North Americans are understandably unprepared for it. The repertory is broad and variable, and it reflects the history and individuality of the country's distinct regions. Much of the produce is local and seasonal, not yet genetically engineered. Mexico's European-and-Indian soul feels the intuitions of neither bare-bones Victorianism nor Anglo-Saxon productivity.

Frankly, Mexican fare and its attendant customs can be so unexpectedly different that many first-time visitors to our next-door neighbor find themselves taking refuge in the Denny's or the continental dining rooms simply from the stun of its rich diversity. But with the most rudimentary introduction, the unexpected can become anticipated. And then, perhaps, comfortable and magnetic, as it has for me.

MEXICO'S CULINARY HERITAGE

When the first Spaniard set foot on New World soil, he was, without knowing it, breaking the seal on a highly developed world of altogether different plants, animals and people. Fully six and a half millennia earlier, the humans that had hunted and gathered on this continent began to settle into agricultural ways, and through those centuries they developed one of the major horticultural systems in the history of humankind.

The earliest foods to emerge in the agricultural camp were some beans and a squash that at first seemed good only for its meaty seeds, then for its golden flowers and tender leaves, and finally for its edible pulp. Nutritive, tasty chiles were added, and, within a short thousand years or two, the primal kernels of the corn cob—the builders and sustainers of American civilization—had been tamed from the tiny wild grain.[1] "In focusing their attention on maize, beans, and squash," say Peter Farb and George Armelagos in *Consuming Passions*, "the domesticators thus merely had to copy a natural model. Both in their habits of growth and in the nutrition they offer, the three plants complement one another."[2]

Now, the way those early domesticators had developed for making edible their domestic and wild-gathered produce would probably not have stimulated anyone's culinary curiosity. But by 1519, when the Spaniards made their conquering march into the future home of Mexico City, all that had changed.

The peoples that made up the Meso-American empires had orchards full of avocados, coconuts, papayas, pineapples, prickly pears and a long list of others whose names don't ring familiar in our ears. Their farms grew the father of our red tomato and a little green husk "tomato"; there were chiles, manioc, sweet potatoes, four kinds of squash, peanuts and at least five major strains of beans. *Epazote* was the herb of preference (as it is today), and there were huge quantities of amaranth and *chía* seeds to make into porridge and unleavened cakes.

The Aztecs' domination was felt far and wide in this part of America. They had subjugated all the competition from Yucatán to barren Northern Mexico, but it was a top-heavy domination that sucked all but the guts out of many of the neighboring societies. Everyday people were on a subsistence diet of sweet or chilied *atole* (porridge), some beans and the necessary allotment of tortillas; meat was scarce and fruit only a little less so.[3] When shortages came, the people's recent emergence from the less civilized life of nomadic gatherers showed through: The whole system lacked a fundamental stability.

But in the face of all this uncertainty, the lordly houses had tables set with such brilliant flavors and ingeniously constructed dishes that their presence is still felt in the best Mexican kitchens. Beyond the simple boiled or pit-cooked domestic turkeys, Muscovy ducks, venison and little dogs, these households commanded all manner of wild quails and peccary, pigeons and a remarkable variety of fish and shellfish from the coasts as well as local waters.[4]

Cortés described the dishes at Emperor Montezuma's table as being of four classes: meat, fish, herbs and fruit.[5] The great, good Friar Sahagún was more detailed in his astoundingly thorough enthnography of that early Aztec society. He detailed two basic sorts of sauces for the stewed dishes that simmered in

❖ ───

[1] Paul C. Mangelsdorf, Richard S. MacNeith and Gordon R. Willey, "The Origins of Agriculture in Middle America," *Handbook of Middle American Indians*, ed. Robert Waushope (Austin, TX: University of Texas Press, 1964), vol. 1, pp. 430–431.

[2] Peter Farb and George Armelagos, *Consuming Passions* (Boston: Houghton Mifflin, 1980), p. 202.

[3] Jacques Soustelle, *Daily Life of the Aztecs on the Eve of the Conquest*, trans. Patrick O'Brian (Stanford: Stanford University Press, 1961), pp. 148–154.

[4] Ibid.

[5] Hernán Cortés, *Conquest: Dispatches of Cortés from the New World*. Intro. and commentary by Irwin Blacker (New York: Grosset and Dunlap, 1962), p. 61.

the traditional earthenware *cazuelas*. One was thickened with ground pumpkin-seeds and flavored with red chiles and tomatoes—called *pipián* in the mid 1500s when Sahagún wrote, and still known by that name today. The second was a kind of chile sauce or tomato sauce, depending on your perspective and the proportions of ingredients.[6]

Most royal homes served this kind of highly flavored food with tortillas of all sorts. Some were smooth, others made from rough-ground corn. The cooks prepared *tlacoyos* and *gorditas* like the ones popular today; and Aztecs apparently loved *tamales* and turnovers as much as their modern ancestors do.[7]

The greatest concentration of royal households was in the capital, Tenochtitlán. And there is little doubt that the streets of this beautiful city were some of the most active in the world of that time. The market was massive enough to hold sixty thousand souls buying and selling, estimated Hernán Cortés.[8] It was filled with incalculable variety, and varieties of variety, according to Sahagún. Beans, fish, chiles, meat . . . even prepared stews and sauces, roasted meats and guacamole.[9] The whole must have been spectacular, and, in spite of the passing of four centuries and disparate rulers, it sounds not unlike the aggressively sensual offerings in and around the colossal Merced market at the center of present-day Mexico City.

The first city was cultured—albeit from a different source than our culture—and, perhaps for the first time, the Spaniards encountered a sect that thought *them* rather barbaric. Of course, the opposite was true in other respects, but it's clear from what was written down by Cortés and his soldier Bernal Díaz del Castillo that the refinements of the Aztec ruling class were impressive. They both described the banquets with myriad dishes, the ceremonial handwashing, the beautiful red and black dishes and the gilded chocolate cups filled with that foaming, exotically flavored drink of nobles.[10]

By a decade after the 1521 fall of Tenochtitlán, the Mexican natives had already adopted a new set of flavors into their existing large assortment. There seemed to be an "absence of strong cultural resistance to the introduction and use of foreign plants," as one researcher found recently when he tried to discover what had become of so many of those pre-Columbian crops in modern Mexico.[11]

---

[6] Fray Bernardino de Sahagún, *General History of the Things of New Spain*, trans. and annotated by Arthur J. O. Anderson and Charles E. Dibble (Santa Fe, NM: The School of American Research, 1953), vol. 9, pp. 37–40.

[7] Ibid., and Ana M. de Benítez, *Cocina prehispánica* (México, D.F.: Ediciones Euroamericanas, 1974), pp. 34–48.

[8] Cortés, op. cit., p. 55.

[9] Sahagún, op. cit., vol. 10, pp. 65–94.

[10] Bernal Díaz del Castillo, *The Conquest of New Spain*, trans. J. M. Cohen (Harmondsworth, Middlesex: Penguin Books, 1963), pp. 224–227; and Cortés, op. cit., p. 61.

[11] Angel Palerm, "Agricultural Systems and Food Patterns" in Robert Waushope, ed., *Handbook of Middle American Indians*. (Austin, TX: University of Texas Press, 1967), vol. 6, p. 44.

Spice traders brought cinnamon, black pepper and cloves; everyone wanted the common European thyme, marjoram and bay leaves.[12] As early as the second voyage of Columbus, the first load of wheat, chickpeas, melons, onions, radishes, salad greens, grapes, sugar cane and fruit stones had made their way to America.[13]

Though the Indians knew well the ways of agriculture, they had domesticated only a small selection of animals. So when the Spaniards came with horses, hogs, cattle and chickens, they were welcomed immediately. By the end of Cortés's life, meat was plentiful, wheat bread was cheap, rice was growing where wheat and corn could not; in fact, most all the fruits, vegetables and other new important food crops like sesame seeds, almonds and citrus were in the land.[14]

But several European foodstuffs failed to thrive in America, and that, of course, meant that the Spanish diet found itself in a state of transition perhaps as great as that of the Indians. Olive trees yielded little, so there was little oil; grapevines did quite miserably, which meant—devastatingly for the Spaniards—less wine. The newcomers never lovingly embraced the ubiquitous corn, but their wheat did well and the meat those Iberian cattle ranchers relied on grew at a rate previously unknown.[15]

Bernal Díaz describes a 1538 banquet in the court of the Spanish conquerors that lays bare the early tastes of the Spanish branch of the Mexican family. They had a sweet tooth (Spain had just reconquered its own land from seven centuries of sweet-loving Arab domination), and they served great quantities of marzipan and their other favorites. They made little birds in a pickling sauce (*escabeche*) that Yucatecans still prepare; they put together salads and vegetable dishes; they roasted meats; they set out cheese and bread and dishes made with lots of eggs; and they showed plainly their newly acquired partiality for the cup of chocolate.[16]

For several centuries that strain of Spanish blood stayed as pure as any of them could have hoped for in a land as alluring as Mexico. But all the while, of course, the Indian blood was becoming more mestizo, and stronger, and less content with the pure-white ruling crust. The War of Independence in 1821 was the first blow to the Crown, but not so much to the whites' control. Then, in the revolution of 1910, the world saw a change: the emergence of a new Mexico, a more honestly mestizo Mexico.

The food that the people of this newly emerged country put on their tables had seen a slow, four-century evolution—a flowing together of royal Aztec court tradition, ecumenical Old World Spanish fare and bits and pieces left from

❖ ———

[12] Virginia Rodríguez Rivera, *La comida en el México antiguo y moderno* (México, D.F.: Editorial Pormaca, 1965), p. 10.

[13] Alfred Crosby, Jr., *The Columbian Exchange* (Westport, CT: Greenwood Press, 1972), pp. 67–68.

[14] Ibid., pp. 70, 76–77, 106–108.

[15] Ibid., pp. 71–72, 76, 98.

[16] Bernal Díaz del Castillo, *Historia verdadera de la Nueva España* (Buenos Aires: Espasa-Calpe Argentina, 1955), p. 627.

French, North American and other people's involvement. Perhaps it had seen its first independent life in the kitchens of the ubiquitous convents, where the Spanish nuns had to work hand-in-hand with Indian girls who knew the country's produce. Or it may have been the everyday cooks whose inventiveness led them to pepper their well-proved cooking with all things new. Whatever it was, the roots of today's Mexican food are buried deep in the first native tastes and traditional ways. And like all things that reveal Indian heritage, mestizo Mexican cooking has been a long time in coming out of the back rooms, market *fondas* and street stalls into respectable spots where it can be enjoyed at its delicious best.

THE TAPESTRY OF MEXICAN FLAVOR

The Mexican Marketplace

In the middle of the market, practically any Mexican market, the floor is rough, stained concrete; it's dark enough in the cavernous room that some vendors have turned on the one or two bare, weak bulbs they've strung over their goods to show the blush on the mangoes, the crimson skin of the tomatoes or the fine, green, fresh-dug *cilantro* (coriander). There is a damp coolness that hangs close to the ground and a thick, constantly evolving aroma that hovers and roams; by the end of the day, or the year, the aroma will have become every aroma.

A woman with cropped, curled hair stands a few steps up behind a series of wide sturdy baskets set onto her tiered countertop. Her face is unengaged, as if her spirit had taken refuge elsewhere, until the approach of a potential customer triggers the automatic "*¿Qué va a llevar?*" ("What are you going to take?") into the noisy mixture of identical questions from neighboring stalls. Her bronze hands sweep past her mounds of black or yellow or pinto or white beans, past her large kernels of dried corn, past her rice.

The wave of entreaties follows the customers through the market, through aisles of vegetable sellers whose counters are large angled troughs heaped with small firm-textured potatoes, sweet potatoes, fresh field corn, green-and-tan pumpkins and masses of ripe-smelling tomatoes so perfectly beautiful they could bring tears to a North American eye. The heavy produce gives way to neat piles of *tomatillos,* cactus paddles and round light-green squash, to little pyramids of black- or green-skinned avocados, to bunches of Swiss chard, spinach and dock, to huge mounds of large green chiles to buy by the kilo.

The air gets close and fills with a sanguinary smell at the end of the aisle, where the butchers have their refrigerated cases. You can take the step up onto the wooden platform that lies in front of each stall to peer at the fresh beef, or what's been dried or half-dried; you can point to the part of the pork loin you want, inspect the plumpness of the chickens, survey the age on the sausage or choose the largest eggs.

Someone has dragged in an old wooden table to display his once-a-week sale of goat or lamb. There's another make-shift stand with dried fish and shrimp, and a lady with a three-foot basket of hot *bolillo* rolls she's carried from the bakery.

The fish sellers have easy-to-wash concrete slabs where they set out their snapper, snook, mullet, catfish, shark and mackerel. Perhaps there are little crabs if the market is near the ocean, perhaps shrimp, squid and octopus. Certainly there are a dozen or more varieties awaiting the stewpot or skillet.

In one way or another it all goes into the stewpot or skillet—the beans, dried corn and rice, the vegetables, greens, chicken and the like. For these are the essential components of the Mexican diet, though certainly not what gives that diet its well-known character.

No, it's the chiles—the dried, fresh and pickled chiles, the sweet and the *picante* chiles—that make it seem really Mexican. And the spices like cinnamon, clove, cumin, anise and black pepper; the herbs like *cilantro, epazote,* thyme, bay leaves and marjoram; the sprinkling of milky, acidy, salty fresh cheese; the sharp, raw red or white onion or the freshly squeezed lime juice. Plus that sweet aromatic undercurrent of well-cooked garlic and white onion that runs through most of the dishes on the table. Those are the distinctive flavors that make Mexico's essential nutritional elements taste Mexican. And they're scattered in the market, too, in among the other vegetables or the greens, or set out in small baskets in front of the congregation of spice sellers.

Tradition has taught the cooks how to weave the flavorings together into well-loved combinations that lift the national spirit (or at least reaffirm it). The crowds on the waterfront near downtown Veracruz enjoy tostadas topped with lime-marinated fish with tomato, green chile and fresh coriander; they eat tacos from the tiny *taquerías* and lace them with avocado enriched with tomato, green chile, fresh coriander and lime (guacamole) or with the relishlike *salsa mexicana* of tomatoes, green chile, fresh coriander, onion and a little lime or vinegar. Ripe, raw tomato, green chile, lime . . .

The Mexican tourists come to that port town to order their spicy crab soup (*chilpachole*) with its well-cooked base of pureed tomatoes sparked with *chipotle* or other dried hot chiles. They wouldn't think of leaving without their fish *a la veracruzana* in fresh, chunky tomato sauce mellowed with herbs and simmered with pickled green chiles. At breakfast, they eat fried eggs with the traditional *ranchera* sauce of coarsely pureed tomatoes, onion and green chiles; or perhaps they want their everyday favorite of eggs scrambled with onion, tomato and green chiles. Tomatoes cooked with chiles: The cooks of every region make a sauce with them and brand it with their own methods or special ingredients.

The same is also true, though certainly to a lesser extent, when the tomato is replaced with the small, husk-covered, tart *tomatillo.* It makes bright-tasting sauces and stew bases, flecked with coriander or simmered with *epazote. Tomatillo* and chile: another classic Mexican flavoring.

A fourth is more foreign to the American taste, though once it has burrowed itself into your memory, there is no scent or savor that spells Mexico any more completely. It is found in the celebratory *mole,* with its pulpy puree of rehydrated dried red chile seasoned with cinnamon, cloves and black pepper. And since it's a fiesta dish, the deep-red chile sauce is thickened with nuts and seeds and, of course, flavored with chocolate. But every day, cooks in every region soak their chiles, puree and prepare them to suit their tastes. Mixed with vinegar for a flavorful marinade, seasoned with cumin for a stew, ground with pumpkinseeds for the centuries-old *pipián*—they're all tasty examples of sauces and stews thick with once-dried chiles.

Dishes would all carry the national stamp if they were prepared with these four distinctive combinations of flavors; but without the exuberant, lively, traditional garnishes, the dishes would seem like half-breeds. They need their crunchy raw onion or sprinkling of crumbled, sharp, fresh cheese. Almost no brothy soup would taste quite right without a squirt of fresh lime, perhaps a little dried oregano or spoon of crushed dried chile or diced green chile. Snacks would speak with the wrong accent if there was no crunchy lettuce or fresh cabbage, no chile sauce (the bottled, vinegary stuff or a traditional blend of hot dried chiles, *tomatillos* and garlic). Without the colorful, flavorful contrasts that the garnishes give, nothing would taste or look like the beautiful, traditional fare I'm so partial to.

Ways of the Mexican Kitchen

My tongue tells me it isn't solely the staples and spices that make the flavor, but almost equally as much the way those Mexican foodstuffs are reduced to saucy mixtures or simmered into warm soups or stews. Rudimentary boiling, unsurprisingly, is the way to soften the dried corn, the beans and tough meat, but in the old Mexican kitchen boiling also mixed in the earthy taste of the clay cooking pots they call *cazuelas.* Nowadays, glossier materials are beginning to take the clay's place, so the everyday boiling is simply that: a long, tenderizing bubbling in a pot.

There are two techniques that still give a distinctive Mexican flavor, though. The first I call the *asar* technique, from the verb *asar,* meaning to broil, brown, roast, sear, toast (to offer a handful of English words that convey a little of what happens when the *asar* technique is employed). The large green chiles are flame-roasted, then peeled; dried ones are toasted on a griddle to deepen their flavor and release their aroma into the room. Garlic is turned in its skin on a hot, dry surface beside the tomatoes and *tomatillos;* they blacken and blister, while their flavor concentrates and mellows. Meat is seared on the open fire, and the corn dough called *masa,* in all its forms from tortillas to boat-shaped *sopes,* is cooked on the dry iron or clay surfaces. The flavors intensify, they deepen and take on a savory earthiness.

The second technique that gives Mexican distinction to many cooked dishes is the initial searing of the pureed sauce ingredients, the "frying of the sauce" as I often call it. A little fat in a hot pan, then in goes the chile or tomato puree, and it sizzles vigorously and fries and concentrates into a thick mass. In essence, it takes on a seared quality, that makes, say, a Mexican tomato sauce seem quite unrelated to the slow-simmered Italian spaghetti sauces.

The last of the techniques that set Mexican cooking apart is the grinding. It began millennia ago with corn crushed on a rock slab (*metate*) to make the dough for tortillas. The slab proved good for grinding rehydrated chiles, for nuts and seeds, for cacao beans and even the tender curds of fresh cheese. A bowl-shaped rock mortar (*molcajete*) worked for spices and contained the juices of tomatoes and *tomatillos.* And until recently, it was those hand-powered grinders that blended the nutritious flavorings into the often-used, thick, tasty purees. Now it is the electric blender or spice grinder, with fast-running blades, but the effect isn't the same. The blender whirs and chops it all into small bits, where the old *metate* and *molcajete* crushed the foodstuffs and smoothed them into a paste. In my mind, there is little doubt that the stone slab makes the best *moles,* though it's out of most North Americans' range. The mortar, on the other hand, is manageable and one of the most useful pieces of kitchen equipment: to powder spices so you get their full aroma, or to pound chiles, garlic and tomatoes into a deliciously thick-textured sauce.

Each element—the staples, the flavorings, the garnishes and the cooking techniques—makes it Mexican food; how, when and where it's eaten make it Mexican life.

Regional Tastes

". . . Mexico has a faint, physical scent of her own, as each human being has" was D. H. Lawrence's observation. To me it seems strange, almost paradoxical, that such a singular scent could linger over a country as diverse as Mexico—but it does.

The land mass itself, as it has been arbitrarily contained and divided by modern governments, is only one third the size of our United States. Yet it rises and falls with more variety of plant life and human life, more formations and colors and textures and smells and tastes than any country on earth. Each of Mexico's six regions[17] mixes a distinct aroma into the persistent scent that gives Mexico its

---

[17] I have cut up the country into six regions, each one with its own style of cooking. Some analysts may have drawn the lines a little differently, but rarely will you meet a Mexican who doesn't clearly differentiate six main breeds of his compatriots: Chilango (Mexico City), Tapatío (Guadalajara), Jarocho (Veracruz), Norteño (the North), Yucateco (Yucatan) and Oaxaqueño (Oaxaca). It was those personalities that formed the core of each of my regions. From there, I looked at the natural topographical divisions of the land, the climate and vegetational zones; I matched them with

Mexican unity; each region displays a different facet of the Mexican cook's resourcefulness, tradition and imagination.

Central Mexico illustrates the duality of *lo mexicano:* the Spaniard and the Aztec, the modern and the earth-bound primitive. The famous sparkling candy shops of Puebla line up a few blocks from the old market where the classic, centuries-old *mole poblano* gurgles in huge *cazuelas,* fragrant with dried chiles, herbs and spices. Just miles from Mexico City's most elegant restaurants are the Tolucan Indian produce vendors with their dozens of herbs—both medicinal and culinary—and their colorful array of wild mushrooms.

Southern Mexico, particularly Oaxaca, exhibits a vital Indian heritage. The black-braided Indian cooks mix a remarkable variety of dried peppers into Mexico's most varied sauces and stews. It is savory, well-spiced fare redolent with sweet spices like cloves and cinnamon; it is complex and distinctive, and it's flavored with the sure hand of tradition.

West-Central Mexico is thoroughly mestizo. It is the essence of national flavors drizzled on crispy fried pork *carnitas* or sprinkled in a bowl of *pozole.* It is the home of *mariachis* and tequila, of fried tacos and red-chile enchiladas. It is, perhaps, Mexico's most prominent profile, the one least obviously chiseled from ancient Indian ways.

The Gulf states are warm tropical states that rise up from the well-stocked coastal waters to cool mountains known for growing good coffee. This is the land of simple, well-seasoned cooking—fish with tomatoes, herbs and olives, spicy crab soup, turnovers and butter-fried plantains. There is something of a European character to the spicing and garnishing and there's a Caribbean lilt to the songs that are sung.

The Yucatán, though half on the Gulf and half on Caribbean waters, owes little to either. The Yucatán is Mayan, and its original settlers were a progressive, independent lot. In fact, the Yucatán has remained so independent that the national Mexican scent is faintest there, overwhelmed almost entirely at times by the beloved *achiote* seasoning. The regional specialties are among Mexico's most unusual: from the pork in banana leaves to the egg-stuffed, pumpkinseed-sauced *papadzules,* from wild turkey with *masa*-thickened white sauce to chicken with vinegar and spices. When you taste the delicate balance of Yucatecan seasoning, the complex red-chile sauces traditional in the rest of Mexico seem countries away.

If pressed to choose the culinary element that ties together diverse Northern Mexico, I'd have to say it is fire: smoky hot embers. They give character to fish on the west coast, kid around Monterrey and steaks nearly everywhere. They add char to the rustic taste of beef jerky and chewiness to *chorizo* sausage. Northern flavors are forthright, frontier flavors—just the kind to wrap in warm flour tortillas.

---

ethnic concentrations, histories and state boundaries. And the regional divisions that emerged have proved as useful for capturing culinary distinctions, I think, as they have for all others.

Mexico

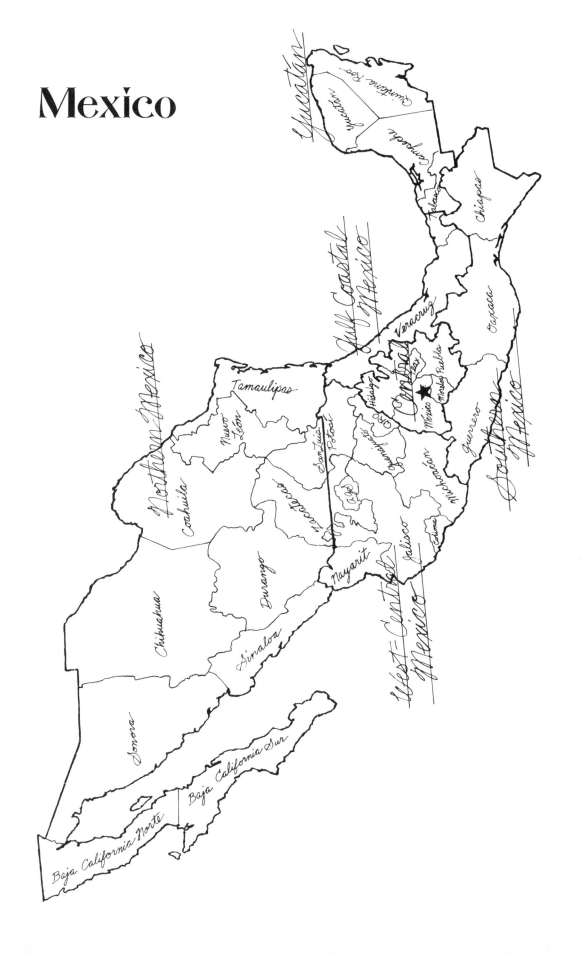

Yucatán

Quintana Roo

Yucatán

Campeche

Tabasco

Chiapas

Gulf Coastal Mexico

Veracruz

Oaxaca

Northern Mexico

Tamaulipas

Nuevo León

Hidalgo

Central Mexico

Tlax.

Morelos Puebla

México

Guerrero

Southern Mexico

Coahuila

San Luis Potosí

Querétaro

Guanajuato

Michoacán

Zacatecas

Ags.

Durango

Jalisco

Colima

Chihuahua

Nayarit

West-Central Mexico

Sinaloa

Sonora

Baja California Norte

Baja California Sur

MEXICO, EATING

As Mexico's independent gastronomical traditions evolved from the remnants of Aztec grandeur and Spanish forcefulness, the countrymen grasped those traditions with tenacity. And, during that evolution, all this feeding and being fed entered as much into the public domain as it stayed in the private one. Today, one of the most noticeable characteristics of the Mexican table is that it's filled with people, exchanging some common spirit and sharing at least this one necessary pleasure.

The sharing takes place in a variety of settings besides the home. If a town has a central square, it will no doubt have a coffee shop (*cafetería*) for basic Mexican nourishment . . . and the mandatory cup of coffee. If there are more than a few dozen people walking the streets, someone will have set up a stand to sell a treacherously good snack that only cooks of that region know how to make well. There will be *restaurantes* with their own Mexican character, and market *fondas* and taco stands (*taquerías*) for folks who aren't too proud to enjoy their fare. Each Mexican eatery has its place in the gastronomical doings.

Restaurantes

If a Mexican eating place carries the name *restaurante* and really is one, it offers a specific blend of service, ambience and fare. More often than not, though, a labeled *restaurante* turns out to be a utilitarian coffee shop (*cafetería*), a polished Continental dining room, or perhaps a more privately indigenous *fonda*. The true Mexican *restaurante* is distinct, though it combines something of all three.

What I call typical, traditional *restaurantes* pop up in urban settings throughout the country, and one of the most characteristic was built in 1916 in the oldest section of Mexico City, behind the Cathedral that sits on the *zócalo*. The sign reads FONDA LAS CAZUELAS: *fonda* for the Mexican hominess provided by the long, glassed-in kitchen that lines one side of the dining room, *cazuelas* for the mammoth earthenware cooking pots steaming-full with the essential patriotic stews. The room is appointed with lovely Mexican tiles and a few bold paintings. There is a bank of jacketed waiters, whose proud professional service begins at about 1:30 P.M. as they usher the first clientele to the boxy, cloth-covered tables and high, ladder-back chairs.

As in many *restaurantes*, tables at Las Cazuelas are set with good crusty *bolillos* and good butter. There's a plate of delicious *entremeses* (appetizers) for the asking: crisp-fried pork rinds that snap and crackle in your mouth; juicy cubes of pork to roll into fresh tortillas, spread with guacamole and garnish with cactus salad; and little deep-fried turnovers stuffed with cheese or potato to dab with the sharp green sauce on the table.

By two-thirty or three o'clock the place is full of office parties, a few businessmen and lots of families; there is an air of celebration at Las Cazuelas, as there has been for decades. The quieter musicians that may show up in other *restaurantes* are replaced here by *mariachis* who ignite the room with voice, trumpets and strings. With their vitality, every table feels like it's in the heart of a party.

Traditionally, midday has been the time to be at home with the family, sharing dinner: a time guarded firmly—in some instances religiously—by parents who want to show their children the integrity of the family's structure while breeding into them a preference for national flavor. From time to time, though, the families move out of the sanctity of their dining room into a respected *restaurante* for a special celebration. It's easy to pick up the conservative tradition they carry with them, and it seems to be catered to unwaveringly in restaurants like Las Cazuelas.

Nearly everyone who writes about Mexicans at table describes the same, uniquely Mexican order of dishes in the traditional midday dinner (*comida*). It's a succession of five preparations (or courses, if you wish) that demonstrates a New World interpretation of European eating patterns. The first dish to come to the table is a bowl of soup, more often than not made with chicken broth. Next is rice, in flavors that range from tomato-red to herb-green, perhaps mixed with diced vegetables or topped with a fried egg. The main dish that follows is frequently stewed fowl or meat in a deliciously forthright sauce, possibly with a few potatoes or vegetables mixed in, and always accompanied by warm tortillas. Before dessert, there is a portion of beans, most chroniclers say; then the meal resolves with a bowl of stewed fruit, pudding or the like.

On the whole, the life force of this Mexican midday *comida* remains alive, but evolving. You sense the strength of its tradition in coffee shops and *fondas* (small eateries serving home-style food), where there is usually a daily, fixed-course meal (*comida corrida*) on the menu. It will frequently follow the traditional pattern, but rarely in these modern times are there any beans, unless the place serves small portions and caters to hard workers.

Las Cazuelas is a full-fledged restaurant, though, not a utilitarian eatery. Most diners there pick out their own courses for a special dinner. They start with appetizers of tender pork pieces, turnovers, avocado or shrimp cocktails, cactus salad or pickled pigs' feet. Perhaps they'll skip the soup (though many Mexicans would contend that you don't have a proper meal without soup), perhaps the rice. Orders go out for the flat steaks called *carne asada*, for *chiles rellenos*, for beef tips with tomato and green chile, for fish *a la veracruzana*, for stewed chicken in *mole* or any number of locally known tomato-, *tomatillo*- or chile-thick sauces; some diners will ask for the variety meats because there is always a good selection that is well prepared.

All this respected fare is consumed with beer or soda pop, even in nice restaurants. There could be a bottle of stalwart Mexican wine, limeadelike sangria or a deliciously sweet *agua fresca* of fresh fruit, tamarind and such. As the members of each party finish their main dishes and move on to rice pudding, flan or sweet fresh-cheese pie, they ask for their syrupy strong cups of spicy coffee. And the big tables of partying co-workers continue to nurse along bottles of brandy and Coke set out on the tables, or they start ritual rounds of tequila.

By six or seven o'clock, Las Cazuelas has seen the last of its diners. The *cazuelas* themselves are close to empty and the *mariachis* pack away their horns, violins and guitars until tomorrow, when it all happens again. Las Cazuelas, like many traditional *restaurantes,* doesn't attract an evening crowd through the poor downtown streets. For a large, late meal, people go where the ambience feels more continental.

Many of the traditional restaurants that hold a vivid place in my memory are specialty regional restaurants. Some of them feel the warm, saline breeze of the Pacific, Gulf or Caribbean and serve seafood from local waters in the locally preferred styles. Some serve thick, good steaks, chewy pork *carnitas* or maguey-wrapped lamb *barbacoa*. Others are bedecked with the handiwork of regional artisans and feature stews, sauces and even some of the legendary *antojitos* (usually *masa*-based snacks) and sweets that hold a special place in the area's culinary repertory.

In the smaller towns, the distinguishing characteristics of restaurants begin to fade. There often aren't the customers for the higher-priced specialties, and the restaurants find themselves doing duty from dawn well into the dark hours, serving eggs and snacks right along with their main-course fare. They call themselves *restaurantes,* but they've taken on the role that, in the cities, belongs to *cafeterías*.

Cafeterías

Cafeterías (or what are *cafés* in Northern Mexico) have nothing to do with the self-serve, steam-table operations of our country. Rather, they are informal, sit-down eating places, and in Mexico they serve a function different from that of the *restaurantes:* They're something like a public social club. While the *restaurante* seems built to preserve the best of venerable tradition, the *cafetería* is a stage for the working out of contemporary Mexican life.

I lived above one of these coffee shops for months in Mexico City. One of the waitresses turned on the fluorescent lights at seven o'clock every morning, and the cooks heated the griddle and the skillets. Not long after, the neighbors and local office workers began to filter in for tall glasses of *café con leche* and plates of saucy *huevos rancheros* or scrambled eggs *a la mexicana* or with *chorizo* sausage. Morning business went at a fast clip there, some customers choosing only a quick liquid breakfast or fare as mundane as corn flakes, or Mexican sweet breads, or thick-crusted *bolillos,* split, toasted and swabbed with butter. There seemed always to be others, also, with that desperately voracious look from too few hours asleep (or too many with a glass at hand), and they asked for the tube-shaped, crispy chicken tacos, tough little steaks (*bistec, carne asada* or *cecina*) and tortillas simmered with spicy green sauce and gobbed with cream, salty cheese and raw onion (*chilaquiles*).

The day slipped on more quietly, but the *cafetería* remained occupied. Men and women sat at the Formica tables, many of them alone or in quiet pairs, drinking espresso or the weaker version they called, appropriately, *americano;* and they stared out the plate-glass front at the uniformed school kids on the overused sidewalks and at the delivery men with full handcarts.

The midday dinner hour at our *cafetería* was more formal than at a lot of them, with tablecloths and a substantial, inexpensive four-dish *comida corrida:* We were, after all, in the heart of the city, where not all men went home for the sacred meal. Most *cafeterías,* whether they'd made up a *comida corrida* or not, kept right on with the coffee, enchiladas, tostadas and sandwiches, nutritive soups, fruit salads, breaded cutlets and other light fare; ours fancied itself a restaurant, at least for a little while.

When night came, I could see the fluorescent lights reflected in the pharmacy window across the street. I could hear the clinking of beer cans on the uncovered tables surrounded by traveling businessmen. When I sat in the middle of it—next to the neighborhood folks in for eggs, tacos, hot cakes, pie, coffee or gossip—it provided, even for me in that foreign land, a sense of community.

The Market and Its *Fondas*

Markets, to people who have not grown up with them, have an unmistakably exotic, bazaarlike air. They are alive with urgent activity, with unrelenting sensory stimulation. The displays of fruit, vegetables and herbs are masses of color and perfume—not pristine works of art, but examples of thriving richness and ingenious display.

And in among all this vital abundance there are always the simple spots for folks to eat—either those who come by to shop or those who work the stalls. They may be little stand-up booths that supply fruit drinks, *tamales* and *masa* porridge (*atole*), tacos or sandwiches; or they might be *fondas* for more substantial food. It is the latter that represent one of the most conservative elements in the community, especially when it comes to how folks nourish themselves. Most don't even post a sign to list the variety they offer; those who eat in them know all too well the local, traditional fare.

Since I've never completely understood the political, economic or social forces involved in choosing one *fonda* over its identical neighbor, I usually follow like a sheep and plant myself at the one that looks busiest. I ask for whatever they have: a bowl of meaty vegetable or vermicelli soup; tripe soup (*menudo*) or hominy soup (*pozole*) or rice with fried egg; meatballs, chicken or innards stewed to community standard in strong *moles* or spicy green- or red-tomato sauces.

The scene is as exotic as the market itself. A haze of frying oil hangs in the sunlight that streams in the market roof. It mixes with the earth smell that rises from underfoot and with the good aromas simmering up from the clay or enameled-metal pots. Deep milky-glass plates hold in the victuals on the dinettes, spoons are in a glass and tiny paper napkins sit in their wrapper. The lady who cooks crisscrosses with the roaming, shawl-wrapped tortilla seller as she carries the flavorful goods to the folks who've stopped.

It's branded, local food. It's a homey, inexpensive meal made daily, and to me it seems as unchangeable as the evasive spirit that makes the feeders and the fed the Mexicans that they are.

Out on the street are the more progressive, modern *fondas,* carrying names like *restaurante* or *cocina económica* ("economical cooking") and *comida familiar* ("family-style food"). Meals are had here in brightly lit rooms that stay open into the night, and their bill of fare is likely to be painted on the wall and targeted at a broader audience.

These eateries are the easily accessible source of the more segregated market cooking, and each day they put together a different set-price, set-menu *comida corrida* that usually features popular local preparations. Like some market *fondas,* they make good enchiladas, *huevos rancheros* and hearty soups. And progressive as they are, they've learned to dress it all up with a radio or jukebox, and with dessert and fried steak and potatoes.

Tacos, *Tortas* and Other Street Food

Late in the evening, after the midday dinner is far in the past, nourishment comes from a new round of public edibles. To some, it may seem surprising that after a late-afternoon dinner there would be any reason to approach the table again, but more than simple bodily sustenance seems to lead the Mexican in that direction. Where tradition and family sanctity are a focus of the *comida,* friends and fun play a role at supper.

The coffee shops will serve a new round of simple eggs and enchiladas, pancakes and sandwiches. Folks will go for walks or sit with people they know over coffee or hot chocolate or beer. Honest fast-food spots fire up their griddles, steamers and charcoal, and street vendors sprout up everywhere.

Taquerías are the definitive snack sellers, and they have certainly come to typify "Mexican food" to many outside Mexico. Most are little more than sidewalk taco hawkers made permanent, with a marginally expanded menu and some places for customers to sit. But that dissuades few people, for they serve that kind of attractively spicy, questionably healthy fare that everyone loves and a mother will rarely make at home.

At one, a vertical skewer of thin-sliced, marinated pork is roasted and charred in front of an open fire, readying it for a young man to slice off in little bits, make into soft *tacos al pastor,* and splash with a strident red-chile sauce, chopped onion and fresh coriander. Another has a steaming table of well-seasoned shreds of pork or tender, gamy goat or lamb to roll into soft tortillas and serve with chunky *salsa mexicana.* At a different type of *taquería*—one that has recently caught the country's attention—meat is grilled for the Northern-inspired *tacos al carbón:* Everything from beef to sausage and little clay dishes of bubbling cheese come off the charcoal broiler. The crowds seem to love the relaxed, frontier flavor and they wash down plates of tacos and bowls of cowboy beans with fruit-flavored *aguas frescas,* soda pop and beer.

Out on the street, a butane-fired griddle lit up with a string of Christmas lights might be searing beef, *chorizo* sausage and potatoes, or strips of chile and onion to offer with a spoonful of *picante* green sauce, some grilled knobby green onions, plus lime to squeeze over it all. A young man just a few steps away could be roasting field corn over a tub of coals or slicing fruit into paper cones. A women could be fanning the charcoal-fired brazier that warms her steamer of *tamales* or heats her griddle for baking *masa* turnovers. There might be a boy with a little glass case of gelatines, flans and rice puddings . . . perhaps a basket of crisp-fried pork rinds or a tray of nuts and candy. Still, all this variety only scratches the surface of what's found in the cubbyhole eateries and street-food stalls throughout Mexico.

Not all *taquerías* and street-food stalls are nocturnal or festal either. Around schools and bus stations and along busy streets, they often come out with the daylight to supply nourishment for the late-morning *almuerzo.* Some have come to think enough of themselves to add a little breadth to their offerings and change their name to *lonchería* ("lunch counter"), but most feature a distinct brand of soft tacos: *tacos de cazuelas.* They're put together from a variety of shredded meats and diced vegetables that are simmered in casseroles with homey, full-flavored sauces.

There is a final major strain of snack purveyors with a national profile and a product that is as tasty (and certainly as satisfying) as most anything in the snack repertory. *Tortas* are like Mexican-spirited hoagies or submarine sandwiches, and in no way should they be overlooked. At their best, they combine a crusty roll with fried beans, meat or eggs, hot sauce and pickled chiles, keeping pace with the most delicious quick meal.

THE MEXICAN COOKING OF THIS BOOK

When I made my first trip into Mexico as a food researcher, it was with the intent of collecting, exploring and verifying all the recipes that later became my

PBS television series, *Cooking Mexican*. I already knew much of the country from college days studying Spanish literature and Latin American culture, and I had been developing cooking classes out of my recollections from that period—plus a lot of book research, cooking and eating. Graduate school had goaded me into asking more questions than I could answer there in Ann Arbor, Michigan, so I went off with a notebook and an embarrassingly small budget to see what the Mexican people were eating.

My natural inclination, wherever I am, is to look in the grocery stores (or their cultural equivalent) to see what the cooks have to start with. The Mexican market, though, offered me more than raw ingredients; there were prepared-food stalls, too, and the marketplace was surrounded by street-food vendors and small restaurants serving traditional fare. It was really more than just a marketplace: It was a complex system of public buying and selling, of public cooking and eating. Public food, well-loved food that a community had set out as its own.

In those early travels, I discovered that the dishes and menus I came across didn't always match what can be found in Mexican cookbooks in our country. Many writers, it seems, had passed over the deliciously honest, easy-to-find preparations, and they'd missed the Mexican presence that makes the dishes magnetic. Still others had come to their Mexican cooking with American (or even French) techniques, rendering their translations of Mexican traditions somewhat unrecognizable.

So I decided to pull together into a single volume the readily available specialties I'd found all over Mexico, with all the necessary details on where and when to find them, and how to authentically prepare them back home. Before I knew it, I was waist-high in notebooks filled with sample menus from every-day eating places, my lists cataloguing markets in dozens of towns, recipes, photographs, histories and botanical information. I had my diaries of every day, every meal and snack I'd eaten, through the land and back again. Over the last eight years of research, my wife and I have logged literally tens of thousands of miles through Mexico, much of it by bus; we've visited dozens of towns and met hundreds of people. And all along, my goal has remained the same: to explore and chart the breadth of the traditional cooking that lay before me.

Because this is the food of the people, its preparation is not as regimented, sanitized and codified as the *haute cuisine* of professional chefs. The recipes for traditional Mexican fare are more fluid and variable, made of measurements like *un poquito* ("a little") and *bastante* ("enough")—the right amounts to suit your taste, of course, and the powers of your purse. And frequently the making of these general recipes follows a cycle of variations, through all the seasonal changes. But there are always boundaries; there is always the strong force of tradition to guide the cook.

Most visitors would be surprised at the high quality of goods and preparations in markets, small restaurants and street stalls; a good number of the tradition-trained cooks in these places have remarkable talent. Some of the everyday fare, though, can be plain, so I've occasionally worked into the dishes nicer touches I've learned from the growing number of dressier traditional restaurants and from the dozens and dozens of regional cookbooks that are printed throughout Mexico. In all but the most common standard preparations, I've given credit to my sources. Anything that has been changed—ingredients or methods—is always clearly denoted.

As is appropriate for the flexible, traditional Mexican dishes, I have written detailed but concise master recipes for classic preparations, then accompanied them with capsulized suggestions for **Traditional Variations.** I've used the **Cook's Notes** to explain unusual or alternative techniques, to discuss special equipment and to give the details of critical or unfamiliar ingredients. (Additional ingredients, preparation and equipment information is in the illustrated **Glossary** in the back of the book.) Along with many recipes, I've included my own ideas for using traditional preparations in nontraditional ways—**Contemporary Ideas** I call them, because they were developed with an eye toward the contemporary North American table. By spelling out these nontraditional ideas, I am *in no way* indicating that the traditional Mexican dishes aren't perfectly delicious, even preferable; rather, my goal is to show that you can keep the spirit of the Mexican originals while utilizing ingredients or techniques that are popular in the United States. My approach is different from the one adopted by many chefs of the "new" Southwestern cooking, who utilize Mexican ingredients in classical/European preparations; I always start from the classic Mexican sauces and preparations, and I never let myself roam too far away.

I'm sure that there are numerous specialties that I didn't come across, having been either in the wrong place or in the right place at the wrong time; probably there are dishes that I glanced right past, even though they were in my path. There are recipes for dozens of traditional classics that ultimately had to be left out, simply due to lack of space. For all of those regional specialties I haven't even mentioned, I apologize to the Mexicans who claim them as their own.

Though *Authentic Mexican* presents the public image of Mexican cuisine, when the last word is written and the final recipe meets approval, it is Mexican cuisine through Bayless eyes, and the pages are filled with my personal adventure, my private exploration. After many years, I have come to appreciate Mexican cooking on its own terms, with all its beautiful ingenuity and brilliant flavor and texture. It has broadened my culinary horizons in ways I never expected; it's brought me to a deeper respect for the beauty of human nourishment than I could have otherwise hoped for. I wish the same for each person who explores these pages.

SAUCES AND CONDIMENTS

❖

Salsas y Encurtidos

Pickled chiles in glass barrels, Querétaro

Tomatoes, chiles, garlic and onions—they make up the flavor framework around which much of Mexico's culinary accomplishments are built. The four can be found pure—ripe and raw and chopped together in the nationally beloved, relishlike *salsa mexicana*. It's the perfect table sauce (condiment) for tacos and other *antojitos* ("snacks"). Even when the tomatoes have been half-boiled or roasted, the coarse sauce you can make from them retains a typical engaging freshness.

Those four primary ingredients may be taken a step further: ground into a rough puree, then fried in hot fat. That's when their utility dramatically increases. As the mixture sits thick in its skillet, cooks can give it their regional additions, then use it to add sweetness, tartness and depth to an infinite number of dishes. A little broth may be necessary to make it the sauce for enchiladas or *huevos rancheros,* or for setting out in a *salsera* dish. And enough liquid to send it beyond the limits of a spoonable sauce yields the delicious, tomatoey *caldo* ("broth") that frequently comes along with meatballs or *chiles rellenos.*

There is a parallel collection of definitively Mexican *salsas verdes* ("green sauces"), turned out in like fashion and utilized with the same intent. But, with the small, verdant *tomatillos* replacing the red-fleshed tomatoes, the sauces take on an attractive tartness that gives them special distinction.

Chiles—and preparations made thick with them—define the remaining major faction of Mexican sauces. Most are not the explosive, pure-green or crimson chile purees that many of the uninitiated fear. Rather, they start with the milder pods that have ripened and dried before they're stewed with meat into *adobo, pipián* or *mole.* The hotter dried ones may be ground with tomatoes or *tomatillos* to help mitigate against the burning capcaicin that is concentrated in the chile veins; then they're balanced with garlic, herbs and spices before they're set out. But, when you see that lone red-chile sauce on the table . . . no doubt it will be one that bears a certain power in its taste, adding momentary unbridled strength to whatever it is drizzled on.

From earliest record, Mexican food has been a tapestry of color, texture and flavor . . . lots of flavor. It is punctuated with *picante* chiles, liberally enriched with condiments, enlivened with a sprinkling of lime, vinegary pickled peppers, vegetables, onions, even tangy, salty crumbled fresh cheese. But the multitude of Mexican table sauces are one of its true glories in my opinion. They go in or on just about anything, from rice and simply prepared meat or fish, to soup and, of course, all the beautifully Mexican *antojitos.* If your experience with hot sauces has been limited to Tabasco or bottled taco sauce, the traditional collection of *salsas* that follows will vigorously broaden your horizons.

Regional Explorations

The chile-based sauces made for use as condiments show the greatest regional affiliations: In western Mexico and parts of the North, it's frequently a simple sauce of pureed, boiled, very hot *chiles de árbol;* in the same areas, bottled hot red-chile sauce contains a good amount of preserving vinegar; in Yucatán, they bottle vinegary orange-red or green sauces made with the local *habanero* chiles; also, in the same area, they simply grind the fresh chiles—straight—with a little salt and lime juice; in Guadalajara, they turn the *chiles de árbol* into a thick, tart sauce by pureeing them with *tomatillos;* in Oaxaca, they use *tomatillos,* too, but the chile is a local, smoky *chile pasilla;* in Central Mexico, the common black *chile pasilla* becomes a special *borracha* sauce made with *pulque* and served with lamb *barbacoa;* also in Central Mexico, tomatoes figure in red-chile sauces made fiery with hot *guajillos* or smoky *chipotles.*

FRESH TOMATO-CHILE RELISH

Salsa Mexicana

The . . . salsa mexicana *that is offered on all the tables of* fondas *and popular restaurants is a delight of absolute simplicity. . . . With it one can season all that is seasonable.*

——PACO IGNACIO TAIBO I, **Breviario del mole poblano** *[author's translation]*

All over this temperate country, which year-round offers crimson-orange tomatoes with good flavor, a *salsa mexicana* made from ripe tomatoes is a traditional condiment put on tables in *taquerías* and *cafeterías*, bus stations and homey dining rooms.

I've never been keen on tomatoes that fall short of that, like the common, mealy store-bought ones. But when the red fruit is full of perfume, *salsa mexicana* comes across with the balanced strength of sweet tomato, hot green chiles, crunchy onion and aromatic fresh coriander—flavors at the heart of the Mexican kitchen.

This definitive, relishy sauce is available in every region of Mexico, with a texture that ranges from a beautiful coarse puree to an unhappy collection of grape-size pieces. The Yucatecan name for the mixture is *xnipec* (which means, rather picturesquely, "nose of the dog"—see variation recipe); in the rest of Mexico, it can be *salsa cruda, salsa fresca, salsa, chile*, you name it; and in Texas, you get it when you ask for *pico de gallo* (literally "rooster's beak"), which would get you something entirely different in West Central Mexico.

COOK'S NOTES

Techniques
Chopping: A sharp knife will give you small pieces that retain their juice. A food processor or blender leaves good ingredients battered and frothed. Remember, the finer the dice, the more the flavors sing in harmony.

Ingredients
Tomatoes: An aromatic, ripe, red tomato makes the best impact here. In summer I look for vine-ripened round tomatoes, but in the winter I usually get pear-shaped ones because they're often riper (though a little pulpy), or cherry tomatoes, which I ripen on the windowsill and then seed.

Timing and Advance Preparation
Allow 10 to 15 minutes to put the sauce together and a few minutes to let it season. It's at its best for an hour or two, after which the crunch goes out and the onion grows in potency.

YIELD: about 1½ cups

1 *ripe,* large tomato
Fresh hot green chiles to taste (roughly 3 *chiles serranos* or 2 *chiles jalapeños*), stemmed
1 small onion
1 clove garlic, peeled
8 to 10 sprigs fresh coriander (*cilantro*), chopped
Salt, about ½ teaspoon
1 teaspoon cider vinegar or freshly squeezed lime juice

1. *Chopping the ingredients.* Core the tomato, then optionally seed it by cutting across the width and squeezing out the seeds and liquid. Chop it very finely (so that no pieces are larger than ¹⁄₁₆ inch) and scoop into a small bowl. If you want a milder sauce, seed the chiles, then chop very finely and add to the tomatoes. Finely chop the onion and garlic and add to the bowl along with the coriander.

2. *Seasoning the sauce.* Stir in the salt, vinegar (or lime juice) and 1 tablespoon water, then let the flavors mingle for ½ hour or so before serving.

Earthenware condiment dish, Mazatlán

FRESH GREEN *TOMATILLO* SAUCE

Salsa Verde Cruda

This green *tomatillo* version of the table *salsa mexicana* seems even more commonplace in Mexico's snack parlors and street stalls than the red tomato one—partly, I suspect, because the cooked *tomatillos* make it more a sauce than a relish, and because it has a tasty puckeriness that deliciously heightens the flavor of whatever it goes on.

The sauce is frequently within easy reach in *cafeterías*, too, paired with a hot Red-Chile Sauce (page 37) or *Salsa Picante*

TRADITIONAL VARIATIONS

Xnipec: Prepare the sauce as directed, replacing the white onion with red, omitting the garlic (and coriander, if you wish), and replacing the vinegar and water with 2 or 3 tablespoons bitter orange juice (page 340), lime juice or vinegar. Generally, the texture of this mixture is coarser and the chile used is *habanero* (which, as far as I know, is not sold commercially in the United States). Another version of this Yucatecan sauce adds finely chopped cabbage and radish to the mixture.

COOK'S NOTES

Ingredients
Tomatillos: If there is a choice, fresh *tomatillos* give this sauce a livelier flavor and color.

Timing and Advance Preparation
The sauce goes together in 15 or 20 minutes. It's best eaten within 2 hours because the onion can get strong. It may need additional thinning (or even

(page 40). They all get sprinkled on or stirred in, like the salt and pepper on our tables. This fresh green *tomatillo* sauce is a particular favorite in Central Mexico.

YIELD: about 1½ cups

> 8 ounces (5 or 6 medium) fresh *tomatillos,* husked and washed
> OR one 13-ounce can *tomatillos,* drained
> Fresh hot green chiles to taste (roughly 2 *chiles serranos* or 1 *chile jalapeño*), stemmed
> 5 or 6 sprigs fresh coriander (*cilantro*), roughly chopped
> ½ small onion, chopped
> Salt, about ½ teaspoon

1. *The tomatillos.* Boil fresh *tomatillos* in salted water to cover until *barely tender,* 8 to 10 minutes; drain. Canned *tomatillos* only need to be drained.

2. *The puree.* Place the *tomatillos* in a blender or food processor. If you want a milder sauce, seed the chile(s), then chop into small bits and add to the *tomatillos* along with the coriander and chopped onion; if using a blender, stir well. Blend or process to a coarse puree.

3. *Finishing the sauce.* Scrape into a sauce dish, thin to a medium-thick consistency with about ¼ cup water, then season with salt. Let stand for about ½ hour before serving, for the flavors to blend.

Tomatillos

RED-CHILE SAUCE WITH ROASTED TOMATO

Salsa Roja

If the flavors of this *picante* red-chile sauce are well blended, the heat will have been rounded out with a little softening tomato flavor and balanced with a burst of roasted garlic. I've

reblending) if it has set up (from the pectin in the *tomatillos*).

TRADITIONAL VARIATIONS
Chunky Tomatillo Sauce: Prepare the sauce as described, finely chopping the chile, onion and coriander, then adding them to the blended *tomatillos.* If the chopped onion is rinsed, the sauce will sour less quickly.
All-Raw Tomatillo Relish: Prepare the sauce with chopped raw *tomatillos,* adding ¼ cup water before blending. Taste for salt and stir in additional water, if needed.

COOK'S NOTES

Techniques
Balancing the Flavors: To reach the right equilibrium, choose and prepare each ingredient with care: boiled or canned tomatoes make the

come across carelessly made versions that varied from riveting to impotent to heart-burning. But if you follow the directions laid out here, you'll turn out a traditionally spirited table sauce that is an unsurpassed condiment for mouthfuls of charcoal-broiled steak.

Simple red-chile sauces are in the repertory of cooks all over Mexico (save Yucatán, I believe) and they are commonly made with the very hot *chiles de árbol* and softened with *tomatillo* or mellowed with vinegar. This is a version I learned from two infectiously friendly *antojito* makers in Toluca, and I love it.

YIELD: 1 generous cup

> 4 medium (about 1 ounce total) dried *chiles gua-jillos,* stemmed, seeded and deveined
> 2 cloves garlic, unpeeled
> 1 ripe, large tomato, roasted (page 352), peeled, cored and roughly chopped
> ½ canned *chile chipotle,* seeded (optional)
> Salt, about ½ teaspoon

1. *The chiles and garlic.* Tear the *guajillo* chiles into flat pieces, then toast them on a griddle or heavy skillet over medium heat, using a metal spatula to press them flat to the hot surface for a few seconds, then flipping and pressing again. You'll notice a toasted look to each side and perhaps a whiff of smoke when they're ready, but don't burn them or they'll taste bitter.

Lay the unpeeled garlic on the griddle and turn frequently until soft and blackened in spots, about 15 minutes. Cool, peel off the skin and cut in quarters.

2. *Blending the ingredients.* Break the chiles into a dry blender jar, cover and blend on high until pulverized. Add the garlic, roasted tomato, optional *chile chipotle* and ¼ cup water, then blend until very smooth.

3. *Finishing the sauce.* Strain the saurce through a medium-mesh sieve into a small dish, then stir in a little more water, if necessary, to make a light, pourable consistency. Season with salt and let stand for ½ hour to let the flavors mingle.

Earthenware sauce dish (salsera), Michoacán

sauce watery; raw garlic is overpowering here; untoasted chiles lack depth. Even though the *chile chipotle* makes the sauce more *picante,* I like its deep, smoky richness.

Ingredients
Chiles Guajillos: Three large New Mexico or California chile pods could replace the *guajillos,* though they're not as sharply flavored; so you may want to add some crushed red-pepper flakes or cayenne.

Timing and Advance Preparation
You can put the sauce together in ½ hour, but it needs to stand for a little while before serving. Covered and refrigerated, it keeps for 3 or 4 days; warm to room temperature before serving.

TRADITIONAL VARIATIONS
Chile de Árbol Sauce, Baja California–Style: Stem 15 or 16 large *chiles de árbol* (known there as *picos de pájaro*), shake out most of the seeds, boil in salted water with the garlic and a slice of onion for 10 minutes. Drain and puree with the tomato and ¼ cup water; strain. Thin with water to a light consistency and season with salt. This is a *hot* sauce and is frequently made hotter by omitting the tomato and blending with ⅓ cup water.
Chipotle Chile Sauce, Vera-cruz- or Puebla-Style: Prepare the recipe as directed, substituting 2 or 3 canned *chiles chi-potles* (seeded) for the *guajillos.* Don't toast or pulverize the chiles prior to blending with the tomato.

CHIPOTLE CHILE SAUCE

Salsa de Chiles Chipotles

COOK'S NOTES

This is a simple, smoky hot table sauce that is delicious with grilled meats. Made from the smoke-dried *jalapeños* they call *chipotles* (from Nahuatl for "smoked chile"), it is an exceptional composite of flavors—though one that doesn't show up in such a pure form much in Mexico. Instead, the sauce that most frequently enlivens tacos seems to combine the cook's two or three favorite dried chiles, one of which is almost sure to be a *chipotle*. So try it this way, then move on to your own combinations.

YIELD: about ¾ cup

3 medium (about 4½ ounces total) fresh *tomatillos*, husked and washed
2 large cloves garlic, unpeeled
3 canned *chiles chipotles*, seeded
Salt, about ¼ teaspoon

1. *Roasting the tomatillos and garlic.* Lay a square of aluminum foil on a griddle or skillet set over medium heat; set the *tomatillos* on top and turn regularly until soft and blackened in spots, about 10 minutes. While the *tomatillos* are roasting, toast the garlic on an uncovered spot on the griddle or skillet, turning frequently until soft, about 15 minutes; cool, slip off the skin and chop.

2. *Finishing the sauce.* Place the *tomatillos*, garlic, *chipotles* and 2 tablespoons water in a blender jar or food processor and puree. Scrape into a sauce dish, season with salt and stir in a little more water to give it a light, saucy consistency. If a smokier flavor is desired, stir in a teaspoon or two of the sauce from the canned *chiles chipotles*.

Ingredients

Tomatillos: Fresh can be replaced with 3 or 4 canned *tomatillos*, though they won't have a roasted flavor.
Chiles Chipotles: Without them, there's no *chipotle* sauce. If only the tan-colored dried ones are available, toast them until slightly darkened and aromatic, then stem, seed and soak until soft. A small, dark, smoky-smelling, red-brown chile usually sold as *mora* (except in Puebla and Veracruz, where it, too, is called *chipotle*) can also replace the canned *chipotles;* in fact, these are often what are sold in the can as *chipotles.*

Timing and Advance Preparation

You'll need 20 minutes to prepare the sauce and a few minutes to let it season. Covered and refrigerated, it lasts 3 days or more; warm to room temperature before serving.

Regional Explorations

Chipotle sauce in Puebla and Veracruz is often made with tomato rather than *tomatillo*. And in Oaxaca, the smoky *chile pasilla oaxaqueño* performs solo in the sauce, without other chiles to mask its flavor.

CHILE DE ÁRBOL HOT SAUCE

Salsa Picante de Chile de Árbol

It stands in corked liter liquor bottles in markets through West-Central and Northern Mexico, waiting to be taken home to sprinkle on tacos, tostadas or the lot of other snacks, or to dash into White *Pozole* (page 108), *Menudo* (page 109) or any other soup. It lasts indefinitely, unlike the uncooked vegetable-chile blends that also go on the table; it's the closest you'll get to Tabasco sauce—and it is a lot better.

YIELD: about 1¾ cups

> 1¼ ounces (about 50 to 60 mixed-size) dried *chiles de árbol*
> 1½ tablespoons sesame seeds
> 2 tablespoons shelled pumpkinseeds (*pepitas*)
> ¼ teaspoon cumin seeds (or a generous ¼ teaspoon ground)
> 4 large allspice berries (or about ⅛ teaspoon ground)
> 2 cloves (or a big pinch ground)
> 1 teaspoon dried oregano
> 1 scant teaspoon salt
> 2 large cloves garlic, peeled and roughly chopped
> ¾ cup cider vinegar

1. *The chiles and seeds.* Stem the chiles, then roll them between your thumb and fingers, pressing gently to loosen the seeds inside. Break in half, shake out as many seeds as possible, then place in a blender jar.

Heat an ungreased skillet over medium-low. Measure in the sesame seeds and stir for several minutes as they brown and pop; scoop into the blender jar. Add the pumpkinseeds to the skillet. When the first one pops, stir constantly for several minutes, until all are golden and have popped up into a round shape.

2. *Blending the sauce.* Pulverize the cumin, allspice and cloves in a mortar or spice grinder, then add to the blender jar along with the oregano, salt, garlic and vinegar. Blend for several minutes, until the mixture is orange-red and feels quite smooth when a drop is rubbed between your fingers.

COOK'S NOTES

Ingredients
Chiles de Árbol: They're available in most Mexican markets. But if you can't find them, a good sauce can be made with any small, dried hot pepper, like the Mexican *chiles japoneses* or the common little ones frequently labeled just "chile peppers" in the grocery store. For a milder hot sauce, replace ½ ounce of the *chiles de árbol* with 2 *chiles guajillos* or 1 large California or New Mexico chile.

Timing and Advance Preparation
Preparing the sauce takes about 30 minutes. Stored in the refrigerator, it will last indefinitely—even getting better after several weeks. Or pour it into sterilized canning jars, seal and process in a water bath; store indefinitely at room temperature.

Regional Explorations
The labels on commercially made bottled hot sauce in Mexico commonly list *chile de árbol* as well as the thin, piquant *guajillo* called *pulla*, plus, of course, vinegar and spices. In the small west-coast state of Nayarit, a bottle of locally made liquid fire plainly listed sesame seeds and pumpkinseeds among the ingredients; I have added them to my simple well-flavored standard and it makes the best sauce I've had.

3. *Straining and ripening the sauce.* Strain through a medium-mesh sieve, working the solids back and forth and pressing them firmly; there will be a fair amount of chile seeds, skins, sesame hulls and other debris to discard, but be careful that there is nothing liquid trapped within them.

Stir in ¾ cup water, then pour into a bottle, cover and let stand for 24 hours before serving.

QUICK-COOKED TOMATO-CHILE SAUCE

Salsa Cocida de Jitomate

> . . . tomatl, *"certain fruit that serves as a tangy liquid in the stews or sauces"*; *"tomahua, to get fat or grow . . ."*; *"tomahuac, something fat, thick, corpulent"*; *"tomahuacayotl (condition or quality of tomato), fatness, corpulence"* . . .
> ——*SALVADOR NOVO, quoting Molina's Nahuatl dictionary in* **Cocina mexicana** *[author's translation]*

Many gastronomical commentators have singled out the tomato as Mexico's most useful contribution to world cookery . . . even in light of her chiles and chocolate. Tomatoes do, after all, have that fresh tangy sweetness and an ability to cook into a soft-textured mass that offers relief from those old-fashioned glutinous soups and sauces.

The cooks of Mexico's distinct regions boil and roast and fry huge quantities of this fruit-of-the-groping-vine into all sorts of delicious variations on this simple sauce, ones that their people have come to identify as their own. For the basic recipe below, I have culled out a kind of fence-straddling version that works as well to spark up *Huevos Rancheros* (page 113) and Mexican Rice (page 263) as it does for saucing *Chiles Rellenos* (page 245) or Quick-Simmered Tortilla Casserole (*Chilaquiles,* page 172) or for spooning onto tacos.

YIELD: about 2 cups

COOK'S NOTES

Techniques
Blender Tricks: See page 42.

Ingredients
Tomatoes: I prefer to make the sauce with pear-shaped tomatoes to give it more consistency.

Timing and Advance Preparation
The sauce takes 20 to 30 minutes. Covered and refrigerated, it keeps for 4 or 5 days.

TRADITIONAL VARIATIONS
Smooth Tomato-Chile Sauce: When this sauce is the base for a brothier one, the ingredients are thoroughly pureed.
Rustic Tomato-Chile Sauce: Thinly slice ½ medium onion and fry in 1½ tablespoons lard or oil until lightly browned. Add 1 clove garlic (minced) and hot green chiles to taste (seeded and chopped). Raise the heat under the skillet to medium-high, add the tomatoes (coarsely pureed) and stir as the mixture fries and thickens. Season with salt. This version is good with the addition of 2 *poblano* or 3 long green chiles (roasted, peeled, seeded and chopped).

1½ pounds (3 medium-large round, 9 to 10 pear-shaped) *ripe* tomatoes, boiled or roasted (page 352), peeled and cored
OR one 28-ounce can *good-quality* tomatoes, drained
Fresh hot green chiles to taste (roughly 3 to 5 *chiles serranos* or 2 to 3 *chiles jalapeños*), stemmed
½ small onion, chopped
1 large clove garlic, peeled and roughly chopped
1 tablespoon lard or vegetable oil
Salt, about ½ teaspoon

1. *The tomatoes.* For a more refined sauce, seed the tomatoes: Cut them in half across the middle and squeeze out the seeds and liquid. Roughly chop the tomatoes and place in a blender or food processor.

2. *The puree.* If you want a milder sauce, first seed the chiles. Then chop them into small bits and add to the blender or processor, along with the onion and garlic. If using a blender, stir to distribute the ingredients evenly, then process the mixture until pureed (but still retaining a *little* texture).

3. *Frying the sauce.* Heat the lard or oil in a medium-large skillet over medium-high. When it is hot enough to make a drop of the puree really sizzle, add it all at once and stir constantly for about 5 minutes, as the puree sears and cooks into a thicker, more orange-colored sauce. Season with salt and remove from the fire.

QUICK-COOKED *TOMATILLO*-CHILE SAUCE

Salsa Verde

This everyday Mexican *salsa verde* is green from a delicious native berry *(tomatillo)* that frequently bears the name of its

Yucatecan Tomato Sauce: Blend the tomatoes until smooth, then strain. Fry ½ medium onion (chopped) in 1½ tablespoons lard or oil over medium heat. Add the tomato, 3 hot green chiles (only a slit cut in the side), 1 tablespoon bitter orange juice (page 340) or lime juice, and 1 sprig *epazote* (if available); simmer 7 to 10 minutes. Season with salt. Remove the *epazote* and chile before serving.

Regional Explorations
Variations using local chiles (both fresh and dried), available herbs and different cooking methods produce sauces of numerous flavors and consistencies, making strong regional generalizations difficult. A few spots, however, are known for distinctive cooked tomato-chile sauce: In Guadalajara, it's simple, smooth and popular on tacos and the like. Yucatecan cooks make it smooth, too (they often call it *chiltomate*), but with a frequent addition of *epazote*, bitter orange juice and the hot little *habanero* chiles; there, they're also fond of a really chunky sauce with onions and roasted light-skinned *chiles xcatiques*. Epazote figures prominently in the medium-consistency tomato sauce in Oaxaca. And the Veracruz variety sometimes has the smoky overtone of *chipotle* peppers.

COOK'S NOTES

Techniques
Blender Tricks: In blending ingredients of such different consistencies to an even-textured puree, make sure that (1)

very distant relation the tomato. The walnut-size fruit in the papery husk makes a traditional sauce with an especially fresh, tart taste.

Mexican *salsa verde* is prepared by cooks in most of the Republic. Some of them will put it on the table for diners to add *al gusto,* or they'll use it for Chicken Enchiladas (page 154), or they'll simmer it with tortillas to make *Chilaquiles* (page 172). It's always put together in the same general way, though some like to add a big sprig of *epazote* while the sauce is cooking.

YIELD: 2½ to 3 cups

 1 **pound (11 medium) fresh *tomatillos,* husked and washed**
  OR two 13-ounce cans *tomatillos,* drained
 Fresh hot green chiles to taste (roughly 3 *chiles serranos* or 2 *chiles jalapeños*), stemmed
 5 **or 6 sprigs fresh coriander (*cilantro*), roughly chopped**
 1 **small onion, chopped**
 1 **large clove garlic, peeled and roughly chopped**
 1 **tablespoon lard or vegetable oil**
 2 **cups any poultry or meat broth (depending on how the sauce is to be used)**
 Salt, about ½ teaspoon (depending on the saltiness of the broth)

1. *The tomatillos.* Boil the fresh *tomatillos* and chiles in salted water to cover until tender, 10 to 15 minutes; drain. Simply drain canned *tomatillos.*

2. *The puree.* Place the *tomatillos* and chiles (raw ones if using canned *tomatillos*) in a blender or food processor, along with the coriander, onion and garlic; if using a blender, stir well. Process until smooth, but still retaining a *little* texture.

3. *The sauce.* Heat the lard or vegetable oil in a medium-large skillet set over medium-high. When hot enough to make a drop of the puree sizzle sharply, pour it in all at once and stir constantly for 4 or 5 minutes, until darker and thicker. Add the broth, let return to a boil, reduce the heat to medium and simmer until thick enough to coat a spoon, about 10 minutes. Season with salt.

harder items are chopped before blending, (2) the mixture is well stirred before blending, and (3) the blender is first pulsed, then turned on low. Blending should never take more than about 20 seconds.

Timing and Advance Preparation
The sauce can be made in ½ hour. It keeps, covered and refrigerated, up to 4 days.

CONTEMPORARY IDEAS
Herby Tomatillo Sauce: Puree the drained *tomatillos,* 1 large *chile poblano* (roasted, peeled, seeded and chopped), 3 cloves garlic (roasted and peeled) and 10 large leaves fresh basil. Fry and simmer as directed in Step 2. For a more Mexican balance of flavors, replace ½ the basil with a few leaves of *epazote* (or mint) and sprigs of fresh coriander.

Kitchen Spanish
In Mexico, the *tomatillo* may be called anything from *tomate,* to *tomate verde, miltomate,* or *tomate de cáscara* ("husk tomato"), not to mention *fresadilla* in the northeast and *tomatillo* in the northwest.

GUACAMOLE

Clearly, guacamole is the work of perfect art, the legitimate employ of the three Aztec elements that make it up: avocado, tomato and chile.
—*SALVADOR NOVO*, **Cocina mexicana** *[author's translation]*

The soft, ripe avocado, besides being the most unctuous and perhaps most addicting of the native fruits, enjoys a reputation beyond the mixing bowl and crispy corn chip. Its buttery, yellow-olive pulp—whose original Nahuatl name describes the fruit like a plump lamb fry—is said to affect the siring prowess of some men, the temper and quarrelsomeness of others.

The first unadorned bite of perfectly ripe, small, wild avocado spreads over the tongue a comforting texture like custard and a drab-green flavor that hints at strong herbs like bay, thyme and fennel. The tree is part of the laurel family, and its leaves serve flavoring purposes in many Mexicans' cooking.

Even when the wonderfully flavored wild avocados aren't to be had (and the flavor of cultivated avocados is not always as good), I contend that the best way to serve the smooth flesh is barely mashed with a sprinkling of salt, a few pinches of biting onion and hot green chile . . . plus the extra touch of garlic, tomato and fresh coriander, if you feel so inclined. That makes the nationally embraced, traditional concoction that fills tortillas or gets scooped up by thick forkfuls. The second of the guacamole recipes included here serves a function different from that of the more relishy, saladlike, common variety. When blended with *tomatillos*, the avocados become more of a smooth green sauce for tacos and other appetizers, with a rich but refreshing edge and, incidentally, very good keeping qualities.

CHUNKY GUACAMOLE (AVOCADO RELISH)

Guacamole Picado

YIELD: about 3 cups, serving 6 as an appetizer, 12 to 15 as a dip

> ½ **small onion, very finely chopped**
> **Fresh hot green chiles to taste (roughly 2** *chiles serranos* **or 1** *chile jalapeño*)**, stemmed, seeded and very finely chopped**

COOK'S NOTES

Techniques
Flavoring Guacamole: In order to accommodate any avocados you might come up with, I've written a loose recipe. Some of the blander fruits will need a little garlic and/or lime juice—even a drizzling of good olive oil—to make a tasty guacamole.

1 ripe, medium-large tomato, cored and very finely chopped (optional)
1 clove garlic, peeled and very finely chopped (optional)
10 sprigs fresh coriander (*cilantro*), chopped (optional)
3 ripe, medium avocados
Salt, about ½ teaspoon
½ lime, juiced (optional)
Additional chopped onion and fresh coriander, radish slices or roses, and/or a little crumbled Mexican *queso fresco* (page 327) or other fresh cheese like feta or farmer's cheese, for garnish

1. *The preliminaries.* In a medium-size bowl, mix the finely chopped onion and chiles with the optional tomato, garlic and coriander.

2. *The avocado.* Close to the time you are going to serve, halve the avocados lengthwise by cutting from the stem to flower ends, around the pits. Twist the avocado halves in opposite directions to loosen the meat from the pits, then scoop out the pits and reserve. Scrape the avocado pulp from the skins and add it to the bowl.

3. *Finishing the guacamole.* Using your hand or a spoon, roughly mash the avocado while mixing in the other ingredients, making a coarse, thick mass. Flavor with salt, then enough lime juice to add a little zing, if you wish. Return the pits to the guacamole and cover with a sheet of plastic wrap pressed directly onto the surface of the mixture. Set aside for a few minutes to let the flavors blend.

4. *Garnish and presentation.* The guacamole is very attractive in a pottery bowl or Mexican mortar, sprinkled with chopped onion, coriander, radish slices and crumbled fresh cheese; radish roses really dress it up.

Ingredients
Avocados: For notes on varieties, choosing and ripening, see page 324.

Timing and Advance Preparation
Allow 20 to 30 minutes to make the guacamole and, for best results, plan to serve it within an hour. The lime juice helps to slow down the notorious avocado darkening, but not much; Fruit-Fresh and other antioxidants leave a telltale taste behind. So choose a slow-browning variety like Hass, return the pits to the guacamole (they retard darkening), and cover it with plastic wrap pressed directly on the surface to keep out oxidizing air; after a while, you may need to scrape off the thin dark layer that forms across the surface.

Hass avocado

GUACAMOLE WITH *TOMATILLOS*

Guacamole de Tomate Verde

YIELD: about 2 cups

8 ounces (5 or 6 medium) fresh *tomatillos,* husked
and washed
OR one 13-ounce can *tomatillos,* drained
Fresh hot green chiles to taste (roughly 2 *chiles
serranos* or 1 *chile jalapeño*), stemmed, seeded
and roughly chopped
4 sprigs fresh coriander (*cilantro*), roughly chopped
½ small onion, roughly chopped
1 ripe, medium-large avocado
Salt, about ½ teaspoon

1. *The tomatillos.* Boil the fresh *tomatillos* in salted water to cover until *just* soft through, about 10 minutes; drain and place in a blender jar or food processor. Canned *tomatillos* need only be drained and put in the blender or food processor.

2. *The puree.* Add the chile, coriander and onion to the *tomatillos* (and stir, if using a blender). Blend or process to a coarse puree.

3. *The avocado.* Halve the avocado lengthwise by cutting from stem to flower ends around the pit. Twist the halves apart, then scoop out the pit and reserve it. Scrape the avocado pulp from the skin and place in a mixing bowl.

4. *Finishing the sauce.* Mash the avocado until smooth, using a fork or your hand. Scrape in the *tomatillo* puree and mix well. Season with salt, return the pit to the sauce and cover well. Let stand a few minutes to blend the flavors, then serve.

RELISHY CACTUS-PADDLE SALAD

Ensalada de Nopalitos

In spite of its being called a salad, this cactus-paddle preparation is actually used more like a condiment—like a coarse *salsa mexicana* mixed with pieces of cactus. It's very popular in the *fondas* of some markets (certainly a lot more popular than you'd expect any *salad* to be in Mexico).

While Mexicans love condiments and garnishes and adornment, North Americans are fond of salads. So that is how most of you will probably be happiest serving it. I think you'll find the firm texture and pleasantly green flavor of the cactus right for this colorful vinegar-and-oil treatment, as would be green beans, say, or asparagus.

YIELD: 4 servings

> 4 medium (12 to 14 ounces total) fresh cactus paddles (*nopales* or *nopalitos*)
>   OR one 12- to 15-ounce jar cactus pieces, drained and well rinsed
> 1 ripe, medium-large tomato, cored and diced
> ¼ cup diced onion
> 6 sprigs fresh coriander (*cilantro*), chopped

For the dressing:
> 3 tablespoons vegetable or olive oil (or a mixture of the two)
> 1 tablespoon cider vinegar
> A big pinch of dried oregano
> Salt, about ⅛ teaspoon

For completing and garnishing the dish:
> Several romaine lettuce leaves
> 3 tablespoons crumbled Mexican *queso fresco* (page 327), or other fresh cheese like feta or farmer's cheese
> Several pickled *chiles jalapeños,* store-bought or homemade (page 337)
> Several radish slices or roses

1. *The cactus.* Prepare the fresh cactus according to the directions on page 325.

COOK'S NOTES

Ingredients
Cactus: For notes on where to find and how to treat the succulent paddles, see page 325.

Timing and Advance Preparation
With prepared cactus paddles on hand, the salad goes together in 15 minutes or so. It is best when served within a few minutes of being dressed.

TRADITIONAL VARIATIONS
A Cactus Salad from Puebla: Prepare the preceding recipe, substituting 5 to 7 ounces of steamed green beans (ends snipped) for ½ of the cactus and ⅓ cup grated mozzarella (they use a string cheese) for the fresh cheese. Garnish with diced avocado. This salad is frequently made with several teaspoons chopped fresh oregano.

Regional Explorations
Cactus paddles fixed in one way or another are popular in Central and West-Central Mexico. Salady mixtures of the *nopal* reach a pinnacle in Toluca, where one is made with a light *chile guajillo* sauce and fried onions, one with *serrano* chiles and carrots, and one with the standard mix of onions, tomatoes, cheese, radish and fresh coriander; the latter usually has no dressing.

2. *Assembling the salad.* Shortly before serving, thoroughly rinse and drain the *boiled or canned* (but not the roasted) cactus, then mix with the tomato, onion and coriander. Blend together the dressing ingredients by thoroughly whisking or by shaking in a tightly closed jar; taste for salt, then pour over the vegetables and toss to combine.

3. *Garnish and presentation.* Line a decorative platter with the lettuce leaves and heap up the cactus salad in the center. Sprinkle with cheese, arrange the pickled chiles and radishes over the top and serve.

Cactus paddles (nopales)

PICKLED CHILES WITH OTHER VEGETABLES

Chiles en Escabeche

When you taste a pickled chile from the glass barrels in Querétaro, Aguascalientes or San Luis Potosí, or from the beautiful bottled mixtures in Toluca or San Cristóbal de las Cases, Chiapas, the flavor seems so much more lively than the canned pickled *jalapeños* that fill our grocery-store shelves. No doubt it's because the Mexican ones are often made with homemade fruit vinegar and the chiles include a wide variety of sizes and colors.

For the Central Mexican recipe outlined here, the onions and carrots are first fried, then simmered with the chiles in the mild brine. The same method can be used for making pickled vegetables, as described in the variation recipe; the result is attractive and delicious for a picnic or buffet table.

COOK'S NOTES

Techniques
Making Hurry-Up Pickled Chiles: To use the chiles the day they're made, make a slit in the side of each one (or seed and slice them) to allow quicker penetration by the vinegar. The flavor, however, won't be as mellow.

Timing and Advance Preparation
Start a day ahead. Preparation time is about 30 minutes. The chiles will last several months in the refrigerator, if brine covers them.

YIELD: about 2 cups, depending on the chiles used

    3 tablespoons vegetable oil
    5 cloves garlic, peeled
    1 medium carrot, peeled
    6 ounces fresh hot green chiles (40 to 50 *chiles
        serranos* or 12 large *chiles jalapeños*)
   ½ medium onion, sliced ⅛ inch thick
   ½ cup cider vinegar
    2 bay leaves
    1 scant teaspoon mixed dried herbs (such as thyme,
        marjoram and oregano)
    4 black peppercorns, very coarsely ground
      Salt, about ½ teaspoon

1. *Frying the vegetables.* In a medium-size skillet, heat the vegetable oil over medium, add the whole garlic cloves and fry, stirring frequently, for about 3 minutes, until they are lightly browned; remove and set aside. Add the carrot, chiles and onion, and fry, stirring frequently, until the onion is translucent, about 5 minutes.

2. *Simmering the chiles.* Add ½ cup water, the browned garlic, vinegar, bay leaves, herbs, pepper and salt. Cover and simmer over medium-low heat for 8 to 10 minutes, until the carrot is barely tender and the chiles are olive-green. Remove from the fire, pour into a noncorrosive container, cool and season with additional salt, if necessary. Cover and refrigerate for a day before using.

Fresh jalapeño and serrano chiles

TRADITIONAL VARIATIONS

Pickled Vegetables with Chiles: Prepare a *double* recipe as directed, using 4 chiles (total) and ¼ cup oil (total), then adding 3 cups raw vegetables with the liquid: broccoli or cauliflower (stalk cut off, broken into flowerets), green beans (ends snipped, broken into 2-inch pieces), zucchini (ends removed, cut into 1-inch pieces), *jícama* (peeled and cut into 1-inch cubes), or çactus paddles (cooked as directed on page 325 and sliced in ¼-inch strips). In Chiapas, they frequently bottle pickled vegetable mixtures that include hearts of palm.

PICKLED RED ONIONS

Escabeche de Cebolla

I wouldn't want a chicken-topped *Panucho* (page 166) or a plate of Pork Pibil (page 234) unless I could have it topped with these sweet-and-sour, richly spiced red onions. They are at practically every Yucatecan meal, and I know Deann uses a Yucatecan dinner as an excuse to make a big batch of them to have around for sandwiches and just about any other snack. To summarize: They are delicious.

YIELD: about 1⅓ cups

    1 small (6-ounce) red onion, sliced ⅛ inch thick
    ¼ teaspoon black peppercorns
    ¼ teaspoon cumin seeds
    ½ teaspoon dried oregano
    2 cloves garlic, peeled and halved
    ¼ teaspoon salt
    ⅓ cup cider vinegar

    1. *Parboiling the onion.* Place the thinly sliced red onion in a saucepan with salted water to cover, bring to a boil, time 1 minute, then remove from the heat and drain.

    2. *The pickling.* Coarsely grind the peppercorns and cumin in a mortar or spice grinder, then add to the saucepan, along with the remaining ingredients. Pour in just enough water to barely cover the onions, bring to a boil over medium heat, time 3 minutes, then remove from the heat and pour into a small, noncorrosive bowl. Let stand several hours before using.

Techniques
Blanching the Onions: This step removes some of the onion's harshness, leaving the finished pickled onions sweet and delicious.

Timing and Advance Preparation
The 15-minute onion preparation should be done several hours ahead. Covered and refrigerated, the onions will last for weeks.

HOMEMADE THICK CREAM

Crema Espesa

It isn't uncommon to see three or four buckets of cream in Central, West-Central and Tabascan markets: from thin, sweet and fresh to well ripened, thick and tangy. It's all heavy cream—not the light, low-butterfat "cream" that is cultured for sour cream here—so it has a richer, glossier texture. And you can bet it's not pasteurized, because the process would have killed the natural bacteria that preserves and thickens the riper cream.

To me, this thick, ripe cream (similar to the French *crème fraîche*) is one of the great pleasures of Mexican cooking—drizzled on Fresh-Corn *Tamales* (page 185), Butter-Fried Plantains (page 295), Quick-Simmered Tortilla Casserole (*Chilaquiles,* page 172) or simple fried tacos and such. Mixing a little milk or cream into our commercial sour cream is a passable substitute here, but nothing like the smoother, less acidic taste of this recipe.

YIELD: about 1 cup

> 1 cup whipping cream
> 2 teaspoons buttermilk

1. *Preparing the cream.* Pour the cream into a small saucepan, set over low heat and stir just until the chill is off; *do not* heat above 100° (lukewarm). Stir in the buttermilk and pour into a glass jar.

2. *Ripening the cream.* Set the lid on the jar (but don't tighten it) and place in a warm (80–90°) spot. Let the cream culture and set for 12 to 24 hours, until noticeably thicker (perhaps almost set like yogurt or sour cream). Stir gently, screw on the lid and refrigerate at least 4 hours to chill and complete the thickening.

COOK'S NOTES

Techniques
Culturing Cream: Don't let the cream get too hot or the culture will die and the cream will simply spoil. It's true that any active culture (yogurt, sour cream, buttermilk) can replace what was destroyed in pasteurization. Buttermilk is my favorite thickening/souring culture, however; it seems to work more slowly, giving the cream a chance to develop a ripe flavor but not much acidity.

Timing and Advance Preparation
Start a full day ahead (or longer, if the incubating spot is cool). The cream will keep for 1½ weeks or more, covered and refrigerated.

Painted gourd drinking cups, Oaxaca

BASIC MEAT PREPARATIONS, FLAVORINGS AND BROTHS
❖
Chorizos, Carnes Saladas, Caldos y Recados

Meat stall, Oaxaca

In order to have a ready supply of meat—or to keep it from spoiling before the whole animal could be brought to the pot or pan—each culture learned to salt, brine or smoke what it raised or hunted. Even now, in the age of refrigerated preserving, we hang on to our cured meats—simply because their tastes have given a familiar character to our food.

Mexico never really went the smoking or brining routes. But long-grained slices of salted beef (*cecina*) are a staple, and fully dried beef (*carne seca*) is a Northern specialty. It's the chile, however, that preserves Mexican meat with more distinctiveness than any of the world's other approaches, in my opinion. Ground with vinegar and smeared on thin-sliced pork (*carne enchilada*) or mixed with ground pork (*chorizo* sausage), it flavors as it preserves.

Spaniards brought the know-how for raising pigs and making *chorizo*, though the Mexican sausages have evolved into an independent life from their less spicy, smoked Spanish counterparts. Toluca is the undisputed capital of Mexican *chorizo* making, both the typical red and an unusual green variety; and they make blood sausages and head cheese there—very good versions of the types popular throughout the Republic. In the northwest, a lesser-known meat preparation, *chilorio*, is a chile-seasoned shredded pork that is packed with a good amount of fat to preserve it, like the French *rillettes*.

There is also a large variety of seasonings and sauce bases available to Mexican cooks. Yucatecans cook by seasoning paste (*recado*) alone, it often seems; many of their specialties rely on one of their three seasoning pastes. In much of Mexico, pastes for different *moles* are prominently displayed for buyers to dilute and simmer at home; in Puebla, this approach reaches its zenith: There are dark, monolithic masses of *mole poblano, adobo, pipián,* green *mole* and on and on.

In spite of the fact that pure, powdered dried chiles are widely available, seasoned chile powder doesn't play a part in traditional Mexican cooking. In much of the Yucatán, however, where premixed seasonings are a way of life, mixtures of herbs and spices for their savory *escabeches* are frequently available. And in eastern Oaxaca and Chiapas, expensive tablets of preground, brick-red *achiote* seeds are judiciously portioned out into rice and sauce mixtures to give them that beautiful hue.

While making preservable *mole* pastes may not seem all that practical at home, *chorizo* is quite simple and will be better than most anything you can buy. Chile marinade (*adobo*) for seasoning meat is little work, it keeps indefinitely in the refrigerator and it is useful in putting together quick meals with an authentic taste. And the Yucatecan seasoning pastes are easy—and essential—for most Yucatecan dishes. Recipes for all of them are here, plus a few broths you'll need along the way.

CHORIZO: THE FAMOUS MEXICAN SAUSAGE

. . . anyone who has seen the grubby [pigs] from the Hot Lands—put together with monstrous long snouts and frightful fangs, thin, lumbering, with dry, acrid meat—and who has also contemplated the pigs that are raised in Toluca—snub-nosed, fat, handsome—will understand why the good chorizo *and the good car-nitas can only be eaten [there].*
———ALFONSO SÁNCHEZ GARCÍA, **Toluca de chorizo** *[author's translation]*

It is certainly like no other sausage: fragrant with herbs and spices, rich and tender with deep-red chile, and pleasantly sharp with a touch of vinegar. It hangs in undulating strings all over Toluca (like waves of the Nile, says Sr. Sánchez García)—in the butchers' counters that border one of the big market buildings and in the beautifully packed taco stalls a few buildings over. And it's in the little downtown stores that sell Tolucan treasures like fresh *asadero* cheese (flavored with *epazote* and *chile manzano*), jars of colorful pickled vegetables, and bottles of orange-flavored liqueur called *moscos*. Strings of *chorizos:* red with dried peppers and uniquely green with *tomatillos,* fresh coriander and hot chiles—either of them textured with peanuts, almonds, raisins or pine nuts.

Of course, Toluca doesn't have a corner on *chorizo* or *longaniza* (as a cheaper, often untied brother is called). The little Oaxacan sausages, tied in 1½-inch rounds, are deliciously sweet and spicy. The Yucatecan sticks of *longaniza* from Valladolid are smoky and closer in appearance to pepperoni. And Chiapas has a stunning array of nearly unacculturated smoked and fresh Spanish-style meats, from *butifarra* sausage to good hams. Those are the highlights; lesser sausage specialties string on and on.

But none of those other specialties compares with the proudly nationalistic *chorizo.* Sr. Sánchez García swells up with the refrain:

And what is it that Toluca—the Mexican ground—added to the Spanish chorizo *to produce the non plus ultra of* chorizos? *The answer is in the flavor, undoubtedly . . .*
First: the flavor of the corn that the luminous Tolucan valley produces, fil-tered, by natural alchemy, [through] to the meat of our pigs.
Second: the flavor of the exciting, sweet, sour, dried red chile that . . . [is] the essence of mole *with turkey.*
Third: the flavors and aromas of the herbs, . . . chosen and united in the Mexican ways; the touch of strong coriander seeds, the freshness of ginger and, above all else, the careful process, the observance of certain rules, the little details of seasoning, etc., that constitute the artistic contribution of the Tolucan pork butchers to the singularity of their chorizo. *[author's translation]*

TOLUCAN CHILE-FLAVORED SAUSAGE

Chorizo Toluqueño

Chorizo sits prominently on the mixed-grill combination plates in places known for charcoal fires; other places it gets scrambled invitingly into fresh eggs (page 116), or browned with crispy potatoes (page 134). One of my favorites, though, is *chorizo* on a plate of good melted cheese (page 82), with a stack of fresh-baked flour tortillas to roll it all in.

The *chorizo* recipe that follows, for the deliciously flavored Tolucan variety, is based on one in Velázquez de León's *Platillos regionales de la República Mexicana.*

YIELD: about 1½ pounds fresh sausage; about 1 pound after air-drying for 36 hours

- ⅓ pound pork fat, cut into ½-inch cubes
- 2 medium (about 1 ounce total) dried *chiles anchos,* stemmed, seeded and deveined
- 2 medium (about ⅔ ounce total) dried *chiles pasillas,* stemmed, seeded and deveined
- A generous ¼ teaspoon coriander seeds (or about ¼ teaspoon ground)
- ½ inch cinnamon stick (or about ½ teaspoon ground)
- ⅛ teaspoon cloves (or a generous ⅛ teaspoon ground)
- ¾ teaspoon dried oregano
- A generous ¼ teaspoon black peppercorns (or about ⅓ teaspoon ground)
- ⅛ teaspoon freshly ground nutmeg
- ⅛ teaspoon ground ginger
- 2 tablespoons good-quality paprika
- 1 generous teaspoon salt
- 3 cloves garlic, peeled and finely minced
- ⅓ cup cider vinegar
- 8 ounces lean, boneless pork loin, cut into 1-inch cubes and chilled
- 8 ounces lean, boneless pork shoulder, cut into 1-inch cubes and chilled
- 4 to 5 feet of hog casings in 1 or 2 pieces, for stuffing the sausage (optional)

COOK'S NOTES

Techniques

Aging and Drying: The overnight refrigeration is simply to blend the flavors; at the end of it, the sausage is usable, though the texture will be crumbly because of the high moisture content. Aging the sausage produces a firm, compact texture and mellower flavor.

An Alternative Unstuffed, Refrigerated Aging: Without a sausage stuffer, place the sausage in a colander, set in a bowl, cover and refrigerate for 2 days. Excess liquid will drip off or evaporate and the flavors will improve.

Ingredients

The Chiles: Anchos are essential; if *pasillas* aren't available, replace them with an extra *ancho.*

Hog Casing: Many grocery stores make their own sausage and will sell you casings, usually salt-packed in 1-pound containers. They keep at least 6 months, refrigerated.

Equipment

Meat Grinder and Sausage Stuffer: I use the commonly available Kitchen Aid meat grinder and sausage stuffer that fits on the heavy-duty mixer. Any meat grinder will work, and you can get some of them with sausage-stuffing attachments. Without a meat grinder, I'd use a food processor for grinding and opt for the refrigerated aging.

1. *The pork fat.* Place the pork fat in the freezer (to firm it for easy chopping) while preparing the seasonings.

2. *The chiles and other seasonings.* Set a griddle or heavy skillet over medium heat, then tear the chiles into large flat pieces. A few at a time, lay the chiles on the hot surface, press them down with a metal spatula until they blister and change color, flip them over and press down to toast the other side. Cool until crisp, then crumble them into a spice grinder (or blender fitted with the miniblend container). Measure in the coriander seeds, cinnamon stick, cloves, oregano and black peppercorns, and pulverize. Sift through a medium-mesh sieve into a large bowl, add the nutmeg, ginger, paprika and salt, then stir in the garlic and vinegar.

3. *Grinding and flavoring the meat.* Set up a meat grinder fitted with the coarse grinding plate. Mix together the pork loin, shoulder and fat, then run through the grinder and into the bowl with the seasonings. Mix the meat and seasonings thoroughly, cover and refrigerate overnight. (Before using or stuffing the sausage, fry a little, taste it, then add more salt, if necessary.)

4. *Optional stuffing and aging.* If the casings were packed in salt, soak for an hour before stuffing. According to manufacturer's directions, set up the meat grinder with the funnellike sausage-stuffing attachment.

Rinse the casings, then check each piece for leaks by running water through it; either cut the casing where there are leaks or discard the piece. (To be useful, a casing should be at least 30 inches long, with no leaks.)

Thread 1 piece of casing over the sausage-stuffing attachment, leaving a 3-inch overhang. Begin feeding the sausage through: When it comes through the end of the attachment, clamp off the casing so that the sausage collects and stretches the casing to a 1-inch diameter; if there is an air bubble, stop the machine and work it out. Feeding the sausage through the grinder in an uninterrupted flow, slowly move the casing away from the stuffer as the sausage fills out a continuous 1-inch diameter link. When the sausage is about 6 inches long, pull off an extra inch of casing and squeeze through the meat, completing one link and starting another. Continue until all of the sausage meat has been cased, stopping to thread on more casing as necessary.

Stuffing chorizo sausage into casing

Timing and Advance Preparation

Start at least 24 hours (preferably 3 days) ahead and allow about 45 minutes to make the sausage, then 30 to 45 minutes to stuff it. Wrapped and refrigerated, the sausage will keep for a week or so.

TRADITIONAL VARIATIONS

Tolucan Chorizo with Nuts and Raisins: Prepare the sausage as directed; before stuffing, stir in ¼ cup *each* raisins, toasted almonds (coarsely chopped) and toasted peanuts or pine nuts.

Chorizo with Spirits: Josefina Velázquez de León, in her 1946 edition of *Salchichonería casera* recommends adding 2 tablespoons grain alcohol (you could use vodka, though it's not as strong). It has a nice effect on the meat and adds another bit of preservative; with this addition of liquid, the sausage must be air-dried.

Either twist the links several times to separate them or tie pieces of string between them. Hang in a cool, dry, airy place for about 36 hours or until dry to the touch and somewhat firm. Set a dish underneath to catch drips.

Wrap in plastic and refrigerate until ready to use.

THIN-SLICED STRIPS OF BEEF, FRESH OR DRIED TO JERKY

Cecina de Res y Carne Seca

My butcher in Oaxaca could brandish her long steel knife with grace and speed, unfolding a thick slab of beef round into thin sheets for curing. She salted them, then hung them above her counter for customers to buy fresh (for tough little steaks) or dry (to roast and gnaw, or to stew). With a little age, the flavors mellowed and deepened—like those of a well-aged steak.

Her thin-cutting-with-the-grain is a time-honored approach to making rather tough fresh meat into something more versatile. The method is used for pork and venison as well as beef, and it's the method employed north of the border for the Old West's jerky.

Sheer lack of familiarity made me hesitant to tackle this preparation until I was forced to, after having been smitten with a love for Burritos with Shredded Jerky (page 141) and the Scrambled Eggs with Shredded Jerky (page 117). Now, I almost always have some on hand. Once you get the feel of the thin-slicing procedure (it may seem awkward at first, if you've not done a lot of meat cutting), you'll find jerky easily managed in your kitchen. This recipe is one I learned in Baja California.

YIELD: about 1¼ pounds thin-sliced beef or about 7 ounces jerky

    A 1½-pound piece eye of round
    1½ teaspoons salt
    1 tablespoon freshly squeezed lime juice
    1½ teaspoons dried oregano

COOK'S NOTES

Techniques
Accordian-Cutting Meat: There is really nothing tricky about this technique, but it does require a little practice. Work slowly, slicing with firm, back-and-forth, sawing motions. The firmly held hand compacts the meat and holds it in place, making it much more manageable. If you work carefully, there is little risk of cutting yourself.

Drying the Beef: Some recipes direct you to hang it in the sun during the day, then bring it in at night; a cool, dry kitchen window works well, also. High humidity keeps the meat from drying and can cause it to spoil.

Ingredients
Eye of Round: This cut is the right size for home *cecina* making. A comparable alternative is a solid piece of round or sirloin tip roast.

Timing and Advance Preparation
Plan on 20 to 30 minutes to prepare the meat, then ½ hour for seasoning and anywhere

1. *Accordian-cutting the meat.* Using a very sharp knife (such as a boning, filleting or slicing knife), trim the ends, top and bottom of the meat to make them flat, giving you a roughly loaf-shaped chunk (weighing about 1¼ pounds). Reserve the scraps for another use.

Lay the meat so that its length (and the grain) runs crosswise in front of you. Place one hand firmly on top of the meat, then begin slicing at one end, parallel to the work surface and ⅛ inch below the top (and, as you guessed, ⅛ inch below the level of your hand).

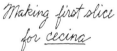

Making first slice for *cecina*

Making second slice for *cecina*

Work your way across the meat, but stop ⅛ inch short of the other end; *do not cut through.* Remove your knife, turn the meat 180° and start a second cut across, ¼ inch below the top. When you've cut across about 1 inch, open out the top slice, bending it on the ⅛-inch "hinge" that you left at the end. Lay your hand firmly on the newly exposed top and continue cutting across, again ⅛ inch below the surface, below your hand. Stop ⅛ inch from the end, turn the meat around and begin a third slice ¼ inch below what is now the top. Cut across 1 inch, unfold the second slice, then continue your cut, ⅛ inch below your firmly held hand. Work your way back and forth across the meat, leaving ⅛-inch hinges at the end of each slice, until the entire piece has been stretched out to a long, ⅛-inch-thick piece of meat.

Finished thin-sliced *cecina*

2. *Salting and aging.* Mix together the salt, lime juice and oregano, stirring until the salt has mostly dissolved. Spread out

from 12 to 48 hours for aging, depending on the meat's intended use. Fully dried jerky will keep for several months, loosely wrapped at a cool room temperature.

TRADITIONAL VARIATIONS
Chile-Dried Beef: Mix 2 teaspoons pulverized, toasted *chile guajillo* or New Mexico chile with the salt-lime-oregano flavoring; add a little cayenne, if you wish. Prepare the meat as directed in Steps 1 and 2, coating it with the chile seasoning, then hanging it to dry.

Regional Explorations
Northern Mexico is the equivalent of our cowboy West, and likewise it's the land of jerky. Dried beef is so commonly used there that the process has been industrialized: The meat is force-dried and tenderized, giving it the look of a horsehair blanket.

This basic preparation is known widely in Mexico: *cecina* when fresh (a term also used to refer simply to the with-the-grain slicing) and *carne seca* or *cecina oreada* when dried. Oaxaca follows a different lead: The thin-sliced beef is *tasajo* and pork (usually smeared with chile paste) is *cecina.*

the meat, smear the mixture on both sides, then refold into its original shape. Let stand ½ hour.

Unfold the meat and hang it to dry in a dry place with good air circulation.

3. *For cecina (fresh or half-dried strips of beef).* For dishes that call for *cecina*, let the meat dry a few hours or overnight. Cut into manageable-size pieces, cover and refrigerate; to ensure that the meat doesn't dry any further, you may lightly rub both sides with oil.

4. *For carne seca (jerky).* For dishes that require jerky, let the meat hang for at least 48 hours. If you plan to keep it for an extended period, let it hang several days longer, then loosely wrap and store in a cool, dry place.

SHEETS OF PORK IN CHILE-SPICE MARINADE

Carne de Puerco Enchilada

The chile and vinegar tenderize the meat and give it that incomparable Mexican savor; the spices and herbs make it rich-tasting and attractive.

As in jerky-making, slicing the meat for this preparation is easily mastered, and there's nothing tricky about the marinade. The finished sheets of pork can be enjoyed simply fried like pork steaks and served with Roasted Pepper *Rajas* (page 278) on the side, or they can be fried and sliced for tacos (page 136).

YIELD: a generous pound

> A 1¼-pound piece of lean, boneless pork loin
> ⅓ cup Red-Chile Marinade (*Adobo*, page 64)

1. *Trimming the meat.* Using a sharp knife (such as a boning, filleting or slicing knife), trim off the cap of fat that covers one side of the pork loin. On the other side of the loin, there may be a strip that runs the length and has a different texture than the solid loin meat: Separate it by running your hand down the membrane that connects it to the loin, then cut it off and reserve for pork fillings and the like. If there is membrane

COOK'S NOTES

Techniques
Cutting the Meat: See the note on page 57.

Ingredients
Pork Loin: Some cooks replace it with boneless pork shoulder because the latter is juicier when cooked. It is also harder to cut, though. A pound of thin-cut boneless pork steaks is a nice alternative for those not wanting to tackle the accordian cut; they won't be cut with the grain, though, so the texture will be different.

Timing and Advance Preparation
If the marinade (*adobo*) is ready, the meat will take 20 to 30 minutes to slice and coat. Start at least 4 hours ahead, so the meat has time to marinate.

Regional Explorations
There are trays of the pork—thin, long-grained slices, smeared with the well-spiced paste—sitting under the butchers' ropes of *chorizo* sausage in Tuxtla Gutiérrez, Oaxaca, Aca-

or fat covering any of the surfaces, trim it off. The piece of loin should now be clear, solid meat from one end to the other.

2. *Slicing the meat.* Slice the meat "accordian" fashion, into a single ⅛-inch-thick strip, as described in Step 1 on page 58.

3. *Coating and marinating the meat.* Coat the meat with *adobo* and restack it: Spread a scant tablespoon of the paste over the center of a small plate, lay the bottom layer of meat over it, spread with a thin cap of *adobo,* fold over the next layer of meat, spread with *adobo,* and so on, until the meat has been restacked with a little *adobo* between all layers. Spread the top and sides with *adobo,* cover with plastic wrap and refrigerate for several hours or, preferably, overnight.

Dried ancho chiles

SHREDDED POACHED CHICKEN

Pollo Deshebrado

The muscular Mexican birds are nearly always poached to get them tender—even before turning them into fried chicken. They practically raise themselves all over the country, they're quick to stew and shred, and the result is easy to stretch into filling for tortilla-wrapped snacks to feed an army.

YIELD: about 3 cups (18 ounces) for a whole chicken, 1⅓ cups (8 ounces) for a medium breast

For a whole chicken:
- ½ medium onion, roughly chopped
- 7 cups water
- 1 teaspoon salt
- 1 medium (3½-pound) chicken, quartered (page 225)
- 1 teaspoon mixed dried herbs (such as marjoram and thyme)
- 3 bay leaves

pulco and Chilpancingo, in Guadalajara, Aguascalientes, San Luis Potosí and points in between. The sliced pork may be replaced with little ribs, for roasting or braising; or the sheets of pork may be stacked on a vertical skewer, roasted in front of a gas or charcoal fire (like Greek *gyros*) and shaved off for *tacos al pastor.*

Kitchen Spanish
The names seem to change with the landscape: *cecina* in Oaxaca, *carne de puerco enchilada* in Guerrero, and *carne de puerco adobada* in many other spots. Of course, that makes it sound more codified than the free-roaming variants really are.

COOK'S NOTES

Techniques
Timing Poached Chicken: Unlike the free-ranging Mexican chicken, the American "hothouse" chicken needs to be carefully timed—especially the breast—so it comes out tender but moist. The chicken is juiciest when cooled in the broth.

Timing and Advance Preparation
A whole poached chicken will be ready in 25 minutes, plus an hour for optional cooling in the broth and 10 minutes for boning and shredding. Covered and refrigerated, it will last for 2 or 3 days.

For a chicken breast:
- ¼ medium onion, roughly chopped
- 3 cups water
- ½ teaspoon salt
- 1 medium (about 1-pound) whole chicken breast, halved
- ½ teaspoon mixed dried herbs (such as marjoram and thyme)
- 2 bay leaves

1. *Preliminaries.* Place the onion, water and salt in a saucepan (a 4-quart one for a whole chicken, a 2-quart for a breast) and bring to a boil.

2. *Cooking the chicken. If cooking a whole chicken:* add the dark-meat quarters. Skim off any foam that rises during the first few minutes of simmering, add the herbs and bay leaves, partially cover and simmer over medium heat for 10 minutes. Add the breast quarters (plus additional hot water to cover, if necessary), skim off any new foam that rises once the liquid returns to a simmer, partially cover and simmer for 13 minutes.

If cooking only chicken breast: Add the breast quarters (plus additional hot water to cover, if necessary). Skim off any foam that rises during the first minute of simmering, add the herbs and bay leaves, partially cover and simmer over medium heat for 13 minutes.

Remove the pot from the fire and let the chicken (whether whole bird or just breast) cool in the broth, if there is time.

3. *Shredding the chicken.* Skin and bone the chicken, then shred the meat into small pieces. Sprinkle with salt before using, unless directed otherwise in your recipe.

BROTH

Caldo

One lesson kitchen history has taught us is that good cooking requires good broth, and in my opinion, the little artificially flavored bouillon cubes don't count. Most Mexican broths aren't as rich as their relatives, the French stocks; in fact, a really strong stock can unbalance the flavors of many Mexican preparations. Soups need the richest broths, while Mexican sauces can take those that are weaker.

COOK'S NOTES

Timing and Advance Preparation
Allow at least 2 hours to make a decent broth (preferably 4 hours for beef or pork broth). Covered and refrigerated, it will keep 4 or 5 days.

Since meats in Mexican cooking are frequently simmered until tender, many dishes create their own broths. When they don't, here's how you proceed.

YIELD: about 1½ quarts

>   2 pounds meaty poultry, pork or beef bones or
>   odd pieces (plus poultry innards—excluding
>   the liver—for poultry broth)
>   1 small onion, thinly sliced
>   2 cloves garlic, peeled and halved
>   2 bay leaves
>   1 teaspoon mixed dried herbs (such as marjoram
>   and thyme)
>   8 black peppercorns, very coarsely ground
>   1 small carrot, sliced (optional)
>   1 rib celery, roughly chopped (optional)

1. *Preliminaries.* Place the bones and so forth in a large saucepan, add the onion, garlic and 3 quarts water and bring slowly to a simmer. Skim off all the grayish foam that rises during the first few minutes of simmering, then add the bay leaves, herbs, peppercorns, and the carrot and celery, if you are using them.

2. *Simmering, straining and degreasing.* Partially cover and simmer gently over medium-low heat for at least 2 hours (the liquid should reduce to about 1½ quarts); pork or beef broth will have a better flavor if simmered 4 hours, adding water as necessary to keep the quantity at no less than 1½ quarts.

Strain through a fine-mesh sieve and discard the solids. If there is time, let cool, refrigerate for several hours, then scrape off the congealed fat. Otherwise, let stand several minutes, then spoon off the fat that rises.

FISH BROTH

Caldo de Pescado

One of the most important ingredients in a really good fish soup or sauce is a well-made fish broth. This version that I've developed is rich without being strong or fishy, it has additions that enhance the piscine flavor, and it has a nice, reddish-brown hue. In Mexico, the heads and bones are always sold beside the

---

CONVENIENT VARIATION
Doctored-Up Canned Chicken Broth for Soup: In a small saucepan, fry the onion in a little oil until soft, add the garlic and cook 2 minutes. Add 3 bay leaves, ½ teaspoon mixed dried herbs, 6 coarsely ground peppercorns, the optional carrot and celery and 1 quart good-quality canned chicken broth (low in MSG and salt). Simmer, partially covered, for 30 minutes, then strain.

COOK'S NOTES

Techniques
Simmering Fish Broth: Unlike other broths, fish broth gets bitter and strong if simmered more than 20 or 25 minutes.

fillets and such; in the United States, you need to call ahead to the fish markets to have them reserved.

YIELD: about 2 quarts

2 pounds fish heads (gills removed) and bones
1 rib celery, roughly chopped
1 small onion, sliced
1 medium-large carrot, roughly chopped
2 large cloves garlic, peeled and halved
2 tablespoons vegetable oil
1 small dried *chile ancho,* stemmed and seeded (optional)
1 ripe, medium-large tomato (or 1½, if you're not using the *chile ancho*), sliced
   OR ⅔ 15-ounce can tomatoes (or an entire 15-ounce can, if you're not using the *chile ancho*), drained and roughly chopped
2 bay leaves
1½ teaspoons mixed dried herbs (such as thyme and marjoram)
4 sprigs fresh coriander (*cilantro*)
½ teaspoon black peppercorns, very coarsely ground
¼ teaspoon aniseed
4 strips of orange zest (orange rind only, *no white*), each about ½ inch wide and 2 inches long

1. *Preliminaries.* Rinse the heads and bones, then place in a large saucepan along with the celery, onion, carrot, garlic and vegetable oil. Stir to coat the fish and vegetables lightly with oil, place over medium heat, cover and cook, stirring occasionally, for 8 minutes.

2. *Simmering, straining and degreasing.* Uncover and add the *chile ancho,* tomato, bay leaves, herbs, spices and orange zest. Pour in 10 cups water, partially cover and simmer gently over medium to medium-low heat for 20 minutes.

Strain through a fine-mesh sieve and discard the solids. Skim off the fat that rises and it is ready to use.

Ingredients

Fish Heads and Bones: They must be fresh and have the bloody gills (which cloud the broth) removed. Avoid overly strong or oily fish like most salmon, mackerel and bluefish.

Timing and Advance Preparation

It takes 40 minutes to prepare the broth. Covered and refrigerated, it keeps 3 days.

TRADITIONAL VARIATIONS

Sopa de Pescado: Half a recipe of this delicious broth can be turned into about 1½ quarts very good Mexican fish soup: Fry 1 small onion (sliced) in a little olive oil until lightly browned, then add 2 medium-small tomatoes (roasted or boiled, cored, peeled and chopped) or a 15-ounce can of tomatoes (drained and chopped); cook until reduced and thick. Add the broth and a big sprig *epazote* (or ½ teaspoon dried oregano); simmer 20 minutes. Add 1 to 1½ pounds boneless, skinless fish fillets (cubed) and simmer gently for several minutes, until the fish is tender (½ pound of the fish can be replaced with 12 whole clams and ½ pound shrimp or tender-simmered squid or octopus for a *sopa de mariscos*). Serve with wedges of lime, plus a bowl of chopped onion and fresh coriander to sprinkle on. This is also good with ½ cup sliced, pitted green olives and/or 3 medium boiling potatoes, added with the broth.

RED-CHILE MARINADE

Adobo

This marinade brings to life Chile-Marinated Pork (page 59) and Fish *Adobado* in Cornhusks (page 218). It lasts indefinitely in the refrigerator, since vinegar, chile and salt are three preservatives that for centuries have been put to work in Mexican kitchens. I keep it around to spread on pork chops or ribs that I marinate and bake slowly, and it's an excellent quick marinade for a flavorful, meaty fish fillet, gently pan-fried or charcoal-grilled.

I developed this recipe while living in Oaxaca. My butcher gave me some of her *adobo* to use as a guide and told me how she made it. Though she called for all *guajillos,* I've used some of the sweeter *anchos* as well (as many cookbooks suggest).

YIELD: 1 generous cup

- 8 cloves garlic, unpeeled
- 4 medium (about 2 ounces total) dried *chiles anchos,* stemmed, seeded and deveined
- 6 medium (about 1½ ounces total) dried *chiles guajillos,* stemmed, seeded and deveined
- ½ inch cinnamon stick (or about ½ teaspoon ground)
- 1 clove (or a pinch ground)
- 10 black peppercorns (or a scant ¼ teaspoon ground)
- 2 large bay leaves, broken up
- ⅛ teaspoon cumin seeds (or a generous ⅛ teaspoon ground)
- ½ teaspoon dried oregano
- ½ teaspoon dried thyme
- 1½ teaspoons salt
- ¼ cup cider vinegar

Toasting the chiles and garlic. Roast the garlic cloves on a griddle or heavy skillet over medium heat, turning frequently, until blackened in spots and *very* soft, about 15 minutes. Remove, cool, skin and roughly chop.

While the garlic is roasting, tear the chiles into flat pieces and toast them a few at a time: Use a metal spatula to press them firmly against the hot surface for a few seconds, until they blister, crackle and change color, then flip them over and press them flat to toast the other side.

2. *Soaking the chiles.* Break the chiles into a small bowl, cover with boiling water, weight with a plate to keep submerged and soak 30 minutes. Drain, tear into smaller pieces, place in a blender jar and add the garlic.

3. *Finishing the adobo.* In a mortar or spice grinder, pulverize the cinnamon, cloves, peppercorns, bay leaves and cumin. Add to the chiles along with the oregano, thyme, salt, vinegar and 3 tablespoons water. With a long series of blender pulses, reduce the mixture to a paste: Run the blender for a few seconds until the mixture clogs, then scrape down the sides with a spatula and stir; repeat a dozen times or more until the mixture is smooth. Don't add water unless absolutely necessary or this marinating paste won't do its job well. Strain the paste through a medium-mesh sieve into a noncorrosive container with a tight-fitting lid. Cover and refrigerate.

meat] *adobada,* however, can vary widely in sauciness. To make a generalization (which is not always easy with a cuisine as fluid and uncodified as Mexico's), a meat *en adobo* is stewed and saucy; a meat *adobada* (sometimes *enchilada*) is smeared with a chile marinade . . . then baked, broiled, fried or roasted.

YUCATECAN SEASONING PASTES

Recados Yucatecos

Recado: *a combination of different spices . . . that are necessary for cooking.*
——**Diccionario de mejicanismos** *[author's translation]*

They sit in dense mounds, piled and pressed into colorful plastic dishpans in the numerous market spice stalls in Mérida, Yucatán. A brick-red, an olive-amber and a coal-black.

The first has the flavor of the red *achiote* seeds that grow plentifully in the peninsula in pods that resemble the fruit of the horse chestnut. They're ground with the definitive lot of Yucatecan herbs and spices (oregano, black pepper, cloves, cumin) plus garlic and a little vinegar. The combination is one of the tastiest, most likable and most popular flavorings in Yucatán—whether smeared on chicken, pork or fish for baking in banana leaves (page 233) or added to *tamales* (page 189) and stews. In books published as early as 1832, I've come across this *recado* . . . so cooks in the area have had a long tradition of cooking with preblended spices. This red one goes by *recado rojo* ("red *recado*") as well as *adobo de achiote* ("*achiote* seasoning").

The second flavoring is the gentlest to nonnative tongues, made entirely of garlic and spices (usually including a good pinch of native allspice and sometimes cinnamon). When you buy preportioned packets, they're labeled *recado de bistec* ("steak *recado*"); but as far as I can tell, the seasoning is most often used in the local *escabeche* dishes (page 230). It is so much easier than the other two pastes that cooks who are really proud of their *escabeches* make it from scratch.

The black paste, called *recado negro* ("black *recado*"), *chirmole* or *chilmole*, is the most exotic and indigenous-tasting of the flavorings. It's made black from carbonized—that is, black-burnt—chiles, then it's enriched with a little *achiote*, the spices and garlic. The cooks use it in a ground-pork "stuffing" (*but negro*) that's part of the more famous *pavo en relleno negro* (literally "turkey with black stuffing"). "Eating it is an act of faith," says R. B. Read in his *Gastronomic Tour of Mexico,* "since you can't tell what you're putting in your mouth, but you're aided considerably by the fact that, somehow, it's delicious."

This is the triad of flavorings that distinguish most of the traditional Yucatecan dishes. I've included recipes for the first two pastes, since you'll find need for them in several preparations in following chapters.

YUCATECAN *ACHIOTE* SEASONING PASTE

Recado Rojo

YIELD: ¼ cup

- 1 tablespoon *achiote* seeds (page 324)
- 1 teaspoon black peppercorns (or a scant 1½ teaspoons ground)
- 1 teaspoon dried oregano
- 4 cloves (or about ⅛ teaspoon ground)
- ½ teaspoon cumin seeds (or a generous ½ teaspoon ground)
- 1 inch cinnamon stick (or about 1 teaspoon ground)
- 1 teaspoon coriander seeds (or a generous teaspoon ground)
- 1 scant teaspoon salt
- 5 cloves garlic, peeled
- 2 tablespoons cider vinegar
- 1½ teaspoons flour

1. *The spices.* Measure the *achiote* seeds, peppercorns, oregano, cloves, cumin, cinnamon and coriander seeds into a spice grinder and pulverize as completely as possible; it will take a minute or more, due to the hardness of the *achiote*. Transfer to a small bowl and mix in the salt.

2. *The seasoning paste.* Finely mince the garlic, then sprinkle

COOK'S NOTES

Techniques
Grinding Achiote: Because *achiote* seeds are very hard, they are best pulverized in a high-speed spice grinder; unless they are reduced to a powder, the paste will be gritty. Second choice: a blender fitted with a miniblend container: Prepare a double batch, pulverizing the *achiote* and spices first, then blending in the garlic (roughly chopped) and, finally, the vinegar and flour. A mortar requires lots of energy: Grind the seeds a teaspoon at a time, transferring them to a small bowl; grind the spices, then add in the ground *achiote* and the garlic, flour and vinegar, and pound to a paste.

Timing and Advance Preparation
The paste can be finished in 15 minutes, but should be made several hours ahead. Refrigerate if not using within 2 days; it keeps well for months.

it with some of the spice mixture and use the back of a spoon or a flexible spreader to work it back and forth, smearing it into a *smooth* paste. Scrape in with the remaining spice powder, then mix in the vinegar and flour.

Scoop into a small jar, cover and let stand several hours (or, preferably, overnight) before using.

YUCATECAN MIXED-SPICE PASTE

Recado de Bistec

YIELD: about 3 tablespoons

- 12 cloves garlic, unpeeled
- 1 teaspoon black peppercorns (or a scant 1½ teaspoons ground)
- ¼ teaspoon allspice berries (or a generous ¼ teaspoon ground)
- ¼ teaspoon cloves (or a generous ¼ teaspoon ground)
- ¼ teaspoon cumin seeds (or a generous ¼ teaspoon ground)
- 2 teaspoons dried oregano
- ½ teaspoon salt
- 1 tablespoon cider vinegar
- 1 teaspoon flour

1. *The garlic.* Roast the unpeeled garlic on a griddle or heavy skillet set over medium heat for about 15 minutes, turning frequently, until blackened outside in spots and *very* soft inside. Remove, cool, then slip off the skin.

2. *The herbs and spices.* Measure the black pepper, allspice, cloves, cumin and oregano into a mortar or spice grinder and pulverize thoroughly. Transfer to a small bowl and add the salt.

3. *The seasoning paste.* Finely mince the garlic, then sprinkle with some of the spice mixture and use a flexible spreader or the back of a spoon to work it back and forth, mashing it to a *smooth* paste. Scrape in with the remaining spice powder, then work in the vinegar and flour.

Scrape into a small jar, cover and let stand for several hours (or, preferably, overnight) before using.

COOK'S NOTES

Timing and Advance Preparation
This paste goes together in 20 minutes, but is best made several hours ahead. It keeps well for months, but should be refrigerated.

Kitchen Spanish
For those who speak non-Mexican Spanish, the common *recaudo,* which means "seasonings" elsewhere, has become *recado* in much of Mexico; and, yes, *recado* also means "message."

TORTILLAS

Tortilla makers, Guadalajara market

Within a quarter of a century after the Spaniards brought wheat to the New World, it was written that bread in Mexico City was as good and cheap as what you could find in Spain. Not exactly what one would expect in a country that from time immemorial had put a tortilla in each person's hand several times every day. But the locals readily picked up the new custom, and still today the daily wheat bread in Mexico City is some of the best—the crisp-crusted rolls (*bolillos*) split on top and tapered at both ends. They're made a lot like French bread, though not as light inside . . . and the butter you get to spread on them is flavorful and delicious.

Those who haven't traveled through Mexico often don't realize that some kind of French-style bread is available in all parts of the country, and that it comes to the table in most all restaurants, especially those in the cities. Certainly, tortillas continue to nourish the provincial masses, they're generally preferred for everyday eating, and the best traditional restaurants invariably have a woman rhythmically baking tortillas all during the dining hours, so they'll be perfectly fresh. But the split-topped *bolillos* or the softer, double- or triple-humped *teleras* hold a firm place in everyone's eating, especially when eating out. The bread is generally nice and light in old colonial cities. But through the North and down to the Gulf, *bolillos* frequently lack the crisp crusts (and, in the North, can be quite sweet). In the Yucatán peninsula, the bakers know nothing of *bolillos* and *teleras:* They make long loaves of French bread (called, appropriately, *franceses*) and soft, light dinner rolls.

But tortillas are known everywhere, and they're the same thin, unleavened, griddle-baked cakes of fresh *masa* in most all locales. Except, as I was startled to discover, in Juchitán, Oaxaca, where the tortillas approach ¼-inch thickness, and are slapped onto the inside wall of a hot, barrel-shaped, clay oven and baked. There is nothing to compare to their earthy, slightly smoky taste when they're retrieved from the oven; certainly they are the most unusual tortillas I know in Mexico.

What follows here are detailed recipes for making the traditionally thin tortillas (I doubt many would have the tandoori-style oven for the Juchitecan tortillas), using the easily available *masa harina* as well as fresh *masa*. Then we proceed to the Northern-style tortillas made of wheat flour, and the fried corn tortillas for tostadas and chips. Any of them in their homemade versions make a meal truly memorable, especially just-baked tortillas from fresh *masa* or soft, warm, flour tortillas.

Crusty Mexican roll (bolillo)

MAÍZ IN THE MEXICAN KITCHEN

Perhaps it was, as some experts claim, the small, wild Mexican grass *teocincle* that mothered our big ears of corn: *teocincle* from Nahuatl *teo* ("god") and *cincle* ("corn"). Perhaps it was another grain, long since forgotten, that the hungry early inhabitants of the land tamed for their staple. Whatever the seed, they learned through the millennia to grow their precious plant with good-size ears and take full advantage of its nutrients.

They dried the starchy corn during the days of its harvest, then boiled it little by little, day by day, to soften it for their teeth and their stomachs. Then a change came somewhere along the way: They learned that adding a little of the lime they burned from sea shells and limestone took off the kernel's hard-to-digest hulls—and wood ashes could do the same, they discovered.

And their bodies felt more strength: The corn now gave them more minerals like niacin, more protein at their service, perhaps more calcium. They had made the one nutritionally energizing discovery that could yield a strong race: *nixta-malización* (from the Nahuatl *nextli*, "ashes").

Today, the process is still used when preparing the corn that becomes the smooth dough of tortillas, the coarse dough of *tamales* and the whole hominy that goes into soups like *pozole*. The kernels are boiled with a little slaked lime (*cal*), the hull quickly turns yellow, and softens, then what's left of it—and all the lime—is washed away.

Though the ingredients and process involved here are quite unfamiliar to North Americans, I've included these recipes because they are at the very heart of the Mexican kitchen: Without *masa* there would never have been a Mexico as we know it—certainly nothing like Mexican cooking. If there is a tortilla factory around, the ingredients are accessible; and with accessible ingredients, at least once you should try the *tamal* dough or the hominy cooked from scratch . . . just to feel the corn in your fingers and smell the age-old fragrance of lime and dried corn.

Slaked lime, dried corn and clay
colander for washing corn

DOUGH FROM DRIED CORN FOR TORTILLAS OR *TAMALES*

Masa Para Tortillas o Tamales

YIELD: 2¼ to 2½ pounds

> 1½ **pounds (1 quart) dried white field (flint or dent) corn (page 343)**
> 2 **tablespoons slaked lime (page 346)**

1. *Cleaning the corn.* Measure the corn into a colander and rinse to remove the chaff.

2. *The lime mixture.* Measure 2 quarts water into a large (4-quart) *noncorrosive* pan, set over high heat, add the lime and stir to dissolve.

3. *Boiling the corn.* Stir the corn into the lime water and remove any kernels that float. When the liquid returns to a boil, reduce the heat and simmer: for tortilla dough about 2 minutes, for *tamal* dough 12 to 15 minutes. Remove the pan from the heat and let soak: for tortilla dough let stand covered for several hours (or, preferably, overnight), for *tamal* dough about 1 hour.

4. *Washing the corn.* Pour the corn into a colander and set under running water. With both hands, thoroughly work through the corn, carefully rubbing off what remains of the gelatinous yellow hulls and letting the debris wash away. Continue until *all* is white again (except the dark, pointed germ end of each kernel); drain well. The hulled and cleaned, half-cooked corn is now called *nixtamal* in Spanish.

5. *Grinding the corn. For tortilla dough:* Set up a plate-style mill (see Equipment in **Cook's Notes**), adjusting it for the finest grind. Place the corn in the hopper and grind it through, a process that will take some time (probably 30 minutes) and some endurance. The damp grindings that come from between the plates should be smooth, not gritty. When all the corn has been ground, work in enough water (generally between ⅔ and ¾ cup) to make the *masa* into a medium-soft consistency dough. (Tortilla factories occasionally have a second machine for *amasando*—that is, kneading and smoothing the dough; the final working undoubtedly makes the lightest tortillas.)

For tamal dough: Spread the drained corn onto a towel and pat thoroughly dry with another towel. Grind the dried corn

COOK'S NOTES

Techniques

Making Masa for Tortillas vs. for Tamales: When preparing corn for tortilla *masa*, don't cook it too long or the resulting dough will be heavy and lack the characteristic light, malleable body. The long soaking ensures that the corn is properly penetrated; the kernels will *not* be soaked completely through, however. For *tamales,* the corn is cooked a little longer, not soaked much, then usually dried so that a coarse, damp meal can be ground. This method of making *masa* for *tamales* works well at home, but tortilla factories generally use the same corn they've prepared for tortilla dough and simply grind it less smooth.

NOTE: When a recipe in this book calls for *masa* (that is, unless a recipe calls specifically for *masa* for *tamales*), always use *masa* for tortillas.

Washing the Corn: This step should be completed carefully and thoroughly; insufficient washing will result in yellow-colored *masa* that tastes of the slaked lime.

Hand-Grinding Tortilla Dough: This process is, shall we say, labor-intensive. It takes me as long as driving across Chicago to my favorite tortilla factory (and it isn't nearly as enjoyable). When I do the hand-grinding, though, I dry and pregrind the corn in the food processor (as if making *tamal* dough), then moisten it and grind it through the mill.

through a plate-style mill (see Equipment in **Cook's Notes**), adjusted for a medium to medium-fine grind. Or grind it in 4 batches in the food processor, pulsing each batch 5 or 6 times, then letting the machine run for *several minutes* until the corn is reduced to a meal that resembles damp hominy grits. Place the damp meal in a large bowl, then work in enough water (generally about ⅔ cup) to make a stiff dough.

HALF-COOKED HOMINY FOR *POZOLE*

Nixtamal Para Pozole

YIELD: enough to make about 4 quarts when fully cooked

> 2 pounds (5½ cups) dried white field (flint or dent) corn (page 343)
>
> 2½ tablespoons slaked lime (page 346)

1. *Cleaning, boiling and washing the corn.* Clean the corn and prepare the lime mixture as directed in Steps 1 and 2 of the preceding recipe. Boil it as you would for making *tamales* (Step 3); let stand for a few minutes, then wash (Step 4). The corn is now called *nixtamal.*

2. *Optional de-heading for "flowered" hominy.* For the hominy used in soups like *pozole* and *menudo*, the cleaned corn is ready to be slowly simmered in unsalted water as directed in the various recipes. Or, for the most attractive hominy, pick off the head (the pointed germ end of each kernel)—a step that not only eliminates the hard inner kernel, but lets the corn splay (or "flower," as they say in Spanish) into an attractive shape.

Equipment

The Plate-Style Mill for Grinding Tortilla Dough: I've had two of these corn/grain mills over the years: one with metal plates and one with stone. While the metal plates are fine for grinding meal, stone seems to be the only tool that will reduce the soaked corn to a smooth paste. Mine is the Corona brand hand-powered mill; it can be ordered through most health-food stores that stock equipment. Corona also makes electric corn mills.

Timing and Advance Preparation

For *tamal* dough or whole-kernel hominy, start about 1½ hours ahead (2¼ hours ahead if you plan to pick the heads off the corn for "flowered" hominy); you'll be actively involved for a third of the 1½ hours. For tortilla dough, boil the corn the night before, then clean and grind it (which will take at least ½ hour) the following day. Tortilla dough needs to be used the day it is made; *tamal* dough or half-cooked hominy will keep for 2 or 3 days, covered and refrigerated. Both can be frozen.

Mesquite-wood and cast-iron tortilla presses

MAÍZ:
MEXICO'S DAILY BREAD

The thick scent of *masa* being ground from once-dried corn is unmistakable, and the flavor of the fresh-baked tortillas it produces is a definitive Mexican experience. Tortillas have kept away hunger when other nourishment was scarce; they have been useful as wrappers and scoops for eggs and beans and what have you; they have thickened soups and stews; and on occasion they have even served as tableware, when brittle and cupped under a pile of salt.

For the Mexican provider who needs fresh tortillas once (sometimes twice or three times) a day, the tortilla factory's modern electric mills, rolling dies and automated baking conveyors add up to a little easier life. The one thing modernization can't promise, though, is the same thick tenderness of tortillas patted by well-practiced hands. It has been done the same way for centuries: She pinches off a nut of fresh, soft *masa* and begins to clap it from one damp hand to the other, those fingers held stiff, with the slightest cup and spring to the palm. Clap and turn, clap and turn, until the malleable *masa* has been coaxed to a thin, even, saucer size. It takes hundreds of tries to learn the right touch, and like learning a new language, few can truly master it, I think, after adulthood arrives.

When Mexicans talk on and on about the soft tortillas of their innocent years, when they sing the praises of that elemental nourishment, no doubt they think of handformed, griddle-baked cakes, those that sit on familiar dining room tables, moist and fragrant in a heavy towel.

Regional Explorations

In the Yucatán and Gulf, *tortilleras* pat their cakes onto a piece of plastic (originally banana leaf) instead of hand to hand. Some places you'll see the hinged press replaced with a complicated-looking belted and levered contraption, and frequently the tortillas will come through a hand-cranked pair of rollers with a round die on one of them. Mostly, though, the masses are satisfied with the near-white, near-fine, medium-thin tortillas that come off automated machines around markets or dotted through neighborhoods everywhere; in places like Yucatán, they even seem to be satisfied with tortillas made from the powdered *masa*. I can think of two exceptions: the Guadalajara market, where thick, yellowish tortillas are still pressed out one at a time and griddle-baked; and Oaxaca, where vendors around the market sell cloth-lined baskets of *blanditas,* the whitest, smoothest-ground, thinnest tortillas imaginable. They are among the most refined in the country and tortilla purists are willing to pay a hefty price for them. Some of Mexico's most interesting tortillas, however, are Tabasco's thick ones: the size of a salad plate and made from *maíz nuevo,* half-dried corn. The dough is coarse and the hefty, baked cakes are quick-fried and topped with sweet, browned garlic—tortillas *al mojo de ajo,* they call them, and they're unforgettably delicious.

All through the Central highlands and most of West-Central Mexico, you'll find blue (sometimes red) corn used for *masa,* and in a few places they go for a yellow-grained corn. These are mostly for special-occasion tortillas, though; for everyday eating, everyone seems drawn to the smooth, supple, light-colored cakes that represent half the daily volume that feeds the country.

CORN TORTILLAS

Tortillas de Maíz

For most of us North Americans, there is a proud feeling of accomplishment when we can pass around a basket of steaming homemade tortillas to enjoy with our meals. With powdered *masa harina* so widely distributed these days, more of us have learned how wonderful a fresh-baked tortilla is. And with the fresh-ground dough (*masa*) becoming available from *tortillerías* in so many communities, it won't be long until the freshest-tasting home-baked tortillas are part of many of our lives. Though tortillas take some time to prepare, it's time well spent— at least on special occasions. Other times, store-bought factory-made tortillas can be served as the authentic accompaniment (and if they're steam-heated as described on page 353, they'll be very good indeed); and store-bought tortillas are fine, generally even preferable, for most of the *antojitos* like enchiladas.

YIELD: 15 tortillas

> 1 **pound fresh** *masa* **for tortillas, store-bought or homemade (page 71)**
> **OR 1¾ cups** *masa harina* **mixed with 1 cup plus 2 tablespoons hot tap water**

1. *The dough.* If using *masa harina,* mix it with the hot water, then knead until smooth, adding more water or more *masa harina* to achieve a very soft (but not sticky) consistency; cover with plastic and let rest 30 minutes

When you're ready to bake the tortillas, readjust the consistency of the fresh or reconstituted *masa* (see Techniques in **Cook's Notes**), then divide into 15 balls and cover with plastic.

2. *Heating the griddle.* Heat a large, ungreased, heavy griddle or 2 heavy skillets: one end of the griddle (or one skillet)

COOK'S NOTES

Techniques
Adjusting the Consistency of the Dough: You want the dough to be softer than shortbread dough (or Play-Doh, if that rings a louder bell), about like a soft cookie dough (though it isn't sticky). Reconstituted *masa harina* should be as soft as possible, while still having enough body to be unmolded; it should feel a little softer than perfectly adjusted fresh *masa. Masa* is not elastic like bread dough, but fresh *masa* will have a little more body than a dough made from *masa harina.* Because the dough dries out readily, it is necessary to add water from time to time; tortillas made from dry dough usually won't puff much, and they'll be heavy and somewhat crumbly.
Unmolding: If the tortilla breaks when you peel off the plastic, the dough is too dry. If the tortilla refuses to come free from the plastic, either you've pressed it too thin or the dough is too soft.
Griddle-Baking: If the lower heat isn't low enough, the tortilla will bubble and blister immediately and the result will be heavy. If the higher heat isn't high enough, the tortilla will not puff, which also means it will be somewhat heavy. Don't leave the tortilla for too long

over medium-low, the other end (or other skillet) over medium to medium-high.

3. *Pressing.* Cut 2 squares of heavy plastic to fit the plates of your tortilla press. With the press open, place a square of plastic over the bottom plate, set a ball of dough in the center, cover with the second square of plastic, and gently flatten the dough between. Close the top plate and press down gently but firmly with the handle. Open, turn the tortilla 180°, close and gently press again, to an even ¹⁄₁₆-inch thickness.

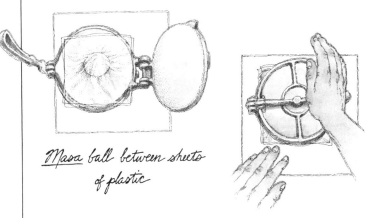

Masa ball between sheets of plastic

Pressing out the masa ball

4. *Unmolding.* Open the press and peel off the top sheet of plastic. Flip the tortilla onto one hand, *dough-side down,* then, starting at one corner, gently peel off the remaining sheet of plastic.

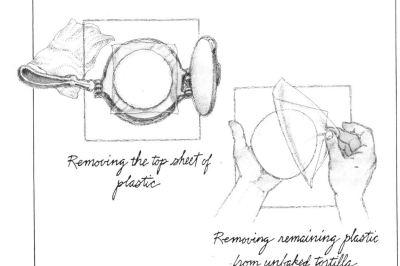

Removing the top sheet of plastic

Removing remaining plastic from unbaked tortilla

before flipping it the first time; it will dry out and then not puff.

Getting Tortillas to Puff: After you flip the baking tortillas the second time, pressing on them lightly with your fingertips or the back of your spatula will encourage the two layers to separate.

Equipment

Tortilla Presses: See page 343.

Ingredients

Masa vs. Masa Harina: While fresh *masa* is unsurpassed for taste and texture, *masa harina* makes good tortillas, though ones with a certain toasted flavor and a slight graininess.

Timing and Advance Preparation

Masa harina dough should be made at least ½ hour ahead (though it will keep for several hours at room temperature). Allow 15 to 30 minutes to press and bake the tortillas, depending on your proficiency and amount of griddle room. The hot tortillas can be wrapped in foil—towel and all—and kept warm in a *low* oven for an hour or so. To reheat cold tortillas, see the directions on page 353.

5. *Griddle-baking.* Lay the tortilla onto the cooler end of the griddle (or the cooler skillet). In about 20 seconds, when the tortilla loosens itself from the griddle (but the edges have not yet dried or curled), flip it over onto the hotter end of the griddle (or onto the hotter skillet). When lightly browned in spots underneath, 20 to 30 seconds more, flip a second time, back onto the side that was originally down. If the fire is properly hot, the tortilla will balloon up like pita bread. When  lightly browned, another 20 or 30 seconds, remove from the griddle (it will completely deflate) and wrap in a towel.

Press, unmold and bake the remaining balls of *masa,* placing each hot tortilla on top of the last and keeping the stack well wrapped.

6. *Resting.* Let the wrapped stack of tortillas rest for about 15 minutes to finish their cooking, soften and become pliable.

WHEAT-FLOUR TORTILLAS

Tortillas de Harina

The first homemade wheat-flour tortillas I remember tasting were in Morelia, Michoacán, of all places—far away from the Northern states where these are common. Outside the glass-enclosed kitchen of the Silla de Cerro *cabrito* restaurant, you could watch one cook care for the roasting kid and another rhythmically roll out ball after ball of white dough—four or five passes, and they were ready to bake on the iron griddle, where they ballooned beautifully. Like the best of them, those tortillas were steaming, tender and savory-tasting.

After a lot of experimenting through the years I think that the lightest and tastiest flour tortillas are the simplest ones—those made from part lard and cooked over a fairly high heat. No baking powder, no milk and no low-fat approaches. They are easy to make once you get the feel of the process; your rewards will match the effort, too, since they are so much better than the bready ones in the grocery-store packages.

YIELD: 12 tortillas

COOK'S NOTES

Techniques
Combining Fat and Flour: If this isn't done thoroughly (until no particles of fat remain visible), the tortillas will have an irregular texture.
Preparing the Dough in a Food Processor: Measure the flour and fat into the bowl of a food processor. Pulse several times, then run until the fat is thoroughly incorporated. Dissolve the salt in ⅔ cup warm water. With the machine running, pour the liquid through the feed tube in a steady stream. Let the machine run until the dough has collected into a ball. Test the consistency: If it is too stiff, divide the dough into several pieces, sprinkle with a tablespoon of water and process until it

¾ **pound (2¾ cups) all-purpose flour, plus a little extra for rolling the tortillas**
5 **tablespoons lard or vegetable shortening, or a mixture of the two**
¾ **teaspoon salt**
about ¾ cup very warm tap water

1. *The dough*. Combine the flour and fat in a large mixing bowl, working in the fat with your fingers, until *completely* incorporated. Dissolve the salt in the water, pour about ⅔ cup of it over the dry ingredients and immediately work it in with a fork; the dough will be in large clumps rather than a homogeneous mass. If all the dry ingredients haven't been dampened, add the rest of the liquid (plus a little more, if necessary). Scoop the dough onto your work surface and knead until smooth. It should be a medium-stiff consistency—definitely not firm, but not quite as soft as most bread dough either.

2. *Resting*. Divide the dough into 12 portions and roll each into a ball. Set them on a plate, cover with plastic wrap and let rest at least 30 minutes (to make the dough less springy, easier to roll).

3. *Rolling and griddle-baking*. Heat an ungreased griddle or heavy skillet over medium to medium-high heat.

On a lightly floured surface, roll out a portion of the dough into an even 7-inch circle: Flatten a ball of dough, flour it, then roll forward and back across it; rotate a sixth of a turn and roll forward and back again; continue rotating and rolling until you reach a 7-inch circle, lightly flouring the tortilla and work surface from time to time.

Lay the tortilla on the hot griddle (you should hear a faint sizzle and see an almost immediate bubbling across the surface). After 30 to 45 seconds, when there are browned splotches underneath, flip it over. Bake 30 to 45 seconds more, until the other side is browned; *don't overbake the tortilla or it will become crisp*. Remove and wrap in a heavy towel. Roll and griddle-bake the remaining tortillas in the same manner, stacking them one on top of the other, wrapped in the towel.

Palm tortilla basket and cloth

forms a ball again. No additional kneading is necessary.
Griddle-Baking: The temperature is all important: It must be hot enough to puff the tortillas quickly; if the tortilla balloons up into a pillow, all the better, since the more bubbles the lighter the end result.

Ingredients
Lard and Shortening: In my opinion, flour tortillas made from all vegetable shortening are bland, but those made with all lard are a little crumbly and heavy. My favorite tortillas are made with 2½ tablespoons of each.

Timing and Advance Preparation
The dough preparation takes 15 minutes and should be begun 45 minutes before you start baking; covered and refrigerated, the dough will keep for several days. Allow about 30 minutes for rolling and baking. If you don't plan to serve the tortillas right away, wrap the cloth-covered tortillas in foil and keep them warm in a *very low* oven; they will hold for an hour or more.

A NOTE ON REWARMING FLOUR TORTILLAS
Though they're not *quite* as good as the fresh-baked ones, flour tortillas can be made ahead; refrigerate them wrapped in a plastic bag. To reheat, wrap stacks of 6 or 8 flour tortillas (either homemade or store-bought) in foil and reheat them in a 325° oven for 15 to 20 minutes.

CRISP-FRIED TORTILLAS AND CHIPS

Tostadas y Tostaditas (o Totopos)

I've heard it said that North America's favorite flavor is crisp, so perhaps it's no wonder that we've perfected the crisp chip snack. Yes, it's *our* tortilla factories that have learned to make up drier, thinner tortillas (often made of rather coarse-ground *masa*), especially for frying to a crisp light snap that almost melts in your mouth.

Mexicans, on the whole, don't seem to be as enthralled with the concept of crisp. So they fry sturdier, meatier tortillas, cut up for chips *(tostaditas)* or left whole for tostadas.

For the exigencies of the North American audience, I've tackled fried chips and tostadas in considerable detail, ensuring that what you turn out will be crisp and light.

YIELD: 8 tostadas, or chips for 2 or 3 people

> 8 corn tortillas (page 353), preferably stale, store-
>   bought ones
> Vegetable oil to a depth of 1 inch, for deep-frying
> Salt, as desired

1. *Drying the tortillas.* For chips, cut the tortillas into 4 to 6 wedges; for tostadas, leave them whole. Spread into a single layer, cover lightly with a dry towel to keep them from curling, and let dry until very leathery.

2. *Frying.* Heat the oil to 380°. For tostadas, lay the tortillas in the oil one at a time, flip them after about 30 seconds, then fry them until they are *lightly* browned and completely crisp, about 30 seconds longer. For chips, distribute a few wedges of tortilla over the oil and stir them nearly constantly to keep them separate, for 45 seconds to 1 minute, until *lightly* browned and completely crisp. Tostadas/chips are not done until nearly all bubbling has stopped.

Remove from the oil, shaking off the excess, and drain on paper towels. While the chips are warm, sprinkle with salt, if you like.

COOK'S NOTES

Techniques

Drying the Tortillas: If the tortillas are moist at all, they will turn out greasy. Completely dried—that is, hard—tortillas come out greaseless but *very* crunchy.

Deep-Frying: If the oil temperature ever drops below 360°, the tostadas or chips will usually turn out greasy. If possible, fry in a heavy pan (to stabilize the heat) and use a thermometer. The color of the tortillas will be darkened only slightly when the tostadas/chips are ready; if fried until clearly brown (rather than golden brown), they will taste burnt.

Timing and Advance Preparation

Plan an hour or so for drying the tortillas; frying goes quickly. You can keep them warm in a low oven for ½ hour, but they're best soon after frying. Leftovers may be stored in an airtight container for a day, then rewarmed in the oven.

Regional Explorations

In Tuxtla Gutiérrez, Chiapas, the delicate tostadas rival the Stateside beauties. In Guadalajara, you'll find more substantial crisp-fried tortillas by the bin load. Some places, tortillas are simply toasted to a chewy crispness, rather than fried. The most famous are Tehuantepec's *totopos* (a word used to refer to chips in much of Mexico): They're made from coarse-ground *masa* that's patted out, slapped onto the walls of barrel-shaped clay ovens that resemble the East Indian *tandoor*, and dried.

APPETIZERS AND SALADS

❖

Entremeses y Ensaladas

Las Cazuelas restaurant, Mexico City

Very early in my Mexican adventure, I came face to face with fiestas and delectable food and the joyous celebration that works the two together. In the capital, I'd found my way through the narrow old streets into the front door of Fonda las Cazuelas restaurant. I'd moved past the glassed-in kitchen, with its massive mortars and earth-brown clay cooking pots, into a ladder-back chair at a cloth-covered table; the noisy dining room always seemed ready to burst apart with each blast of the *mariachi*'s trumpet. A plate of appetizers came, then my first taste of thick and foamy *pulque* (fermented juice of the maguey plant), or perhaps little shots of tequila and the spicy *sangrita* chaser. The tables were set for ten, fifteen, twenty-five, and we all bit into our appetizer-size *masa* turnovers with special relish; we made thick, soft tacos from golden-brown pork *carnitas,* from guacamole, from cactus salad and crisp pork rind. We ordered more of it all, with more to drink. And only later on that holiday afternoon did we think about a chicken leg in red or green *mole, chiles rellenos* or flan and cinnamon-flavored sweet coffee.

They set out an *entremés* (or, as it's often called, *entremés ranchero*—"ranch-style appetizer") in other Mexico City restaurants, I discovered; in fact, they put together good starters most anyplace where there's something to celebrate. Sunday afternoons we ate nothing but *entremeses,* it seemed, when we went for pit-cooked lamb out south of the capital. For birthdays, we went to Mexico City's elegant Hacienda de los Morales and enjoyed the savory *masa* boats (*sopes*) while sitting in the courtyard. On the coasts, we got the cocktails of mixed seafood, or the *seviches,* or the shredded fish or crab preparations called *machacas* or *salpicones.* In the North, it was always a plate of melted cheese with peppers and *chorizo* to start off a roast-kid dinner. And in mountainous Chiapas, there were plates of ham, allspice-flavored sausage (*butifarra*), blood sausage and locally made cheese. They are all delicious, hearty and varied, and, like many of our appetizers, they are reserved for special meals—when the commonplace preliminary bowl of soup (that every good Mexican wife and mother includes in a "proper" meal) can be overlooked.

Mexico also offers a collection of highly prized *entremeses* for the adventurous: beautiful gratinéed crepes with the black corn mushrooms (*huitlacoche*) or squash blossoms in the elegant restaurants of Central Mexico; salads of smoked gar (*pejelagarto*) in Tabasco; crisp-fried maguey worms in Puebla; toasted grasshoppers in Oaxaca; tiny fresh-water lobsterettes (*acosiles*) in Toluca; fried minnowlike *charales* in Michoacán; and the abundant pickled pigs' feet and pork rind in the West-Central states. It easily goes on and on, because every area has something special for fiesta.

There is—or was—a great tradition in the *pulque* parlors and *cantinas* of deliciously spicy *botanas* (literally "corks" or "stoppers") for the patrons to enjoy. Though that isn't my territory, I go for the similar nibbles they sell on the streets—mostly on weekends, at night or during fiestas: the pumpkinseeds and chile-coated peanuts, the spears of cucumber or slabs of *jícama* with lime and chile, the fruit salads. And, of course, the myriad *masa* snacks that are known as *antojitos* (pages 119–192). In their own ways, all of them can be brought in from the street or taco stands and put out as appetizers on a well-set table.

Out-and-out first courses—a small portion of just about anything, coming before the main course—doesn't really fit into the formal Mexican meal, for it would have to usurp the place of the prized soup. But for a special occasion (or simply when it seems appropriate), it's always possible to slip in a little *entremés* first.

And a salad? If you're a health-conscious Mexican you might want to have one for a lunch or supper, as they do in other parts of the world. Most Mexicans I know, however, have their only salad sprinkled on their tacos or other snacks; and if you calculate it out, I think you'd find they eat a fair amount of salad indeed.

I've included in this chapter a couple of the very few traditional salads. I have refrained, however, from tackling the baroque Christmas Eve salad of beets, *jícama,* radish, banana, lettuce and numerous other ingredients that don't really seem to go together; some cooks surely make it, but I've not met them. Cookbooks from Mexico always list a number of European- and North American–sounding salads, but they have no place in the country's public food. Nontraditionally, however, I like to serve simple green salads with many of my Mexican meals, so I've worked up several distinctive dressings I think go well with the traditional flavors of other dishes. You'll find them at the end of the chapter.

Recipes from other chapters that work well as appetizers, first courses and salads: all the soups (pages 93–110), of course, and the lighter *antojitos* (pages 119–192), plus Fish *Adobado* in Cornhusks (page 218), Oysters in *Escabeche* (page 220), *Chiles Rellenos* (page 245), Chunky Guacamole (page 44), Cactus-Paddle Salad (page 47), Pickled Vegetables with Chiles (page 49).

MELTED CHEESE WITH ROASTED PEPPERS AND *CHORIZO*

Queso Fundido con Rajas y Chorizo

Topped with roasted peppers and aged *chorizo,* the melted cheese is a simple, perfect filling for flour tortillas; it can be your main course for a light meal, or it fits in before Steak *a la Tampiqueña* (page 243), with a sweet fruit ice (page 300) for dessert.

It's a famous Northern dish (especially in Monterrey, where they call it *queso flameado*) and it's served up in eating places that feature glowing grills for the slow, smoky roasting of *cabrito* ("kid") and the quick melting of cheese in shallow earthenware plates. There, the cheese is a flavorful *queso asadero* ("broiling cheese") that is stringy like mozzarella when melted. The dish is popular in Northern-style *taquerías* throughout the country, though, and just about any of the good Mexican melting cheeses will be used.

YIELD: enough to fill 6 to 8 flour tortillas, serving 4 to 6 as an appetizer, 2 to 3 as a light main course

>   2   tablespoons vegetable oil
> ½   small onion, thinly sliced
>   1   fresh *chile poblano,* roasted and peeled (page 337), seeded and sliced into thin strips
>   4   ounces (½ cup) *chorizo* sausage, store-bought or homemade (page 54), casing removed
>   8   ounces (2 heaping cups) melting cheese (page 328) like mozzarella and/or Monterey Jack, cut into ½-inch cubes

1. *Heating the pan.* Turn the oven on to 375° and set an 8- to 9-inch pie pan or gratin dish in the lower third to heat while you prepare the toppings.

2. *The chiles and chorizo.* In a medium-small skillet, heat *half* the oil over medium. Add the sliced onion and cook, stirring frequently, until the onion is lightly browned, about 8 minutes. Stir in the pepper strips, cook several minutes until they're softening, then scoop the mixture into a small bowl. Measure the remaining oil into the skillet and reduce the heat to medium-

COOK'S NOTES

Techniques
Heating the Pan: The pan is heated so the cheese melts quickly and evenly without overcooking.

Ingredients
Chile Poblano: Local or seasonal chiles are frequently utilized in this dish: a couple of long green chiles or *chiles chilacas* can replace the *poblano.*

Timing and Advance Preparation
The dish can be ready in about ½ hour. The cheese may be cubed in advance, and the chile mixture and *chorizo* can be cooked; if refrigerated, warm the latter two to room temperature before adding to the cheese.

CONTEMPORARY IDEAS
Queso Fundido with Roasted Peppers and Fresh Herbs: Prepare the dish as directed, using a mixture of whole-milk mozzarella and Monterey Jack or Italian Fontina cheese, and replacing the *poblano* with red, yellow or long green peppers (roasted, peeled, seeded and sliced); if desired, replace the *chorizo* with another flavorful sausage. Sprinkle with chopped fresh herbs (thyme, oregano, basil and the like) just before serving.

low. Add the *chorizo* and gently fry until done, about 10 minutes, breaking up any clumps as it cooks. Drain off excess fat and set the skillet aside.

3. *Melting the cheese.* Remove the hot pan from the oven and spread the cheese cubes in a shallow layer over the bottom. Bake for about 10 minutes, until the cheese is just melted. Remove the pan from the oven and sprinkle on the chile-onion mixture and the *chorizo*. Bake for 4 or 5 more minutes to heat the vegetables and meat, then carry the hot, bubbling *queso fundido* to the table for people to scoop into warm flour tortillas, roll up and eat.

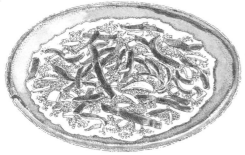

Queso fundido

LIME-MARINATED MACKEREL WITH TOMATO AND GREEN CHILE

Seviche de Sierra

To my tongue, there is nothing more refreshing than the clean, fresh taste of *seviche,* whether it is made in the saucy, tomatoey Acapulco/west-coast style or with the chunky simplicity of the east-coast versions. Because it is light and mild, *seviche* is a good way to ease into the rich or spicy Mexican sauces. It's good as picnic fare too (kept in a cold thermos), or served in the backyard before a cookout.

My recipe for the classic mackerel *seviche* in fresh-tasting tomato "sauce" is based on one published in Mexico's *Gastrotur* magazine. The less saucy versions are in the notes; they're a little dressier since they can be served on a lettuce-lined plate, but they're also good served simply on tostadas for a stand-up hors d'oeuvre.

YIELD: about 4 cups, 6 servings

COOK'S NOTES

Techniques
Filleting and Skinning Fish:
See the notes on page 211.

Ingredients
The Fish: Sierra is in the mackerel family, closely related to Spanish mackerel and king-fish; either can be substituted. Alternately, you can choose practically any meaty saltwater fish like striped bass, grouper (sea bass on the West Coast), and halibut or fluke (a large flounder). Most critical is that your fish be impeccably fresh.

Timing and Advance Preparation
You need to start at least 4 hours ahead, though I highly recommend letting most any

1 pound *very fresh,* boneless, skinless *sierra* or other
   fish fillets (see Ingredients in Cook's Notes)
1 cup freshly squeezed (*not bottled*) lime juice
   (roughly 6 to 8 limes)
½ medium onion, finely diced
1 ripe, medium-small tomato, cored and chopped
   into ¼-inch dice
16 to 20 meaty, flavorful green olives (preferably
   medium *manzanillos*), pitted and roughly
   chopped
Fresh hot green chiles to taste (roughly 2 *chiles
   serranos* or 1 *chile jalapeño*), stemmed, seeded
   and finely chopped
1 to 2 tablespoons finely chopped fresh coriander
   (*cilantro*) or parsley
1 cup good-quality tomato juice
3 tablespoons vegetable oil, preferably part olive
   oil
1 teaspoon dried oregano
Salt, about ½ teaspoon
Sugar, about 1 teaspoon (optional)
Sprigs of fresh coriander (*cilantro*) or parsley, or
   some diced avocado, for garnish

1. *Marinating the fish.* Run your finger down the groove in the center of each fillet, feeling for the stubby ends of tiny rib bones. To remove them, run a sharp knife along the groove just to one side of the bones, cutting the fillets in half lengthwise. Then, from the halves containing the stubby ends, cut off the thin strips of flesh in which the bones are embedded and discard them. Cut the fillets into ⅜-inch cubes and place in a noncorrosive bowl.

Pour the lime juice over the fish, mix thoroughly, cover with a sheet of plastic wrap pressed directly on the surface of the fish, and refrigerate 4 hours, or overnight, to "cook" the fish. To ascertain if the fish is ready, break apart a cube of fish: If it is still raw-looking inside, it needs to marinate longer.

2. *Finishing the seviche.* Shortly before you are planning to serve, drain the fish thoroughly. Mix in the chopped onion, tomato, olives, green chile, fresh coriander or parsley, tomato juice, oil and oregano. Season with salt and the optional sugar, cover and refrigerate until serving time.

When you are ready to serve, spoon a portion of the *seviche* into each of 6 small bowls. Garnish with sprigs of fresh coriander, sprigs of parsley or diced avocado.

fish marinate overnight (or up to 2 days). The remaining preparation requires less than ½ hour and should be completed shortly before serving.

TRADITIONAL VARIATIONS

Seviche for Tostadas: Chop the fish into tiny pieces, then marinate it as described. Finish according to the directions, reducing the tomato juice to a tablespoon or two and the oil to 1 tablespoon.

Shrimp Seviche: For less saucy *seviche,* chop 1 pound raw shrimp (peeled and deveined) into ½-inch pieces; marinate for 12 hours in the lime juice, mixed with ½ red onion (chopped) and ½ teaspoon *each* coarsely ground allspice and black peppercorns. Drain, mix in 1 *jalapeño* (chopped), 2 tablespoons chopped fresh coriander (*cilantro*), 2 teaspoons vinegar and 3 tablespoons olive oil. Toss with salt and 1 avocado (peeled, pitted and cubed), and serve on leaves of lettuce.

CONTEMPORARY IDEAS

Scallop Seviche with Chipotle: Marinate 1 pound bay scallops with red onion and spices as described in the shrimp *seviche* variation. Drain, mix in 2 canned *chipotle* peppers (seeded and chopped), a little fresh oregano, 2 teaspoons vinegar and 3 tablespoons olive oil. Toss with salt and 1 avocado (peeled, pitted and cubed).

Kitchen Spanish

I use the spelling *seviche* because it is common and sanctioned by the *Diccionario de mejicanismos.* It may be true, as the late Mexican gastronome

Mexican lime juicer

SHREDDED-BEEF SALAD WITH AVOCADO AND *CHILE CHIPOTLE*

Salpicón de Res Poblano

They make incredibly good *tortas* of this *salpicón* at a snack shop in colonial Puebla: a crackling-crisp bun full of meaty, shredded brisket dressed with olive oil *vinagreta* and topped with smoky *chipotle* chiles, a good slice of avocado and milky fresh cheese. In Mexico City, the famed Fonda el Refugio restaurant beautifully arranges those same basic components and serves them as a salady appetizer or a light main course. That's how I've chosen to present the delicious *salpicón* here, and I can make a special meal out of it—especially in summer—with nothing more than Chile-Marinated Vegetable Tostadas (page 165) to start and a Creamy Fresh-Coconut Dessert (page 285).

YIELD: about 3 cups, serving 4 as an appetizer, 2 or 3 as a light main course

For the meat mixture:

- 1 pound flank steak or brisket, well trimmed and cut into 2-inch squares
- 1 clove garlic, peeled and quartered
- 1 fresh *chile serrano* (or ½ fresh *chile jalapeño*), sliced (optional)
- 2 bay leaves
- ½ teaspoon mixed dried herbs (such as marjoram and thyme)
- ¼ teaspoon freshly ground black pepper
- A generous ½ teaspoon salt
- 1 small onion, diced
- 2 small (about 6 ounces total) boiling potatoes like the red-skinned ones, quartered

Amando Farga claimed, that Captain Vasco Núñez de Balboa discovered it in the South Seas in 1513 and christened it the homophonous *cebiche*, from *cebar* ("to penetrate"); but that still doesn't affect the fact that it's generally spelled *seviche*.

COOK'S NOTES

Ingredients
Chiles Chipotles: These are what make the dish really sing; if they are unavailable, substitute 4 pickled *jalapeños* and 2 tablespoons chopped fresh coriander *(cilantro)*.

Timing and Advance Preparation
Beginning-to-end preparation time is about 2 hours, only about ½ hour of it active. Though at its best when prepared shortly beforehand, the dish may be completed through Step 3 a day ahead and refrigerated. Let warm to room temperature before finishing Step 4; if the potatoes have absorbed most of the dressing, mix up a little more to pour over it all.

TRADITIONAL VARIATIONS
Yucatecan Dzik de Res: Prepare the meat as directed in Step 1, then dice and add ½ medium red onion, 4 large radishes, hot green chile to taste and 1 small tomato. Toss with 2 tablespoons chopped fresh coriander *(cilantro)*, 6 tablespoons bitter orange juice (page 340) and salt to taste.

For the dressing:
  ¾ cup olive oil
  ¼ cup cider vinegar
  ½ teaspoon salt
  ¼ teaspoon freshly ground black pepper

To finish the dish:
  6 leaves romaine lettuce
  1 ripe avocado, peeled, pitted and sliced
  4 canned *chiles chipotles,* halved and seeded
  ½ cup (2 ounces) crumbled Mexican *queso fresco*
        (page 327) or other fresh cheese like feta or
        farmer's cheese
  3 or 4 radish roses, for garnish

1. *The meat.* Bring 3 cups water to a boil in a medium-size saucepan, add the squares of meat and skim off any grayish foam that rises to the top during the first few minutes of boiling. Add the garlic, optional chile, bay leaves, herbs, pepper, salt and *half* of the onion, and simmer over medium to medium-low heat for an hour or so, until the meat is tender. If there is time, let cool in the broth. Drain and discard all but the meat; then shred the meat into long, thin strands.

2. *The potatoes.* While the meat is cooking, boil the potatoes in salted water to cover until they are *just* tender, about 15 minutes. Cool under running water, peel off the skins if you wish, then dice into ½-inch bits. Add to the meat, along with the remaining onion.

3. *The dressing.* Measure the dressing ingredients into a small bowl or a jar with a tight-fitting lid. Whisk or shake to thoroughly blend, then pour ⅔ of the dressing over the meat mixture. Stir, cover and let stand ½ hour.

4. *Completing the dish.* Just before serving, line a platter with 4 of the romaine leaves; slice the remaining 2 to make a bed in the center. Taste the meat-potato-onion *salpicón* for salt, then scoop it into a mound over the sliced lettuce. Decorate with slices of avocado alternating with *chile chipotle* halves, then re-mix the rest of the dressing and drizzle it over the whole affair. Sprinkle with the cheese, decorate with the radish roses, and the *salpicón* is ready to serve.

CONTEMPORARY IDEAS

Beef and Jícama Salpicón: Prepare the recipe through Step 3, omitting the potatoes and adding, along with the onion in Step 2, 1 cup matchstick-cut *jícama,* 4 sliced radishes and ⅓ cup diced green onion. Serve on lettuce leaves garnished with the diced *chipotle* and drizzled with the remaining dressing.

Kitchen Spanish

In Spanish, *salpicón* means "hodgepodge," or "splash" or "spatter." In the Mexican kitchen, that translates as a mixture with shredded beef or chicken in Central Mexico, shredded beef and eggs in Acapulco, well-seasoned shredded crab on the east coast, shredded venison with bitter orange juice in Tabasco, even a spicy condiment mixture in Yucatán.

MIXED VEGETABLE SALAD WITH LIME DRESSING

Ensalada Mixta

There are times when *arugula, mâche* and *radicchio* don't have the appeal of a homey, Mexican mixed-vegetable salad laid out with hard-boiled eggs, avocado and a sprinkling of fresh cheese. Something like it is served in most coffee shops and restaurants in the country's larger cities—where European colonialism is fully rooted. "Salad" to the rest of Mexico is little more than the combination of raw greens and vegetables that decorates tacos, enchiladas, *pozole* and the like.

This simple, flexible recipe can accommodate most anything that might be on hand. While the typical Mexican vegetable-cooking method is boiling, I've found it easier to steam here. This salad is delicious and beautiful served before Fish with Peppers and Cream (page 216).

YIELD: about 6 cups, 6 servings

About 2 cups (total) of any or all of the following:
    Carrots, peeled and sliced diagonally ⅛ inch thick
    Small boiling potatoes like the red-skinned ones, sliced ⅛ inch thick
    Beets, peeled and sliced ⅛ inch thick

About 2 cups (total) of any or all of the following:
    Green beans, ends snipped and cut in half
    Peas, fresh or (defrosted) frozen

About 2 cups (total) of any or all of the following:
    Radishes, stem- and root-ends removed, sliced paper-thin
    Cucumbers, peeled, seeded (if desired) and sliced ⅛ inch thick
    Tomatoes, cored and sliced ⅛ inch thick

For the dressing:
    3 tablespoons freshly squeezed lime juice
    ½ cup vegetable oil, preferably part olive oil
    ½ teaspoon salt

COOK'S NOTES

Timing and Advance Preparation
The time involved depends on the number of vegetables you choose and how quickly you can prepare them: Allow about 1 hour. The cooked vegetables may be prepared a day ahead, the raw vegetables several hours in advance. Dress the salad at serving time.

A generous ¼ teaspoon freshly ground black pepper

1½ tablespoons finely chopped fresh coriander (*cilantro*) or flat-leaf parsley (optional)

For the garnish:

6 leaves romaine or leaf lettuce

1 small bunch of watercress, large stems removed (optional)

1 hard-boiled egg, sliced ⅛ inch thick

1 thick slice of red onion, broken into rings

2 tablespoons crumbled Mexican *queso fresco* (page 327) or other fresh cheese like feta or farmer's cheese (optional)

1. *The vegetables.* In a large saucepan, set up a vegetable steamer over an inch of water and set over medium-high heat. When the water begins to boil, place the prepared carrots, potatoes and/or beets in separate shallow piles on the steamer rack. (If using beets, keep them away from the others, or you'll have a lot of red vegetables.) Steam, tightly covered, until the vegetables are tender but still retain a little firmness, 8 to 12 minutes, depending on their cut and condition. If one vegetable is done before the others, remove it with a large spoon or tongs. Cool the vegetables in separate groupings on a large tray.

Next, steam the green beans and/or fresh peas, tightly covered: 5 to 8 minutes for beans, anywhere from 4 to 20 minutes for the peas (depending on their size and freshness). When the green vegetables are done, remove them and cool with the other vegetables. Frozen peas need only be defrosted and set aside.

In a large bowl, mix together the radishes, cucumbers and/or tomatoes with the *well-drained,* cooked vegetables.

2. *The dressing.* A few minutes before serving, measure the lime juice, oil, salt, pepper and optional fresh coriander or parsley into a small bowl or a jar with tight-fitting lid; whisk or shake until thoroughly blended. Pour onto the vegetables and mix well.

3. *Garnish and presentation.* Line a large serving platter with lettuce leaves. Once again, toss the vegetable mixture with the dressing, then scoop it onto the platter. Garnish the edges with the optional watercress. Top with slices of hard-boiled egg, rings of red onion, and a sprinkling of the optional fresh cheese.

SPICY *JÍCAMA* SALAD WITH TANGERINES AND FRESH CORIANDER

Ensalada de Jícama

*J*ícama—the large, bulbous, woody-looking root vegetable—has something of a raw potato texture and a slightly sweet apple taste. And when it's one of the small (¾-pound) fresh-dug variety that comes out in the fall, it needs nothing more than the street vendor's squeeze of lime and sprinkling of salt and hot chile powder. In West-Central Mexico, restaurants sometimes offer *jícama* prepared with orange and *cilantro* (*pico de gallo*), and everywhere in the Republic the street-side fruit-salad sellers mix it with cantaloupe, watermelon, papaya and the like.

The refreshing recipe that follows is from a street vendor in Mérida, Yucatán; it goes well with other Yucatecan dishes like Stacked Tortillas with Shark and Tomato Sauce (page 161) or Chicken *Pibil* (page 233) and white rice.

YIELD: 6 to 8 cups (depending on the ingredients chosen), 6 to 8 servings

- 1 small (1-pound) *jícama,* peeled and cut into ¾-inch cubes
- ½ cup bitter orange juice (page 340)
- ¼ teaspoon salt
- 1 red-skinned apple, cored and cut into ¾-inch cubes (optional)
- ½ small cantaloupe, peeled, seeded and cut into ¾-inch cubes (optional)
- 3 tangerines, peeled, broken into sections and, if you wish, seeds cut out
- About 2 tablespoons roughly chopped fresh coriander (*cilantro*)
- Powdered dried chile, about 1 teaspoon (see Ingredients in Cook's Notes)
- 2 or 3 small leaves romaine lettuce, for garnish

1. *Marinating the jícama.* Place the *jícama* in a large noncorrosive bowl, pour in the bitter orange juice and sprinkle with salt. Toss well, cover and let stand at room temperature for an hour or so.

COOK'S NOTES

Ingredients

Jícama: If none is available, you can make a nice salad (though one that lacks the gentle sweetness and open crunchy texture) by substituting small fresh turnips and/or daikon radish.

Powdered Dried Chile: *Jícama* gets sprinkled with the fiery-hot powdered *chile seco* in Yucatán and *chile de árbol* most everywhere else. I like to use the less-hot powdered New Mexico or California chiles, then add a little cayenne to bring up the heat level.

Timing and Advance Preparation

The dish should be started 1½ hours before serving, though you will spend only about ½ hour actively working on it.

TRADITIONAL VARIATIONS

Pico de Gallo: This West-Central version of *jícama* salad is named "rooster's beak" because everything is chopped up. Marinate the *jícama* in ¼ cup lime juice and a little salt. Toss with 2 small seedless oranges (segmented and cubed), fresh coriander and powdered chile. I've also had an elegant version of sliced *jícama* laid out on a platter, alternating and overlapping with rounds of orange and cucumber; the whole assemblage was sprinkled with lime, coriander and chile.

CONTEMPORARY IDEAS

Cress and Jícama Salad: Cut ½ small *jícama* and an equal portion daikon radish into

2. *Finishing the salad.* About 15 minutes before serving, add the apple, cantaloupe, tangerines and fresh coriander to the bowl and mix thoroughly. Toss the mixture every few minutes until time to serve. Season with powdered chile, and add more salt and fresh coriander, if desired. Toss one final time and scoop the salad into a serving dish lined with romaine leaves.

matchsticks, and marinate in the bitter orange juice. Drain, reserving the juice. Blend together *half* the juice, an equal portion of olive oil and ½ *chile serrano.* Toss with *jícama* mixture, a large bunch of cress (large stems removed) and a little chopped fresh coriander.

jícama

NONTRADITIONAL SALAD DRESSINGS

AVOCADO DRESSING

YIELD: about 1⅓ cups

This thick, creamy dressing is just right for raw or blanched vegetables or over firmer lettuces like romaine.

  ½ ripe avocado, peeled and pitted
  1½ tablespoons freshly squeezed lime juice
  1½ tablespoons cider vinegar
  2 tablespoons chopped fresh coriander *(cilantro)*
  1 clove garlic, peeled and roughly chopped
  ⅔ cup vegetable oil
  1 large egg yolk
  The green top of 1 green onion, thinly sliced
  2 tablespoons cream
  Salt, about ½ teaspoon

Combine the avocado, lime juice, vinegar, coriander, garlic and oil in a blender or food processor, and process until smooth.

Whisk the yolk in a medium-size bowl until broken up, then slowly whisk in the avocado mixture, about a tablespoon at a time, to achieve a light mayonnaise consistency. Add the green onion and cream, then season with salt. Cover and refrigerate; if it becomes too thick during storage, whisk in a little more cream.

Hass avocado

ROASTED GARLIC DRESSING

YIELD: about ¾ cup

This simple vinegar-and-oil dressing goes beautifully with mixed fresh greens or matchsticks of *jícama* tossed with watercress and red onion. The rich-tasting Italian balsamic vinegar really enhances the roasted garlic flavor; look for it at any specialty food shop.

    3 large cloves garlic, unpeeled
    3 tablespoons balsamic vinegar
    ⅔ cup olive oil
    ¼ teaspoon freshly ground black pepper
    Salt, about ½ teaspoon

    1. *The garlic.* Roast the garlic on a griddle or heavy skillet over medium heat, turning occasionally until blackened in spots and soft, about 15 minutes. Cool, then slip off the skin.
    2. *The dressing.* Combine the garlic and the rest of the ingredients in a blender or food processor, and process until smooth. Taste for salt. Cover and store at room temperature.

LIME-*CILANTRO* DRESSING

YIELD: about 1 cup

This tart, creamy dressing is as tasty on a tossed salad of mixed lettuces as it is on steamed mixed vegetables.

> Two 2-inch strips of lime zest (green rind only), ¼ inch wide
> 2½ tablespoons freshly squeezed lime juice
> 2 small cloves garlic, peeled and roughly chopped
> ½ fresh *chile serrano,* seeded and roughly chopped
> 1½ tablespoons chopped fresh coriander (*cilantro*)
> ⅔ cup vegetable oil
> 3 tablespoons crumbled feta (or "natural"—no gum—cream) cheese
> Salt, about ½ teaspoon (depending on the saltiness of the cheese)

In a blender, whiz all ingredients until smooth. Taste for salt. Cover and refrigerate.

Fresh coriander (cilantro)

LIGHT AND HEARTY SOUPS

❖
Sopas, Caldos, Pozoles y Menudos

Traditional restaurant, San Luis Potosí

Mexican soups are a delicious, homemade-tasting, justly renowned lot of nourishment. By mixing the flavorful broth from the ever-stewing bird, pig or steer with the pulpy puree of good tomatoes, garlic and onions, Mexican cooks have created a delicious base for a brilliant variety—from cactus paddle to wild mushroom, from the ubiquitous vermicelli to soups thick with cheese. They've seasoned their offerings with little bundles of fresh thyme, marjoram and bay leaves brought from the markets and with large sprigs of leafy *epazote*. And they've worked their special magic with a squirt of fresh lime, slices of avocado, a little aromatic fresh coriander, sharp raw onion or toasted dried chile. These are spectacular soups, for people who love flavor and texture.

Soup—a *big* steaming bowl of soup—is an inextricable prelude to a traditional Mexican meal: "Don't you want a little soup to start?" the waiters always ask when you've failed to order it. The homey restaurant's set-course *comida corrida* would be almost unimaginable without at least one offering; most of the cookbooks plow immediately into dozens of soup recipes—perhaps with no reference to other starters at all.

The most characteristic soup in Mexico, in my opinion, is the classic *sopa de tortilla:* It shows the full range of traditional flavors and contrasting textures. The common, Spanish-style toasted-garlic soup plays a major role, too, as does the smoky-tasting vegetable-chicken *caldo tlalpeño* and the sprightly *sopa xóchitl*, with its bouquet of fresh condiments. And just about everywhere on the coasts (and inland, too), the simple, Mexican-flavored fish and shellfish chowders are popular: from fruits-of-the-sea *sopa de mariscos* and West-Coast oyster stews, to the fish-filled *caldo largo* of Veracruz, the *picante*, dark *caldo de camarón* (made with dried shrimp) that's available in several locales, and the Gulf Coast crab *chilpachole* I love so much. Mexico's favorite cream soup, undoubtedly, is made of fresh corn and flecked with rich *chile poblano*.

The cooks of each region have developed their own soupy specialties with what is locally available and prized: The Yucatecan tortilla soup (*sopa de lima*), is flavored with the fragrant lime called *lima agria;* the Central/West-Central *barbacoa* sellers serve a rich broth (*consomé*) they've collected from below their pit-roasting lamb or goat; Gulf, Southern and Yucatecan Mexico like a black bean soup now and again; Oaxacan cooks work up a popular broth with the squash-vine runners (*guías*); in Chiapas the specialty is a delicious, thick soup studded with the herb *chipilín*, corn and fresh cheese; in the North it's a comforting broth made with jerky or cheese; and throughout Central Mexico it's frequently an unctuous broth laden with marrow (*sopa de médula*), or lenten soups of fava bean (*caldo de habas*) and cactus paddles with egg (*nopales navegantes*).

And often in Mexico a large soup bowl holds the whole meal. In the markets and pedestrian eateries the offerings are chanted: the simple beef stew (*caldo de res,* or *puchero* in Yucatán) and one made of chicken (*caldo de pollo*); a hearty soup-stew with red-chile broth (*mole de olla*) for those in Central Mexico; or another with innards (*chocolomo*), should you find yourself in Campeche.

One year, my friends gave me a traditional Guerrero-style birthday, starting shortly after dawn. Flowers were tacked around my door and the chorus of "Las Mañanitas," the early-morning birthday song, pushed me out of bed and down to the kitchen for a shot of mescal and a huge, seven o'clock festal bowl of pork and hominy soup. The party could continue all day, I knew, with round after round of *pozole* . . . of mescal; the folks in Guerrero could live exclusively on this nourishment, it seemed to me.

Pozole, like the beloved, hearty tripe soup *menudo,* really is something special: a beautiful one-bowl meal to serve when a crowd comes, a rustic specialty to eat from the street stands at night or, in the case of *menudo,* the morning after. Both soup-stews are informal, high-spirited fiesta foods, like *tamales,* say, rather than the respectable platter of celebratory *mole.* But of the two, *pozole*—in any of the national colors (white, red or green)—is my favorite. It offers more of the contrasting textures—soft-cooked and crunchy-raw—and each guest gets to doctor it up *al gusto,* as the Spanish saying goes.

In the pages that follow, there is a good selection of recipes for traditional soups—both the lighter ones to serve before the main course and the rustic classics to make a meal on. In Mexico, I often find the portion of those lighter, meal-starting soups too large to precede three more courses. To me, those portions seem just about right to feature for an informal supper or winter lunch, together with some of the delicious *masa* snacks (pages 119–192).

For soup recipes in other chapters, see "Soups" in the Index.

Kitchen Spanish

North Americans are often confused when they see brothy soups and rice listed together on menus under the heading *"sopas."* The former are the *sopas aguadas* ("liquid soups"), the latter *sopas secas* ("dry soups"). Traditionally, "liquid" precedes "dry" in the *comida;* here, though, I've broken them up for North American readers, moving rice dishes in with vegetables. Perhaps (at the risk of sounding simplistic) the initially brothy look of simmering rice explains the categorization.

STED TORTILLA P WITH FRESH CHEESE AND *CHILE PASILLA*

Sopa de Tortilla

This is a quintessentially Mexican soup that's composed in the nicer *cafeterías* and restaurants across the Republic. Its base is the familiar broth from stewed chicken, plus crisp strips of tortillas and a bit of toasted dried chile. What adorns it is a homey parade of whatever is traditional or available: ingredients as simple as cubed fresh cheese or chicken, or as luxurious as thick cream, squash blossoms, *chicharrones* and avocado.

In small portions, this soup makes a nice beginning to a special meal of Duck in Pumpkinseed *Pipián* (page 225), Zucchini with Toasted Garlic (page 274) and Pecan Pie with Raw Sugar (page 289). Or add chicken and serve it as a hearty main course.

YIELD: 6 to 7 cups, 4 to 6 servings

    2 tablespoons lard or vegetable oil
    1 medium onion, sliced
    2 cloves garlic, peeled
    1 ripe, medium-small tomato, roasted or boiled
        (page 352), cored and peeled
        OR ½ 15-ounce can tomatoes, drained
    1½ quarts good broth, preferably poultry (page
        61)
    Salt, the quantity will vary depending on the sal-
        tiness of the broth
    4 to 6 corn tortillas, preferably stale, store-bought
        ones
    ⅓ cup vegetable oil
    1 to 2 dried *chiles pasillas*, stemmed, seeded and
        deveined
    8 ounces (about 2 cups) cubed Mexican *queso fresco*
        (page 327) or other fresh cheese like farmer's
        cheese, or even Muenster or Monterey Jack
    1 large lime, cut into 4 to 6 wedges

1. *The broth flavoring.* In a medium-size skillet, heat *1 table-spoon* of the lard or oil over medium-low. Add the onion and

COOK'S NOTES

Techniques
Frying Tortillas: See page 78.

Ingredients
Corn Tortillas: See page 353. *Chile Pasilla:* This traditional Central Mexican addition becomes the smoky *chile pasilla oaxaqueño* in Oaxaca, the *chile ancho* in Michoacán, and perhaps other not-too-hot dried chiles in your kitchen; fry and crumble the pods you find, but don't be tempted by chile powder.

Timing and Advance Preparation
With broth on hand, the soup can be ready in less than 1 hour. It may be prepared through Step 2 several days in advance, then covered and refrigerated.

whole garlic cloves, and fry until both are a deep golden-brown, 12 to 15 minutes. Scoop into a blender jar or food processor, add the tomato and process until smooth.

Heat the remaining tablespoon of lard or oil in the same skillet over medium-high. When hot, add the tomato mixture and stir constantly until thick and considerably darker, about 5 minutes. Scrape into a large saucepan.

2. *The broth.* Stir the broth into the tomato mixture, partially cover and simmer for ½ hour over medium-low heat. Season with salt.

3. *The garnishing ingredients.* If the tortillas are fresh or moist, let them dry out for a few minutes in a single layer. Slice them in half, then slice the halves crosswise into strips ¼ inch thick. Heat the ⅓ cup vegetable oil in a medium-small skillet over medium-high. When hot, add the tortilla strips and fry, turning frequently, until they are crisp. Drain on paper towels. Cut the chiles into 1-inch squares and fry in the hot oil *very briefly,* about 3 or 4 seconds; immediately remove and drain, then place in a small serving bowl.

4. *Assembling the soup.* Just before serving, divide the cheese among 4 to 6 bowls, and top with the fried tortilla strips. Ladle on the hot soup and serve right away. Pass the toasted chile separately, along with the lime (the juice of which brings out the flavors of the soup).

Tortilla soup with garnishes

GARBANZO-VEGETABLE SOUP WITH SMOKY BROTH AND FRESH AVOCADO

Caldo Tlalpeño

First, there is smoke and the prickle of *picante;* then meaty, mealy garbanzos and earthy root vegetables; finally, calming

CONTEMPORARY IDEAS

Tortilla Soup with Fresh Goat Cheese: Prepare the soup as directed, doubling the tomatoes, replacing the vegetable oil with olive oil, adding 3 sprigs fresh thyme along with the broth and replacing the fresh cheese with goat cheese.

Regional Explorations
This soup is found most commonly in Central and Southern Mexico, where it may be called *sopa azteca* (or *sopa tarasca* in Michoacán). In Yucatán, a similar soup is called *sopa de lima* because it is served with *lima agria* ("bitter" *lima*).

COOK'S NOTES

Techniques
Simmering Picante Chiles in Soups: If you add the chile much before serving, the piquancy can increase so that a once-mild broth can pack a walloping punch.

broth and the soothing bits of oily avocado. It's a soup with the savoriness of the vegetable-studded broth that collects below pit-roasted *barbacoa*—the broth that was likely the inspiration for *caldo tlalpeño*.

This recipe, based on the version served at the Bola Roja restaurant in Puebla, makes a good first course before Beef Tips *a la Mexicana* (page 241) or Fish with Toasted Garlic (page 215). Or serve large bowls for a main course, with Deep-Fried *Masa* Turnovers (*quesadillas*, page 143).

YIELD: about 2½ quarts, 6 generous servings

>   2   quarts good chicken broth (page 61)
>   1   large (1¼-pound), whole chicken breast
>   1   teaspoon mixed dried herbs (such as marjoram and thyme)
>   1   tablespoon lard or vegetable oil
>   1   medium onion, diced
>   1   large carrot, peeled and diced
>   1   large clove garlic, peeled and minced
>   One 15-ounce can garbanzos (chickpeas), drained and rinsed
>   1   sprig *epazote* (see Ingredients in Cook's Notes)
>   Salt, the quantity will vary depending on the saltiness of the broth
>   Canned *chiles chipotles* to taste (roughly 1 to 2 chiles), seeded and thinly sliced
>   1   ripe, medium avocado, peeled, pitted and diced
>   1   large lime, cut into 6 wedges

1. *The broth.* Place the broth and chicken in a 4-quart saucepan and bring to a simmer over medium heat. Skim off any grayish foam that rises during the first few minutes of simmering, add the herbs, cover and simmer 13 minutes.

Remove the chicken breast, skin and bone it, then tear the meat into thick shreds and set aside. Strain the broth and skim off all the fat that rises to the top.

2. *Finishing the soup.* Wash the pan, set it over medium heat, and add the lard or oil, onion and carrots. Cook, stirring occasionally, until the onions begin to brown, about 7 minutes. Add the garlic and cook 1 minute longer. Stir in the broth, garbanzos and *epazote*, partially cover and simmer for 30 minutes. Season with salt.

3. *Garnishing the soup.* Just before serving, add the chile and shredded chicken to the simmering soup. Let them heat through, then ladle the soup into bowls, top with diced avocado, and serve accompanied by wedges of lime.

Ingredients

Epazote: The bitter herb adds another dimension to the soup, but it can be omitted; the results are still very good. *Chiles Chipotles:* Without them this soup really loses something. If canned chiles are unavailable, dried ones (toasted and soaked) are an option, should you find them. Or prepare the *sopa xóchitl* variation.

Timing and Advance Preparation

If the broth is on hand, the soup takes ½ hour to make and ½ hour to simmer. It may be prepared through Step 2 a couple of days ahead; refrigerate the broth and chicken separately, both well covered.

TRADITIONAL VARIATIONS

Sopa Xóchitl: To prepare this soup named for the Aztec goddess of flowers, complete the recipe through Step 2, omitting the carrots and adding 2 tablespoons raw rice with the broth. When ready to serve, add the chicken and a handful of squash blossoms (cleaned of all the stamens), if you have them; simmer several minutes, until the blossoms are tender. Garnish with diced avocado, a little chopped fresh coriander, chopped raw onion, chopped fresh *jalapeño* and a wedge of tomato.

Kitchen Spanish

After years of searching, I still haven't discovered how this soup got its name. There seems a thread of connection, though, between the Mexico City suburb of Tlalpan, its famous barbacoa sellers and the meaning of the Nahuatl word *tlalpan* ("on land").

FRESH CORN CHOWDER WITH ROASTED PEPPERS

Crema de Elote

With its smooth, rich texture punctuated with bits of green chile and sharp fresh cheese, this was the most popular soup I served while I was chef of Lopez y Gonzalez restaurant in Cleveland. Its richness goes well before Charcoal-Grilled Chicken (page 228), with fresh fruit ice (page 300) or Pecan Pie with Raw Sugar (page 289) for dessert.

A rather plain-tasting bowl of this chowder is ubiquitous in Mexican *cafeterías*, largely because Campbell's can be purchased everywhere. A homemade version, however, seems to be listed most frequently on *comida corrida* menus in Central and West-Central Mexico.

YIELD: about 1 quart, 4 servings

> 3 **large ears fresh sweet corn**
>   **OR 2½ to 3 cups frozen corn, defrosted**
> 4 **tablespoons unsalted butter**
> ½ **medium onion, finely chopped**
> 2 **cloves garlic, peeled and minced**
> 1½ **tablespoons cornstarch**
> 2 **cups milk, plus a little more if necessary**
> 2 **fresh *chiles poblanos,* roasted and peeled (page 337), seeded and finely diced**
> 1 **cup Thick Cream (page 51) or whipping cream**
> **Salt, about 1 teaspoon**
> ½ **cup (2 ounces) crumbled Mexican *queso fresco* (page 327) or other fresh cheese like feta or farmer's cheese**
> 2 **tablespoons chopped flat-leaf parsley, for garnish**

1. *Preparing the corn.* For fresh corn, husk and remove all of the corn silk, then cut the kernels from each cob with a sharp knife; transfer to a blender or food processor. Scrape all the remaining bits of corn from the cobs, using the end of a spoon and add to the rest. There should be between 2½ and 3 cups of corn. Simply place defrosted frozen corn in the blender or processor.

2. *The corn puree.* Heat *half* of the butter in a small skillet

COOK'S NOTES

Ingredients

Sweet Corn and Mexican Field Corn: Because sweet corn isn't popular in Mexico, the soup is traditionally made with non-sweet field corn, which has enough natural starch to thicken the soup. I've adapted this recipe from *Recetario mexicano del maíz,* substituting sweet corn, though the taste is obviously sweeter. Field-corn soup—no sugar added—tastes a little like one made from potatoes.

Chile Poblano: Three long green chiles can be substituted for the *poblanos,* though their flavor isn't as pronounced.

Timing and Advance Preparation

This soup takes only about 45 minutes. Though best when just made, it keeps for several days, covered and refrigerated; reheat *slowly,* thinning with additional milk, if necessary.

over medium. Add the onion and fry until soft, 6 or 7 minutes, then stir in the garlic and cook a minute longer. Scrape the mixture into the corn in the blender or processor, along with the cornstarch and ¼ cup water. Process until smooth. (With a blender, you'll have to pulse the machine and stir the contents several times—but do not add more liquid; there is enough moisture in the corn once the blades can get at it.)

Melt the remaining 2 tablespoons of butter in a medium-large saucepan set over medium heat. Add the corn puree and stir constantly for several minutes, until quite thick.

3. *Finishing the soup.* Whisk in the milk, partially cover and simmer 15 minutes over medium-low heat, stirring often.

When the soup is ready, strain it through a medium-mesh sieve. Rinse out the pan, return the strained soup to it and stir in the diced *chile poblano* and cream. Season with salt and simmer over medium-low heat for 10 minutes longer, stirring frequently.

When you are ready to serve, thin the soup with additional milk if it is thicker than heavy cream, then ladle into small, warm soup bowls. Garnish with the fresh cheese and chopped parsley, and serve at once.

SPICY CRAB SOUP

Chilpachole de Jaiba

Jaibas, the little live blue crabs, come to the Veracruz market tied into bundles, ready for boiling, picking and stuffing, or for stewing into a rich-tasting, spicy *chilpachole*. This recipe, given to me by a waitress in Veracruz, is one of the least complicated I know; I think its simplicity (and the bit of *chipotle* pepper) best shows off the crab. For a special dinner, serve it before Green Pumpkinseed *Mole* (page 203); or more simply, serve it with *Picadillo* Turnovers (page 150).

YIELD: about 1½ quarts, 4 to 6 servings

    8 medium (2 to 2½ pounds total) live blue crabs (see Ingredients in Cook's Notes*)*
    3 cloves garlic, unpeeled

TRADITIONAL VARIATIONS

Corn Soup with Various Flavors: A large tomato (peeled and diced) can go in with the chiles; all or half of the milk may be replaced with chicken broth.

CONTEMPORARY IDEAS

Corn Soup with Shrimp: Prepare the recipe using 1 red and 1 *poblano* pepper (both roasted, peeled, seeded and sliced); add 1 tomato (peeled and diced) along with the peppers. Just before serving, add 6 ounces shrimp (peeled, deveined and diced), cook 2 or 3 minutes, then serve garnished with crumbled goat cheese or feta.

COOK'S NOTES

Techniques
Simmering Chile in Soups: See page 97.

Ingredients
Live Blue Crabs: Live blue crabs are available in many ethnic markets (especially Oriental ones); choose *lively* ones and cook them the day you buy them. If they are unavailable, you may substitute 1 large Dungeness crab: If it is alive, boil, clean and pick it as you would the blue crabs. A frozen one will be cooked; simply defrost it, clean and pick it, then use the shells to make your

2 ripe, medium-small tomatoes, roasted or boiled (page 352), cored, peeled and roughly chopped
OR one 15-ounce can tomatoes, drained and roughly chopped
½ small onion, roughly chopped
2 tablespoons olive oil
1 large sprig *epazote* (see Ingredients in Cook's Notes)
Canned *chiles chipotles* to taste (roughly 1 to 2 chiles), seeded and chopped
Salt, about ½ teaspoon
1 to 2 limes, cut into wedges

1. *Cooking the crabs.* Bring 2 quarts water to a boil in a soup pot or kettle, drop in the crabs and quickly set the lid in place. Once the water returns to a boil, reduce the heat to medium. After 5 minutes, the crabs should have changed from their mottled blue to a brilliant red; if not, let them cook a minute or two longer. Remove the crabs to a tray and set the broth aside in its pan.

2. *Cleaning the crabs.* First, remove the crab bodies from the shells: Working with one crab, break off all the legs and claws where they join the body, then pry back the small pointed flap (the "apron") on the underside and break it off. Grasp the outer shell and, with your other hand, take hold of the body itself—your thumb at the front where the eyes are, your fingers at the back where you broke off the flap. Pry the two apart. If there is any orange-colored roe sticking to the shell, scrape it into a bowl; place the body in a second bowl, and the legs, unwashed shell and flap in a third; crack the claws and add them to the bowl with the roe. Continue with the remaining crabs.

Next, remove the meat from each body: With a small spoon, scrape off any roe that is sticking to the bodies and add it to what you've already collected. Pull off and discard the white fingerlike gills (also called "dead-man's-fingers") that are attached to each side. Break the bodies in half, then pick out the lump of crab meat that is attached toward the front of each half, inside where the claws joined the body. Stand the body halves on their sides (on the joints where the legs were attached) and split them in half, exposing the meat inside. Use your finger or a small pick to run between the quill-like filaments and fish out the crab meat. Add it to the bowl with the roe, being careful to remove any bits of chipped shell or filament.

Add the picked bodies to the bowl with the shells.

broth (Step 3). Another possibility is to use 6 ounces of crab meat and 4 to 6 crab legs, but the broth won't be as rich unless you substitute 1½ quarts fish broth (page 62) for the crab broth in Step 4.

Epazote: When the herb is unavailable, either omit it, add several sprigs of flat-leaf parsley (not to give the same flavor, but to give *some* flavor) or sprinkle a little oregano into the broth as it is simmering.
Chiles Chipotles: Other chiles are frequently used: the small dried *japoneses* (or other hot dried chiles), or hot green chiles like the *jalapeño*. Use them in small quantities: If dried, soak in hot water, then puree with the soup base (Step 4); if fresh, seed and add to the blender.

Timing and Advance Preparation
Depending on your crab-picking speed, the soup can take from 1 to 2 hours, plus an additional 1½ hours of simmering. It may be prepared a day in advance, through Step 4: Refrigerate the broth and the crabmeat and legs separately, both covered.

TRADITIONAL VARIATIONS
Chicken Chilpachole: In Puebla and vicinity, they prepare the soup by poaching a chicken (page 60), then using the broth in place of the crab broth in Step 4. They serve whole pieces of chicken in the soup, though it's easier to eat when the chicken is served in boneless chunks.
Shrimp Chilpachole: Prepare the soup beginning at Step 4,

3. *Finishing the broth.* Add the bowl of picked shells to the broth, cover and simmer over medium-low heat for 30 minutes. Strain through a fine-mesh sieve, set the broth aside and discard the shells. Wash and dry the pan.

4. *The soup base.* Roast the unpeeled garlic on an ungreased griddle or heavy skillet over medium heat, turning frequently, until the cloves are soft and blackened in spots, about 15 minutes. When cool enough to handle, slip them out of their skins and place them in a blender or food processor with the tomatoes and onion. Process until smooth.

Heat the olive oil in the soup pot or kettle over medium-high. When hot enough to make a drop of the puree sizzle sharply, add it all at once. Stir nearly constantly for about 4 minutes, as the puree sears and thickens. Then add the broth and the *epazote*, cover and simmer gently over medium-low heat for 30 to 45 minutes.

5. *Finishing the soup.* About 15 minutes before serving, remove the *epazote* and skim off any fat that is floating on the broth. Stir in the chopped *chipotles,* re-cover and simmer for 10 minutes. Season with salt.

Finally, add the crab meat, claws and any roe. Cover and let the crab heat in the broth for about 5 minutes. Ladle up bowlfuls for your guests, each with bits of crabmeat and several of the claws to be fished out and picked at the table. Pass the lime wedges for the guests to squeeze into the soup to suit their own tastes.

SHRIMP-BALL SOUP WITH ROASTED PEPPER AND TOMATO

Sopa de Albóndigas de Camarón

The simple Mexican flavors of this west-coast specialty are clean and invitingly uncomplicated. The soup is substantial—just the kind of thing to serve before some simple Crispy-Fried Tacos (page 139) or *Enchiladas Suizas* (page 154); ripe, aromatic Strawberries with Cream (page 296) would be my choice for dessert.

Along Mexico's upper west coast, near Topolobampo in the Sea of Cortés, shrimp are so plentiful that the cooks use them

substituting fish broth (page 62) for the crab broth. Peel and devein about 1 pound shrimp (though in Mexico it's common to serve this rustic soup with unshelled shrimp), then cook them in the broth for a few (roughly 3 to 6) minutes just before serving.

Regional Explorations
All around the Gulf Coast, from Alvarado, Veracruz, to Tampico, crabs are generally the first choice for making *chilpacholes*. (In Tampico the crab broth is thickened with *masa* and the soup is called *chimpachole*.) In some places the cooks replace crab with fish or shrimp, and in Puebla there's even a chicken *chilpachole* offered.

COOK'S NOTES

Techniques
Chopping Shrimp: Warm shrimp will turn to mush, so be sure that they are well chilled. I prefer to chop the shrimp with a sharp knife, simply because I like the even, coarse texture that the knife cuts give.

Ingredients
The Right Ones: All the ingredients need to be the best quality—especially the fish broth.

to fill up soups, to shred for taco fillings and to grind for shrimp balls or cakes. This is a recipe for the latter, which re-creates a delicious version I had in Mazatlán; it is a combination of recipes I found in several Spanish-language publications.

YIELD: about 1½ quarts, 4 servings

8 ounces shrimp, *well chilled*
¼ small onion, *very finely* chopped
¼ ripe, medium-large tomato, cored, seeded and finely chopped
1 large egg yolk
2 tablespoons flour
½ teaspoon dried oregano
A generous ½ teaspoon salt
1 tablespoon vegetable oil
1 small onion, thinly sliced
1 medium fresh *chile poblano,* roasted and peeled (page 337), seeded and sliced into thin strips 1 inch long
1 ripe, medium-small tomato, roasted or boiled (page 352), cored, peeled and roughly chopped
OR ½ 15-ounce can tomatoes, well drained and roughly chopped
About 4½ cups (½ recipe) fish broth (page 62)
Salt, about ¾ teaspoon
¼ cup loosely packed, roughly chopped fresh coriander (*cilantro*)
1 to 2 limes, quartered

1. *The shrimp mixture.* Peel the shrimp and devein them by running a knife down the back to expose the dark intestinal track and scraping it out. Chop them finely: To chop by hand, use a large, sharp knife to cut the shrimp in small bits, then rock and chop, working the knife back and forth for several minutes, until the shrimp forms a coarse-textured paste. For machine chopping, either run the shrimp through the meat grinder fitted with the fine plate or use a food processor to chop the shrimp into a coarse puree (do it in two lots, pulsing 4 to 5 times for each lot). Place the shrimp in a mixing bowl.

Add the onion, tomato, egg yolk, flour, oregano and salt, and mix thoroughly. Cover and refrigerate until you're ready to finish the soup.

2. *The broth.* In a large saucepan, heat the oil over medium. Add the onion and fry until just browning, about 7 minutes.

The soup is a combination of simple flavors and every one must shine.
Shrimp: Here is a good place to use the small shrimp, if you have the patience to peel and devein them. If shrimp are unavailable or prohibitively expensive, you might want to substitute scallops or a gelatinous fish like monk fish.
Chile Poblano: Though a *poblano* is the best flavor for the soup, 2 large, long green chiles would be my second choice.

Timing and Advance Preparation
If the fish broth is ready, you'll need 45 minutes to prepare the soup. The brothy soup base (Step 2) can be prepared a day or two ahead, covered and refrigerated; prepare and cook the shrimp balls just before serving.

TRADITIONAL VARIATIONS
Tortas de Camarón Fresco: On the west coast of Mexico you often find the shrimp mixture formed into cakes, dredged in flour or crumbs and fried. They can be served as is, with hot sauce and a salad, or with about 1½ cups Quick-Cooked Tomato-Chile Sauce (page 41), or with the sauce used for Fish *a la Veracruzana* (page 212).

Add the chile strips and tomato and fry for 3 or 4 minutes longer to reduce the liquid a little.

Stir in the broth, bring to a boil, cover and simmer 15 minutes over medium-low heat to blend the flavors. Season with salt.

3. *Finishing the soup.* Fifteen minutes before serving, poach the shrimp in the gently simmering broth: Drop in rounded tablespoons of the shrimp mixture, simmer gently for 8 to 10 minutes, then remove from the fire.

Ladle the soup into bowls and sprinkle with the chopped coriander. Serve with the lime wedges on the side.

Pozole bowl and condiment dishes, Guerrero

PORK, CHICKEN AND HOMINY SOUP WITH GROUND PUMPKINSEEDS

Pozole Verde

Through the steeply mountainous terrain of Guerrero, from Acapulco up through Taxco, Thursday is green *pozole* day, a day to close up shop in midafternoon and adjourn to small *pozole* "restaurants"—many of them only makeshift arrangements of tables and chairs that go public only this one day a week. The big earthernware bowls they serve are thick with hominy and redolent with ground pumpkinseeds and rich herbs—without exception, my favorite of the *pozoles*. We ate it once, back in the winding streets above Tixtla, with *botanas* ("drinking snacks") of tender sliced tongue and the region's famous little crispy tortilla boats (*chalupitas*) with sweet-sour pickled *chipotles*. And since it was Guerrero, there were shots of mescal, some of it made deliciously smooth by adding *nanches* (chokecherries).

The very traditional recipe that follows was taught to me by Abaku Chautla D. in Almolonga, Guerrero. It is a meal in itself: Some light tostadas (pages 163–166) and Flan (page 283) are all you need to make it really special.

YIELD: 8 to 9 quarts, 10 to 12 typically hefty servings

COOK'S NOTES

Techniques

Pressure-Cooking Hominy: You can save time by completing Step 1 in a large pressure cooker. Cook the hulled corn in 5 quarts water for about 1 hour, until nearly tender. Transfer to a stockpot, add enough water so everything floats freely, and continue with Step 2.

Adding Salt to Pozole: Add salt only when the hominy is fully tender; adding it too early will toughen the kernels.

Adding Shredded Meat to the Soup: Shredded meat disintegrates and mats together when simmered in the soup, so add it just before you plan to serve.

Ingredients

Dried Corn and Canned Hominy: Canned hominy may be easy, but the aroma and texture of the home-cooked kernels make the longer process worth the effort. Another alternative to the softer-textured

2 pounds (about 5½ cups) dried white field corn, prepared as Half-Cooked Hominy using slaked lime (page 72)
    OR 4 quarts canned hominy, drained and rinsed
8 ounces lean, boneless pork shoulder, in a single piece
About 8 ounces pork neck (or other pork) bones
1 small (2½-pound) chicken, halved
2⅔ cups (12 ounces) hulled, untoasted pumpkin-seeds (*pepitas*)
1 pound (about 11 medium) fresh *tomatillos*, husked and washed
    OR two 13-ounce cans *tomatillos*, drained
Fresh hot green chiles to taste (roughly 6 *chiles serranos* or 3 *chiles jalapeños*), stemmed and seeded
1 medium onion, roughly chopped
2 large sprigs *epazote* (see Ingredients in Cook's Notes)
4 large leaves *ashoshoco* or 2 small leaves *hoja santa* (see Ingredients in Cook's Notes)
2 tablespoons lard or vegetable oil
Salt, about 1 tablespoon

For the condiments:
1 cup diced red onion
⅓ cup dried oregano
2 ripe avocados, peeled, pitted and diced in ½-inch chunks
2 cups *chicharrón* (crisp-fried pork rinds), broken into 1-inch pieces (optional)
12 to 15 Crisp-Fried Tortillas (*Tostadas*, page 78)
4 limes, cut into quarters

1. *The hominy.* As directed on page 72, parboil the dried field corn with slaked lime, clean off the hulls, and, if you like, pick off the heads. Place in a large stockpot or soup kettle with 7 quarts of water, bring to a boil, partially cover and simmer over medium-low heat until the corn is nearly tender, 3 to 4 hours. Add water periodically to bring it back to its original level.

Canned hominy simply needs to be drained and rinsed.

2. *The meat. Using dried corn:* When the corn is nearly tender, add the meat, bones and chicken. After the liquid returns to a boil, skim off the foam for several minutes. Partially cover and

canned hominy is the lime-treated, half-cooked *maíz nixtamalado* (often just called *nixtamal*), available in the refrigerated cases or freezers of some Mexican groceries; simply rinse 8 cups of it and simmer until tender. For notes on purchasing dried field corn and slaked lime, see page 343 and page 346, respectively.

Pumpkinseeds: In Almolonga, the *pozole verde* is prepared with a store-bought green powder made of unhulled pumpkinseeds. Because the home-ground, unshelled seeds come out coarser (and the *pozole* grittier), I have called for hulled seeds.

Epazote: This isn't a dominant flavor here, so when unavailable, you can replace it with parsley.

Ashoshoco and Hoja Santa: The former is closely related to the long-leafed herb called plantain; if you're a forager, you likely know where you can pick some to add its pleasant, sharp herbiness. *Hoja santa* is *Piper sanctum*, a member of the black-pepper family, and its anisey flavor can be replaced by 1½ cups of fennel bulb *tops* (feathery green part only) plus ½ teaspoon freshly ground black pepper. Some cooks use neither of these herbs in their *pozole verde.*

Timing and Advance Preparation
While the soup should be started 8 hours or more before serving time, the active preparation time is only about 1 hour (unless you choose to prepare your own hominy). It may be prepared a few days in advance, the meat and soup refrigerated separately, covered. Slowly reheat and thin, if necessary, just before serving.

simmer 3 hours, adding water periodically to bring it back to its original level. Then taste the corn: If it is *thoroughly* soft and the kernels are splayed open, you are ready to proceed; if it is still firm, let it cook another hour or so.

Using canned hominy: Measure 7 quarts water into a kettle or stockpot and add the meat, bones and chicken. Bring to a boil, skim off the foam for the first 5 minutes of simmering, partially cover and cook over medium-low heat for 3 hours. Add water periodically to bring it back to its original level.

While the meat is cooking, complete Steps 3 and 4.

3. *The pumpkinseeds.* Heat a large (12-inch) skillet for a few minutes over medium-low. Add the pumpkinseeds in a shallow layer and, when the first one pops, stir them constantly for several minutes, until all have popped and turned a golden color. Remove the seeds to a large bowl.

4. *The soup-base puree.* Cook fresh *tomatillos* until tender in salted water to cover, about 10 minutes. Drain either the fresh or canned *tomatillos* and add to the pumpkinseeds, along with the green chile, onion and herbs. Remove 2 cups of broth from the pot and pour over the mixture. Scoop half the mixture into a blender jar and blend until smooth; if the mixture is too thick to move through the blades, add *a little more* broth to get it going again. Strain through a medium-mesh sieve, then repeat the pureeing and straining with the rest of the mixture.

Set a large skillet over medium-high heat and measure in the lard or oil. When hot enough to make a drop of the puree really sizzle, add it all at once and stir constantly for about 7 minutes, until it has darkened some and thickened noticeably. Remove from the fire.

5. *Finishing the pozole verde.* Remove the meat and bones from the pot and set aside to cool. Stir the pumpkinseed mixture into the pot. *If you are using canned hominy, add it now.* Let simmer for an hour, stirring frequently to ensure that nothing is sticking on the bottom.

While the soup is simmering, skin and bone the chicken and pork, removing all the fat; shred the meat into large strands.

Fifteen minutes before serving, season the soup with salt (hominy requires considerable salt) and add the shredded meat to the pot. Place the condiments on the table in small serving dishes. Finally, dish up a large bowl of the *pozole verde* for each guest and pass the condiments for each to add *al gusto.*

CONTEMPORARY IDEAS

Pozole Verde to Begin a Meal: This is such an elegant-tasting soup that I recommend making it without meat to serve as a first course. Prepare *half* the quantities called for as follows: Simmer the hulled hominy from Step 1 in 3 quarts unsalted beef broth; prepare and fry the soup-base puree, then add it to the simmering broth when the hominy is tender; simmer 1 hour, season and serve in small bowls with the garnishes. (Using canned hominy, prepare and fry the soup-base puree using beef broth, then thin it to a light consistency with more broth, add the drained canned hominy and simmer for 1 hour.)

PORK AND HOMINY SOUP WITH RED CHILE AND FRESH GARNISHES

Pozole Rojo

When hominy is simmering with pork and dried red chile, the aromas are wonderfully mouth-watering. A big bowl of the rich soup, topped with its crunchy fresh vegetables, makes a full informal meal for those who like good eating. I'd start with a *Jícama* Salad (page 89) or Cactus-Paddle Salad (page 47) and finish with one of the ice creams (page 298).

While any Mexican will say "Guadalajara" as fast as you can say *"pozole,"* this soup is supper and weekend food most everywhere in the Republic, save Yucatán. White *pozole* (simmered without the red chile) is the typical Guadalajara version, where the adorning sprinkle of oregano is often omitted. My first choice is this full-flavored Michoacán recipe—which comes from a transplanted vendor at the Coyoacán prepared-foods market in Mexico City.

YIELD: 8 to 9 quarts, 10 to 12 large servings

2 pounds (about 5½ cups) dried white field corn, prepared as Half-Cooked Hominy using slaked lime (page 72)
    OR 4 quarts canned hominy, drained and rinsed

½ small (about 4 pounds) pig's head, well scrubbed and halved
    OR 3 medium (about 2½ pounds total) pigs' feet, well scrubbed and split lengthwise, plus 1½ pounds meaty pork neck bones

1½ pounds lean, boneless pork shoulder, in a single piece

4 large cloves garlic, peeled and minced

4 large (about 2 ounces total) dried *chiles anchos,* stemmed, seeded and deveined

4 large (about 1 ounce total) dried *chiles guajillos,* stemmed, seeded and deveined

Salt, about 1 tablespoon

COOK'S NOTES

Techniques
See the technique notes on page 104.

Ingredients
Dried Corn and Canned Hominy: The details of which to choose are on page 104.
Pig's Head: For anyone who's eaten a genuine *pozole* made with pig's head, there is little doubt that the latter is what provides a lot of its richness. But since a great number of Stateside cooks wouldn't want the head in their kitchens (much less in their stewpots), I've given an alternative of pigs' feet (which adds a similar richness).
Dried Chiles: It isn't uncommon for the soup to be made with all *guajillos* or all *anchos.* Use 6 *anchos* or 12 *guajillos;* the *anchos* make it sweeter, the *guajillos* sharper. If neither is available, use 9 California or New Mexico chiles.

Timing and Advance Preparation
Start the soup at least 8 hours ahead, most of which is devoted to unattended simmering. The soup can be made several days in advance: Store the meat and soup separately, covered and refrigerated. Reheat the soup and add the meat just before serving.

For the condiments:

    ½ medium head of cabbage, cored and very thinly sliced
        OR ½ head iceberg lettuce, cored and very thinly sliced
    8 to 10 radishes, thinly sliced
    1½ cups finely chopped onion
    About ⅓ cup dried oregano
    2 to 3 large limes, cut into wedges
    15 to 20 Crisp-Fried Tortillas (*Tostadas,* page 78)

1. *The hominy.* Prepare the Half-Cooked Hominy or canned hominy as described in Step 1 on page 72.

2. *The meat. Using dried corn:* When the corn is nearly tender, add the pig's head (or pigs' feet and neck bones), the pork shoulder and the garlic. Cook as described in Step 2 on page 72, until the corn is tender.

Using canned hominy: Measure 7 quarts of water into a kettle or stockpot and add the pig's head (or pigs' feet and neck bones), the pork shoulder and the garlic. Cook as described in Step 2 on page 72, until the corn is tender.

3. *The chiles.* Tear the chiles into large, flat pieces and toast them, a few at a time, on a griddle or heavy skillet set over medium heat, using a metal spatula to press them firmly against the hot surface until they crackle and blister, then flipping them over and pressing them down again. Remove to a bowl, cover with boiling water, weight with a plate to keep them submerged and soak 30 minutes.

Drain, place in a blender jar and add ½ cup water; blend until smooth. Strain through a medium-mesh sieve into the simmering soup, then mix well.

Generously season the soup with salt (hominy requires considerable salt) and let simmer for another hour or so.

4. *Finishing the soup.* Remove the pig's head (or pigs' feet and neck bones) and the pork shoulder from the simmering broth. When cool enough to handle, remove the meat from the pig's head, discarding the bones, fat and cartilage (or for pigs' feet, remove and discard the cartilage and bones, then chop what remains into 1-inch pieces). Roughly shred all the meat.

Just before serving, reseason the soup with salt. Add the meat to the pot and let simmer a few minutes to reheat.

Ladle the soup into large bowls, top each one with a portion of shredded cabbage or lettuce and some sliced radishes. Pass the onion, oregano and lime wedges separately for each guest to add to his or her taste. The tostadas are a crunchy accompaniment to enjoy between big spoonfuls of the soup.

TRADITIONAL VARIATIONS

White Pozole: Frequently around Guadalajara, in Guerrero and in other parts of Mexico, the soup is made according to the preceding recipe, omitting the red-chile puree. In this version, it is always served with powdered red chile (like *chile de árbol* or *chile piquín*) and/or a *salsa picante* like the one on page 40. And in parts of Guerrero, a raw egg is stirred in, then the soup is garnished with avocado, oregano, red onion and the juice of bitter *lima*.

Kitchen Spanish

The name as well as this centuries-old method for preparing corn comes from the Aztecs. In Nahuatl, *pozolli* means "foam"; to Aztec eyes, the opened (or "flowered") hominy apparently bore a resemblance to something frothy.

RED-CHILE TRIPE SOUP WITH FRESH GARNISHES

Menudo Rojo

I scooted onto a bar stool in a spiffy-looking marketplace *fonda* in Tampico. To tell the truth, I'd never seen one of these places with an espresso machine and ceiling fans before. It was Saturday morning and the crowd was spooning down bowls of weekends-only *mondongo* (the Gulf Coast name for this popular tripe soup), so I followed the lead. And before I left town, I'd returned for several more bowls of their tender tripe in well-flavored broth, as well as some chats with the well-fed owner, whose recipe follows here.

Though most people associate *menudo* with Northern states (where it is frequently made without the red chile and with an addition of hominy), versions of this hearty soup show up everywhere. It's most commonly eaten in the morning (the high vitamin B content, I've read, is good for hangovers); if you're adventurous, serve it for brunch with Quick-Simmered Tortilla Casserole (*Chilaquiles,* page 172) and fresh papaya; or make a supper of it, with Chunky Guacamole (page 44) and hot corn tortillas.

YIELD: a generous 2 quarts, 4 large servings

- **2 pounds fresh beef tripe (see Ingredients in** Cook's Notes)
- **About 1 tablespoon salt**
- **1 large lime, juiced**
- **1 small cow's or medium pig's foot, split lengthwise (see Ingredients in** Cook's Notes)
- **1 pound marrow bones, cut in 1-inch cross sections**
- **6 cloves garlic, peeled and chopped**
- **½ medium onion, chopped**
- **2 teaspoons dried oregano**
- **4 medium (about 1⅓ ounces total) dried *chiles cascabeles norteños* or California/New Mexico chiles, stemmed, seeded and deveined**
- **A generous ½ teaspoon cumin seeds, ground**
- **Salt, about 1 teaspoon**

Techniques
Cleaning and Blanching the Tripe: Tripe in the United States has usually been parboiled as well as treated with lye (which cleans and bleaches it in a way similar to the Mexican home method of scrubbing with salt and lime juice). So ours needs little further cleaning, though some advise blanching it (as in Step 1) to eliminate unpleasant odors.

Ingredients
Tripe: Ethnic markets always carry it. Of the four kinds of tripe, our Chicago Mexican markets only carry the porous honeycomb tripe and a darker, smoother one they call *moreno.* The first is tender and cooks quickly; the second is more flavorful.
Cow's or Pig's Foot: Some recipes don't call for it, but it adds a nice texture to the broth.
Chiles Cascabeles Norteños: These are common Northern chiles (large, smooth-skinned, mild and maroon-colored) that are very similar to our California or New Mexico chiles. Also, 3 *chiles anchos* may be used, as they would be in Monterrey.

Timing and Advance Preparation
Plan 3 or 4 hours to prepare the soup, only 1 hour of which will require your active involvement. *Menudo* keeps well for days, covered and refrigerated.

For the condiments:

> 2 small limes, quartered
> About ½ cup chopped onion
> Several tablespoons dried oregano
> 1 tablespoon or so powdered hot chile, such as cayenne or *chile piquin*

1. *The tripe.* Wash the tripe thoroughly in several changes of warm water. Place it in a large bowl, sprinkle with the 1 tablespoon salt and the lime juice; vigorously work the salt and lime into the tripe with a scrubbing motion. Let stand 30 minutes, then wash the tripe again in several changes of warm water.

Slice the tripe into small pieces about 2 inches long and ½ inch wide. Place in a large kettle or stockpot, cover with several quarts of cold water, bring to a boil, then simmer over medium heat for 10 minutes. Pour into a colander set in the sink, let drain a minute, then return to the pan.

2. *Simmering the tripe.* Add the cow's or pig's foot, the marrow bones and 3 quarts water. Bring to a boil, reduce the heat to medium-low and skim off the foam that rises during the first few minutes of cooking. Add *half* the garlic to the pot along with the onion and oregano; partially cover and simmer until the tripe is very tender, 2 to 3 hours.

3. *The chile flavoring and final preparations.* When the tripe is nearly tender, heat a griddle or heavy skillet over medium. Tear the chiles into flat pieces and toast them a few at a time by laying them on the hot surface, pressing them flat with a metal spatula for several seconds, until they blister and color a little, then flipping them over and pressing down for a few seconds more. Place them in a small bowl, cover with boiling water, weight with a plate to keep them submerged, and soak 30 minutes.

Remove the cow's or pig's foot and all the marrow bones from the broth, then skim off any fat floating on top. If you wish, let the foot cool a little, then cut out and discard all the bone and cartilage, chop what remains into small pieces and return it to the pot.

Drain the chiles and place them in a blender jar with the remaining garlic and the ground cumin. Add ⅓ cup of the *menudo* broth, blend until smooth, then strain through a medium-mesh sieve into the pot. Season with salt, partially cover and simmer 30 minutes.

4. *Serving the soup.* When you are ready to serve, place the condiments in small bowls on the table. Serve large bowls of the steaming soup and pass the condiments for each guest to add to his or her liking.

TRADITIONAL VARIATIONS

Menudo with Hominy: As described on page 72, prepare 5 ounces (¾ cup) dried field corn as Half-Cooked Hominy. Simmer in 3 quarts water until nearly tender, about 3 hours. Add the blanched tripe, foot and bones, skim, add the flavorings, then cook slowly until the tripe is tender. Finish the soup as directed in Step 3.

EGGS

❖

Huevos

Open air *cafetería*, Veracruz

Even before I'd learned anything firsthand about Mexican victuals, I knew that the breakfasts were legendary. The fried eggs with *picante* tomato sauce (*huevos rancheros*) were robust and delicious, and so were the scrambled ones with chiles, onions and tomatoes. Everyone in my part of the country loved them with soft corn tortillas—buttered, salted and drizzled with hot sauce.

When I visited Mexico, I found those same dishes everywhere. Scrambled eggs were on plates, in tacos, laid into rolls for *tortas*. They were served anytime during the morning, anytime during the evening, in coffee shops, market *fondas,* taco and *torta* shops. When I ordered my first afternoon fixed-course *comida corrida,* they asked if I wanted a fried egg with the rice course. At the juice bars, they offered to blend an egg with the fresh-fruit smoothies. And a good many of the stewed taco fillings at the snack-shop cubby holes near the markets were filled with eggs. How could the country survive without eggs, I wondered.

All around the country, all kinds of regional egg dishes show up on menus: an omelet in brothy, *epazote*-flavored red-chile sauce (*huevos a la oaxaqueña*) in Oaxaca; scrambled eggs with smoked gar (*huevos con pejelagarto*) in Tabasco; baked eggs with shrimp and oysters (*huevos malagueños*) in Yucatán; shredded beef, eggs and light chile sauce (*salpicón acapulqueño*) in Acapulco and other spots; scrambled—literally "thrown"—eggs with black beans (*huevos tirados*) in Veracruz; and a rather peculiar "cake" of sweet-spiced eggs and pork in broth with a dollop of smoky Oaxacan *chile pasilla* sauce (*higaditos*) in Tlacolula, Oaxaca.

Others came along that were less memorable, as did two that have become my favorites: the Northern crispy shredded jerky with scrambled eggs, garlic, onion and chiles (*machacado con huevo*) and the delightful, busy layering of tostada, beans, eggs, tomato sauce, ham, peas and cheese known as *huevos motuleños* in Southern and Yucatecan Mexico.

In our home, Mexican egg dishes frequently show up on the table for quick suppers or lunches. Our favorite recipes for the Mexican classics are all included in this chapter.

For egg recipes in other chapters, see "Eggs" in the Index.

Keys to Perfect Egg Cooking

Beating Eggs for Scrambling: The more you beat them the less texture they'll have and the drier they'll seem. I beat them only enough to combine the yolks and whites. Also, adding a little liquid (water, milk, cream, sour cream, yogurt, what have you) will make them lighter.

Getting the Heat Right: Medium heat is a detriment to eggs, making them lifeless and rubbery. Scrambling should be done over medium-low heat for small soft curds or in a *hot* pan over medium-high heat, *gently* and slowly stirring, for large tender-but-firm curds (the latter is what I call for most frequently, especially for taco fillings).

EGGS COOKED "TO TASTE"

Huevos al Gusto

Happily, there are three distinctive, delicious "tastes" in national Mexican egg cooking that go beyond the simple fried, scrambled or *tibio* (half-raw boiled) eggs that abound. At least two of the three are common in bus-station food bars and other utilitarian cookeries through the whole country: one batch of eggs scrambled full of hot *serrano* peppers, tomatoes and crunchy onions (*huevos a la mexicana*), and another made fat and soft with *chorizo* sausage (*huevos con chorizo*). Filled into a pliable tortilla or crusty bun, either one satisfies much longer than the brightly displayed synthetic sweets that compete with them at lunch counters.

The third egg dish is also quite simple, though it does consume more of the cook's energy and so is promoted to the domain of the Republic's coffee shops and restaurants. *Huevos rancheros* starts with fried eggs on soft tortilla beds, then the ensemble is dribbled with a fresh-tasting tomato sauce that always seems to announce the regional (or economic) orientation of the one who prepared it.

RANCH-STYLE EGGS WITH TOMATO-CHILE SAUCE

Huevos Rancheros

You can almost bet that anything *ranchero* or *a la ranchera* will come in a coarse, *picante* tomato sauce—what you might expect for "ranch" style. The *picante* can be little *serranos* (or *habaneros* in Yucatán), dried *chiles de árbol*, even *chipotles* or long green chiles—whatever happens to be the regional choice or the find of the moment.

I can't think of serving *huevos rancheros* without *Frijoles Refritos* (page 269), tropical fruit and lots of *Café con Leche* (page 316).

YIELD: 4 servings

COOK'S NOTES

Techniques
Quick-Frying Tortillas: See page 153.

Timing and Advance Preparation
Start to finish, *huevos rancheros* takes about 15 minutes, if the sauce is on hand. To be at its best, the dish must be served at once.

About 2 cups (1 recipe) Quick-Cooked Tomato-
Chile Sauce (page 41 or any of the accompanying variations)
4 medium-thick corn tortillas, store-bought or
homemade (page 74), preferably stale
¼ cup vegetable oil, plus a little more if needed
8 large eggs
Salt and freshly ground black pepper, as desired
2 tablespoons crumbled Mexican *queso fresco* or
queso añejo (page 327), or cheese like feta,
farmer's cheese or mild Parmesan
A little chopped parsley, for garnish

1. *The preliminaries.* Warm the sauce in a small saucepan
over medium-low heat, covered. If the tortillas are fresh, let
them dry out in a single layer for a few minutes. Heat the oil
in a large, well-seasoned skillet over medium-high; when quite
hot, quick-fry the tortillas one at a time, 2 or 3 seconds per
side, just to soften them. Drain on paper towels, wrap in foil
and keep warm in a low oven. Reduce the heat under the skillet
to medium-low and let it cool for several minutes.

2. *The eggs.* Break 4 eggs into the skillet and let them cook
slowly until set, sunny-side up. (If you want the eggs cooked
more uniformly top and bottom, cover the skillet for a time.)
Sprinkle with salt and pepper, then transfer the cooked eggs to
a baking sheet and keep them warm with the tortillas. Add a
little more oil to the pan, if necessary, then fry the remaining
eggs in the same fashion.

3. *Assembling the dish.* Set a tortilla on each of 4 warm plates.
Top with 2 fried eggs, then spoon the sauce over the tortilla
and *whites* of the eggs, leaving the yolks exposed. Last, sprinkle
with the crumbled cheese and chopped parsley, and carry to
the table.

**TRADITIONAL
VARIATIONS**
*Huevos Rancheros with Other
Sauces:* You can replace the to-
mato sauce with about 2 cups
Quick-Cooked *Tomatillo* Sauce
(page 42) or Northern-Style
Red-Chile Sauce (page 250).

Huevos rancheros

SCRAMBLED EGGS WITH MEXICAN FLAVORS

Huevos a la Mexicana

Like *ranchero, a la mexicana* invariably brings to mind a list of ingredients: tomatoes, chiles and onions—all chopped and chunky. And like eggs with *chorizo,* these eggs *a la mexicana* make a perfect trio with steaming, soft corn or flour tortillas and Fresh Green *Tomatillo* Sauce (page 36). To dress them up for a special breakfast, scoop them into a decorative bowl and top with a few onion rings, a little chopped parsley and crumbled fresh cheese. Unadorned, at the privacy of your own table, they are very good with toast and coffee.

YIELD: 2⅔ cups, 4 servings

> 3 tablespoons lard, vegetable oil, bacon drippings, fat rendered from *chorizo,* or even butter
> Fresh hot green chiles to taste (roughly 3 *chiles serranos* or 1 large *chile jalapeño*), stemmed
> 1 small onion, diced
> 1 ripe, medium-large tomato, cored and diced
> 8 large eggs
> About 1 scant teaspoon salt

1. *The flavorings.* Melt the lard or other fat in a medium-size skillet set over medium heat. For a milder dish, seed the chiles, then chop them finely and add to the skillet, along with the onion and tomato. Cook, stirring frequently, until the onion has softened but is not brown, about 5 minutes. Reduce the heat to medium-low.

2. *The eggs.* Beat the eggs with the salt, just enough to combine the whites and yolks. Add them to the skillet and scramble until they are as done as you like. Taste for salt, then scoop them into a warm dish and serve right away.

COOK'S NOTES

Ingredients
Green Chiles: The *serrano* or *jalapeño* are common, but not exclusive; each region uses its locally favored variety. So follow suit and use what's available or desirable.

Timing and Advance Preparation
This simple dish can be ready for the table in 15 to 20 minutes, and doesn't require any ingredients that aren't already on hand in most flavor lovers' kitchens.

TRADITIONAL VARIATIONS
Scrambled Eggs with Shrimp: Prepare the dish as directed, adding 1 cup (6 ounces) peeled, deveined, chopped raw shrimp to the cooking vegetables.
Huevos con Nopales: Prepare the recipe as directed, adding 1 cup sliced, cooked cactus paddles (page 325) to the vegetables while they are cooking.

CONTEMPORARY IDEAS
Spicy Scrambled Eggs with Avocado, Bacon and Cheese: Add 8 slices crumbled, cooked bacon to the cooked vegetables, then add the eggs and scramble until nearly set. Stir in 1 cup cubed Monterey Jack cheese, letting it soften before scraping the eggs into a warm serving dish. Garnish with diced avocado and chopped fresh basil or oregano.

SCRAMBLED EGGS WITH MEXICAN SAUSAGE

Huevos con Chorizo

For months, Deann and I lived over a coffee shop, whose early-morning aromas collected in the halls outside our place: simmering *chilaquiles* with *epazote*, coffee from the espresso machine, frying bacon and fragrant *chorizo*. A few steps down the stairs and I was ready for *huevos con chorizo* or *chilaquiles* every morning.

Predictably, the best renditions of the simple scrambled-egg dish outlined here are served where the best *chorizo* is made: Toluca, Oaxaca and, to me, the Spanish settlement of Perote, Veracruz. For serving ideas, please see the introduction to Eggs *a la Mexicana* (page 115).

YIELD: 2⅔ cups, 4 servings

> 8 ounces (about 1 cup) *chorizo* sausage, store-bought or homemade (page 55), casing removed
> 1 tablespoon vegetable oil
> 1 small onion, chopped (optional)
> 1 ripe, medium-large tomato, cored and chopped (optional)
> 8 large eggs
> About ½ teaspoon salt (or less if the *chorizo* is very salty)

1. *The flavorings.* In a medium-size skillet, cook the *chorizo* in the oil over medium-low heat, stirring occasionally to break up clumps. When it is done, about 10 minutes, remove it with a slotted spoon, then discard all but about 2 tablespoons of fat from the skillet (or add vegetable oil to bring it to that quantity). Add the optional onions and tomato and cook, stirring frequently, until the onion begins to soften, about 7 minutes. Return the *chorizo* to the pan.

2. *The eggs.* Beat the eggs with the salt, just enough to combine the whites and yolks. Add to the skillet and scramble until done to your liking. Taste for salt, then scoop into a warm dish and serve quickly.

COOK'S NOTES

Timing and Advance Preparation

You need only 20 minutes to prepare this dish—scarcely long enough to steam-heat the requisite stack of corn tortillas.

TRADITIONAL VARIATIONS

Eggs, Chorizo and Rajas: Prepare the flavorings as directed in Step 1, slicing the onion (rather than chopping it) and adding 1 large *chile poblano* (roasted, peeled, seeded and sliced). Complete the recipe as directed and garnish with crumbled fresh cheese and chopped flat-leaf parsley, if you like.

CONTEMPORARY IDEAS

Eggs, Chorizo and Mushrooms: I think *chorizo* goes well with some of the meaty "wild" mushrooms now available (like *shiitakes*). Chop them and fry with the *chorizo*, then finish the dish as directed. Garnish with crumbled fresh cheese and a little fresh or dried oregano.

Coffee can, Veracruz

SHREDDED BEEF JERKY WITH SCRAMBLED EGGS AND CHILE

Machacado con Huevo

To my taste, this Northern specialty is the most delicious of all the egg dishes. I love the aged flavor of jerky that has been shredded and fried crisp; mix it with eggs, and I've found my dish for any simple meal. To make it breakfast, I add fruit, flour tortillas and coffee; for supper, I put out a salad, tortillas and beer. And I always offer a little *Salsa Picante* (page 40) to sprinkle on.

The name *machacado* means "crushed," which aptly describes what happened to the jerky when I learned to prepare it in San Ignacio, Baja California Sur; there, my instructor showed me how to pound the jerky with a large flat stone to shred it quickly.

YIELD: about 2½ cups, 4 servings

> 2 ounces beef jerky, store-bought or homemade (page 57)
> 6 large eggs
> 3 tablespoons lard or vegetable oil, plus a little more if needed
> 1 small onion, diced
> 1 fresh *chile poblano,* roasted and peeled (page 337), seeded and diced
> 1 ripe, medium-small tomato, cored and diced
> 2 cloves garlic, peeled and minced
> Salt, about ½ teaspoon (depending on the saltiness of the jerky)

1. *The meat.* Lay the jerky on a baking sheet and set under a heated broiler. In 1 to 3 minutes, depending on the thickness and dryness of the jerky, the fat will bubble on the top and the edges will be lightly browned and crispy.

Cool the meat, then tear into thin shreds. Now, reduce the shreds of meat to fluffy, fine threads: Either pound them a little at a time in a mortar (it should look like a coarse, loose felt), or process them in 2 or 3 batches in the blender, pulsing the

COOK'S NOTES

Techniques
Roasting the Jerky: The heat softens the jerky slightly, making it easier to shred and giving it a browned flavor. Overroasted jerky crumbles rather than shreds.
Shredding the Jerky: When a chewy piece of jerky is reduced to fine threads, it develops a pleasant texture. The threads should be visible to the eye and about ½ inch long: Coarse shredding means chewy jerky; very fine shredding gives a pre-chewed, gritty texture.

Ingredients
Jerky: Further information is on page 345. If jerky is unavailable, use ½ pound brisket, simmered until tender, then finely shredded as directed on page 131. Complete Steps 2 through 4, browning the meat *with* the onions.
Chile Poblano: Other chiles are frequently used in this dish: 2 long green chiles (roasted, peeled, seeded and diced) or hot green chiles to taste (seeded and diced).

Equipment
Shredders: I prefer to pound the meat in my large basalt mortar because I get the best control and don't run the risk of finely chopped meat. Without a mortar, I'd choose a blender: Be careful to only *pulse* the machine. Market vendors told me they shredded with a mill (like the one used for corn-tortilla dough); their results looked good.

machine on and off *quickly,* until the meat looks like a fluffy heap of light-brown threads. There should be 1 cup.

2. *The eggs.* Beat the eggs just enough to combine the yolks and whites; set aside.

3. *Browning the meat and vegetables.* Heat the oil in a medium-large skillet over medium-high. Add the diced onion and fry, stirring frequently, until beginning to brown, about 5 minutes. Add the threads of meat, reduce the heat to medium and stir frequently until the mixture is well browned and crispy, 5 to 7 minutes more.

Add the chile, tomato and garlic and stir for 2 minutes. Reduce the heat to medium-low and add a little more oil if all has been absorbed.

4. *Finishing the dish.* Pour the eggs into the pan and scramble until done to your liking. Taste for salt, then scoop the mixture into a warm serving bowl and carry to the table.

Timing and Advance Preparation
This dish takes about ½ hour to make; that can be reduced to 15 minutes if Step 1 is completed ahead. Store prepared jerky at room temperature, lightly covered.

Lava rock and earthenware mortars
(molcajete and chirmolera)

SNACKS MADE OF CORN MASA

❖

Antojitos

Gordita vendors, San Luis Potosí

> **Antojo:** *Whim, [passing] fancy, caprice, fad. . . . Sudden craving . . .*
> —Diccionario moderno español-inglés *(Larousse)*

They are the "typical, popular, provincial" snacks, as the *Diccionario de mejicanismos* calls them: the grilled-meat-and-onion tacos, fried *masa* boats with sausage and hot sauce, the *seviche* tostadas or turnovers stuffed with mushrooms or cheese. They are the internationally known collection of Mexican dishes that the outside world, for the most part, thinks to be the sum total of Mexico's culinary adventure. No *moles,* no fish *a la veracruzana* or pork *pibil* in banana leaves; all outsiders seem to know is a combination plate of tacos, enchiladas and tostada . . . fun for the moment, as the name *antojito* implies, but no cuisine to be taken seriously.

And they are not serious, like the sophisticated *moles* and all; nor do they represent the breadth of Mexican cooking any more than hamburgers, hot dogs and pizza sum up what American cooks can do. Rather, they are pure, flavorful, colorful spontaneity mixed with a good portion of vital camaraderie. And that, quite certainly, is at the heart of *lo mexicano.*

It took years for me to shed the inaccurate stereotype of Mexican cooking that I'd garnered from my hometown restaurants and recipes clipped from newspapers and magazines. It probably didn't happen until I lived in Mexico City and fell into the rhythms of my neighborhood: There was an eleven o'clock bustle to the street vendors for a *masa* turnover, a stew-filled soft taco or a seafood cocktail. At night, a bank of *taquerías* opened up several blocks away, completely open little storefronts with big frying tables for meat tacos. In Alameda Park, farther on, the ladies set up their charcoal braziers to roast corn or, if it was a holiday, to bake *masa* boats or heat syrup for the thin fritters called *buñuelos.* Late morning and evening and practically anytime Sunday, waves of people took to the streets to have their public snacks, to eat the filling creations made by someone else, to eat in the company of others—an enjoyable affirmation of cultural solidarity, perhaps . . . of cultural distinctiveness, certainly. At whatever time, these were light meals to be eaten away from home, when the solemn nutritional concerns of the afternoon *comida* were far away.

Mexico's regional *antojitos* are among the most enjoyable preparations in the country's vast repertory. Cooks in every area mix up corn dough in some special way, then fry, griddle-bake or steam it to suit their tastes, and give it a whimsically descriptive name and a sparkling garnish. The more twists and turns, the more variety of filling, the more decoration and ornamentation, the more it will excite this country of exuberant eaters. In regions where the variety of *antojitos* swells, the snack shops and more festive restaurants sometimes collect them all onto one "combination plate" named for the region. But for the most part, they remain singular specialties, featured streetside or in the marketplaces, snack parlors and coffee shops.

Antojitos are quite firmly fixed in the public domain, and the preparation of many of them relies on a special piece of good-size equipment, like the large frying table so commonly used by street sellers, the massive hardwood charcoal fires and the vertical spits for layered pork. So what I've included in this chapter is a representative batch of regional, traditional *antojitos* that I found could be turned out well in a home kitchen.

Kitchen Spanish

Because eating *antojitos* is built inextricably into the fiesta spirit, many Mexican cooks often connect the other fiesta dishes—*mole, barbacoa, pozole, menudo*—to the *antojito* category. To keep things neat and tidy, I've included only *masa*-based snacks as *antojitos*. Also, turning things around, nicer restaurants often take the *masa*-based *antojitos*—which usually function as light meals—prepare them in smaller portions, and put them on the tables along with the appetizers. Clearly, this is a remarkably versatile category.

TACOS

Most Mexicans I know just laugh when they think about the crisp *U*-shaped tacos heaped with ground beef, lettuce and American cheese—the ones that come with beans and rice and pass for a Mexican "dinner" in the United States. They're a long way from the authentic double thickness of corn tortillas—a little greasy from the griddle—wrapped around a biteful of meat, sprinkled with sharp sauce and a little fragrant onion and fresh coriander (*cilantro*). And enjoyed standing up, as a tasty snack.

So what exactly is a taco, that most well known of Mexican culinary inventions? Simply answered by one expert, it is improvised cooking wrapped in a tortilla. And, in my opinion, it is remarkably good not only because a fresh-baked corn tortilla is so good, but also because Mexican cooks have a natural talent for putting together dabs of this and that.

In Mexico, the corn tortillas for tacos can be steaming soft and folded over thick stews (*tacos de cazuela*), griddle-cooked meats, potatoes or eggs (*tacos de la plancha*), charcoal-grilled beef, pork or chicken (*tacos al carbón*), or steamed *barbacoa* or beef head meat (*tacos a vapor*). The tortillas can be quick-fried (to ensure that they don't dry out), then folded over a little ground meat, fresh cheese or chile-seasoned potatoes and packed in a cloth-lined basket to sell on the street (*tacos de canasta*). The tortillas can be rolled around a filling and fried crisp to make *tacos dorados*. Or they can be replaced with soft flour tortillas to make burritos or *tacos de harina*. Folded or rolled, fried, half-fried, quick-fried or soft, filled with practically anything that will fit—they're all tacos to someone in Mexico.

Soft tacos are the most common of the lot, and when it comes to serving them (which I find myself doing frequently), I focus on the spirited informality, putting the components out for help-yourself buffets at parties or on a simply set table for impromptu lunches or suppers. I plan 3 or 4 tacos per person, plus some accompaniments. For a group of 4, I'd make 2 fillings; for 8, I'd make 3 or 4. As a general rule, 1 cup of filling makes about 4 tacos; plan 2 thin (or one thick) corn tortillas or 1 flour tortilla per taco.

Recipes from other chapters that work well as soft taco fillings: Melted Cheese with Peppers and *Chorizo* (page 82); Shredded Beef Salad with Avocado (page 85); Eggs *a la Mexicana* (page 115); Eggs with *Chorizo* (page 116); Scrambled Eggs with Shredded Jerky (page 117); Brains with Mexican Seasonings (page 147); Stewed Mushrooms (page 149); Chile-Marinated Vegetables (page 165); Chicken or Pork *Pibil* (page 233); Chicken *Barbacoa* (page 235); Shredded Pork *Tinga* (page 248); *Carne con Chile Colorado* (page 250); Pork *Carnitas* (page 252); Goat or Lamb *Birria* (page 256).

SOFT TACOS WITH FILLINGS FROM THE EARTHENWARE POT OR GRIDDLE

Tacos de Cazuela y de la Plancha

In Spanish bars, they put out dishes of warm and cool mixtures made with seafood, vegetables and the like: *tapas,* to spoon onto your plate and enjoy with a drink. *Tacos de cazuela* are a sort of Mexican equivalent, though they fill in more as a tortilla-wrapped light meal than as a preprandial snack.

Just about any of the thick-sauced meat dishes ("stews," as we might call them) for which the different regions are known can show up in stands that sell *tacos de cazuela,* so these tacos often have quite interesting and varied fillings. And if the vendor keeps them warm in thick earthenware vessels (*cazuelas*), the scene can be as beautiful as the tacos are tasty. Unfortu-

COOK'S NOTES

Regional Explorations
While the griddle fillings are more or less similar throughout the country, fillings from the homey *cazuelas* show regional distinctiveness as these few examples illustrate: in Querétaro—*rajas* of *chile poblano* in tomato sauce, eggs with dark *chile pasilla* sauce, cactus paddles in light red-chile sauce; in Veracruz—chicken or beef with *chipotle* peppers, blood sausage with onion and tomato, cactus paddles with pork or scrambled eggs, pickled pigs' feet; in Toluca—stewed greens like spinach and dock, mush-

nately, earthenware is fast being replaced by enamelware and even steam tables in towns like Hermosillo, Sonora and Veracruz.

I've seen big griddles for *tacos de la plancha* on the streets of most Mexican cities, save those in Yucatán. One beautiful stand has for years been set up on the wharf in Veracruz: Spread on the counter that's hooked to the front of the butane-fired griddle is a thick carpet of fresh flat-leaf parsley; on top sits a rock mortar full of guacamole followed by help-yourself bowls of *chile de árbol* sauce, *salsa mexicana,* peeled cucumbers, lime wedges and radishes. It's a fragrant sight and the little steak-and-onion, tripe or *chorizo* tacos are delicious.

An equally delicious and varied assortment of *cazuela* and *plancha* soft taco fillings begins after the following general directions.

Preparing the Tortillas: Steam-heat corn tortillas as described on page 353; keep them warm in the steamer in a very low oven, and bring them out as needed. Flour tortillas should be heated as directed on page 77; keep them in a very low oven and bring them out a few at a time. It is customary that vendors of *tacos de la plancha* will heat *very fresh* small corn tortillas directly on the lightly greased griddle. In addition to warming them, the little bit of grease makes them more pliable and less given to falling apart.

How to Serve Soft Tacos: For a small group, simply set out hot tortillas and pass the fillings in warm bowls. Complete the meal with *Frijoles Refritos* (page 269) and a salad. For a large, informal, come-and-go party, set out a number of fillings on warming trays or in small chafing dishes (always include 1 or 2 cold or room-temperature ones; also *Seviche* (page 83) or Shredded Beef Salad with Avocado (page 85) fit here nicely). Have a good supply of different sauces like Guacamole with *Tomatillos* (page 46), *Salsa Mexicana* (page 35) and *Salsa Picante* (page 40) set nearby; Roasted Pepper *Rajas* (page 278) go well with the griddle-cooked fillings. Frequently replenish baskets of flour and corn tortillas. Prepare griddle-cooked or other last-minute fillings in small batches throughout the party. Set out some forks for those who decide to eat the fillings without tortillas. *Charro* Beans (page 270) ladled into cups and Mixed Vegetable Salad (page 87) or *Jícama* Salad (page 89) always seem welcome. Sweet Fresh-Cheese Pie (page 288) and a bowl of fruit would make a sweet, simple ending to the party.

rooms with green chiles, pork rind in tomato or *tomatillo* sauce, squash blossoms; in Mexico City—green and red *mole* with chicken, squash with pork, *salpicón* of chicken or beef, *rajas* of green chile with potatoes and eggs; in Mérida, Yucatán—shrimp, octopus or whelk in lime *vinagreta* or in *escabeche,* octopus in its ink, meaty fish like *cherna* in mayonnaise with peas, fish in tomato sauce.

SCRAMBLED EGGS AND POTATOES IN TANGY GREEN SAUCE

Huevos y Papas con Rajas en Salsa Verde

This earthy combination of well-browned potatoes, roasted chiles, scrambled eggs and *tomatillo* sauce is a delicious brunch or supper dish served with *Frijoles Refritos* (page 269) and corn tortillas. It comes from a literal hole-in-the-wall, no-name, stand-up *taquería* in downtown Mexico City, where none of the dishes has a name more complicated than "potatoes and eggs" or "pork and zucchini." The talented ladies who cook there, though, really know the Mexican secret of brilliantly flavored, beautifully textured taco fillings.

YIELD: about 3½ cups, enough for 12 tacos, serving 4 as a light main course

> ½ recipe Quick-Cooked *Tomatillo* Sauce (page 42), prepared as directed in Step 1 below
> 3 small (about 10 ounces total) boiling potatoes like the red-skinned ones, halved
> 4 large eggs
> A generous ¼ teaspoon salt
> 2½ tablespoons lard or vegetable oil
> ½ cup (about 2 ounces) crumbled Mexican *queso fresco* (page 327) or other fresh cheese like feta or farmer's cheese, plus a little extra for garnish
> ½ small onion, thinly sliced
> 2 large fresh *chiles poblanos,* roasted and peeled (page 337)

1. *The preliminaries.* Prepare the ½ recipe *tomatillo* sauce as directed on page 43, through Step 2; measure out the broth and salt called for in the sauce recipe and combine them.

Simmer the potatoes in salted water to cover just until tender, about 15 minutes. Drain, run under cold water to cool, peel if you wish, then cut into ¾-inch dice.

2. *The eggs.* Beat the eggs with the salt, just enough to combine the whites and yolks. Heat *half* the lard or oil in a large, well-seasoned or Teflon-coated skillet over medium-high.

COOK'S NOTES

Ingredients
Chiles Poblanos: If necessary, they can be replaced with 3 large, long green chiles (roasted and peeled) or 4 *jalapeños* (seeded and sliced); add the latter with the onions.

Timing and Advance Preparation
The dish takes about an hour, though not every minute is active. Steps 1 and 2 may be completed ahead; cover and refrigerate the components. Finish the dish just before serving; if necessary, the completed dish can be gently reheated.

TRADITIONAL VARIATIONS
Potatoes and Rajas: For a nice side dish to serve with eggs or meats, prepare the potatoes as described in Step 1, then brown with the onions and chiles (Step 3) and season with salt. It makes about 3 servings.

When hot, add the eggs and stir every 3 seconds or so (as when making an omelet) until set; to form large curds, the cooking must go quickly without much stirring. Scrape the eggs into a small bowl, stir in the crumbled cheese, and set aside. Clean the skillet.

3. *Frying the mixture.* About ½ hour before serving, heat the remaining generous tablespoon lard or oil in the skillet over medium. Add the onion and diced potatoes, and fry, stirring frequently to ensure that nothing sticks to the pan, until the mixture is *well browned,* about 15 minutes. While the potatoes are browning, stem and seed the chiles, then slice them into ⅛-inch strips. Add to the potato mixture and increase the heat to medium-high.

4. *Adding the sauce.* When the mixture begins to sizzle with a little added fervor, pour in the *tomatillo* puree from Step 1. Stir gently for 4 or 5 minutes while the sauce sears and boils vigorously to a thicker, darker mixture. Add the salted broth, bring to a boil, reduce the heat to medium and simmer until the sauce is thick enough to coat the other ingredients. Add the eggs and cheese, simmer for a minute or so, spoon into a serving dish, sprinkle with a little crumbled cheese and serve.

Tomatillos

ZUCCHINI AND PORK WITH MEXICAN FLAVORS

Calabacitas con Puerco

This typically Mexican-flavored dish, from that Mexico City no-name *taquería* I love, is something I'm sure most Mexicans have prepared or eaten numerous times; the corn, *epazote* and fresh cheese make it especially good. It is a perfectly substantial main-course taco filling and needs nothing more than tortillas and a green salad to make a complete meal. Or chop the meat and vegetables larger, and serve it as a casserole.

YIELD: about 3½ cups, enough for 12 tacos, serving 4 as a light main course

CONTEMPORARY IDEAS

Potatoes, Zucchini and Rajas in Creamy Green Sauce: Prepare the *tomatillo* sauce and potatoes as directed in Step 1, reserving ½ cup broth (rather than 1 cup) with the *tomatillo* puree. In vegetable oil in a large skillet, brown the potatoes with the onions and 2 diced zucchini. Add the chile, increase the heat to medium-high, then stir in the *tomatillo* puree as directed in Step 4. Add the broth plus ½ cup Thick Cream (page 51) or whipping cream. Simmer until thickened, then serve sprinkled with fresh cheese.

COOK'S NOTES

Techniques
"Sweating" Zucchini: See page 273.

Ingredients
Chile Poblano: If this chile isn't available, prepare the dish with 2 long green chiles (roasted, peeled, seeded and diced) or as many hot green chiles (seeded and diced) as you can take.

1 pound (4 small) zucchini, ends trimmed and cut in ¾-inch dice

2 tablespoons lard or vegetable oil, plus a little more if necessary

1 pound lean, boneless pork shoulder, trimmed of fat and cut into ⅜-inch pieces

1 small onion, thinly sliced

2 cloves garlic, peeled and minced

1 ripe, medium-large tomato, roasted or boiled (page 352), peeled, cored and diced

1 large fresh *chile poblano,* roasted and peeled (page 337), seeded and diced

The kernels cut from 1 large ear of fresh sweet corn (about 1 cup)
OR 1 cup frozen corn, defrosted

1 teaspoon mixed dried herbs (such as oregano, marjoram and thyme)

2 bay leaves

1 sprig *epazote* (optional)

Salt, if necessary

3 ounces (1 scant cup) Mexican *queso fresco* (page 327) or other fresh cheese like mild domestic goat or farmer's cheese, cut into ½-inch cubes

1. *"Sweating" the zucchini.* Place the zucchini in a colander, toss with salt and let stand for 20 to 30 minutes, to rid it of excess liquid.

2. *Browning the meat.* In a large skillet, heat the lard or oil over medium-high. When hot, add the pork in a single layer; stir occasionally for about 7 minutes, until well browned, then remove to a small bowl.

3. *Finishing the dish.* Add a little more lard or oil to the pan, if necessary, reduce the heat to medium, then add the onions and cook, stirring frequently, until they have browned, about 7 minutes. Stir in the garlic, cook for a minute or so, then add the tomato. Let the mixture cook, stirring occasionally, for 5 minutes.

Rinse the zucchini and dry on paper towels. Add to the to-mato mixture, along with the browned meat, the chiles and the corn. Measure in the herbs, bay leaves, *epazote* and 1½ cups water. Reduce the heat to medium-low and simmer for about 30 minutes, until the meat is tender and the juices have been almost completely consumed. Taste for salt. Scoop into a serv-ing dish and top with the cubes of fresh cheese.

Timing and Advance Preparation

Allow 1½ hours to prepare the dish, about half of which is un-attended simmering. The dish may be simmered a day or so ahead, covered and refriger-ated; reheat slowly in a covered saucepan, then garnish with the cheese.

TRADITIONAL VARIATIONS

Minor Variations on the Cala-bacitas Theme: The pork may be omitted, making it a nice vegetable dish to accompany a simple meat; replace the water with 1 cup chicken broth. Beef can replace the pork, as can boneless chicken breast. (With the latter, add the browned cubed chicken breast to the simmering vegetables only 5 minutes before serving and use chicken broth in place of water.)

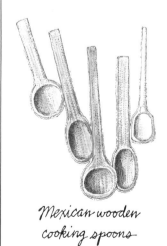

Mexican wooden cooking spoons

SHRIMP WITH LIME DRESSING AND CRUNCHY VEGETABLES

Camarones a la Vinagreta

The refreshing simplicity of this soft taco filling, based on a recipe given to me by a Yucatecan *taquería* cook, makes it a perfect complement to some of the richer fillings. Also, it's a delicious first course, hors d'oeuvre or picnic offering. With warm tortillas or good bread and a creamy potato salad, it makes a very good summer supper.

YIELD: about 3 cups, enough for 12 tacos, serving 4 as a light main course

For the shrimp:

   1 lime, halved
   ½ teaspoon black peppercorns, very coarsely ground
   ¼ teaspoon allspice berries, very coarsely ground
   3 bay leaves
  12 ounces good-quality shrimp, left in their shells

For completing the dish:

   ½ small red onion, cut into ¼-inch dice
   1 ripe, medium-small tomato, cored and cut into ¼-inch dice
   5 radishes, finely diced
  1½ tablespoons finely chopped fresh coriander (*cilantro*)
  2½ tablespoons freshly squeezed lime juice
   5 tablespoons vegetable oil, preferably half olive oil and half vegetable oil
   ½ teaspoon salt
  2 or 3 leaves romaine or leaf lettuce, for garnish
  Sprigs of coriander (*cilantro*) or radish roses, for garnish

1. *The shrimp.* Squeeze the two lime halves into a medium-size saucepan, then add the two squeezed rinds, the black pepper, allspice, bay leaves and 1 quart water. Cover and simmer over medium-low heat for 10 minutes.

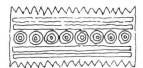

COOK'S NOTES

Timing and Advance Preparation
Preparation time is about 1¾ hours, most of which is devoted to the shrimp quietly marinating. The shrimp and vegetables can be prepared early in the day: Refrigerate separately, *well covered*. Dress the salad up to 1 hour before serving.

TRADITIONAL VARIATIONS
Fruits of the Sea a la Vinagreta: Squid or octopus (simmered until tender, then cubed), shelled cooked crawfish, crabmeat or any meaty fish (poached and cubed) can be used in this dish: Replace the cooked shrimp with 10 ounces (1⅔ cups) cooked seafood.

CONTEMPORARY IDEAS
Shrimp, Jícama and Roasted Chiles a la Vinagreta: Prepare the recipe as directed, replacing the tomato with 1 cup diced *jícama* and adding 1 large *chile poblano* or 2 long green chiles (roasted, peeled, seeded and thinly sliced) and 2 tablespoons minced fresh chives. Garnish with orange segments if you wish.

Raise the heat to high, add the shrimp, re-cover and let the liquid return to a full boil. Immediately remove the pan from the heat, hold the lid slightly askew and strain off all the liquid. Re-cover tightly, set aside for 15 minutes, then rinse the shrimp under cold water to stop the cooking.

Peel the shrimp, then devein them by running a knife down the back to expose the dark intestinal track and scraping it out. If the shrimp are medium or larger, cut them into ½-inch bits; place in a bowl.

2. *Other preliminaries.* Add the red onion, tomato, radish and coriander to the shrimp. In a small bowl or a jar with a tight-fitting lid, combine the lime juice, oil and salt.

3. *Combining and serving.* Shortly before serving, mix the dressing ingredients thoroughly, then pour over the shrimp mixture. Toss to coat everything well, cover, and refrigerate or set aside at room temperature.

Line a shallow serving bowl with the lettuce leaves. Taste the shrimp mixture for salt, scoop it into the prepared bowl and serve, garnished with sprigs of coriander or radish roses.

Olive oil, Baja California

COLD CHICKEN AND AVOCADO WITH *CHILE CHIPOTLE*

Pollo, Aguacate y Chile Chipotle en Frío

Here is a variation on *salpicón* (page 85), from a *taquería* in Mexico City, which pairs chicken and vegetables with the perfect combination of avocado, *chile chipotle,* and well-dressed salad. Serve it as a summer main course with warm tortillas, a big fruit salad and, nontraditionally, a bottle of Gewürztraminer. Or carry it unmixed to a picnic, toss it as directed in Step 2 and serve with crusty French bread.

COOK'S NOTES

Ingredients

Chiles Chipotles: In Mexico City, dishes like this often utilize pickled (not *adobo*-packed) *chipotles*. Without any *chipotles* at all, this dish loses many of its special qualities, though a nice salad can be made using pickled *jalapeños* and chopped fresh coriander *(cilantro)*, if desired.

Chunky Guacamole (page 44)

Relishy Cactus-Paddle Salad (page 47)

From top to bottom: Tolucan *Chorizo* Sausage (page 55);
Potatoes with *Chorizo* Sausage (page 134)

From top left to right: *chile ancho*, Red-Chile Marinade (page 64),
Mexican cinnamon, *chile guajillo*, cloves, Mexican oregano, bay leaves, Yucatecan
Mixed-Spice Paste (page 67), garlic, vinegar, coriander seeds, black pepper,
achiote seeds, Yucatecan *Achiote* Seasoning Paste (page 66), cumin seeds

Shrimp-Ball Soup with Roasted Pepper and Tomato (page 102)

From top to bottom: Slivered Beef with Well-Browned Onions (page 135);
Pan-Fried Chicken Livers with *Tomatillo* Sauce (page 130);
Cold Chicken and Avocado with *Chile Chipotle* (page 128)

Deep-Fried Cheese *Quesadillas* (page 143)

Stacked Tortillas with Shark, Black Beans and Tomato Sauce (page 161)

YIELD: about 3½ cups, enough for 12 tacos, serving 4 as a light main course

1 **chicken leg-and-thigh quarter or 1 large breast half**
½ **teaspoon salt**
2 **small (about 6 ounces total) boiling potatoes like the red-skinned ones, halved**
2 **medium (about 6 ounces total) carrots, peeled and cut into 1½-inch lengths**
¼ **cup cider vinegar**
1 **teaspoon dried oregano**
½ **teaspoon salt**
2 to 4 **canned *chiles chipotles,* seeded and thinly sliced**
¼ **small onion, finely diced**
4 **large romaine lettuce leaves, sliced in ⅜-inch strips, plus several whole leaves for garnish**
1 **ripe avocado, peeled, pitted and diced**
¼ **cup vegetable oil**
1 **slice of onion, broken into rings, for garnish**

1. *The chicken mixture.* Bring 2 cups water to a boil in a medium-size saucepan, add the chicken and salt, skim off the foam that rises as the water returns to a boil, partially cover and simmer over medium heat—23 minutes for the dark meat, 13 minutes for the breast. If there is time, cool the chicken in the broth.

Boil the potatoes and carrots in salted water to cover until they are just tender, 12 to 15 minutes. Rinse for a moment under cold water, strip off the potato skins, if you wish, then cut the potatoes and carrots into ⅜-inch dice. Place in a large mixing bowl.

Skin and bone the chicken, then tear the meat into large shreds and add to the potatoes.

Skim off all the fat on top of the broth, then measure 3 tablespoons of broth into a small bowl. Stir in the vinegar, oregano and salt. Pour the dressing over the chicken mixture and add the sliced *chiles chipotles* and chopped onion. Stir, cover and let stand for 45 minutes, refrigerated or at room temperature.

2. *Finishing the dish.* Shortly before serving, mix the sliced lettuce and diced avocado into the chicken mixture. Drizzle with oil and toss lightly. Taste for salt.

Line a serving platter with the remaining romaine leaves and pile on the chicken mixture. Decorate with the onion rings and serve.

Timing and Advance Preparation
The active preparation time is less than 45 minutes, though you'll need to start a couple of hours before serving. The chicken mixture can marinate overnight, covered and refrigerated; complete the final dressing within 15 minutes of serving.

TRADITIONAL VARIATIONS
Variations on the Salpicón Theme: The proportions and selection of the main ingredients should be kept loose. Meats such as ham and leftover pork or beef roast can easily be substituted for the cooked chicken.

CONTEMPORARY IDEAS
Smoked Chicken Salad with Avocado and Chipotle: Replace the cooked chicken with 4 or 5 ounces (about ⅔ cup) diced smoked chicken. Serve on plates lined with lightly dressed curly lettuce leaves.

PAN-FRIED CHICKEN LIVERS WITH *TOMATILLO* SAUCE

Azadura con Salsa Verde

In Querétaro, *cazuela* fillings are set out in every little doorway or cubbyhole eatery for spooning into rolls, rolling into tortillas or stuffing into puffed *masa* cakes called *gorditas*. One filling is frequently the pan-fried chicken livers, which I think are a perfect match for *tomatillo* sauce.

Served with tortillas and *Jícama* Salad (page 89), *azadura* (literally "innards") makes a good light supper (or even brunch, served with warm, sliced hard-boiled eggs).

YIELD: about 2½ cups, enough for 10 tacos, serving 3 or 4 as a light main course

½ recipe Quick-Cooked *Tomatillo* Sauce (page 42), prepared as directed in Step 1 below
1 pound (2 cups) chicken livers
About ⅓ cup flour
About ½ teaspoon salt
2 tablespoons lard or vegetable oil
½ medium onion, thinly sliced
¼ cup finely chopped onion mixed with 1 tablespoon chopped fresh coriander (*cilantro*)

1. *The sauce.* Prepare the sauce as directed on page 43, simmering it an additional 5 minutes (a total of about 15 minutes) until it is the thickness of tomato ketchup. Remove from the fire and set aside.

2. *Frying the livers and onion.* About 15 minutes before serving, rinse the livers and pull or cut off all the fat and connective tissues. Cut in half, then dry on paper towels. Scoop the flour onto a large plate and sprinkle with salt.

Heat the lard or oil in a large (12-inch) skillet over medium. Add the onion and fry for about 5 minutes, until translucent. Raise the heat to medium-high. Quickly toss the livers in the flour, shake off the excess and lay in a single layer in the skillet. Fry for 3 to 4 minutes per side, until nicely browned and a large liver is just pink—not bloody and red—when cut into.

a few Mexican beers

3. *Finishing the dish.* While the livers are frying, reheat the green sauce over low, adding a tablespoon or so of water if it has thickened beyond a pourable consistency.

Scoop the fried livers onto a deep, warm serving plate and spoon on the warm green sauce. Sprinkle with the onion and coriander and serve right away.

NORTHERN-STYLE SHREDDED BEEF WITH TOMATOES

Carne Deshebrada a la Norteña

Mexican cooks throughout the Republic boil and shred beef for snacks, though nowhere do they prepare it as frequently or as well seasoned as in Northern Mexico. Besides being rolled into soft tacos, meaty shreds of beef with tomatoes, chile and green onions are the unnamed filling for Crispy-Fried Tacos (page 78) called *flautas* there, and for the flour tortilla–wrapped *Chivichangas* (page 142) of the northwest. Served with flour tortillas, *Frijoles Refritos* (page 269) and a salad, this shredded beef is a satisfying meal.

YIELD: about 2½ cups, enough for 10 tacos, serving 3 or 4 as a light main course

1 pound lean, boneless beef chuck, flank or brisket, well trimmed and cut into 1½-inch pieces
1 teaspoon salt
1 medium onion
3 cloves garlic, peeled
3 tablespoons lard or vegetable oil
2 ripe, medium-small tomatoes, roasted or boiled (page 352), cored, peeled and chopped
    OR one 15-ounce can tomatoes, drained and chopped
2 large green onions, root ends removed and chopped in ¼-inch pieces
Fresh hot green chiles to taste (roughly 2 or 3 *chiles serranos* or 1 or 2 *chiles jalapeños*), stemmed, seeded and finely chopped
Salt, about ½ teaspoon

COOK'S NOTES

Techniques
Shredding Boiled Beef: In contrast to the soft-textured chuck (which can be easily shredded between your fingers), flank and brisket are dense enough that they require some ingenuity (though they make good, meaty *carne deshebrada*). Tear the meat into small pieces, then pulse *small batches* 3 or 4 times in a food processor; or tear the meat into small pieces, stab into a piece with a fork (to secure it firmly on the cutting board) and claw at it with a second fork until finely shredded. The fork shredding gives the nicest texture.

Timing and Advance Preparation
Start making this filling at least 2 hours ahead; plan on about 40 minutes of active involvement. It can be prepared up to 4 days ahead, covered and refrigerated.

TRADITIONAL VARIATIONS
Beef and Green-Chile Filling: The hot green chiles can be replaced with 3 or 4 long green chiles or 2 or 3 large *chiles poblanos* (either should be roasted, peeled, seeded and chopped).

1. *The meat.* Bring 2 quarts water to a boil in a large saucepan, add the meat and salt, then skim off any grayish foam that rises during the first few minutes of simmering. Slice *half* of the onion and halve *1 clove* of the garlic; add to the meat. Partially cover and simmer over medium to medium-low heat until the meat is very tender, 45 minutes to 1½ hours, depending on the cut. Let the meat cool in the broth, if there is time. Strain the liquid and spoon off all the fat that rises to the top; set the broth aside. Finely shred the meat (see Techniques in **Cook's Notes**), then dry with paper towels.

2. *Finishing the shredded beef.* Dice the remaining onion and mince the remaining garlic. Heat the lard or oil in a large, heavy skillet over medium-high. When hot, add the onion and shredded beef and stir frequently for 8 to 10 minutes, until well browned. Reduce the heat to medium, add the garlic, tomatoes, green onions and chiles, and cook, stirring frequently, until the tomatoes have softened, about 4 minutes. Stir in ⅔ cup of the reserved broth, then simmer until the liquid has evaporated, 10 to 15 minutes. Season with salt and it's ready.

MINCED PORK WITH ALMONDS, RAISINS AND SWEET SPICES

Picadillo Oaxaqueño

Though this filling is made of ground meat, it's rich with tomatoes and sweet spices, and it's textured with raisins and almonds. Oaxacan *picadillo* is a far cry from the soupy, undistinguished hamburger-and-potato *picadillos* commonly available throughout Mexico. It makes a delicious filling for *Chiles Rellenos* (page 245) and *Picadillo* Turnovers (page 150) as well as simple soft tacos. The name, by the way, comes from the verb *picar*, "to mince."

YIELD: about 3⅓ cups, enough for 12 tacos, serving 4 as a light main course

    1½ **pounds (3 medium-large) ripe tomatoes, roasted or boiled (page 352), cored, peeled and roughly chopped**
        OR one 28-ounce can tomatoes, undrained
    1½ **tablespoons vegetable oil**
    1 **medium onion, finely diced**

Veracruz-Style Shredded Pork Filling: Use 1 pound lean, boneless pork shoulder in place of the beef. Complete the recipe as directed, replacing the green onions and green chiles with 2 canned *chiles chipotles* (seeded and sliced) and 2 or 3 pickled *chiles jalapeños* (seeded and sliced).

Flavorful Shredded Chicken Filling: Poach 2 chicken breasts as directed on page 60, reserving the broth; skin, bone and coarsely shred. Follow Step 2 of the preceding recipe, adding the chicken when the broth is nearly reduced.

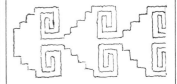

COOK'S NOTES

Ingredients
Coarse-Ground Meat: To avoid the high fat and water content, I buy pork shoulder (or, for Northern-Style *Picadillo,* beef chuck), trim it, then run it through a meat chopper or chop it in small batches in the food processor.

Timing and Advance Preparation
Allow about an hour to prepare the filling, at least half of which is for relatively unattended simmering. The finished *picadillo* can be covered and refrigerated for 3 or 4 days before using.

1 clove garlic, peeled and minced

1½ pounds lean, coarse-ground pork (see Ingre-
    dients in Cook's Notes)

½ teaspoon black peppercorns (or about ¾ tea-
    spoon ground)

1 inch cinnamon stick (or about 1 teaspoon
    ground)

5 cloves (or about ⅛ teaspoon ground)

¼ cup raisins

4 teaspoons cider vinegar

¼ cup slivered almonds

Salt, about 1 teaspoon

1. *The tomatoes.* For a *picadillo* using peeled fresh tomatoes, place them in a blender or food processor with ⅓ cup water, then process until smooth. Using canned tomatoes, simply puree them with their liquid.

2. *The meat.* Heat the oil in a large skillet over medium. When hot, add the onion and cook until soft, about 5 minutes. Stir in the garlic and cook 2 minutes longer. Add the pork in a thin layer and fry, stirring frequently, until cooked and lightly brown. (If quite a bit of fat has rendered from the meat, drain it off.)

3. *Finishing the picadillo.* Pulverize the pepper, cinnamon and cloves in a mortar or spice grinder, then add to the skillet along with the tomato puree, raisins and vinegar. Simmer until reduced to a thick, homogeneous mass, 30 to 45 minutes, depending on the juiciness of the tomatoes.

Toast the almonds for about 10 minutes in a 325° oven, stir into the filling, season with salt, and it's ready.

Cinnamon sticks (canela)

TRADITIONAL VARIATIONS

Northern-Style Picadillo: Complete Step 2 as directed (ignore Step 1), increasing the garlic to 4 cloves and replacing the pork with coarse-ground beef. Stir in one 15-ounce can tomatoes (drained and chopped), 2 teaspoons mixed dried herbs, ½ teaspoon ground black pepper, ¼ cup raisins, 20 to 25 green olives (pitted and chopped) and salt to taste. Simmer until all the liquid has evaporated.

Shredded Pork Picadillo: Simmer 1½ pounds cubed, boneless pork shoulder in salted water until very tender. Strain, cool and finely shred the meat. Prepare the recipe as directed, replacing ground pork with the shredded. (You will need a little more oil.)

Oaxacan Picadillo with Fried Plantain: Prepare the recipe as directed. While the filling is simmering, fry 1 small, very ripe plantain (diced) in a little vegetable oil over medium heat until browned. Add to the filling with the almonds.

CONTEMPORARY IDEAS

Red-Chile Picadillo: Toast and soak 4 large *chiles anchos* (stemmed and seeded). Reduce the tomatoes to ¾ pound (or a 15-ounce can) and blend with the drained chiles; strain. Prepare the *picadillo* as directed in Steps 2 and 3, adding the chile mixture where the tomatoes are called for and simmering over medium-low heat.

POTATOES WITH MEXICAN SAUSAGE

Papas y Chorizo

There is a bare glass bulb that hangs over most of the outdoor taco stalls, and it casts its unfocused illumination on an earthy scene that smells of fire and substance. Sausage and potatoes sizzle on the metal and crackle out that unmistakable, penetrating savor; alongside are piles of chiles whose piquancy you can feel. These are the environs for tacos, nighttime street tacos, and the enjoyment of them is as much for the oily tortillas and energizing sauce as it is for the taste of comradeship, green earth and hot fires.

Traditionally, this potato-*chorizo* filling is paired with Fresh Green *Tomatillo* Sauce (page 36), plus a sprinkling of fresh coriander (*cilantro*) and chopped onion. Untraditionally, it makes a good stuffing for mushroom caps.

YIELD: about 3 cups, enough for 12 tacos, serving 4 as a light main course

> 4 medium-small (about 1 pound total) boiling potatoes like the red-skinned ones, halved
> 2 tablespoons vegetable oil
> 8 ounces (1 cup) *chorizo* sausage, store-bought or homemade (page 55), casing removed
> 1 small onion, diced
> Salt, if necessary

1. *The potatoes.* Boil the halved potatoes in salted water to cover until just tender, 12 to 15 minutes. Drain, peel if you wish, then cut into ¾-inch dice.

2. *The chorizo.* Heat the oil in a large skillet set over medium-low, add the *chorizo* and cook, stirring to break up any clumps, until done, about 10 minutes. Remove from the pan, leaving behind as much fat as possible. Pour off all but enough fat to coat the bottom of the pan.

3. *Finishing the mixture.* About 20 minutes before serving, fry the onions and potatoes over medium heat until well browned, about 15 minutes; regularly scrape up any sticking bits of potato so they won't burn. Add the *chorizo* to the potatoes, stir well and let heat for several minutes. Season with salt, if necessary, and you're ready to serve.

COOK'S NOTES

Timing and Advance Preparation
Start to finish, this filling can be prepared in about 40 minutes. Complete the first two steps up to a day ahead, reserving the *chorizo* fat; cover and refrigerate the components. Complete Step 3 shortly before serving. The finished dish can be kept warm in a low oven, lightly covered with foil, for ½ hour; or it may be reheated in a shallow layer, uncovered, in a 400° oven, just before serving.

TRADITIONAL VARIATIONS
Potatoes and Chorizo with Varied Flavors and Textures: Choose any or all of the following: Add 1 large tomato (roasted or boiled, peeled and chopped) to the browned potato mixture, let it reduce a little, then add the *chorizo*; add ¼ cup water along with the cooked *chorizo* to give the filling a more homogeneous texture; add 1 large *chile poblano* (roasted, peeled, seeded and sliced) shortly before adding the *chorizo*.

CONTEMPORARY IDEAS
Chorizo, Potato and Plantain: Prepare the recipe as directed, replacing *half* the potatoes with a scant cup of diced ripe plantain (frying them all together in Step 3), and adding a few raisins, toasted slivered almonds, and/or *chile chipotle* (seeded and sliced).

SLIVERED BEEF WITH WELL-BROWNED ONIONS

Bistec Encebollado

Portable, butane-fired griddles show up at dusk in parks and on street corners through most of the country, penetrating the outdoor odors with the aroma of searing meat and sweet browned onions. This is an easy dish to get a passion for, served in hot flour or corn tortillas, with a little Chunky Guacamole (page 44) or Red-Chile Sauce (page 37).

YIELD: about 2 cups, enough for 12 tacos, serving 4 as a light main course

> 1 **pound thin-cut pan-fryable steaks like those called sandwich steaks or flip steaks, or even skirt steaks (see Ingredients in** Cook's Notes)
> **Salt and freshly ground black pepper, as desired**
> **About 3 tablespoons vegetable oil**
> 1 **large onion, diced or sliced**
> 2 **large cloves garlic, peeled and minced**

1. *The meat.* Trim the beef of excess fat and sprinkle with salt and pepper. Over medium-high, heat enough vegetable oil to nicely coat the bottom of a large, heavy skillet. When it is searingly hot, brown the steak for 1 to 2 minutes on each side; for cuts like skirt, be careful not to cook past medium-rare. Remove to a wire rack set over a plate and keep warm in a low oven; reduce the heat under the skillet to medium.

2. *The onion.* Add the onion to the skillet and cook, stirring frequently, until a deep golden-brown, about 10 minutes. Stir in the garlic and cook 2 minutes longer.

3. *Finishing the mixture.* Cut the meat into thin strips (across the grain, for skirt steak); for tougher cuts of meat, cut into ½-inch pieces. When the onion mixture is ready, add the beef to the skillet and stir until heated through. Season with salt and serve in a deep, warm bowl.

COOK'S NOTES

Techniques
Searing the Meat: If you sear the meat in a *hot* pan, you'll get a nice flavor and a good crust; if the pan isn't hot, you'll find pale meat simmering in its juices.

Ingredients
The Meat: The Mexican *bisteces* often used in this preparation are taken from the tougher cuts (frequently the round) and pounded. Choose thin round steaks (often sold as breakfast steaks, sandwich steaks, flip steaks, wafer steaks or perhaps under other names) and pound them if necessary; or choose any thin steak tender enough to pan-fry. I like trimmed skirt steak because of its flavor and texture. Frequently, Mexican street vendors use the sheets of Thin-Sliced Beef (*Cecina*, page 57); it's tougher, so they chop it into small pieces.

Timing and Advance Preparation
About 25 minutes are needed to make this dish; nothing can be prepared in advance.

CONTEMPORARY VARIATIONS
Minor Variations on the Theme: The meat may be marinated (see page 244). It may also be fried in olive oil. Red onions may replace white, 4 *roasted* cloves of garlic could be used instead of raw ones. And strips of just about any roasted and peeled chile could be stirred in with the meat.

PAN-FRIED CHILE-MARINATED PORK

Puerco Enchilado a la Plancha

COOK'S NOTES

I know of this quintessentially Mexican-flavored filling not from the mobile street griddles, but from the more permanent bus-station and market *taquerías* in Toluca, Oaxaca, San Luis Potosí and Chilpancingo, Guerrero, where chile-marinated pork is a specialty. It's at its best laid across a fresh tortilla, sprinkled with Fresh Green *Tomatillo* Sauce (page 36) and topped with Roasted Pepper *Rajas* (page 278).

YIELD: about 2 cups, enough for 12 tacos, serving 4 as a light main course

> About 1 pound (1 recipe) **Chile-Marinated Pork** (page 59)
> About 2 tablespoons **vegetable oil**

1. *Frying the meat.* Cut the meat into lengths that will fit into your skillet, then smooth the *adobo* marinade into a light, even coating.

About 15 minutes before serving, set a large skillet over medium heat and measure in the oil (there should be enough to coat the bottom nicely). When it is hot, lay in as much meat as will comfortably fit in the pan, and fry until cooked through: Meat that is ⅛ inch thick will take about 2 minutes per side.

Remove the meat to a wire rack set over a large plate, and keep warm in a low oven. Continue frying batches of the meat, adding a little more oil to the skillet, if necessary. After the last batch has been fried, let the meat rest for a couple of minutes in a low oven.

2. *Serving.* The moment you're ready to serve, cut the meat across the grain into thin strips, place in a deep, warm bowl and carry to the table.

COOK'S NOTES

Techniques
Frying Chile-Coated Meat: Choose a well-seasoned (or Teflon-coated) skillet and keep the fire at medium, so the *adobo* ("chile marinade") won't stick and burn. With a light coat of *adobo,* a good layer of oil in the right pan and a medium heat, any bits of *adobo* that come off into the oil will not burn during at least two batches of frying.

Timing and Advance Preparation
The marinated pork can be ready in 15 mintues; it shouldn't be fried in advance.

SOFT TACOS WITH FILLINGS FROM THE CHARCOAL GRILL

Tacos al Carbón

For years, would-be sophisticates of the Mexican food scene have looked right over the wood fires and the heaps of smoldering charcoal that seared thin slabs of meat and radiated their heat into pots of beans and *pozole* and *menudo*. In Mexico, the gourmands still mostly brush that cooking aside as primitive—good only for a steak or slow-roasted kid, but not for serious cooking. But I was reared in a family that put bread on its table by putting hickory-smoked meats on the tables of others, so I've always been more captivated by what a smoky fire can do than by any powers of a blue gas flame or a safe electric burner.

Charcoal-grilled meat (and tacos made from it) has been a specialty of the North for a long time. But the spreading popularity of *tacos al carbón* has led people to put in *taquerías* with charcoal grills across much of the country; many even serve the Northern flour tortillas, if they can get them.

Tacos al carbón is an easy summer supper or picnic: Just prepare a couple of side dishes to fill in, then charcoal-grill some skirt steak according to the recipe that follows (or prepare one of the variations) and bring it to the table for the hungry to make into solid "main course" tacos. If given half a chance, I'd choose to invite 8 or 10 people for a relaxed afternoon cookout, but first I'd make sure my grill was the right size. It should be large enough to hold a 12-inch square of aluminum foil for cooking the green onions, an 8-inch-diameter pot for beans, another pot for warm corn tortillas, and have space left over for grilling the meat. To the side, you need a cutting board and knife, plus an easily accessible spot for all the condiments. Build the bulk of your fire under the open part of the grill, letting a few coals stay below the foil and the two pots. Grill some onions slowly, then heap them up entirely on the foil. Pass small bowls of beans, then grill your prepared meat(s) a little at a time, serving each batch with onions and a stack of hot tortillas.

Preparing the tortillas: About 20 minutes before serving, steam-heat the corn tortillas as described on page 353. Just before serving, set them to the back of the grill (where they will keep warm for 45 minutes or longer). Griddle-heated tortillas are

COOK'S NOTES

MENU SUGGESTIONS
I lean toward serving most everything off the grill: the different meats that follow, Charcoal-Grilled Baby Onions (page 277), Grill-Roasted Corn (page 272) and Roasted Pepper *Rajas* (page 278) with the peppers prepared on the grill. *Charro* Beans (page 270) are always welcome, as are Melted Cheese with Peppers and *Chorizo* (page 82), guacamole (page 44 or 46), *Salsa Mexicana* (page 35), *Chipotle* Chile Sauce (page 39) and/or Red-Chile Sauce (page 37); Pickled Red Onions (page 50) aren't traditional with this fare, but they're delicious. Summer dessert means an ice or ice cream (pages 298–301) to me. Add beer, *Jamaica* "Flower" Cooler (page 307) and Pot-Brewed Coffee (page 315), and the meal will be as memorable as any could be.

common with *tacos al carbón* (see page 123), but they are generally impractical for home grilling. Flour tortillas are also traditional with this Northern-bred fare: Heat them in packages of 8 to 10, as directed on page 77. Keep them warm in a very low oven and bring them out a package at a time.

CHARCOAL-GRILLED SKIRT STEAK

Arrachera al Carbón

Skirt steak, in my opinion, is one of the most delicious, beefiest-tasting cuts of meat, if it's a good-quality outside piece and well trimmed. Charcoal-grilled, daubed with Fresh Green *Tomatillo* Sauce (page 36) or Chunky Guacamole (page 44) then wrapped with Roasted Pepper *Rajas* (page 278) in a flour tortilla—it is nearly the same as the Texan *fajitas* that have become very popular in many parts of the United States. Meat for *fajitas* is frequently marinated, as described on page 244.

Though *arrachera* ("skirt steak") is commonly used only in northeastern Mexico (especially around Monterrey), cooking thin sheets of beef over charcoal is popular throughout the North and everywhere Northerners have set up *taquerías*. In Hermosillo, Sonora, in fact, street vendors of *tacos de bistec* have elaborate chimney-covered charcoal grills built into pushcarts with customized condiment jars to hold *salsa roja*, *salsa mexicana*, cucumbers, red onions and radishes. Nearly everywhere, tacos of charcoal-grilled meat are accompanied by lime wedges to squeeze over them.

YIELD: about 2 cups, enough for 12 tacos, serving 4 as a light main course

> 1 pound trimmed skirt steak, cut into 3-inch lengths (see Ingredients in Cook's Notes)
> 1 lime, halved
> Salt and freshly ground black pepper, as desired

COOK'S NOTES

Techniques
Trimming Skirt Steak: If you get an untrimmed piece, strip off the elastic membrane, then trim off the surface fat and all the *very tough* silvery tissue.

Ingredients
Skirt Steak: This is the diaphragm muscle: a flat 4- or 5-inch-wide piece of meat, a foot or longer, with a clearly visible grain. There is an inner and an outer piece, the latter being a little more tender and flavorful. In Mexican markets in the United States, it may be called *arrachera*, *carne para asar* ("meat for broiling"), *bistec ranchero* ("ranch-style steak") or *fajitas* (literally "sashes"), and it is frequently butterflied, making two *very* thin steaks. For this recipe, I recommend nonbutterflied, small, outer skirt steaks. Other candidates for grilling are listed on page 243; each will work for these tacos, but the texture will be different.

Timing and Advance Preparation
Skirt steak takes only a few minutes to prepare; the trimming can be done in advance.

1. *Preliminaries.* Trim the meat of most fat and all the silvery tissue, then cover and refrigerate until grilling time. About 30 minutes before serving, light your charcoal fire and let it burn until the coals are very hot.

2. *Grilling the arrachera.* About 10 minutes before serving, squeeze a little lime over the meat, then sprinkle with salt and pepper. Grill over the hot coals for 2 or 3 minutes per side, depending on the thickness of the meat and heat of the fire; the meat is best grilled to medium-rare.

3. *Cutting and serving the arrachera.* Set the steak to the back of the grill (where it isn't hot enough to continue cooking), and let stand several minutes to reabsorb the juices. Then cut it across the grain into ¼-inch slices; or, alternatively, chop it into ½-inch pieces. Scoop into a small warm bowl and serve right away.

Earthenware bean pots (olla)

CRISPY-FRIED TACOS

Tacos Dorados

With the predictable regularity of changing traffic signals, people in the cities come to sit together in the brightly lit Mexican coffee shops they know as *cafeterías*. These are spots for the tasty snacks that are common indoors, like tostadas and the cylindrical, crispy, chicken-filled *tacos dorados* (or *tacos de pollo*) with guacamole and thick cream.

This typical version makes a great light meal with the addition of *Frijoles Refritos* (page 269). For a special winter supper, serve them with bowls of Shrimp-Ball Soup with Roasted Pepper (page 102).

YIELD: 12 tacos, serving 4 as a light main course

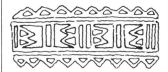

COOK'S NOTES

Ingredients
Corn Tortillas: See page 353.

Timing and Advance Preparation
With chicken and guacamole ready, the tacos take 45 minutes. You can make the filling a day in advance; cover and refrigerate. The tacos may be rolled 1 hour ahead; fry them just before serving.

1 ripe, large tomato, roasted or boiled (page 352), cored, peeled and roughly chopped
    OR about ¾ 15-ounce can tomatoes, drained and roughly chopped
½ small onion, roughly chopped
1 clove garlic, peeled and roughly chopped
1 tablespoon lard or vegetable oil
1 large (1¼-pound) whole chicken breast, cooked, skinned, boned and shredded (page 60)
Salt, about ½ teaspoon
12 corn tortillas, preferably thin store-bought ones
¾ cup vegetable oil
8 large leaves romaine lettuce, for garnish
½ cup Thick Cream (page 51) or commercial sour cream thinned with 2 tablespoons milk or cream
About 1½ cups (½ recipe) Chunky Guacamole (page 44) (optional)
1 tablespoon crumbled Mexican *queso fresco* or *queso añejo* (page 327), or other cheese like feta or farmer's cheese, for garnish
Several radish slices or roses, for garnish

1. *The filling.* Combine the tomato, onion and garlic in a blender or food processor and process until very smooth. Heat the tablespoon of lard or oil in a medium-size skillet over medium-high. When quite hot, add the puree and stir constantly until it is thick and reduced, about 4 minutes. Stir in the chicken, remove from the heat and season with salt.

2. *Assembling the tacos.* If the tortillas are moist, let them dry out in a single layer for a few minutes. Heat ¼ cup of the oil in a medium-size skillet over medium-high. When quite hot, quick-fry the tortillas one at a time to soften them, 2 to 3 seconds per side. Drain well on paper towels. Place 2 tablespoons of filling across each tortilla, roll up and secure with toothpicks (sliding them into the flap while holding them almost parallel to it). Cover with plastic wrap.

3. *Frying the tacos.* Add the remaining ½ cup of oil to what is in the skillet and heat over medium-high. When quite hot, lay in *half* the tacos. Fry, turning occasionally, until all sides are lightly browned and crispy, about 4 minutes. Drain on paper towels and keep warm in a low oven while frying the remainder.

4. *Garnish and presentation.* Line a platter with *half* the romaine leaves; slice the remainder into ⅜-inch strips and spread

TRADITIONAL VARIATIONS

Northern-Style Beef Flautas: Replace the chicken filling with ½ recipe Northern-Style Shredded Beef (page 131), completing this recipe as directed.

Flautas of a Different Sort: Choose 24 *very thin* corn tortillas. Prepare the recipe as directed, forming long *flautas* by overlapping 2 quick-fried tortillas about 2 inches, then spreading the filling down the length and rolling up very tightly. Fry in a *large* skillet.

Regional Explorations

From Guadalajara north, tacos are generally folded and fried, frequently with pork inside; anything with a tubular look gets called a *flauta* (literally "flute") and is often filled with beef. In Guerrero, there are thin rolled *taquitos* stuffed with ricotta. And in Mérida, Yucatán, the cooks fill crisp tortilla tubes (resembling Italian *cannoli* shells) with ground-meat *picadillo* and douse them with tomato sauce (*codzitos*). Only on the northern border do U-shaped, hamburger-stuffed tacos show up; I think it's clear which way the influence is going.

over the center. Arrange the tacos side by side over the lettuce and drizzle with cream. Dollop the optional guacamole down the center and sprinkle with cheese and/or radish slices; arrange the optional radish roses decoratively.

Crispy-fried tacos

BURRITOS WITH SPICY SHREDDED JERKY

Burritos de Machaca

Deann and I had driven hundreds of uneventful miles, most of it through sun-bleached expanses of Baja California's fascinating, unpopulated terrain; so it was a pleasure to roll into the cool, shaded center of San Ignacio. We found a place to eat and rest, and, like most every little eating place we'd passed, the menu consisted mostly of *burritos de machaca*. But in this isolated town, we got the real stuff: Rather than serving up the easy boiled-beef version I expected, the owner-cook took down a piece of homemade beef jerky, roasted and pounded it, fried it with vegetables and rolled it into flour tortillas. It is her recipe for jerky that is on page 57, and her recipe for this rustic, full-flavored burrito filling.

Served as a light main course, these burritos need only a little *Salsa Picante* (page 40), a green salad and some *Charro* Beans (page 270) to make a very memorable meal.

YIELD: 8 to 10 burritos with about 2½ cups filling, serving 3 to 4 as a light meal

COOK'S NOTES

Techniques
See page 117.

Ingredients
Jerky: See page 345. If jerky is unavailable, use 1 pound brisket, simmered until tender, then finely shredded as directed on page 131. Complete Step 2, browning the meat with the onions.
Chile Poblano: Other fresh chiles frequently appear in *machaca:* 2 long green chiles (roasted, peeled, seeded and diced) or hot green chiles to taste (seeded and diced).

Timing and Advance Preparation
This dish takes a little over ½ hour. The shredding and chopping can be done in advance, but complete the filling just before serving.

8 to 10 flour tortillas, store-bought or homemade (page 76)

For the filling:
   4 ounces beef jerky, store-bought or homemade (page 57)
   5 tablespoons lard or vegetable oil, plus a little more if needed
   1 large onion, diced
   2 fresh *chiles poblanos,* roasted and peeled (page 337), seeded and diced
   2 ripe, medium-small tomatoes, cored and diced
   3 cloves garlic, peeled and minced
   Salt, about ½ teaspoon (depending on the saltiness of the jerky)

1. *The tortillas.* If the tortillas are not hot, heat them as directed on page 77.

2. *The filling.* About ½ hour before serving, broil and shred the jerky as described in Step 1 on page 117 (there should be about 2 cups).

Heat the lard or oil in a medium-large skillet over medium-high. When quite hot, add the onion and fry, stirring frequently, until beginning to brown, about 5 minutes. Add the jerky, reduce the heat to medium and stir frequently until the mixture is *well browned,* 5 to 7 minutes. (If the meat absorbs all the oil, add a little more, so the mixture fries and browns rather than toasts and burns.) Stir in the chile, tomato and garlic and cook several minutes, until the mixture is homogeneous. Season carefully with salt (jerky can vary widely in its saltiness).

3. *The burritos.* When the *machaca* mixture is ready, make the burritos by rolling ¼ cup of filling into each hot flour tortilla. Place them on a warm platter and serve at once.

Fresh poblano chiles

TRADITIONAL VARIATIONS

Burritos with a Variety of Fillings: The *machaca* can be replaced with 2 to 2½ cups of practically any taco filling (pages 124–138), or with a combination of *Frijoles Refritos* (page 269) and a melting cheese like mild cheddar (rolled, covered with foil and baked until the cheese begins to melt).

Chivichangas: In Sonora and vicinity, they make long, thin, crisp-fried burritos—cousins to our large, egg roll–shaped *chimichangas.* Cut four 10-inch, store-bought flour tortillas in half. Divide 3 cups Northern-Style Shredded Beef (page 131) among the halves, roll up tightly and secure with toothpicks. Fry in ⅜ inch hot oil until crisp. Drain, and serve on a bed of sliced lettuce. Strew with chopped tomato and dollop with mayonnaise or my simple avocado mayonnaise: blend 1 avocado, ½ cup mayonnaise, 1 teaspoon fresh lemon juice, a little chopped onion, 4 sprigs fresh coriander (*cilantro*) and salt to taste.

Kitchen Spanish

While burritos are common throughout Northern Mexico, they are called simply *tacos de harina* (literally "wheat tacos") as you approach the east coast, and *burritas* in most Northern-style restaurants outside the North.

TURNOVERS

Quesadillas y Empanadas

Whatever they call them—*quesadillas, empanadas, molotes, tlacoyos,* even *enchiladas* in the confusing jargon of San Luis Potosí—they're deliciously stuffed pockets of Mexican flavor, bearers of well-spiced vegetables, meats and cheese, transporters of chile-spiked hot sauce or smooth guacamole. On the streets or in the markets, they're made for the midmorning *almuerzos* or late-evening *cenas* of folks on their way to or from. In the restaurants, they turn into nice *entremeses* ("appetizers") to have before the more serious eating starts. In my home, I make them with all their regional casings—from corn *masa* to flour-tortilla dough—and I fry or griddle-bake them to offer with drinks, to set in a basket on the table as an informal appetizer or to feature at a light lunch or supper. Following are the recipes for many of the well-known regional varieties.

Keys to Frying Perfect *Masa* Creations

Getting the Oil Temperature Right: As with all frying, work with a heavy pan and a thermometer. Keep the oil at 375°; cool oil means greasy food.

Judging Doneness: Anything made from *masa harina* darkens more quickly than that made from fresh *masa;* so fried *masa harina* creations must be well browned for them to be done. Any *masa* creations will turn out greasy if not fried long enough.

DEEP-FRIED *MASA* TURNOVERS WITH CHEESE

Quesadillas Fritas

The *quesadilla:* crisp-fried so the crunchy exterior gives way to soft, corny *masa* and melted or spicy insides. They're one of Central Mexico's favorite and most common edibles, made everywhere from the capital's finest restaurants to the makeshift snack parlors. Some of the best ones, I think, come from the snack market in Coyoacán, a wealthy sector of Mexico City, where the turnovers are stuffed with everything from tripe to

COOK'S NOTES

Techniques

Frying Quesadillas: These may be shallow-fried in ½ inch vegetable oil over medium-high heat; though, as the filling heats, steam can break through the uncooked top. To avoid greasy fried pies, flip them every ½ minute, cooking both sides evenly. For more notes, see page 78.

the musty, gray-black corn mushrooms (*huitlacoche*) and back home to the simple *queso* ("cheese") that gives the *quesadilla* its name.

Though powdered *masa harina* is not my favorite, it works well here. For an easy special supper, serve *quesadillas* with *Tlalpeño* Soup (page 97); and you always need a little Guacamole with *Tomatillos* (page 46), Red-Chile Sauce (page 37), or Fresh Green *Tomatillo* Sauce (page 36) to daub on them.

YIELD: 12 medium turnovers, serving 4 as a light meal, 6 as a hearty appetizer

For the dough:
1 **pound fresh** *masa*
    OR 1¾ **cups** *masa harina* **mixed with 1 cup plus 2 tablespoons hot tap water**
2 **tablespoons lard or vegetable shortening**
¼ **cup flour** (⅓ **cup if using** *masa harina*)
A **generous** ½ **teaspoon salt**
1 **scant teaspoon baking powder**

For the filling:
10 **ounces (about 2½ cups) grated melting cheese (page 328) like Monterey Jack or a mild cheddar, plus 12 leaves** *epazote* **(optional)**
    OR 10 **ounces (about 2½ cups) crumbled Mexican** *queso fresco* **(page 327) or other fresh cheese like farmer's cheese, plus 12 leaves** *epazote* **(optional)**
    OR **about** 1½ **cups (1 recipe) of any** *quesadilla* **filling (pages 145–149)**

For frying:
Vegetable oil to a depth of 1 inch

1. *The dough.* If you are using *masa harina*, mix it with the hot water, cover and let stand 20 to 30 minutes. Mix the fresh or reconstituted *masa* with the lard or shortening, flour, salt and baking powder. If necessary, correct the consistency of the dough, as described in detail on page 74. Divide into 12 balls and cover with plastic wrap.

2. *Forming the quesadillas.* Divide the filling into 12 portions; if you are using cheese, press each portion into a flat oval about 2 x 2½ inches. Using a tortilla press, flatten a ball of the dough between sheets of plastic to make a medium-large (5-

Timing and Advance Preparation
It takes about 45 minutes to prepare the cheese-filled turnovers; allow 30 minutes longer to reconstitute *masa harina*. If the filling is a *dry* one, the turnovers can be formed a day ahead, coverd and refrigerated. Fry the *quesadillas* when you're ready to eat them; if held too long in a warm oven they become tough.

TRADITIONAL VARIATIONS
Griddle-Baked Quesadillas: Prepare the dough as directed in Step 1, using **fresh** *masa* and omitting the flour and baking powder. Heat a griddle (or heavy skillet) over medium. Press out a tortilla using a tortilla press, then unmold it (see page 74 for details) and lay it on the griddle. When it loosens itself (about 30 seconds), spoon 2 tablespoons of the filling on one side, then fold the uncovered side over and seal around the filling by pressing the edges together. When browned underneath (about 2 minutes), flip and bake 2 or 3 minutes longer, until the folded edge feels firm and dry. Serve immediately.

Easy Griddle-Baked Cheese Quesadillas: These are popular through much of Mexico, especially the North (where they're often made with flour tortillas). Frequently, fried onions, roasted peppers, shredded beef or chicken, slivered ham, even slivers of steak or flaked fish will go in with the cheese. Heat a griddle over medium and lightly oil it. Lay on several already-baked tortillas (store-bought or homemade) and spread ⅓ cup (about 1½ ounces) grated melting cheese over each one;

inch), thickish tortilla (further details on the process are on page 75). Remove the top piece of plastic. Lay one portion of filling across half the uncovered tortilla, leaving a ½-inch border around the edge; if the filling is cheese, top with a leaf of the optional *epazote*. Slip a hand under the plastic beneath the uncovered side of the tortilla, then carefully fold the tortilla over the filling. Press the edges together to seal.

Next, peel the plastic off the top of the turnover, then flip the turnover onto one hand, uncovered-side down, and peel the plastic off the bottom. Lay on a tray covered with plastic wrap. Continue making the remaining *masa* balls into turnovers and lay each one several inches from the next to ensure easy retrieval. Cover with plastic.

3. *Frying*. Heat the oil to 375°, then fry the turnovers 2 or 3 at a time, until browned, about 2 minutes per side. Drain on paper towels and keep warm in a low oven until all are ready. Serve right away.

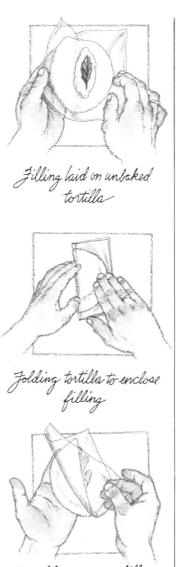

Filling laid on unbaked tortilla

Folding tortilla to enclose filling

Unmolding quesadilla from plastic

top with any of the above-mentioned additions. When the cheese begins to melt, fold the tortillas in half, then griddle-bake until crispy, flipping occasionally.

Regional Explorations
Though most common in Central Mexico, these little turnovers can appear just about anywhere in the country, with whatever fillings the cooks know will please their customers, and with names like *quesadilla*, *empanada* (Southern and Yucatecan Mexico) and *molote* (Puebla and Veracruz).

TURNOVER FILLINGS

Rellenos para Quesadillas

The following fillings come primarily from Central Mexico: Pueblan vendors fill their small, fried turnovers with concoctions heavy in strips of green chile, while their large griddle-baked turnovers get my favorite Shredded Pork *Tinga* (page 248). Near Cuernavaca, the cooks fry *quesadillas* filled with shredded chicken, minced pork or beef *picadillo* (page 132), and black corn mushrooms (*huitlacoche*), as well as the deliciously pungent brains with *epazote,* and the mushrooms with green chile outlined below. In Toluca, large *quesadillas* show up with a filling of squash blossoms; the recipe follows, should you be lucky enough to lay your hands on some of the delicate flowers. And on the coasts, crab, shrimp and poached fish find their way into turnovers. Though I haven't seen them used in Mexico, Northern-Style Shredded Beef (page 131) and Potatoes with *Chorizo* (page 134) are good turnover fillings, too.

POTATOES AND GREEN CHILES

Papas con Rajas

YIELD: about 1½ cups

- 2 small (about 6 ounces total) boiling potatoes like the red-skinned ones, halved
- 1½ tablespoons lard or vegetable oil
- ½ small onion, thinly sliced
- 3 medium, fresh *chiles poblanos,* roasted and peeled (page 337)
- Salt, about ½ teaspoon
- ¾ cup (about 3 ounces) crumbled Mexican *queso fresco* (page 327) or other fresh cheese like mild domestic goat or farmer's cheese

1. *The potatoes.* Simmer the potatoes in salted water to cover until tender, about 15 minutes. Drain, cool under running water, peel and cut into ¼-inch dice.

2. *Frying the mixture.* Heat the lard or oil in a heavy medium-size skillet over medium. Add the onion and potato, and fry, stirring regularly to ensure that nothing sticks to the pan, until the mixture is nicely browned, 10 to 15 minutes.

While the potatoes are browning, seed the chiles and slice them into ⅛-inch strips. Stir them into the potato mixture, season with salt, remove from the fire and stir in the cheese. Scrape into a small dish and cool before using.

COOK'S NOTES

Ingredients
Chiles Poblanos: If these are unavailable, replace them with 4 long green chiles (roasted and peeled) or 4 or 5 of the hotter *chiles jalapeños* (roasted, seeded and deveined).

Timing and Advance Preparation
This filling can be finished in about ½ hour; it keeps well for several days, covered and refrigerated.

TRADITIONAL VARIATIONS
Fresh Cheese with Green Chiles: Mix the sliced chiles with 8 ounces (2 cups) crumbled Mexican *queso fresco* (page 327) or other fresh cheese like mild domestic goat or farmer's cheese and (optionally) 8 leaves *epazote* (chopped).
Scrambled Eggs and Green Chiles: Fry ¼ cup chopped onion in 1 tablespoon lard or vegetable oil until soft, then stir in the sliced chiles and increase the temperature to medium-high. Add 4 eggs (lightly beaten) and scramble until firm; season with salt. Cool before using.

BRAINS WITH PUNGENT MEXICAN SEASONINGS

Sesos con Epazote

YIELD: about 1½ cups

12 to 14 ounces (1 pair beef or 1½ pairs veal) brains

½ large lime, juiced

Fresh hot green chiles to taste (roughly 2 *chiles serranos* or 1 *chile jalapeño*), stemmed, seeded and finely minced

1 large sprig *epazote*, leaves removed and minced (1 generous tablespoon)
OR 6 sprigs fresh coriander (*cilantro*), stemmed and finely chopped

¼ medium onion, finely chopped

Salt, about ¼ teaspoon

1. *The brains.* Soak the brains in cold water for 30 minutes. Drain and peel off the thin outer membrane. Soak in salted water for an hour more and drain again. Place the brains in a medium-size saucepan with enough salted water to cover; add the lime juice. Bring *barely* to a simmer, then cook over medium to medium-low heat for 20 to 25 minutes, until the brains are firm and white when cut into. Cool for ½ hour in their liquid, if there's time. Drain, dry with paper towels and trim off any extraneous tissue.

2. *Finishing the mixture.* In a mixing bowl, coarsely mash the brains. Stir in the chile, *epazote* (or coriander), onion and salt to taste. Cool thoroughly before using.

Epazote

COOK'S NOTES

Techniques
Soaking, Trimming and Poaching the Brains: Soaking brains rids them of excess blood—which can give them an off flavor and color. You may peel off the thin outer layer after the initial soaking or after you poach them (when the brains are more manageable, but the membrane comes off in frustratingly small patches). When poaching, it is important to keep the water at a gentle simmer so the brains don't break apart.

Timing and Advance Preparation
Start the filling at least 3 hours ahead; active involvement is only about ½ hour. Brains should be served the same day they're cooked.

CONTEMPORARY IDEAS

Golden-Fried Brains: Cut the poached, dried brains into ¼-inch cubes and fry in vegetable oil in a large skillet over medium heat until golden. Mix in the remaining ingredients and cool.

STEWED SQUASH BLOSSOMS

Flores de Calabaza Guisadas

YIELD: about 1½ cups

20 good-size, fresh squash blossoms
½ medium onion, diced
Fresh hot green chiles to taste (roughly 2 *chiles serranos* or 1 *chile jalapeño*) stemmed, seeded and finely minced
1 tablespoon lard or vegetable oil
1 medium-large tomato, roasted or boiled (page 352), cored, peeled and chopped
    OR ⅔ 15-ounce can tomatoes, drained and chopped
Several *epazote* leaves, chopped
    OR a small handful fresh coriander (*cilantro*) or parsley, chopped
Salt, about ½ teaspoon
2 tablespoons crumbled Mexican *queso fresco* (page 327) or other fresh cheese like feta or farmer's cheese

1. *The squash blossoms.* Clean the squash blossoms by removing the stamens from inside the flowers and trimming off tough-looking bases (the calyxes). Rinse them well and cut them crosswise into ½-inch sections.

2. *The filling.* In a medium-size skillet set over medium heat, fry the onion and chile in lard or vegetable oil for about 5 minutes, until tender. Add the tomato, along with the sliced flowers and *epazote*. Cover and let the mixture steam over medium-low heat until the flowers are tender, about 8 minutes. Uncover, season with salt and sprinkle with cheese. Scoop into a small dish to cool before using.

Squash blossoms (flores de calabaza)

COOK'S NOTES

Ingredients
Squash Blossoms: See page 351 for the notes on locating, storing and preparing squash blossoms.

Timing and Advance Preparation
Allow about ½ hour to prepare the filling. It can be made 1 day ahead; cover and refrigerate.

STEWED MUSHROOMS WITH ONIONS AND GARLIC

Hongos Guisados

YIELD: about 1½ cups

12 ounces fresh mushrooms, washed and chopped
    into ½-inch pieces
½ medium onion, diced
Fresh hot green chiles to taste (roughly 2 *chiles
    serranos* or 1 *chile jalapeño*), stemmed, seeded
    and finely minced
⅔ cup any poultry broth or water
½ small lime, juiced
1 tablespoon lard, bacon drippings or fat ren-
    dered from *chorizo*
1 ripe, large tomato, roasted or boiled (page 353),
    cored, peeled and roughly chopped
    OR ¾ 15-ounce can tomatoes, drained and
    roughly chopped
2 cloves garlic, peeled and roughly chopped
1½ tablespoons chopped *epazote* (optional)
Salt, about ½ teaspoon (depending on the salti-
    ness of the broth)

1. *Cooking the mushrooms.* Place the mushrooms, onion, chile, broth or water, lime juice and lard or other fat in a medium-size saucepan. Bring to a boil over medium-high heat, cover and cook 3 minutes. Uncover and cook until all the liquid has evaporated and the mushrooms begin to fry in the fat.

2. *Finishing the mixture.* While the mushrooms are cooking, puree the tomato with the garlic in a blender or food processor. When the mushrooms begin to fry, add the tomato mixture and optional *epazote,* and cook about 5 minutes, until the liquid has reduced and the mixture is thick. Season with salt and cool before using.

CRISPY WHEAT-FLOUR TURNOVERS WITH WELL-SEASONED MEAT

Empanadas de Picadillo

COOK'S NOTES

Techniques
Preparing the Dough: The technique notes on page 74 will be helpful.

Timing and Advance Preparation
With the filling on hand, the *empanadas* can be ready to fry in 1 hour, half of which is for the unattended "relaxation" of the dough. If the filling isn't juicy, the *empanadas* can be formed 1 day ahead, covered and refrigerated. Fry them just before serving.

TRADITIONAL VARIATIONS
Empanadas with Local Flavors: Practically all Mexican communities make *empanadas* and fill them with what they have or can afford: 3 cups shredded meat or chicken, Northern-Style Shredded Beef (page 131), lightly cooked vegetables, Roasted Pepper *Rajas* (page 278) and melting cheese (page 328) like Monterey Jack or mild cheddar—the possibilities are inexhaustible.

Through the North, where flour tortillas are a part of the everyday routine, cooks in restaurants and snack shops make turnovers from the wheat-flour dough, folding them over a savory meat filling studded with nuts and olives, then slipping them into the hot oil to fry golden and crispy. After I learned to make them in the northeast, I had hoped to see them more frequently than I did in my journey westward across the northern land. They do, however, show up frequently on my table, served as a light meal with *Salsa Picante* (page 40), guacamole (pages 44 or 46) and a salad or soup like the *Sopa Xóchitl* (page 98). On occasion, I'll make half-size turnovers to pass around as an appetizer or to take on a picnic.

YIELD: twelve 6-inch turnovers, serving 4 as a light main course, 6 as a hearty appetizer

For the dough:
> ¾ pound (about 2¾ cups) all-purpose flour, plus a little extra for rolling the dough
> 3 tablespoons lard or vegetable shortening OR 4 tablespoons unsalted butter
> ¾ teaspoon salt
> About ¾ cup very warm tap water

For filling and frying:
> 1 recipe (about 3 generous cups) Minced-Pork *Picadillo* or Northern-Style *Picadillo* (page 132), *cooled to room temperature*
> Oil for deep frying, to a depth of 1 inch

1. *The dough.* As described in the recipe for flour tortillas on page 77, measure the flour into a bowl, then thoroughly work in the fat. Dissolve the salt in the hot water, then work it into the flour mixture, making a medium-stiff dough. Knead several minutes until smooth.

2. *Resting.* Divide the dough into 12 portions, roll each into a ball, set on a plate, cover with plastic wrap and let rest at least 30 minutes (to make the dough easier to roll).

3. *Forming the empanadas.* On a lightly floured surface, roll out a portion of dough into a 7-inch-diameter circle (details of the process are in Step 3 on page 77). Very lightly brush the perimeter with water, then scoop about ¼ cup of filling onto one side. Fold the uncovered side over the filling, expelling as much air as possible, then press the two edges firmly together. Lay the *empanada* on a baking sheet; continue forming turnovers with the remaining balls of dough. Firmly seal the *empanadas* by pressing the two edges together with the tines of a fork or by making the rope edge described below.

4. *The optional decorative rope edge.* Hold an *empanada* in one hand; with the thumb and first finger of the other hand, pinch out a ½-inch section of the dough on the nearest end, flattening it so that it extends out ¼ inch beyond the rest of the edge. With your thumb, curl over the top half of the pinched-out section of dough (it should look like a wave breaking), then gently press it down to secure it. Now, pinch out the next ½-inch section of dough, curl the top side over, and press it down. Continue until you reach the other end. Fold the last pinched-out section back on itself, finishing the seal. Complete the rope edge on the remaining *empanadas* and return them to the baking sheet.

Pinching out empanada edge

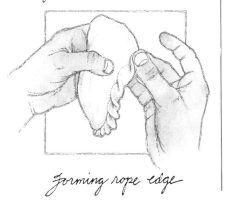

Forming rope edge

CONTEMPORARY IDEAS

Lamb Empanadas with Fresh Coriander: Mix 3 cups shredded lamb (from cubed lamb simmered until tender or from leftover roast) with ½ small onion (finely chopped), 2 tablespoons toasted, ground *guajillo* or New Mexico chile, 3 tablespoons chopped fresh coriander (*cilantro*) and salt to taste. Form the *empanadas* as directed, using the lamb filling; fry and serve with saucy Guacamole with *Tomatillos* (page 46).

Mexican Explorations

Uniformed children home from school, women with fully packed *bolsas,* businessmen and workmen—nearly every member of the Mexican constituency files into the fragrant, glassed-in, self-service bakeries, picks up a tray and a pair of tongs and chooses a mound from the dozens of simple sweet breads, cookies, plain pastries, warm crusty *bolillos* and turnovers in several flavors: apple, pineapple, sweet potato or pumpkin. On Fridays and all through Lent, many of the bakers fill them with tuna before they go into the oven.

5. *Frying the empanadas.* About 15 minutes before serving, heat the oil to 375°. Fry the *empanadas* 2 or 3 at a time, until deep golden, 2 to 3 minutes per side. Drain on paper towels and keep warm in a low oven until all are fried. Serve at once.

Picadillo-stuffed empanadas

ENCHILADAS AND THEIR RELATIVES

Enchiladas y Sus Parientes

Many workers migrated from their West-Central homeland to Los Angeles and to Chicago, where I live, carrying with them a feel for enchiladas of chile-dipped tortillas—quick-fried so the sauce penetrates and adheres, then topped with a little fried potatoes and carrots and sprinkled with cheese. They're light fare, to be eaten gingerly with fingertips; and they're the only enchiladas that show up on the streets.

In Mexico, you'll find enchiladas mostly in coffee shops, though, since many varieties have substantial fillings and are more involved than much of the street food. Still, they've never graduated to a spot in the afternoon *comida:* It seems any dish that involves tortillas or the like will always carry the stigma of inconsequentiality, of being an *antojito*. And that's too bad, since enchiladas make beautiful main courses, featuring a wide variety of traditional fillings and sauces.

This is a collection of four distinctive regional recipes, which I've taken the liberty to group together because all involve dipping tortillas in sauce (though the sauce may not contain much chile or the final dish be called an enchilada). There are the legitimate enchiladas like those in *tomatillo*-chile sauce, *mole* or the West-Central or Northern red-chile sauces; but the same idea is used for

Oaxacan *enfrijoladas* dipped in a savory bean sauce, the tomato-sauced *entomatadas,* the stack of tortillas, black beans and fish they call *pan de cazón,* or even the Yucatecan *papadzules* with their egg stuffing and *pepita* sauce. Many areas have variations on this traditional theme.

There are three approaches to making enchiladas, and I've included a recipe using each one. When the sauce is an uncooked puree of soaked red chiles, the tortillas are dipped before they're fried. For a fully cooked sauce of *tomatillos,* tomatoes or *mole,* the tortillas are quick-fried before dipping (to make them more pliable as well as resistant to quick softening in the sauce). And some cooks with really fresh tortillas and a fully cooked sauce will omit the tortilla frying altogether, simply saucing the fresh tortillas and serving them quickly (before they soften too much). The flavor and texture changes with each approach, so make them all, then begin to work out your own variations on your favorites.

Keys to Perfect Enchiladas

Quick-Frying Tortillas for Enchiladas of the Fried-Then-Sauced Category: The tortillas should be dried until they feel somewhat leathery or they will absorb a lot of oil. Fry them quickly and drain them well: The goal is to "soften" the tortillas, making them pliable enough to roll without cracking; they should not crisp in the least.

Baking Enchiladas: Except for the newly popular *enchiladas suizas,* enchiladas in Mexico are not generally baked: They are put together with warm ingredients just before serving, though they never arrive at the table as piping hot as most North Americans would like. So I recommend baking the enchiladas for a few minutes after they're sauced. But don't leave them too long in the oven or they'll come out mushy, and keep the sauce on the thin side, since it will thicken a little during baking.

Kitchen Spanish

In Spanish, to *enchilar* something is, in some way or another, to get chile all over it; a *tortilla enchilada* (or just plain *enchilada* for short) is one of the common corn cakes that is dipped in a chile-spiked sauce, rolled or folded, filled or not; and it can have as many possible flavors as there are Mexican sauces.

For the purpose of this book, I have developed my own functional definition, though: Any of the sauced tortilla dishes get lumped together under the heading *enchilada.* It is my valiant attempt to bring order to linguistic chaos. Where shape is definitive in Mexico, anything *rolled* in a tortilla is a *taco,* sauced or not; a simple tortilla dipped in sauce might be called an enchilada in those places—but it would only be folded or quartered, not rolled or stuffed. Some places they differentiate the dipping sauce in the name: *enfrijolada* for a sauce of *frijoles* ("beans"), *enmoladas* for a sauce made of *mole,* and so on. And to complicate things further, sometimes you'll run into the sauced tortilla *folded* over a filling and called an *envuelto.* Most cookbooks from Mexico seem to welcome all this complication and contradiction and will list virtually the same recipe various times under the different regional names, often with only the shape modified.

CHICKEN-FILLED ENCHILADAS WITH TANGY *TOMATILLO* SAUCE

Enchiladas Verdes

Here is a recipe for the classic Mexican enchiladas, the ones that combine a flavor that is traditionally tart and piquant with the mealy meatiness of corn tortillas, the tenderness of chicken and a sharp, salty adornment of aged Mexican cheese. They're rolled up and sauced in *cafeterías* (especially the new, bright chain restaurants) everywhere—and with above-average fervor in the heartland sections of Central and West-Central Mexico. They're simple to make, easy to enjoy and attractively filling. Make a traditional supper of them by adding some *Frijoles Refritos* (page 269), a plate of crunchy *jícama* with lime, and beer or iced tea.

YIELD: 4 to 6 servings

About 2¾ cups (1 recipe) Quick-Cooked *Tomatillo* Sauce (page 42)
1 large (1¼-pound), whole chicken breast, cooked, skinned, boned and shredded (page 60)
¼ cup Thick Cream (page 51) or commercial sour cream
1 tablespoon finely chopped onion
Salt, about ¼ teaspoon
12 corn tortillas, preferably store-bought
¼ cup vegetable oil, plus a little more if needed
⅓ cup (about 1½ ounces) Mexican *queso añejo* (page 327) or other cheese like feta or mild Parmesan
2 slices onion, broken into rings, for garnish
Several radish slices or roses, for garnish

   1. *The sauce and the filling.* Heat the *tomatillo* sauce in a small, covered pan over low. Warm up the chicken in a separate pan over low heat (sprinkled with a little water so it won't dry out), then stir in the cream or sour cream, onion and salt; set aside off the fire, covered.
   2. *The tortillas.* If the tortillas are moist, let them dry out for a few minutes in a single layer. Heat the oil in a small skillet

COOK'S NOTES

Techniques
Enchilada Making: See page 153.

Ingredients
Corn Tortillas: See page 353.

Timing and Advance Preparation
With the *tomatillo* sauce and chicken on hand, the enchiladas can be ready in about ½ hour. Though not really sanctioned, these enchiladas can be partially made ahead: Quick-fry the tortillas, but *don't dip them in the sauce;* fill and roll them, then cover and refrigerate; bring to room temperature, cover with foil and bake 10 minutes at 350°; cover with hot sauce and bake 5 minutes longer, then garnish and serve.

TRADITIONAL VARIATIONS
Enchiladas Suizas: Prepare the recipe as directed, adding 1 cup Thick Cream (page 51) or whipping cream to the *tomatillo* sauce. Top the enchiladas with 6 ounces (1½ cups) grated melting cheese (page 328) like mild cheddar or Monterey Jack and bake 10 minutes uncovered at 400°. Omit the other garnishes.
Entomatadas: Prepare a *smooth* Quick-Cooked Tomato-Chile Sauce (page 41), add ¾ cup poultry broth and simmer until it is a medium consistency. Make the enchiladas as directed, substituting the tomato-chile sauce for the *tomatillo* one. Versions of these are popular in Oaxaca and across the North.

over medium-high. When sizzlingly hot, quick-fry the tortillas to soften them, one at a time, for 2 to 3 seconds on each side. Drain on paper towels.

3. *Assembling the enchiladas.* About 20 minutes before serving, preheat the oven to 350°. Pour a cup of the warm sauce into a plate. Lay a tortilla in the sauce, flip it over, lay a scant 2 tablespoons of the filling across the center and roll it up (fingertips are most efficient here). Transfer to a baking dish, then continue filling and rolling the rest of the tortillas. Pour the remaining sauce over the enchiladas, being careful to cover the ends.

4. *Baking.* Immediately cover the dish with foil and bake just long enough to heat through, about 10 minutes. Sprinkle the enchiladas with the crumbled cheese, decorate with onion rings and radishes, and serve right away.

Chicken enchiladas

RED-CHILE ENCHILADAS WITH CHEESE AND VEGETABLES

Enchiladas a la Plaza

For the most part, the hands of West-Central and Northern cooks move toward the dried chile pods whenever enchiladas are requested. They transform the chiles into a muscular, uncooked sauce, dip in the tortillas, then quick-fry them in hot oil, searing the flavors into the thin corn cakes. The star here is the chile-flavored tortilla and not so much what fills it. A little cheese or thick cream might go in or on (as described in the simple variation that accompanies this more involved recipe); perhaps a fried egg might go over the top (*enchiladas montadas*) or even a spatulaful of richly seasoned vegetables.

Seafood Enchiladas: In the northwest, they frequently replace the chicken with 1¼ cups flaked, poached, boneless fish (like sea bass, halibut, cod—even chopped shrimp or shredded crab). Complete the recipe as directed.

TRADITIONAL NORTH AMERICAN VARIATIONS

Cheese Enchiladas: Use 1 pound grated mild cheddar or Monterey Jack in place of the chicken filling (grated onion may be added, but no cream). Complete the recipe as directed, baking the enchiladas until the cheese melts. The *tomatillo* sauce may be replaced with 2½ cups of Northern-Style Red-Chile Sauce (page 250). A little cheese may be sprinkled on the enchiladas before baking.

COOK'S NOTES

Techniques
Frying Chile-Dipped Tortillas: First, use a well-seasoned pan; second, keep the heat no higher than medium; and third, use a sauce no thicker than *light* canned tomato sauce. If any bits of stray sauce begin to burn, clean your pan and heat a little more oil before continuing.

The latter variation (from the state of Michoacán) is the dressiest and most famous of the lot. Though this very good recipe comes from a restaurant waitress in Morelia, I'd never pass up the chance to have this dish at the nighttime prepared-foods plaza that is its namesake.

For a meatless meal, serve the enchiladas with *Frijoles Refritos* (page 269) and a malty, half-dark Dos Equis beer.

YIELD: 4 to 6 servings

For the enchiladas:
>   12 corn tortillas, preferably store-bought

For the sauce:
>   4 large cloves of garlic, unpeeled
>   4 medium (about 1 ounce total) dried *chiles guajillos,* stemmed, seeded and deveined
>   6 medium (about 3 ounces total) dried *chiles anchos,* stemmed, seeded and deveined
>   ¼ teaspoon black peppercorns (or a generous ⅓ teaspoon ground)
>   ¼ teaspoon cumin seeds (or a scant ⅓ teaspoon ground)
>   2 cups any poultry broth, plus a little more if needed
>   Salt, about 1 teaspoon
>   Sugar, a big pinch, if necessary

For the vegetables:
>   2 medium-small (about 8 ounces total) boiling potatoes like the red-skinned ones, peeled and diced into ½-inch pieces
>   2 medium-large (about 8 ounces total) carrots, peeled and diced into ½-inch pieces
>   3 tablespoons cider vinegar
>   1 teaspoon salt

For the condiments:
>   ½ small head (about 10 ounces) cabbage
>   3 tablespoons cider vinegar
>   2 tablespoons vegetable oil
>   ½ teaspoon salt
>   2 thin slices onion, broken into rings
>   ½ cup (about 2 ounces) crumbled Mexican *queso fresco* (page 327) or other fresh cheese like feta or farmer's cheese

Soaking the Chiles: Because there is little in this sauce to balance the astringency of the chiles, the pods are soaked longer (to remove excess harshness).

Ingredients
Corn Tortillas: See page 353.
Dried Chiles: This sauce is frequently made with all *anchos* or all *guajillos.* The latter is similar to a sauce made of 12 large New Mexico or California chiles.

Equipment
Enchilada-Frying Pan: These enchiladas are commonly prepared in what I call a frying table: a large metal rectangle with a shallow well in the center. The heat is under the well, where the frying is done; the flat sides keep food warm (and catch spatters). A wok is similar (though deeper and lacking the flat sides); if the wok is well-seasoned, the chile sauce doesn't stick, and if large, the enchilada frying goes quickly.

Timing and Advance Preparation
Start 2 hours before serving, though you won't be actively involved all that time. The sauce may be prepared several days ahead, covered and refrigerated. The vegetables and garnishes may be prepared early in the day you're serving; cover and refrigerate. Complete the final two steps just before serving.

For finishing the dish:
   4 to 5 tablespoons vegetable oil, plus a little more
      if needed

1. *Preliminaries.* If the tortillas are moist, lay them out to
dry a little, then wrap in plastic.

2. *The sauce.* Heat a heavy skillet or griddle over medium,
then lay the garlic on one side to roast. Tear the chiles into flat
pieces and, a few at a time, press them against the hot surface
with a metal spatula, flip them over and press again; you'll hear
them crackle and see them blister and change color. Remove to
a bowl, cover with boiling water, weight down with a plate to
keep them submerged, and soak for at least 1 hour, preferably
2 or 3.

Turn the garlic frequently for 15 minutes or so, until blackened a little and soft within. Remove, cool, peel and place in a
blender jar. Grind the peppercorns and cumin seeds in a mortar
or spice grinder and add to the garlic.

Drain the chiles, squeezing gently. Add to the blender jar
and measure in 1½ cups of the poultry broth. Blend until
smooth, then strain into a large bowl through a medium-mesh
sieve. Season with salt and with sugar (if the sauce is bitter or
sharp). Add additional broth to thin to the consistency of a
light tomato sauce.

3. *The vegetables.* Place the potatoes and carrots in a medium-size saucepan, cover with water and add the vinegar and
salt. Simmer over medium until tender, about 15 minutes, then
drain thoroughly and set aside.

4. *The garnishes.* Core the cabbage, slice it very thinly and
place in a bowl. Mix the vinegar, oil and salt, then toss with
the cabbage. Set aside, together with the onion rings and
crumbled cheese.

5. *Frying the enchiladas.* About 15 minutes before serving,
divide the cabbage mixture among 4 dinner plates, spreading it
into a bed in the center. Heat 3 tablespoons of the vegetable
oil in a large skillet or wok (see Equipment in **Cook's Notes**)
over medium. When hot, dip both sides of a tortilla into the
sauce, then lay it in the oil; do the same with 1 or 2 more, if
they will fit into your pan. After about 20 seconds, flip the
tortillas over, fry another 20 seconds, fold them in half, then
in half again lengthwise. Lift them out, draining as much of
the oil back into the pan as possible, lay on a baking sheet and
keep warm in a low oven. Fry the remaining tortillas in the
same manner, adding more oil as necessary.

6. *Finishing the dish.* Add a little more oil to the skillet or
wok, then scoop in the potatoes and carrots along with 2 or 3

**TRADITIONAL
VARIATIONS**
*Chicken Enchiladas a la
Plaza:* Add 1 cup shredded
cooked chicken to the vegetables in Step 6.
Enchiladas con Crema: Prepare the enchiladas without the
vegetables, dressing or cabbage. Top with ¾ cup Thick
Cream (page 51), 1 cup crumbled Mexican *queso fresco* (page
327) or other fresh cheese like
feta or farmer's cheese, some
chopped onion and fresh coriander (*cilantro*).

tablespoons of leftover sauce. Stir frequently until the vegetables are warm, 3 or 4 minutes.

Place 3 enchiladas over the cabbage on each plate. Divide the fried vegetables over the enchiladas, then strew with the onion and cheese and serve.

PORK-FILLED ENCHILADAS WITH ORANGE-RED *MOLE*

Enchiladas de Coloradito

When I want to introduce friends to the authentically Mexican world of rich red-chile sauces, I don't head straight for the elaborate *mole poblano;* instead, I make this smooth and mild Oaxacan *mole coloradito.* The recipe comes from a particularly good Oaxacan cook, a Zapotec Indian woman, whose savory pork filling and no-fry method of enchilada preparation make the dish all the more attractive.

For an informal meal, serve these *enchiladas de coloradito* with a big salad and a dessert of fresh fruit with Thick Cream (page 51).

YIELD: 4 to 6 servings, with 2½ to 3 cups of sauce

For the meat:
- 12 ounces lean, boneless pork shoulder, cut into 1-inch cubes
- 1 teaspoon salt
- ½ teaspoon mixed dried herbs (such as marjoram and thyme)
- 1 thick slice onion, roughly chopped

For the coloradito *sauce:*
- 7 medium (about 3½ ounces total) dried *chiles anchos,* stemmed, seeded and deveined
- 5 cloves garlic, unpeeled
- 2 slices firm white bread
- 1 ripe, large tomato, roasted or boiled (page 352), peeled and cored
  OR ¾ 15-ounce can tomatoes, drained

COOK'S NOTES

Techniques
Enchilada Making: See page 153.

Ingredients
Chiles Anchos: There is no substitute for their sweetness in this sauce.
Plantain: To ensure that your plantain is very ripe, buy it a week or so before you need it. If *ripe* plantain is unavailable, substitute a very green banana. Don't fry it; just add it with the tomato-chile mixture.
Corn Tortillas: See page 353.

Timing and Advance Preparation
Preparing the filling, sauce and enchiladas requires 1½ to 2 hours. Filling and sauce may be made several days in advance, covered and refrigerated. Complete Step 4 in the ½ hour before serving.

1 small onion, roughly chopped
1 generous teaspoon dried oregano
3 cloves (or a big pinch ground)
3 black peppercorns (or a big pinch ground)
½ inch cinnamon stick (or a scant ½ teaspoon ground)
1½ tablespoons lard or vegetable oil
Salt, about ½ teaspoon
Sugar, about 1 tablespoon

For finishing the filling:
1 small (about 3 ounces) boiling potato like a red-skinned one, peeled and cut into ¼-inch dice
3 tablespoons lard or vegetable oil
1 medium onion, diced
½ ripe plantain, peeled and cut into ¼-inch dice (see Ingredients in Cook's Notes)
1 ripe, medium-large tomato, roasted or boiled (page 352), peeled and cored
OR ⅔ 15-ounce can tomatoes, drained
Salt, about ½ teaspoon
Freshly ground black pepper, about ¼ teaspoon

For finishing the enchiladas:
12 corn tortillas, preferably store-bought
1 cup (about 4 ounces) crumbled Mexican *queso fresco* or *queso añejo* (page 327), or cheese like feta, farmer's or a mild Parmesan
About ¼ cup diced onion

1. *The meat.* Bring 4 cups of water to a boil in a large saucepan, add the pork, then skim off the foam that rises during the first few minutes of simmering. Add the salt, herbs and onion. Partially cover and simmer over medium heat until the meat is tender, about 45 minutes. When the meat is done, remove it, then strain the broth and skim off all the fat that rises to the top.

2. *The coloradito sauce.* Cover the seeded *chiles anchos* with boiling water, weight with a plate to keep them submerged and let reconstitute for 30 minutes. Place the unpeeled garlic cloves on a griddle or small skillet set over medium heat and roast for about 15 minutes, turning frequently, until blackened in spots and soft to the touch. Cool, then slip off the papery skins and place in a blender jar. Darkly toast the bread and tear into small pieces. Add to the blender along with the tomato, onion and

TRADITIONAL VARIATIONS

Enchiladas de Mole: Much less time-consuming but still delicious, replace the filling in the recipe with about 1⅔ cups Shredded Chicken (page 60). For the more common *enchiladas de mole,* fill steam-heated corn tortillas with chicken, then sauce them with 2½ to 3 cups *Mole Poblano* (page 197) or *Mole Rojo* (page 201), following the guidelines in Step 4.

CONTEMPORARY IDEAS

Duck Enchiladas with Coloradito: Replace the pork with about 8 ounces (1½ cups) boneless, skinless roast, smoked or Chinese barbecued duck (½ large duck should do it). Complete the recipe as directed in Steps 2 through 4, adding the duck with the tomato mixture in Step 3.

Kitchen Spanish

Asking for enchiladas in Oaxaca usually gets you ones like these (sprinkled with fresh cheese and parsley, but without filling). *Enmoladas* follow suit, with black *mole* replacing the *coloradito* and *entomatadas* have a ladle of tomato sauce—no *mole* at all.

oregano. Grind the cloves, peppercorns and cinnamon in a mortar or spice grinder and add to the mixture.

Drain the soaked chiles, *set aside 1 to use in the filling* and add the remainder to the blender, along with ½ cup of the reserved pork broth. Blend until smooth, then strain through a medium-mesh sieve.

Heat the 1½ tablespoons lard or oil in a large saucepan set over medium-high. When it is hot enough to make a drop of the puree sizzle fiercely, add it all at once, and stir for several minutes as the mixture fries and concentrates. Stir in 2½ cups of the pork broth, partially cover and simmer over medium-low heat for 45 minutes. When the sauce is ready, season it with salt and sugar and, if necessary, thin it with some of the remaining pork broth to achieve a medium consistency.

3. *The filling.* While the sauce is simmering, prepare the filling. Boil the potato in salted water until tender, about 5 minutes, and drain. When the pork is cool enough to handle, trim off the fat and shred with your fingers.

Heat the remaining lard or oil in a large skillet over medium. Add the shredded meat, potato, onion and plantain. Stir often, scraping the bottom of the skillet to dislodge any sticky bits, until the mixture is a rich golden-brown, about 8 minutes.

While the meat mixture is frying, combine the remaining tomato and the single reserved chile in the blender, and process until smooth. Add the puree to the browned mixture and stir constantly for several minutes as the filling thickens. Remove from the fire, season liberally with salt and pepper, cover and keep warm in a low oven.

4. *Finishing the enchiladas.* Steam-heat the tortillas as described on page 353, and heat the sauce over low.

Just before serving, remove the hot filling from the oven and raise the temperature to 350°. Two or 3 at a time, lay the steaming tortillas in front of you, spoon a heaping tablespoon of the filling down the center of each one, roll up and lay in a warm baking dish, seam-side down. When all have been filled and rolled, spoon the *coloradito* sauce over them and warm in the oven for 5 minutes or so.

Sprinkle the enchiladas with the cheese and onion and carry to the table.

STACKED TORTILLAS WITH SHARK, BLACK BEANS AND TOMATO SAUCE

Pan de Cazón

This stack of tortillas, tangy tomato sauce, fish and black beans is a favorite in snack shops and informal restaurants all over the Yucatán Peninsula—especially in Campeche, where shallow-water sand sharks (dogfish) called *cazónes* are abundant. It's a simple but tasty combination, and one that is fairly quick to prepare. Serve it with *Jícama* Salad (page 89) and a glass of Almond-Rice Cooler (page 309) for a traditional-tasting meal.

Chiles habaneros are requisite additions to Yucatecan tomato sauces—bobbing about to spread a little chile cheer. Since they're used whole, they don't give much of their special herby taste; but they're always fished out and set proudly atop the dish. (EATER BEWARE.) They're difficult to find in the United States, so I recommend using *serranos*.

YIELD: 6 servings as a snack or light meal with other accompaniments

    1 cup (about ½ recipe) *Frijoles Refritos* made with
          black beans (page 269)
    About 4 cups (2 recipes) Yucatecan Tomato Sauce
          (page 42)
    3 fresh *chiles habaneros* or *chiles serranos,* roasted
          (page 337)
    12 corn tortillas, preferably store-bought
    3 tablespoons bitter orange juice (page 340)
    6 leaves *epazote,* finely chopped
    12 ounces boneless, skinless shark steak, prefera-
          bly 1 inch thick
    Salt, about ½ teaspoon

  1. *Preliminaries.* Heat the beans in a small, covered saucepan over low. Warm the tomato sauce over low heat in a similar covered pan; make a small slit in the side of each of the chiles and add to the sauce. Steam-heat the tortillas as directed on page 353.

  2. *The fish.* Bring 3 cups of salted water to a boil and add

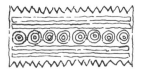

COOK'S NOTES

Techniques

Enchilada Making: See page 153. An additional note: You may find it easier to work with the tortillas if they are quick-fried (Step 2, page 154) rather than steam-heated; they hold together a little better in transferring from baking sheet to plate.

Ingredients

Corn Tortillas: See page 74.
Epazote: Since the flavors are simple here, the *epazote* comes through clearly. But when it can't be found, either leave it out or use a little flat-leaf parsley in its place.
Shark: In the Campeche market, you can buy roasted chunks of *cazón*, almost black from the fire but moist and sweet-tasting within. Their flavor is perfect in this dish because the smoke and char don't let the fish get lost in the beans and sauce. If possible, charcoal-broil the fish rather than boil it, or replace it with about 10 ounces of meaty smoked fish, such as albacore. If fresh shark is unavailable, choose swordfish, tuna or the milder halibut or cod.

Timing and Advance Preparation

If the sauce and beans are prepared in advance, the dish can be finished in a little over ½ hour. The fish may be prepared a day ahead, covered and refrigerated. Heat the ingredients (Step 1) and complete Step 3 just before serving.

2 tablespoons of the bitter orange juice, *half* the *epazote* and the shark. Cover and simmer over medium heat for 10 minutes. If possible, let the fish cool in the broth.

Drain off the liquid, remove the fish and break it into rather small shreds. Place it in an ovenproof bowl, season with salt and mix in the remaining tablespoon of bitter orange juice and the rest of the *epazote*. Cover with foil, set in the oven, and turn it on to 350°.

3. *Finishing the dish.* Oil a baking sheet and lay out 6 hot tortillas on it. Spread each with 2 rounded tablespoons of beans, then top with a portion of the warm fish mixture and a spoonful of the sauce. Top each serving with a second tortilla and spread a little sauce over it.

Cover with foil and bake for about 8 minutes, just to heat through. Transfer each serving to a warm dinner plate, ladle some of the remaining sauce over each one and garnish with the roasted chiles from the sauce.

Epazote

OTHER SNACKS

Otros Antojitos

The whimsical names of the "little whims" (as *antojito* literally translates) continue to multiply: The cooks and eaters never stop thinking up picturesque and unflattering christenings for the ways they pinch and push, fry, bake and steam their corn dough. A favorite game of Mexican writers is to list off those names, line after line after line, never bothering to let you know that they're all variations on a handful of styles.

After exploring the major approaches to *antojitos* in the preceding sections, we're now face to face with the *masa* boats (*sopes* and *garnachas,* just two of their many names), the delicious fat tortillas (*gorditas*) that puff like pita bread to hold their fillings, the infamous hoagielike sandwiches called *tortas* and the widely popular, quick-simmered tortilla casserole (*chilaquiles*) that makes an everyday lunch or supper in our house. They're as adaptable as all the other *antojitos;* they're appetizers, snacks, light meals and, in the case of *chilaquiles,* even side dishes.

No collection of *antojitos* would be representative if it didn't at least nod in the direction of tostadas. I have eaten crisp-tender little 4-inch tostadas with lime-cured meat in Tuxtla Gutiérrez, Chiapas; thick 6-inch tostadas of pickled pigs' feet and pork rind in the West-Central states; the stuffed *panuchos* of Yucatán; and the huge Oaxacan toasted—not fried—*clayudas* that serve as a dinner plate for a rich array of unusual toppings. But never, I must admit, did I come across anything in Mexico like the California version of tostadas: the crisp flour-tortilla baskets filled with enough lettuce salad to feed several indulgent people. No, in Mexico, tostadas are simply crispy food conveyors made of corn tortillas—the consumable little plates used by many street vendors. In the coffee shops, they may be piled a little higher to serve as a light meal rather than a light snack; or in a refined traditional restaurant, they may be delicately topped with a little something spicy, to go with drinks.

What follows in this chapter, then, pretty well fills out the traditional Mexican *antojito* offerings.

CHICKEN TOSTADAS WITH FRESH VEGETABLES AND CREAM

Tostadas de Pollo

This recipe's simple layering of crisp tortilla, fried beans, chicken, sour cream and a little well-dressed salad is a mainstay of coffee shops throughout Mexico (and even up into the fast-food restaurants north of the border). It is satisfying and tasty, but certainly seems less adventurous than a pigs' feet tostada made on the hefty, salty, West-Central–style fried tortillas. And what could be more refreshing than the *seviche* tostadas served under the hot sun on practically any Mexican beach?

The coffee-shop version detailed below makes a nice lunch or supper dish. Lightly topped tostadas often accompany Green *Pozole* (page 104) in Guerrero and I also think they go well with a brothy soup like *Tlalpeño* Soup (page 97). This is one dish that isn't too filling for a dessert like Sweet Fresh-Cheese Pie (page 288).

COOK'S NOTES

Techniques
Tostadas and Temperature: While most Americans think of food as hot or cold, Mexicans generally consider a cool room temperature perfect for tostadas. Warming the beans past room temperature would seem superfluous to them, I would guess, so omit the step if you wish.

Timing and Advance Preparation
With beans and shredded chicken on hand, you can have the tostadas ready in 20 minutes. Both the beans and the chicken can be prepared in advance, covered and refrigerated; but the tostadas are best

YIELD: 12 tostadas, serving 4 as a light meal

12 Crisp-Fried Tortillas (*Tostadas,* page 78)
1 large (1¼-pound), whole chicken breast, cooked, skinned, boned and shredded (page 60)
About 2 cups (1 recipe) *Frijoles Refritos* (page 269)
2 tablespoons cider vinegar
6 tablespoons vegetable oil, preferably part olive oil
¼ teaspoon salt
A big pinch of freshly ground black pepper
2½ to 3 cups sliced lettuce, preferably romaine
1 cup Thick Cream (page 51) or commercial sour cream thinned with 3 to 4 tablespoons milk or cream
½ cup chopped onion
1 ripe, large avocado, peeled, pitted and diced
2 ripe, medium-small tomatoes, cored and sliced or diced
¾ cup (3 ounces) crumbled Mexican *queso fresco* or *queso añejo* (page 327), or cheese like feta, farmer's cheese or mild Parmesan

1. *Preliminaries.* About 25 minutes before serving, fry the tortillas as directed on page 78. Sprinkle the chicken with salt, if desired. Warm the beans over low heat, adding a little water if they're overly thick. Thoroughly whisk together the vinegar, oil, salt and pepper, then toss the lettuce with this dressing.

2. *Assembling the tostadas.* Spread a generous 2 tablespoons of warm beans over each crisp tortilla. Top with a little chicken, then add a thick drizzle of cream, some onion and avocado. Top each tostada with dressed lettuce, tomato and a sprinkling of cheese. Serve at once.

Chicken tostadas

when completed shortly before serving.

TRADITIONAL VARIATIONS

Black-Bean Tostadas with Thick Cream: A dressy way to serve beans is to prepare 2 cups (1 recipe) *Frijoles Refritos* made with black beans (page 269), then divide them between 6 crisp-fried tortillas and drizzle on ½ cup Thick Cream (page 51) or commercial sour cream thinned with a little cream. End with crumbled Mexican *queso añejo* (page 327) or cheese like feta or Parmesan, plus a little chopped onion. Serve at once.

Seviche Tostadas: Prepare *Seviche* following the variation recipe for tostadas (page 84); divide it between 10 to 12 crisp-fried tortillas and garnish with a sprig of fresh coriander (*cilantro*) and a few drops of *Salsa Picante* (page 40).

CHILE-MARINATED VEGETABLE TOSTADAS

Tostadas de Chileajo

In Oaxaca and Guerrero, *chileajo* (literally "chile-garlic") is a well-known simple sauce of mild chile, lots of garlic, sweet spices and a dash of vinegar. Roadside eateries near Taxco stew iguana and rabbit in it; and market-day street vendors around the Oaxaca valley mix it up with vegetables and serve it on tostadas. Here's a traditional recipe for the latter, based on one from Guzmán's *Tradiciones gastronómicas oaxaqueñas*. These tostadas are good served before Fresh Corn Chowder with Shrimp (page 100), with a fresh fruit ice (page 300) for dessert. Or, for a summer meal, serve the cool vegetables by themselves, with poached fish or smoked chicken.

YIELD: 12 tostadas, serving 6 as a hearty appetizer

- 4 medium (about 1 ounce total) dried *chiles guajillos,* stemmed, seeded and deveined
- 6 large cloves garlic, unpeeled
- 3 ounces (about 1 cup) green beans, ends snipped, and chopped in ½-inch lengths
- ⅔ cup peas, fresh or (defrosted) frozen
- 2 small (about 6 ounces total) boiling potatoes like the red-skinned ones, diced in ½-inch pieces
- 2 small (about 4 ounces total) carrots, peeled and diced in ½-inch pieces
- 2 cloves (or a big pinch ground)
- ⅛ teaspoon black peppercorns (or a scant ¼ teaspoon ground)
- ½ teaspoon oregano
- 1 tablespoon lard or vegetable oil
- 1½ tablespoons cider vinegar
- Salt, about ½ teaspoon
- Sugar, about ½ teaspoon
- 12 Crisp-Fried Tortillas (*Tostadas,* page 78)
- ¼ cup (about 1 ounce) Mexican *queso añejo* (page 327) or cheese like feta or mild Parmesan
- ½ small onion, thinly sliced

1. *The chiles and garlic.* Cover the chiles with boiling water, weight with a plate to keep them submerged, soak 30 minutes, then drain. While the chiles are soaking, place the unpeeled garlic on a griddle or heavy skillet over medium heat. Turn frequently for about 15 minutes, until blackened in spots and soft. Cool, then slip off the skins. Place the garlic and chiles in a blender jar and set aside.

2. *Preparing the vegetables.* In a large saucepan, bring several quarts of salted water to a boil over high heat. One at a time, boil the vegetables *just until tender* (you can use the same water for each batch): first the green beans for 3 to 5 minutes, then the *fresh* peas for 4 to 20 minutes (depending on their freshness and maturity), then the potatoes for about 5 minutes, and last, the carrots for 5 to 8 minutes. As each group of vegetables is done, scoop it out, run under cold water to stop the cooking, then drain on paper towels. Transfer to a mixing bowl (along with the defrosted peas, if using them).

3. *Finishing the sauce.* Grind the cloves and black pepper in a mortar or spice grinder; add to the chile mixture in the blender jar along with the oregano and ½ cup water. Blend until smooth, then strain through a medium-mesh sieve.

Heat the lard or vegetable oil in a medium-small skillet over medium-high. When quite hot, add the chile mixture and stir constantly until somewhat darker and noticeably thicker, 2 to 3 minutes. Reduce the heat to medium-low, add the vinegar and enough water to give the sauce the consistency of thin ketchup, and simmer for a minute to blend the flavors. Season with salt and sugar, then cool.

Mix the sauce into the vegetables. If there is time, cover and let stand for a few hours before serving.

4. *Finishing the tostadas.* When you are ready to serve, scoop 2 heaping tablespoons of the vegetable mixture on each crisp-fried tortilla and sprinkle with a little cheese and onion.

HALF-FRIED TORTILLAS WITH BLACK BEANS, CHICKEN AND PICKLED ONIONS

Panuchos Yucatecos con Pollo

The appeal of these special little tostadas is the way they crisp underneath while the thin top layer of the tortilla melds with

COOK'S NOTES

Ingredients
Tortillas: If I can't be sure that my brand of store-bought, factory-made tortillas will be puffed, I'll make them myself for this dish—even though store-bought tortillas are preferable for frying. If your torti-

the beans; strew that with a little chicken in *escabeche* and the result is remarkably delicious. Everyone, from market vendors to the best regional restaurateurs, serves them in Mérida, Yucatán, and they are popular up the Gulf Coast through Veracruz.

This recipe is based on the version served at Los Almendros restaurant in Mérida, where the *panuchos* occasionally come with a welcomed sprinkling of lettuce over the top. For a special Yucatecan meal, serve them before Pork *Pibil* (page 234) and Creamy Fresh-Coconut Dessert (page 285). Or use them as a main course with a fruit salad and Mexican Rice Pudding (page 286).

YIELD: 12 *panuchos*, serving 4 as a light meal, 6 as a hearty appetizer

> 12 *puffed* corn tortillas (see Ingredients in Cook's Notes)
> About 2 cups (½ recipe) Shredded Chicken in *Escabeche* (page 230)
>   OR 1⅓ cups salted Shredded Chicken (page 60), plus about ⅔ cup (½ recipe) Pickled Red Onions (page 50)
> About ¾ cup (⅓ recipe) *smooth Frijoles Refritos* made with black beans (page 269)
> ⅔ cup vegetable oil
> 1½ cups loosely packed, sliced leaf lettuce
> 6 pickled *chiles jalapeños*, either store-bought or homemade (page 48), stemmed, seeded, deveined and sliced into thin strips (optional)

1. *Opening a pocket in the tortillas.* Lay out the tortillas in a single layer, turning them every few minutes, until they have lost any moistness and feel leathery. Do not let them dry until they curl or begin to harden.

Lay a tortilla face-side up on the counter (face-side is the one with the *thin*, puffed cap and small, dark splotches). Using a thin knife, near the edge make an incision into the pocket between the two layers. Following the line that marks the separation of the layers (most tortillas won't have puffed all the way to the edge), cut about ⅓ of the way around the perimeter.

Next, open the two layers of the tortilla into as full a pocket as possible by sliding a few fingers through the opening and *very gently* prying apart the two sides. (Should the tortilla rip,

llas don't puff much and you have difficulty prying the two layers apart, try heating the tortillas on a griddle set over medium-high, flipping them frequently until they stiffen and brown a little. Then cut into them and pry the two layers apart.

Timing and Advance Preparation
All toppings except the lettuce can be prepared ahead and refrigerated. It takes ½ hour or so to prepare the tortillas for stuffing and frying; if wrapped well, they can be done a day ahead and refrigerated. Fill the tortillas with beans within an hour of serving or they'll be tough when fried; slice the lettuce and complete Step 3 shortly before serving.

TRADITIONAL VARIATIONS
Panuchos with Other Traditional Toppings: In the preceding recipe, the chicken may be replaced by about 1⅓ cups shredded Chicken or Pork *Pibil* (page 233 or 234). Occasionally, sliced hard-boiled egg is slipped into the pocket, on top of the beans.
Panuchos with Picadillo or Shark: A common market variation replaces the chicken with 1½ cups minced pork or beef *picadillo* (page 132); splash with 1 tablespoon Yucatecan Tomato Sauce (page 42) before sprinkling with lettuce, Pickled Red Onions (page 50) and *jalapeño* strips. Some recipes call for the same layering, but with 1⅓ cups shredded, cooked shark (you could use any meaty fish) in place of the *picadillo*.

Regional Explorations
Often, *panuchos* outside Mérida

stop at once and either discard the tortilla or, if the rip is small, use the tortilla with whatever size pocket it has.) Open pockets in the remaining tortillas.

2. *Stuffing the tortilla and other preliminaries.* About 45 minutes before serving, drain the juice from the chicken in *escabeche* and set it out at room temperature; or, if using shredded chicken, set it out with the pickled onions.

Spoon 1 tablespoon of the beans into the pocket of each tortilla, then press gently on the tops to spread out the beans. Stack the stuffed tortillas and cover with plastic wrap.

3. *Frying and topping the panuchos.* Heat the vegetable oil in a large skillet over medium-high. When it is hot enough to make the edge of a tortilla sizzle sharply, begin frying the *panuchos* 2 or 3 at a time, face-side up, until crisp underneath, about 3 minutes. Drain them for a minute upside down on paper towels, then flip them over so they're face-side up; keep warm in a low oven until all are fried.

Lay the *panuchos* on a warm serving platter. Divide the sliced lettuce over them, top with chicken in *escabeche*, or shredded chicken and onions in *escabeche*, then strew with the optional pickled *jalapeño*. Serve immediately.

CRISPY *MASA* BOATS WITH *CHORIZO* AND FRESH TOPPINGS

Sopes Tapatíos

These tender little *masa* boats, so much a part of Guadalajara's snack-shop and street-food fare, are one of the most beautiful displays of classic Mexican flavors and textures: a variety of typical toppings—from soft and meaty to crunchy, raw and *picante*—spread in a crispy, silver dollar–size shell of good corn *masa*.

The easy, uncommon forming method I've outlined below is one I learned at a Loredo restaurant in Mexico City; there they serve *sopes* as appetizers. They're great to pass around at a cocktail party, along with little *Seviche* Tostadas (page 164) and

are simply black-bean tostadas with chicken shreds or ground beef—except those in the Villahermosa and Campeche markets. There, they're made from two very thin, raw tortillas pressed together with beans or meat between them; they're fried, topped with sauce and other condiments, and taste delicious—like a cross between *panuchos* and soft *salbutes*, another Yucatecan specialty.

COOK'S NOTES

Techniques
An Alternative, More Common Method of Forming Sopes: Divide the dough into 18 balls, pat them into 2½-inch-diameter discs ¼ inch thick, and bake them for 1½ minutes per side. Cool, then pinch up a border around the perimeter, breaking through the cooked layer and molding up some of the soft *masa* below; fry as directed. They are a little heavier than the split variety.
Frying Masa Creations: See page 143.

Nuevo León–Style *Tamales* (page 186). Or make a light meal of them with a bowl of Shrimp-Ball Soup with Roasted Peppers (page 102).

YIELD: 24 *sopes,* serving 8 to 12 as an appetizer

For the dough:

    1¼ **pounds fresh *masa***

        OR 2¼ cups *masa harina* mixed with a scant 1½ cups hot tap water

    2 **tablespoons lard or vegetable shortening**

    ⅓ **cup flour (plus 1 tablespoon for *masa harina*)**

    ¾ **teaspoon salt**

    1 **teaspoon baking powder**

For finishing the sopes:

    1 **cup Brothy Beans (page 267), coarsely pureed with a little of their broth**

    8 **ounces (about 1 cup) *chorizo* sausage, store-bought or homemade (page 55), casing removed**

    Vegetable oil to a depth of ¾ inch, for frying

    About 1¼ cups (1 recipe) Fresh Green *Tomatillo* Sauce (page 36)

    ½ **cup (about 2 ounces) crumbled Mexican *queso fresco* or *queso añejo* (page 327), or cheese like feta, farmer's cheese or mild Parmesan**

    1 **cup thinly sliced romaine lettuce**

    3 **or 4 radishes, thinly sliced**

1. *The sope shells.* If you are using the *masa harina,* mix it with the hot water, cover and let stand 20 to 30 minutes. Mix the *masa* (fresh or reconstituted) with the lard or shortening, flour, salt and baking powder, kneading until all ingredients are thoroughly combined. If necessary, adjust the consistency of the dough with a little water; page 74 has the details. Divide the dough into 12 balls, place them on a plate and cover with plastic wrap.

Heat a griddle or heavy skillet over medium. Cut a square of heavy plastic (like that used for freezer bags). Lay it out in front of you, flatten one of the balls onto it, then gently pat and press it into an evenly flat disc, ⅜ inch thick and 2½ inches in diameter. With the fat little tortilla still on the plastic, flip it over onto one hand, dough-side down, and peel off the plastic.

Lay the tortilla on the hot griddle or skillet and bake for about 2 minutes per side, until lightly browned; it will still be

Timing and Advance Preparation

Allow about an hour to complete the *sopes* (plus 20 to 30 minutes more if using *masa harina*). The shells can be completed up to 2 days ahead, covered and refrigerated. The beans, of course, can be cooked in advance, as can the *chorizo;* rewarm them, prepare the other toppings and fry the *sopes* just before serving.

TRADITIONAL VARIATIONS

Sopes with a Variety of Toppings: If the ingredients are finely chopped, practically any taco filling (pages 124–141), *quesadilla* filling (pages 146–149), even eggs (*a la Mexicana* [page 115], with *Chorizo* [page 116], or with Shredded Jerky [page 117]) can fill *sopes*.

CONTEMPORARY IDEAS

Plantain Sopes with Shredded Pork: In many cookbooks from Mexico, *sope* dough is made with flavorful additions: Boil 1 medium-ripe, large plantain in salted water until very tender, 30 to 40 minutes. Drain, cool and puree in a food processor. Mix with ¾ pound *masa,* ½ cup Mexican *queso fresco* or fresh farmer's cheese, and the lard, flour, salt and baking powder called for in the recipe. Form, bake (over *low* heat, 3 to 4 minutes per side), split, pinch and fry the *sopes.* Top each one with a generous tablespoon of the Shredded Pork *Picadillo* (page 132) and a little crumbled fresh cheese.

Regional Explorations

A *sope* by any other name . . . can show up elsewhere in Mexico: *picadas* (literally "picked at") in Veracruz; *pellizcada* (lit-

soft and uncooked inside. Pat out and bake the remaining 11 *masa* balls in the same fashion.

With a thin, sharp knife, slice each tortilla in half, as you would an English muffin. With the cooked-side down, pinch up a ¼-inch-high border around each disc, molding the pliable uncooked *masa* from the center. Cover the *sopes* with plastic wrap so they won't dry out.

2. *Preparing the toppings.* About ½ hour before serving, warm the beans in a small covered pan and set in a low oven; if they're not the consistency of thick bean soup, either simmer briefly, uncovered, or stir in a few drops of water or broth. In a small skillet, cook the *chorizo* in 1 tablespoon of the vegetable oil over medium-low heat, breaking up any clumps. When it is done, about 10 minutes, drain off the fat, cover and place in the oven.

3. *Frying the shells.* Heat the ¾-inch depth of vegetable oil to 360°. Fry the *sope* shells 3 or 4 at a time until lightly browned, about 45 seconds; they should be a little crunchy on the outside, but still tender and moist within. Drain on paper towels and keep warm in the oven.

4. *Finishing the sopes.* When you are ready to serve, layer the fillings in each *sope* shell in this order: 2 teaspoons beans, 1 heaping teaspoon *chorizo,* a scant tablespoon *tomatillo* sauce, 1 teaspoon cheese, a little lettuce and a couple of radish slices. Serve immediately.

aged and fresh Mexican cheese (queso fresco and queso añejo)

PUFFED *MASA* CAKES STUFFED WITH CHILES AND CHEESE

Gorditas de Chile con Queso

The fat *masa* cakes bake and puff on a thick slab of steel set over charcoal, there are a dozen or more fillings lined up in

erally "pinched at") around Central, Southern and Gulf Coastal Mexico; *garnachas* from the capital out through Yucatán; *chalupas* (literally "boats") in Puebla and vicinity (though the everyday *chalupas* don't have pinched borders); *memelas* (literally "oblong, thick tortillas") on the streets in Oaxaca; *gorditas* (literally "little fat ones") in Hermosillo, Sonora; *migadas* (literally "picked to pieces") around Tampico. And, of course, plain, unqualified *sope* is understood most everywhere, too. All of them are *masa* boats with pinched borders and each has its characteristic toppings. The Guadalajara-style *sopes* outlined here are smaller and more fully filled than the common, 4-inch, lightly sauced and cheese-sprinkled snacks.

COOK'S NOTES

Techniques
The Bake-Then-Fry Approach to Gorditas: While some cooks get their *gorditas* to puff by simply griddle-baking them,

plain-looking earthenware bowls, and the air is cut up by the aromas and streaks of sunlight filtering through uncovered patches in the roof of the San Luis Potosí market. I find myself attracted to this kind of earthy setting when I'm looking for snacks like *gorditas*.

From Querétaro north, *gorditas* are enjoyed with an endlessly evolving lot of fillings; I chose chiles and cheese for this recipe (it's not the melted-cheese dip of Texas) because it is delicious and popular throughout the area. *Gorditas* are good for a light lunch or supper, or to serve before a rustic main course like Lamb *Birria* (page 256).

YIELD: 12 *gorditas* serving 4 as a light meal, 6 as a hearty appetizer

For the filling:
   1 ripe, large tomato, roasted or boiled (page 352), cored and peeled
      OR ¾ 15-ounce can tomatoes, drained
   4 medium-large fresh *chiles poblanos,* roasted and peeled (page 337), seeded and thinly sliced
   1 cup broth, preferably poultry
   8 ounces (about 2 cups) Mexican *queso fresco* (page 327) or fresh farmer's cheese, or even Monterey Jack, cut into ½-inch cubes (see Ingredients in Cook's Notes)
   Salt, about ½ teaspoon (depending on the saltiness of the broth)

For the gorditas:
   1 pound fresh *masa*
      OR 1¾ cups *masa harina* mixed with 1 cup plus 2 tablespoons hot tap water
   2 tablespoons lard or vegetable shortening
   ½ teaspoon salt
   ¼ cup flour (⅓ cup if using *masa harina*)
   1 scant teaspoon baking powder
   Oil to a depth of ¾ inch, for frying
   About 1½ cups thinly sliced romaine or iceberg lettuce (optional)

   1. *The filling.* In a blender or food processor, puree the tomato, then strain through a medium-mesh sieve into a medium-size saucepan. Add the chiles and broth, then simmer over medium heat for about 10 minutes, until the chiles are tender and the liquid reduced to a light coating. Remove from the heat, stir in the cheese and season with salt.

the most foolproof method I've found is that used by the street vendors: Bake a nice crust on them, then pop them in the oil, where they nearly always puff.
Frying Masa Creations: See page 143.

Ingredients
Chiles Poblanos: If *poblanos* aren't to be found, use 7 long green chiles (roasted, peeled, seeded and sliced).
Cheese: Though either the crumbly fresh cheese (*queso fresco*) or the spongy *panela* is generally used for this dish in West-Central and Northern Mexico, you might enjoy a melting cheese (Muenster, Monterey Jack or a mild cheddar) as they do in Chihuahua. Melting cheese, however, is harder to work with as a filling.

Timing and Advance Preparation
Allow 45 minutes or so to prepare the *gorditas* and filling. If using *masa harina*, mix it with water first, so it can rehydrate while you complete the other steps. The filling can be prepared a day or two ahead and refrigerated, covered.

2. *The dough.* If using *masa harina*, mix it with the water, cover and let stand for ½ hour. Mix the lard, salt, flour and baking powder with the fresh or reconstituted *masa*, kneading it until all ingredients are thoroughly incorporated; if necessary, add a little water to correct the consistency of the dough, as described on page 74. Divide into 12 portions, place them on a plate and cover with plastic wrap.

3. *Forming and baking the gorditas.* Set a griddle or heavy skillet over medium to medium-low heat. Place a 7-inch square of heavy plastic (like that used for freezer bags) on your counter and flatten a portion of *masa* onto the center of it. Pat and press the dough into a ⅛-inch-thick disc, 3½ to 4 inches in diameter. With the *gordita* still attached to the plastic, flip it over onto one hand, dough-side down, then carefully peel off the plastic. Lay the *gordita* on the heated griddle or skillet and bake, turning every minute or so, until it is lightly browned and crusty, about 3 or 4 minutes. Cool on a wire rack. Form and bake the remaining portions of *masa* in the same way.

4. *Frying, filling and serving the gorditas.* About 20 minutes before serving, heat the oil to 375°. Place the filling in a low oven to heat just a little.

When the oil is hot, fry the *gorditas* a few at a time for 1½ minutes, turning frequently, until the two sides have puffed apart about ¾ inch; if they don't puff, you can simply split them with a knife when you serve. Drain on paper towels and keep warm in the low oven while frying the remainder.

When you are ready to serve, use a small, pointed knife to cut an opening into the pocket, going in at the edge and slicing about ⅓ of the way around the perimeter.

Spoon about 3 tablespoons of the warm filling into each *gordita*, then stuff in the optional lettuce. Serve at once.

QUICK-SIMMERED TORTILLA CASSEROLE WITH GREEN OR RED SAUCE

Chilaquiles Verdes o Rojos

It's the slight chewiness of the tortillas I think you'll enjoy, run through as they are with the flavor of broth, tomatoes,

COOK'S NOTES

Techniques
Drying and Frying Tortillas: See page 353.

Ingredients
Corn Tortillas: They should not be too thin, or they will disintegrate as they simmer.

tomatillos and chiles. And then there's the drizzling of thick, glassy cream. *Chilaquiles* are a favorite choice in coffee shops from the U.S. border to Guatemala—simmered with a locally popular sauce, plus an endless variety of chunky vegetables, meat, eggs and sausage. The Guadalajara market cooks keep *cazuelas* of them on hand during morning hours; after a long simmering, they take on the texture of a coarse *polenta*. And the standard Mexico City version calls for a spicy *tomatillo* sauce and a whole sprig of *epazote* in every portion—apt ingredients for a dish whose name means "chiles and herbs" in Nahuatl.

This simple restaurant version of *chilaquiles*, which I learned in the capital, plays an unchanging role in morning food. It also makes a nice supper when paired with a salad and/or Pan-Fried Chile-Marinated Pork (page 136); it can even replace enchiladas in Steak *a la Tampiqueña* (page 243).

YIELD: 2 servings as a main course, 4 when accompanied by other dishes

> 6 medium-thick (5 to 6 ounces total) corn torti-
>   llas, preferably stale, store-bought ones
> ⅓ cup vegetable oil
> 1½ cups Quick-Cooked *Tomatillo* Sauce (page 42)
>   or Quick-Cooked Tomato-Chile Sauce (page
>   41)
> ½ cup chicken broth for the *tomatillo* sauce, 1 cup
>   for the tomato sauce
> ½ cup boneless, cooked chicken (page 60), cut in
>   chunks (optional)
> 1 large sprig *epazote* (optional)
> Salt, about ¼ teaspoon
> ¼ cup Thick Cream (page 51) or commercial sour
>   cream thinned with a little milk or cream
> 2 tablespoons crumbled Mexican *queso fresco* or
>   *queso añejo* (page 327), or cheese like feta,
>   farmer's cheese or mild Parmesan
> 1 thin slice onion, broken into rings

1. *The tortillas.* Cut the tortillas into eighths. If they are moist, dry them out for a few minutes in a 350° oven, until quite leathery.

Pour the oil into a medium-size skillet set over medium-high heat. When hot enough to make the edge of a tortilla sizzle, add *half* the tortilla pieces. Turn them frequently until they are lightly browned and nearly crisp, then remove and drain on paper towels. Fry and drain the remaining tortilla pieces in the

Timing and Advance Preparation

These *chilaquiles* require only 20 minutes to prepare when the sauce is on hand; the tortillas may be fried in advance. *Chilaquiles* won't retain their good texture for long, so simmer them shortly before serving.

TRADITIONAL VARIATIONS

Chilaquiles with Scrambled Eggs and Rajas: Fry ½ medium onion (sliced) and 2 *chiles poblanos* (roasted, peeled, seeded and sliced) until tender; break in 3 eggs and scramble until set. Prepare the *chilaquiles* as directed, adding the egg mixture with the sauce.

Chilaquiles for a Crowd: This is the home-style method (similar to what's called a "dry" tortilla soup). Using *double* quantities: Fry batches of tortillas in ½ inch oil until nearly crisp, drain and place in an 8-inch-square baking dish; heat the sauce and broth and pour over the tortillas, then mix in the optional chicken and *epazote*, and the salt; stir, cover and bake at 350° about 20 minutes. Top with cream, cheese and onions.

same fashion. Reduce the heat to medium-low and discard any oil that remains.

2. *Simmering the chilaquiles.* Return the tortilla pieces to the skillet and add the sauce, broth, optional chicken and optional *epazote.* Stir well to coat the tortillas, cover the skillet and simmer until the tortillas are soft but not mushy, about 5 minutes. Season with salt.

3. *Garnish and presentation.* Scoop the mixture onto a warm serving platter. Drizzle with the cream, sprinkle with cheese and decorate with onion rings. Serve immediately.

LAYERED TORTILLA CASSEROLE

Budín de Tortillas

YIELD: about 6 servings

This delicious lasagnalike variation on *chilaquiles* is often called *budín cuauhtémoc* or *budín azteca.* Quick-fry 12 corn tortillas in a little vegetable oil, 2 or 3 seconds per side, then drain well. Prepare 2 cups Quick-Cooked *Tomatillo* Sauce (page 42), 3 large chiles *poblanos* (roasted, peeled, seeded and sliced, page 336), 1¼ cups Thick Cream (page 51) or thinned commercial sour cream, and 1½ cups (6 ounces) grated melting cheese (page 328) like mild cheddar or Monterey Jack. Line the bottom of a 9-inch-square baking dish with 3 tortillas (slightly overlapping). Top with ¼ of the sauce, cream and cheese, and ⅓ of the chiles; repeat with three more layers (the top will have no chiles). Cover and bake at 350° for about 30 minutes. Strew with onion rings and radish rounds, then serve. About 1½ cups shredded cooked chicken, pork or fish can be layered with the chiles.

CONTEMPORARY VARIATIONS

Chilaquiles with Quick-Fried Chard and Monterey Jack: Stir-fry 1½ cups sliced Swiss chard in a little oil, just until softened. Prepare the *chilaquiles* through Step 2, using Quick-Cooked Tomato-Chile Sauce (made with 2 seeded *chiles chipotles* in place of the green chiles). Mix in the chard, scoop into a baking dish, top with 1 cup grated Jack cheese and broil until the cheese is melted.

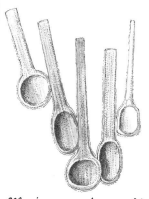

Mexican wooden cooking spoons

TAMALES

[The Lords ate] tamales made of a dough of maize softened in lime, with beans forming a sea shell on top; tamales of maize softened in wood ashes; . . . tamales of meat cooked with maize and yellow chili . . .
——FRIAR BERNARDINO DE SAHAGÚN, 1550s

I have frequently wondered what those *tamales* must have tasted like four and a half centuries ago. Were they made of coarse-ground corn and wrapped like fat cigars in cornhusks, as many are today? Or was the dough smooth (perhaps even stirred over the fire before the *tamales* were formed); could the wrappers have been banana leaves? Might the tightly tied packages have been cooked *in* simmering liquid, as I've seen in Chiapas, rather than steamed above it? Would they have tasted more like a pudding, as do the chokecherry ones they sometimes sell in the Tolucan market? And without the lard brought by the Spaniards, wouldn't the pre-Columbian corn loaves have been heavy and dense?

The yield of the cook's craft, sadly, is a perishable one, which means that the answers to many of my questions will remain incomplete at best. The old cookbooks fail to supply much of the bygone detail that was commonly shared knowledge for writer and reader. And the anthropological records only tantalize us with vague references to different colors, shapes and flavors, before they move on to describe the special varieties of *tamales* that were gifts to the gods during the twelfth month of the Aztecs' eighteen-month year. That was an ancient holiday, as it happened, that coincided rather nicely with the conquerors' All Saints' Day (Day of the Dead, as they call it in Mexico), resulting in the two becoming a thoroughly *mestizo* fiesta—celebrated in honor of all who've gone to the other world, celebrated with an eye to the earthly pleasures of drink and food . . . *tamales* included.

Still today, when people eat *tamales* in Mexico (except perhaps in some big cities), there is at least a hint of fiesta in the air. When family and friends get together to make them, the event is a *tamal*-making-party-before-the-party, a time to take full advantage of the high-spirited company while everyone shares in the special preparations.

For those who don't make their own, *tamales* are often on sale from fragrant steamers along the routes of Sunday-evening strolls (*paseos*) in parks or main squares. In towns where *tamales* are a specialty, the market stalls and coffee shops serve them, hot in their cornhusk or banana-leaf wrappers, frequently with earthenware mugs full of the traditional, warm, *masa*-thickened *atole*, in variations from fruit to nut, chocolate to plain white.

Today this pairing of *tamales* with *atole* has come to seem old-fashioned, so some folks drink soda pop or coffee or hot chocolate with the steamed corn cakes. But during the days when there was only one liquid accompaniment,

Sra. Josefina Velázquez de León wrote her classic cookbook *Tamales y atoles*, filled with recipes for deliciously flavored porridges and the different *tamales* that are the pride of each region.

The majority of the *tamales*—no matter what their filling, flavoring or wrapping—start with a dough of *masa para tamales* ("corn dough for *tamales*") or *harina para tamales* ("cornmeal for *tamales*") made from dried field corn that has been boiled briefly with slaked lime, hulled and coarsely ground: If dried first, it makes meal; if ground wet, the result is a coarse-textured dough.

Good, flavorful, fresh lard is the second ingredient, and it is pliable enough to trap air when beaten, causing the dough to expand as the *tamales* steam and making each bite tender and delicious. The dough is mixed up with a light-flavored broth; and, to help ensure that the *tamales* puff up light and tender, baking powder is stirred in. Baking powder, of course, is of recent manufacture, the long-used leavening (and one still used by some traditional cooks) being the *agua de tequesquite* (a mixture of saltpeter and water in which skins of tomatillos have been boiled).

Having a tamal party: Because *tamales* are so special and can be made ahead, they are ideal for large informal parties—whether you prepare one variety or several. To prepare larger quantities of any of the *tamales,* simply multiply out the recipe, make the dough in a large heavy-duty mixer (using the paddle, not the whisk) and gather together lots of friends to help form the *tamales;* use a large kettle or two for steaming. Small *tamales* can be put out in their wrappers as appetizers, accompanied by fresh vegetables and dip, a *Jícama* Salad (page 89), Cactus-Paddle Salad (page 47) and/or Chunky Guacamole (page 44). Also, *tamales* are substantial enough to be a light buffet main course, served with *Frijoles Refritos* (page 269) or *Charro* Beans (page 270), a Mixed Vegetable Salad (page 87), Flan (page 283), and beer or one of the coolers (pages 307–311); for the sake of tradition, I'd make a warm Chocolate *Atole* (page 317).

Regional Explorations

Coupling my penchant for *tamales* with their endless variety, it would be easy to fill a volume with regional specialties. I have chosen, instead, not to test any reader's patience, including in this list only the most distinctive, easy-to-find ones. **Culiacán, Sinaloa:** large *tamales* with meat and vegetables, plus everyday smaller ones made of sweetened brown beans, pineapple and fresh corn, among others. **Veracruz:** fresh corn *tamales* with pork and the anise-flavored herb *hoja santa*, plus banana leaf–wrapped *tamales* made from smooth *masa*, chicken and the same herb. **Monterrey:** small, cigar-size *tamales* of smooth or coarse dough flavored with red chiles and filled with shredded meat. **Oaxaca:** large, banana leaf–wrapped *tamales* laced with the special Oaxacan black *mole*, plus husk-wrapped ones filled with the local green or yellow *moles*, black beans or the herb called *chepil*. **Yucatán:** very large pit- or oven-baked *tamales* called *pibipollos*, made of smooth-ground *masa* flavored with *achiote* and filled with chicken and/or pork; also, *chanchames* (husk-wrapped *tamales* with *achiote*-flavored filling), *vaporcitos* (a thin layer of *masa* patted on banana leaf, folded over a filling, then steamed), *tamales colados* (a very light, pre-cooked dough of strained *masa* and broth, with a filling of chicken, tomato and *achiote*), among others. **San Cristóbal de las Casas, Chiapas:** *tamales untados* are banana leaf–wrapped *tamales* filled with pork and a sweet, light *mole* (sold at houses that put out a red lantern on Saturday night); *tamales de mumu* are wrapped in cornhusks with a preliminary wrapper of *mumu* leaf (related to the *hoja santa*), among many others. **Michoacán:** the smooth, dense (but tender) unfilled rhomboid shapes called *corundas*, wrapped in the leaves of the corn plant; also, fresh corn *tamales* called *uchepos*. **Northwestern Mexico, especially Pánuco, Veracruz:** huge three- or four-foot *tamales* called *zacahuiles*, made from very coarsely ground corn flavored with red chile, filled with pork, wrapped in banana leaves and baked in a huge, wood-heated oven in special restaurants on weekends. **Central and West Central Mexico:** See the notes on page 182.

TAMAL MAKING

Preparing Cornhusks or Banana Leaves. For cornhusks: Simmer the husks in water to cover for 10 minutes. Weight with a plate to keep them submerged, and let stand off the fire for a couple of hours until the husks are pliable.

When you are ready to form the *tamales*, separate out the largest and most pliable husks—ones that are at least 6 inches across on the wider end and 6 or 7 inches long. If you can't find enough good ones, overlap some of the larger ones to give wide, sturdy, unbroken surfaces to spread the dough on. Pat the chosen leaves dry with a towel.

For banana leaves: Defrost overnight in the refrigerator if they're frozen, then unfold and cut off the long, hard side of the leaf (where it was attached to the central vein). Look for holes or rips, then cut the leaf into unbroken, 12-inch segments.

Set up a large steamer with about an inch of water; loosely roll up the banana-leaf squares, place in the steamer, cover and steam for 20 to 30 minutes, until the leaves are soft and very pliable. Or simply pass the banana leaves slowly over a medium gas flame, one at a time, until they change texture (as the oil rises to the surface) and become more pliable; don't overdo it or they'll become brittle.

Setting up the steamer for tamales. Steaming less than 20 husk-wrapped *tamales* can be done in a collapsible vegetable steamer set into a large, deep saucepan. For larger quantities, you need something like the kettle-size *tamal* steamers used in Mexico (and occasionally sold in the United States); mine is a two-part apparatus, the bottom of the top half of which is perforated for steam to pass through. You can improvise by setting a wire rack on 4 upturned custard cups in a large kettle.

COOK'S NOTES

Techniques

Adding Liquid to the Dough: Stiff dough means crumbly, dry and heavy *tamales*. Dough made of fresh *masa* should be the consistency of a medium-thick cake batter, *but no stiffer;* dough made of the substitute *masa* will be slightly stiffer. It is impossible to give the exact quantity of broth you'll need, since fresh *masa* can vary greatly in its consistency.

Beating the Dough: With all ingredients at room temperature, the dough will be pliable enough to trap lots of air during the beating (ensuring light and tender *tamales*).

Preparing Tamal Dough in a Food Processor: When you are making *tamal* dough with no more than 1 pound of *masa,* you may measure all but the broth into the bowl of the food processor, pulse several times, then run the machine for 30 seconds, stopping to scrape down the sides at least once. With the processor running, pour in the broth in a steady stream. Season with salt. Test the lightness by dropping a little dough into

When steaming banana leaf–wrapped *tamales,* you need lots of space. In Mexico, they use the large steamers described above and stack the *tamales* on top of each other. I prefer to lay the *tamales* in single layers in stacked Chinese bamboo steamers; they cook more evenly and retain their shape better. Lacking the Mexican or Chinese alternatives, improvise a supported-rack assemblage in a kettle.

It is best to line all steamers with extra cornhusks or banana leaves to protect the *tamales* from direct steam contact and to add more flavor. Make sure that there are small openings for drainage, so condensing steam won't pool.

Forming Tamales. To form tamales in cornhusks: First tear extra husks into ¼-inch-wide, 7-inch-long strips—one for each *tamal.* Lay out a large, lightly dried cornhusk with the tapering end toward you. Spread a portion (3 tablespoons or ¼ cup, depending on the recipe) of the dough into about a 4-inch square, leaving at least a 1½-inch border on the side toward you and a ¾-inch border along the other sides (with large husks, the borders will be much bigger). Spoon the filling (if there is one) down the center of the dough. Pick up the two long sides of the cornhusk and bring them together (this will cause the dough to surround the filling). If the uncovered borders of the two long sides you're holding are narrow, then tuck one side under the other; if wide, then roll both sides in the same direction around the *tamal.* If the husk is small, wrap the *tamal* in

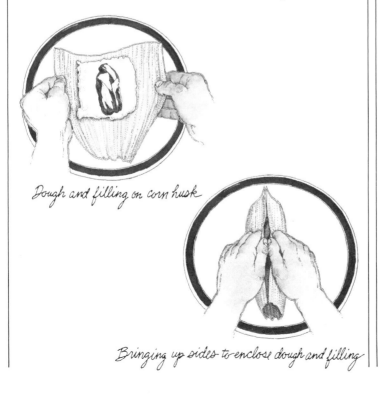

Dough and filling on corn husk

Bringing up sides to enclose dough and filling

cold water: If it sinks, process for a little longer, then test again.

Steaming Tamales: To dispel a common misconception: Unless condensing steam runs directly into one of the husks, a *tamal* with an open end will not be the least bit soggy from its contact with the steam. *Tamales* need uninterrupted medium steam for the first 45 minutes of cooking.

Ingredients

Coarse-Ground Masa for Tamales vs. Smooth Masa for Tortillas and the Substitutes: Though the coarse-ground dough produces the most tender, interestingly textured *tamales,* I sometimes enjoy *tamales* made from the smooth-ground tortilla *masa* (as in Nuevo León–Style *Tamales,* page 186)—so use what you can get. The substitute dough turns out quite an authentic-tasting, light *tamal,* but one that is softer and tastes more like grits than like coarse-ground fresh *masa.*

Lard: Tradition calls for lard in *tamales.* If it is top quality and fresh, it adds a delicious, pleasant taste—even to the sweet ones. Like some Mexican cooks, however, I use part butter in my fresh-corn and sweet *tamales.* If you plan to use vegetable shortening, choose a *tamal* recipe that calls for a flavoring in the dough.

Cornhusks and Banana Leaves: See pages 344 and 325, respectively. Both the husks and the leaves give a distinctive flavor to the *tamales,* so I hesitate to recommend any alternatives. Since banana leaves are more difficult to find, however, I'll pass along that you can replace them with squares of aluminum foil or a second husk. Finally, fold up the empty 1½-inch section of the husk (to form a tightly closed "bottom," leaving the top open), then secure it in place by loosely tying one of the strips of husk around the *tamal*. As they're made, stand the *tamales*

Folding and tying husk-wrapped tamal

on the folded bottom in the prepared steamer. Don't tie the *tamales* too tightly or pack them too closely in the steamer; they need room to expand.

Tamal in steamer lined with husks

To form tamales in banana leaves: First cut a 12-inch length of string for each *tamal*. Then lay out one of the prepared squares of banana leaf, shiny-side up, and spread one portion (usually ½ cup) dough into an 8x4-inch rectangle over it, as shown in the illustration. Spoon or lay the filling over the left side of the

Dough and filling on banana leaf

parchment paper; for the Yucatecan Baked *Tamal* (page 189), simply omit the banana leaves altogether.

Advance Preparation
Finished *tamales* will stay warm for 45 minutes in the steamer on the fire. Or they can be made several days ahead and stored in the refrigerator, well wrapped; they may also be successfully frozen. For the best results, reheat cooked, defrosted *tamales* in a steamer for 10 to 15 minutes.

rectangle of dough, then fold in the right third of the leaf so that the dough encloses the filling. Fold in the uncovered third of the leaf, then fold in the top and bottom. Loosely tie the *tamales* with string and set them in the steamer.

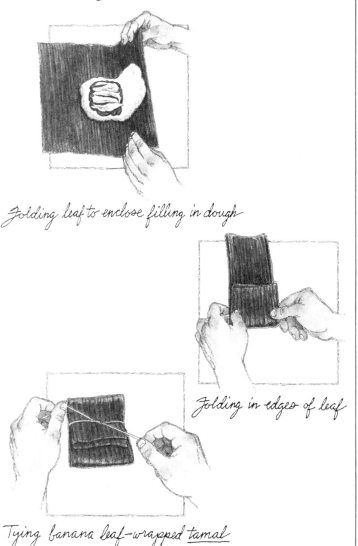

Folding leaf to enclose filling in dough

Folding in edges of leaf

Tying banana leaf-wrapped tamal

Steaming Tamales. When all *tamales* are in the steamer, cover them with a layer of leftover husks or banana leaves; if your husk-wrapped *tamales* don't take up the entire steamer, fill in the open spaces with loosely wadded aluminum foil (to keep the *tamales* from falling down). Set the lid in place and steam over a constant medium heat for about 1 hour for *tamales* made from fresh *masa*, 1¼ to 1½ hours for those made from the substitute. Watch carefully that all the water doesn't boil away and, to keep the steam steady, pour *boiling* water into the pot when more is necessary.

Tamales are done when the husk or leaf peels away easily; *tamales* made from the substitute *masa* may seem a *little* sticky when they are done. Let *tamales* stand in the steamer off the fire for a few minutes, to firm up.

Different ways to form tamales

SUBSTITUTE *MASA* FOR TAMALES

Masa Fingida para Tamales

YIELD: about 2 cups (1 pound) *tamal* dough

⅔ cups (4 ounces) quick-cooking (not instant) grits

¾ cup (3½ ounces) *masa harina*

1. *The grits.* Pulverize the grits in a spice grinder or blender (preferably fitted with a miniblend container) as thoroughly as possible. Transfer to a medium-size bowl.

2. *Finishing the dough.* Stir in 1¼ cups boiling water and let stand 10 minutes. Measure in the *masa harina* and stir until thoroughly homogeneous. Cover and cool to room temperature.

TAMALES WITH CHICKEN AND GREEN SAUCE

Tamales de Pollo y Salsa Verde

It is this style of *tamal* that most of Mexico holds up as exemplary: a white, light, tender, even-textured loaf of coarsely ground corn . . . with just a little flavorful sauce and a few

Alternative Forming Methods for Cornhusk-Wrapped Tamales:
In the United States, our husk-wrapped *tamales* are frequently smaller than those in Mexico because our husks are smaller, having been cut off well above the broad, cupped base. Though the size limits the variations on forming techniques, you can also (1) form the *tamal* in the middle of the husk, roll it up and tie on both ends, or (2) form the *tamal* in the middle of the husk, roll it up, fold in both ends (slightly overlapping them) and tie a string of husk around the middle to hold the ends in place. With our small husks, both variations either make very small *tamales* or constrain them so much that they can't rise.

COOK'S NOTES

Additional Notes
See page 177.

Timing
If the *masa* and fillings are on hand, allow 45 minutes to prepare the *tamales* and 1 to 1½ hours to steam them.

shreds of meat to fill it. Some North Americans may be a little surprised with them, especially if they've been raised with the Texan *tamales* made from flavored dough and lots of saucy insides. Perhaps it takes a couple of bites before you can turn your focus from *filling* to *casing* and begin to enjoy the cake's moist–corn bread texture.

If you're having a *tamal* party as described above, these *tamales*—with chicken and green sauce or with one of the variation fillings—are a must. Or serve them as a first course (removed from their wrappers or presented attractively atop them) before Charcoal-Grilled Chicken (page 228) or Fish with Toasted Garlic (page 215); top the *tamales* with a little *tomatillo* sauce and some chopped onion.

YIELD: about 16 medium-size *tamales,* serving 4 or 5 as a light main course

½ **8-ounce package dried cornhusks**

For the dough:
   4 **ounces (½ cup) good-quality, fresh lard (see Ingredient notes on page 178)**
   1 **pound (about 2 cups) fresh *masa* for *tamales,* store-bought or homemade (page 71) OR about 2 cups (1 recipe) Substitute *Masa* for *Tamales* (page 181)**
   About ⅔ **cup broth (preferably light-flavored poultry broth), at room temperature**
   1 **teaspoon baking powder**
   Salt, **about ½ teaspoon (depending on the saltiness of the broth)**

For the filling:
   1⅓ **cups Shredded Chicken (page 60)**
   ½ **cup Quick-Cooked *Tomatillo* Sauce (page 42)**

   1. *The cornhusks.* Follow the directions on page 177 for soaking the husks, then pick out 16 large ones for wrappers; reserve the remainder for ties and for lining the steamer.
   2. *The dough.* If the lard is very soft, refrigerate it to firm a little. Then, with an electric mixer, beat it until very light, about 1 minute. Add *half* the fresh or substitute *masa* to the lard and beat it until well blended. As you continue beating, alternate additions of the remaining *masa* with douses of broth, adding enough liquid to give the mixture the consistency of a medium-thick cake batter. Sprinkle in the baking powder and enough

TRADITIONAL VARIATIONS

Tamales with a Variety of Fillings: Prepare the *tamales* according to the recipe, replacing the mixture of shredded chicken and *tomatillo* sauce with one of the following:

   1⅓ cups Shredded Chicken (page 60) or pork mixed with about ½ cup Quick-Cooked Tomato-Chile Sauce (page 41)
   1⅓ cups Shredded Chicken (page 60) or pork mixed with about ½ cup medium-thick Red *Mole* (page 201)
   1½ cups Minced Pork *Picadillo* (page 132)
   1½ cups Northern-Style Shredded Beef (page 131) mixed with ¼ cup chopped olives
   8 ounces flavorful melting cheese (page 328) like Monterey Jack or mild cheddar, cut in 2x¼-inch sticks, and mixed with 1 *chile poblano* (roasted, peeled, seeded and sliced)
   1½ cups Roasted Pepper *Rajas* with Tomato (page 278)

Regional Explorations
Though *tamales* of this sort (with the full array of fillings) are emulated by everyone, they are found in greatest concentration in Central and West-Central Mexico. In San Luis Potosí, every *cafetería* has *tamales* filled with pork or ground-meat *picadillo*; in Puebla (as well as Mexico City), they make them with chicken, pork, green chiles and cheese, and flavor them with *mole*, tomato or *tomatillo* sauce. And Aguascalientes serves the same gen-

salt to generously season the mixture, then beat for about a minute more, until about ½ teaspoon of it will float when placed in a cup of cold water.

3. *The filling.* Mix the shredded chicken with the cooked *tomatillo* sauce and set aside.

4. *Forming and steaming the tamales.* Following the directions on page 177, set up a small steamer and line it with cornhusks; then use the dough to form 16 cornhusk-wrapped *tamales* (each will take about 3 tablespoons dough), filling each one with 1½ tablespoons of the filling. Finally, cover the *tamales* with any remaining cornhusks, set the lid in place, and steam for 1 to 1½ hours, until they come free from the husks.

SWEET *TAMALES*

Tamales de Dulce

As incongruous as sweet *tamales* might sound, the entire Republic of Mexico seems to have a passion for them—made exactly like the savory ones, with sugar in place of salt and a few raisins dropped in for filling. The flavor is difficult to compare to anything else, but I can report that I'd rather have one than a croissant or Danish any day.

This recipe, like the preceding one, is traditional; I have learned many details of the preparation from Josefina Velázquez de León's paperback *Tamales y atoles.* When you're having a *tamal* party, the sweet ones should always be included; but they are also very good for a winter brunch, with Eggs *a la Mexicana* (page 115) and Chocolate *Atole* (page 317). Or remove them from their husks, lightly fry in butter, and serve with sour cream, ham and some fruit for a Sunday night supper.

YIELD: about 12 medium-size *tamales,* serving 6 as a snack

eral assortment, but adds chopped vegetables and red-chile sauce.

Kitchen Spanish
This sort of *tamal* generally carries no name other than the filling—except in Puebla, where they call them *tamales cernidos* (literally "sifted *tamales*") because the dough is (said to be) sifted to remove all the hard-to-grind germs of the corn. Most Pueblan *tamal* makers I talked to, though, buy a dry mix that looks like fine grits.

COOK'S NOTES

Additional Notes
See page 177.

Ingredients
Lard, Sugar and Broth:
Truthfully, the sweet-savory combination is delicious, since neither the lard nor the broth mask the sweet *masa* taste. If you really can't imagine it, replace lard and broth with butter and milk, as a few recipes suggest.

Timing
If the *masa* is on hand, it takes about 45 minutes to prepare the *tamales* and 1 to 1½ hours to steam them.

½ 8-ounce package dried cornhusks

For the dough:

4 ounces (½ cup) good-quality, fresh lard, butter,
    vegetable shortening or combination thereof,
    slightly softened

¾ cup sugar

1 pound (about 2 cups) fresh *masa* for *tamales,*
    store-bought or homemade (page 71)
    OR about 2 cups (1 recipe) Substitute *Masa*
    for *Tamales* (page 181)

About ½ cup any light-flavored poultry broth or
    milk, at room temperature

¼ teaspoon salt

1 teaspoon baking powder

For the filling:

¼ to ⅓ cup raisins or candied fruit

1. *The cornhusks.* Follow the directions on page 177 for soaking the husks, then pick out 12 large ones for wrappers; reserve the remainder for ties and for lining the steamer.

2. *The dough.* Beat the lard, butter and/or vegetable shortening with an electric mixer until very light, about 1 minute. Beat in the sugar and *half* the fresh or substitute *masa.* With the mixer on, alternate additions of the remaining *masa* with douses of broth (or milk), adding enough liquid to give the mixture the consistency of a medium-thick cake batter. Add the salt and baking powder, then beat for 1 minute longer, until a little batter floats in a cup of cold water.

3. *Forming and steaming the tamales.* As outlined on page 177, set up a small steamer and line it with cornhusks; then use the dough to form 12 cornhusk-wrapped *tamales* (each will take about ¼ cup dough), filling each one with a few raisins or a little candied fruit. Finally, top the *tamales* with any remaining cornhusks, cover and steam for 1 to 1½ hours, until they come free from the wrappers.

TRADITIONAL VARIATIONS

Coconut or Nut Tamales: Add ⅔ cup grated fresh coconut or chopped pecans, blanched almonds or hazelnuts (toasted) to the dough and complete as directed.

Red-Tinted Tamales: Typically, the dough of sweet *tamales* is "painted" with a streak of diluted red food coloring.

Pineapple Tamales: Prepare the recipe as directed, replacing the broth or milk with 1 cup pureed fresh pineapple.

CONTEMPORARY IDEAS

Dried-Fruit Tamales: Add ⅔ cup chopped dried fruit (apricots, figs, dates and the like), ¼ cup toasted pine nuts and ¼ teaspoon ground cinnamon to the dough, and complete as directed.

Regional Explorations

Sweet *tamales* are made in the style of the Central/West-Central light-textured variety and are most frequently enjoyed in areas known for good *tamales.* Sometimes they show up studded with coconut, pineapple, even bits of candied fruit. In Veracruz, some market stalls have bright-red strawberry ones, and at the Cenaduría San Antonio in Aguascalientes, they include nuts and *rompope* (egg liqueur).

FRESH-CORN *TAMALES*

Tamales de Elote

These *tamales* have a moist, corny flavor that is beautifully enhanced by their fresh-husk wrappers. Straight from the steamer or browned in butter and served with Thick Cream (page 51) and Mexican *queso fresco* (page 327) or *Salsa Picante* (page 40), there is no better eating.

Most all fresh-corn *tamales* in Mexico are made from 100 percent starchy field corn, which has less moisture and more body than our sweet corn. Unfortunately, a cook can't substitute sweet for field and come out with anything but a soupy mess, so I've adopted the alternative approach I discovered at the Pichanchas restaurant in Tuxtla Gutiérrez, Chiapas: Combine *masa* and fresh corn.

YIELD: about 12 medium-size *tamales*, serving 6 as a snack or appetizer

- 2 large ears fresh sweet corn in their husks
- 1 pound (about 2 cups) fresh *masa* for *tamales*, store-bought or homemade (page 71)
  OR about 2 cups (1 recipe) Substitute *Masa* for *Tamales* (page 181)
- 2 ounces (½ stick) unsalted butter, cut into ½-inch bits and *slightly* softened
- 2 ounces (¼ cup) good-quality, fresh lard, cut into ½-inch bits
- 2 tablespoons sugar
- ½ teaspoon salt
- 1½ teaspoons baking powder

1. *The corn and husks.* With a large knife, cut through the ears of corn just above where cob joins stalk. Carefully remove the husks without tearing, wrap in plastic and set aside. Pull off the corn silk and discard. Slice off the corn kernels and place in the bowl of a food processor. Scrape the cobs with the end of a spoon to remove all the little bits of remaining corn and add to the food processor. Process the corn to a medium-coarse puree.

2. *The dough.* Add the fresh or substitute *masa* to the corn, along with the butter, lard, sugar, salt and baking powder. Pulse

COOK'S NOTES

Additional Notes
See page 177.

Techniques
Making the Dough Without a Food Processor: Coarsely puree the corn in two batches in a blender, without adding any liquid. Beat the butter and lard, then add the *masa*, corn and remaining ingredients. Beat until light.

Ingredients
Fresh Corn: Select ears with their husks intact, since the husk is used to wrap the *tamales*. If fresh corn isn't available, replace it with 2 cups frozen corn (defrosted) and wrap the *tamales* in soaked, dried cornhusks.

Timing
If the *masa* is on hand, you'll need less than an hour to make the *tamales* and 1 to 1½ hours to steam them.

TRADITIONAL VARIATIONS
Fresh-Corn Tamales with Picadillo: Prepare about 1¼ cups Minced Pork *Picadillo* (page 132). Make the *tamales* as directed, using 3 tablespoons dough and 1½ tablespoons *picadillo* for each one.
Fresh-Corn Tamales with Rajas and Cheese: Prepare the *tamales* as directed, using 3 tablespoons dough for each one and filling with 1 *chile poblano* (roasted, peeled, seeded and sliced) and 6 ounces melting cheese (page 328) like Monterey Jack or mild cheddar, cut into 3-inch sticks.

the processor several times, then let it run for 1 minute, until the mixture is light and homogeneous.

3. *Forming and steaming the tamales.* As described on page 180, set up a small steamer and line it with the smallest husks. Then use the dough to form 12 unfilled *tamales* (each will take about ¼ cup) wrapped in the largest of the fresh husks (or use 2 overlapping husks if small). (If the husks roll up, becoming difficult to work with, blanch them briefly in simmering water and they will relax.) Set the *tamales* in the husk-lined steamer, top with additional husks, cover and steam for 1 to 1½ hours, until the *tamales* come free from the husks.

Two-part steamer from Mexico

NUEVO LEÓN–STYLE TAMALES

Tamales Estilo Nuevo León

Moister, more compact and shot through with the flavors of dried chile and spices—these are the small *tamales* from the Northern border state of Nuevo León, and they closely resemble the ones I grew up eating in Oklahoma and Texas. In Mexico, they're not the most widely sought-after variety, but I've included this recipe based on one from Velázquez de León's *Cocina de Nuevo León* because it re-creates a taste many of us enjoy.

You could serve them on your own combination plate, *a la norteamericana,* with Cheese *Chiles Rellenos* (page 246), Crispy-Fried Tacos (page 139), *Frijoles Refritos* (page 269) and Mexican Rice (page 263). I also think they make a very good supper, with just a dollop of fried beans and a salad. At a *tamal* party, they're a real hit.

YIELD: about 16 medium-size *tamales,* serving 4 or 5 as a light main course

NOTE: The sugar may be omitted from the dough in these variations. The quantities may be doubled and the *tamales* formed in banana leaves as directed on page 179.

Regional Explorations
At the *veracruzano* restaurant Fonda el Recuerdo in Mexico City, they serve sweet, butter-fried fresh-corn *tamales* topped with fresh cheese. In Veracruz, though, the popular fresh-corn *tamales* are typically unsweetened, unfried and filled with herby pork. Less adorned fresh-corn *tamales* are *pictes* in Chiapas, *uchepos* in Michoacán; they're popular everywhere.

COOK'S NOTES

Additional Notes
See page 177.

Ingredients
Chiles Anchos and Cascabeles: The Northern *cascabeles* are like our California or New Mexico chile pods and can be replaced one for one. If *anchos* aren't available, the sauce can be made entirely of the California/New Mexico variety, though the flavor isn't as rich.

Timing
If the *masa* is on hand, allow about 1¼ hours to prepare the *tamales* and 1 to 1½ hours to steam them.

½ 8-ounce package dried cornhusks

For the filling:

  12 ounces lean, boneless pork shoulder, cut into ½-inch cubes

  1 teaspoon salt, plus about ¼ teaspoon more for the finished sauce

  3 large (about 1½ ounces total) dried *chiles anchos,* stemmed, seeded and deveined

  2 large (about ⅔ ounce total) dried *chiles cascabeles norteños* or California/New Mexico chiles, stemmed, seeded and deveined

  ⅛ teaspoon black peppercorns (or a scant ¼ teaspoon ground)

  ¼ teaspoon cumin seeds (or a generous ¼ teaspoon ground)

  1 large clove garlic, peeled and roughly chopped

  1 tablespoon lard or vegetable oil

  Sugar, about 1 teaspoon

  2 tablespoon raisins (optional)

  ¼ cup roughly chopped, pitted green olives (optional)

For the dough:

  4 ounces (½ cup) good-quality, fresh lard (see Ingredients notes on page 178)

  1 pound (about 2 cups) fresh *masa* for tortillas or *tamales,* store-bought or homemade (page 71) OR 1¾ cups *masa harina* mixed with 1 cup plus 2 tablespoons hot tap water OR about 2 cups (1 recipe) Substitute *Masa* for *Tamales* (page 181)

  1 teaspoon baking powder

  ½ teaspoon salt

1. *The cornhusks.* Follow the directions on page 177 for soaking the husks, then pick out 16 large ones for wrappers; reserve the remainder for ties and for lining the steamer.

2. *The meat and chiles.* Measure 4 cups water into a medium-size saucepan. Bring to a boil, add the pork and salt, skim off any grayish foam that rises during the first few minutes of simmering, partially cover and simmer over medium heat until the meat is very tender, about 40 minutes.

Tear the chiles into large, flat pieces and toast them a few at a time on a griddle or heavy skillet set over medium heat. With

A few Mexican beers

a metal spatula, press them firmly down until they crackle, blister and change color, then flip them over and press them down again. Remove the toasted chiles to a small bowl, cover with boiling water, weight with a plate to keep them submerged and soak 20 minutes.

3. *The filling.* Drain the broth from the meat, let it stand for a few minutes, then skim the fat off the top. Drain the chiles and place them in a blender jar. Measure the spices into a mortar or spice grinder, pulverize and add to the blender along with the garlic and ¾ cup of the broth. Blend until smooth, then strain through a medium-mesh sieve.

Heat the lard or oil in a medium-size saucepan over medium-high. When hot enough to make a drop of the puree sizzle sharply, add it all at once; stir for 4 or 5 minutes, as it sears and thickens. Add ¾ cup of the broth, reduce the heat to medium-low, cover, simmer 15 minutes, stirring occasionally, then season with salt and sugar; there should be about 1 cup of medium-thick sauce.

While the sauce is simmering, break up the meat into coarse shreds. Measure ¼ cup of the sauce into a small bowl to cool, then stir the remainder into the meat, along with the optional raisins and olives. Set aside to cool.

4. *The dough.* If the lard is very soft, refrigerate it to firm a little. Then, with an electric mixer, beat it until very light, about 1 minute. Add *half* the fresh or substitute *masa* and the ¼ cup cooled sauce to the lard and beat until well blended. As you continue beating, alternate additions of the remaining *masa* with douses of the cooled meat broth, ultimately adding about ½ cup, or enough to give the mixture the consistency of medium-thick cake batter. Finally, sprinkle in the baking powder and salt, then beat for about 1 minute, until a little dough will float when dropped into a cup of cold water.

5. *Forming and steaming the tamales.* Following the directions on page 180, set up a small steamer and line it with cornhusks; then use the dough to form about 16 husk-wrapped *tamales* (each will take about 3 tablespoons dough), filling each one with 1½ tablespoons of the meat filling. Finally, cover the *tamales* with any remaining cornhusks, set the lid in place and steam for 1 to 1½ hours, until they come free from the husks.

Dried <u>*ancho*</u> *chiles*

YUCATECAN BAKED *TAMAL* IN BANANA LEAVES

Pibipollo

The rustic-looking big corn cakes, half wrapped in the brittle banana leaves that covered them during baking, sit in baskets or on shelves in half a dozen food stalls in the Mérida market. *Pibipollos* they call them, or a more rhythmic-sounding name in Mayan, and they're redolent with the full-flavored *achiote* seasoning paste and the strong scent of the leaves.

This recipe, based on proportions from the *Recetario mexicano del maíz*, closely replicates one I tasted in nearby Campeche—light, moist, tender and made with coarse-ground (instead of the typical smoother, denser) *masa*. It's a good illustration of how thorough beating makes light *tamales* (even without baking powder).

Pibipollo is the perfect dish to make for an informal Sunday supper with spirited friends. You could pair it with a salad and serve a crisp Corona beer or Almond-Rice Cooler (page 309) to drink.

YIELD: one 8-inch-square *tamal*, serving 4 as a light main course

For the filling:

2 chicken leg-and-thigh portions

1½ teaspoons *Achiote* Seasoning Paste (page 66)

1 sprig *epazote* (see Ingredients in Cook's Notes)

1 ripe, medium-small tomato, roasted or boiled (page 352), cored, peeled and chopped into ½-inch pieces

OR ½ 15-ounce can tomatoes, drained and chopped into ½-inch pieces

⅓ cup (about 3 ounces) fresh *masa* for *tamales*, store-bought or homemade (page 71)

OR a generous ½ cup *masa harina* mixed with 6 tablespoons hot tap water

Salt, about ⅛ teaspoon

For the dough:

6 ounces (¾ cup) good-quality, fresh lard (see Ingredients notes on page 178)

COOK'S NOTES

Techniques

Adding Liquid, Beating the Dough and Preparing It in the Food Processor: See page 177.

Cooking with Achiote: Other recipes may call for coloring oil or lard by frying the whole *achiote* in it. It's common in the Caribbean, but I don't think it adds as much flavor as using the whole seed ground, which is the common Yucatecan method.

Ingredients

Epazote: Though typically Yucatecan, the flavor is light in this dish; replace it, if necessary, with flat-leaf parsley.

Fresh Masa, Lard and Banana Leaves: See page 178.

Timing and Advance Preparation

If the *masa* and *achiote* paste are on hand, you'll need about 1¼ hours to prepare the dish and 1 hour to bake it. The filling may be prepared a couple of days ahead, covered and refrigerated; or the whole dish may be assembled, covered and refrigerated 2 hours before baking. While it can be baked ahead and rewarmed, it is best just after it comes from the oven.

Regional Explorations

There is quite a variety of these big, leaf-wrapped *tamales* sold around the Yucatecan markets, filled with chicken, pork or the little fresh black-skinned bean they call *espelón*. All of them are *pibes* (a catchall term that refers to their originally having

1½ pounds (about 3 cups) fresh *masa* for *tam-ales,* store-bought or homemade (page 71) OR about 3 cups (1½ recipes) Substitute *Masa* for *Tamales* (page 181)
About 1 cup broth (preferably light-flavored poul-try broth), at room temperature
2 teaspoons *Achiote* Seasoning Paste (page 66)
Salt, about ¾ teaspoon (depending on the salti-ness of the broth)

For wrapping the tamal:
2 unbroken, 12-inch squares of banana leaf

1. *The filling.* Measure 3 cups of water into a medium-size saucepan, bringing to a boil and add the chicken. Skim off the grayish foam that rises during the first few minutes of simmer-ing, then add the *achiote* seasoning, *epazote* and tomato. Par-tially cover and simmer over medium heat for 25 minutes; if there is time, let the chicken cool in the broth.

Remove the chicken and *epazote* from the broth, set the pan over medium-high heat and reduce the liquid to 1⅓ cups. Skin, bone and coarsely shred the chicken meat.

Place the fresh or reconstituted *masa* in a blender jar or food processor and pour in ¾ cup of the reduced broth. Cover *loosely* and blend until smooth. Strain through a medium-mesh sieve into the broth remaining in the saucepan, set over medium heat and whisk constantly as the mixture thickens to the consistency of thick white sauce. Remove from the heat, season with salt, stir in the shredded chicken and cool.

2. *The dough.* If the lard is very soft, refrigerate it to firm a little. Then, with an electric mixer, beat it for about a minute, until light. Beat *half* the fresh or substitute *masa* into the lard. With the machine still going, beat in alternate additions of the remaining *masa* and broth, adding enough liquid to give the mixture the consistency of a medium-thick cake batter. Beat in the *achiote* paste and enough salt to generously season the mix-ture. Continue beating until a little of the mixture will float in a cup of cold water.

3. *Forming and baking the tamal.* Preheat the oven to 350°. Trim and steam or flame-soften the squares of banana leaf as described on page 177. Fit 1 piece, shiny-side up, into an 8-inch-square pan, folding the corners so the leaf follows the con-tour of the pan. Spread ⅔ of the dough over the bottom and up the sides, then spoon in the filling. Spread the remaining dough in an 8-inch square on the shiny side of the other leaf, then flip it over onto the pan, completely covering the filling.

been baked in a *pib* ("oven") in the ground), with the everyday chicken-filled *pibipollo* measur-ing in at 10 to 12 inches in di-ameter and a good inch thick.

Mexican cooks know many home-style versions of *tamales de cazuela*—two layers of *masa* with a filling in between, baked tightly covered in a *cazuela* ("casserole"). The *pibipollo* is similar (usually with nothing but banana leaves to contain it), and it's public (rather than home-style) food. In fact, it's one of the most celebrated fiesta dishes in Yucatán (associ-ated most closely with All Saints' Day).

Kitchen Spanish
If, in your own explorations, you become confused by ter-minology, remember that *muc-bipollo, pibipollo, shacabihua, cortados, pib de pollo* or just plain *pibes* all refer to more or less the same special dish.

Fold in the banana leaf that overhangs the edges, then *tightly* cover the pan with foil.

Bake for about 1 hour, until the top leaf comes easily away from the dough. Let stand, covered, for 10 or 15 minutes before serving.

Lava rock grinding stone (metate)

OAXACAN-STYLE *TAMALES*

Tamales Estilo Oaxaqueño

I knew I'd love these *tamales* the first time I smelled the fragrance rise from their steaming pot. Oaxacan María Villalobos showed me how to make them back in 1978 in Mexico City, and the lesson included everything from shopping for the prized, large-kernel corn (*maíz cacahuacincle*) at Merced Market, to grinding the cooked corn for the dough and folding the banana leaves to hold the *mole*-laced insides.

What follows is based on María's recipe, though I've called for Pueblan *mole* in place of the classic black Oaxacan one; peppers for the latter, unfortunately, aren't available in the United States. The *tamales* make a very nice supper dish, nestled in their opened wrappers and served with a dab of *Frijoles Refritos* (page 269), a bowl of fresh greens and the traditional cup of Mexican Hot Chocolate (page 314) or Chocolate *Atole* (*Champurrado,* page 317).

COOK'S NOTES

Additional Notes
See page 177.

Ingredients
Mole: If you make your own *mole,* you can color the dough with the fat skimmed off the *mole* (as they do in Oaxaca) rather than the sauce itself. For flavoring these *tamales,* you could eke by with a good brand of thinned, bottled *mole.*

Timing
With the *masa* and fillings on hand, the *tamales* take about 1¼ hours to make; steaming takes 1 to 1½ hours.

CONTEMPORARY IDEAS
Yucatecan-Style Fish Tamales:
Prepare 1 recipe Yucatecan To-

YIELD: about 10 large *tamales,* serving 5 as a main course
10 unbroken, 12-inch squares of banana leaf

For the dough:

8 ounces (1 cup) good-quality, fresh lard (see Ingredients notes on page 178)

2 pounds (about 4 cups) fresh *masa* for *tamales,* store-bought or homemade (page 71)
OR about 4 cups (2 recipes) Substitute *Masa* for *Tamales* (page 181)

About 1⅓ cups broth (preferably light-flavored poultry broth), at room temperature

1½ tablespoons medium-thick *Mole Poblano* (page 197) (see Ingredients in Cook's Notes)

1½ teaspoons baking powder

Salt, about 1 teaspoon (depending on the saltiness of the broth)

For the filling:

About 1½ cups Shredded Chicken (page 60)

About 1½ cups medium-thick *Mole Poblano* (page 197) (see Ingredients in Cook's Notes)

1. *The banana leaves.* Follow the directions on page 177 for trimming and steaming or flame-softening the squares of banana leaf. Set extra leaves aside for lining the steamer.

2. *The dough.* If the lard is very soft, refrigerate it to firm a little. With an electric mixer, beat the lard for a minute or so, until very light. Beat in *half* the fresh or substitute *masa.* Continue beating as you alternate additions of the remaining *masa* and the broth; add enough liquid to give the mixture the consistency of a medium-thick cake batter. Beat in the 1½ tablespoons *mole* and the baking powder, then generously season the batter with salt. Continue beating the mixture until a little of the mixture will float in a cup of cold water.

3. *Forming and steaming the tamales.* As described on page 177, set up a large steamer and line it with pieces of banana leaves; then, use the dough to form 10 banana leaf–wrapped *tamales* (each will take about ½ cup), filling each one with 2 tablespoons of the chicken and 2 tablespoons of the *mole.* Finally, lay any remaining banana leaves over the *tamales,* cover and steam for 1 to 1½ hours, until they come free from the leaves.

mato Sauce (page 42), simmering it until quite thick. Cut 1 pound boneless, skinless meaty fish fillets (like halibut, sea bass or shark) into small strips. Make the *tamales* as directed, flavoring the *masa* with 2 teaspoons *Achiote* Seasoning Paste (page 66) rather than *mole,* and filling each one with a portion of fish and 2 tablespoons of sauce.

Regional Explorations
These *tamales* are sold, served and eaten everywhere in Oaxaca City—from the market stalls to the nice restaurants. They are moister, perhaps a little more compact than the Central Mexican–style *tamales;* the dough is always flavored a little and the leaves give them a good herby flavor.

MOLES

❖

Mole, Puebla market

Mole, the Spaniards said when they heard the Aztecs call a stew or sauce *molli.* It was a useful, well-used word that continued to stick to many traditional dishes, while the newly arrived words *guisado* and *salsa* landed on preparations with shallower roots, with a less indigenous profile. Today, the word *mole* has survived in *guacamole* (literally "avocado" plus "sauce") and in *molcajete* ("mortar," literally "sauce" plus "bowl") and in dozens of other culinary terms; and, of course, it survives intact as the names of a whole collection of uniquely Mexican main courses.

Is *mole*—that is, does *mole* refer to—the sauce only? Or is it the stew, meat and all? These questions have been debated for hundreds of years, though I'd be inclined to say the point is moot. Mexican sauces are not the "napping" variety—as would be a light butter sauce or hollandaise, say. Rather, the sauces *are* the dish—the bulk, the vegetables, the flavorings, the nutrition. And anyone who's been served a plate of *mole poblano* anywhere but the most elegant restaurants knows that the "sauce" comes in what seems inordinately large quantities. The sauce and the stew, it seems to me, are one and the same.

Of course, all this historical detail amounts to little when you say *mole* today . . . when you say *mole poblano.* Nonnatives immediately think "chocolate chicken," while natives' mouths water to visions of a dark, complex sauce made of dried chiles, nuts, seeds, flavoring vegetables, spices and, yes, a bit of chocolate. The famous Pueblan specialty, originally called *mole de olores* ("fragrant *mole*"), took its place of origin as a surname, but today one need only say *mole* to be understood as meaning *mole poblano.*

Should you summon the energy to move past the lauded Pueblan dish, other *moles* are available at easy reach—spanning the spectrum of culinary colors and textures and flavors. But not just any Mexican stew/sauce seems to qualify: They're always cooked sauces, rather than the condiments we spoon onto tacos; they're red-chile sauces, or ones thick with nuts and seeds, or ones made special with herbs and spices. Like *mole poblano,* many are egalitarian celebration dishes of long standing; they're as at home in market *fondas* as they are in refined restaurants.

Some sort of dark red (roughly Pueblan-style) *mole* is made all through Mexico. In Yucatán, it's known but certainly not indigenous; there is, however, a local *chirmole* (literally "chile" plus "sauce")—a pungent, black chile stew/sauce—but its flavor is very different from that of any other *mole.* Many regions know a green *mole* made with *tomatillos,* green chiles, herbs and nuts or seeds to thicken and add flavor. And some have the simple *clemole* (literally "hot" or "cooked" plus "sauce"), though it isn't really a public-food offering. Then comes Oaxaca with its seven *moles:* black, two brick-red ones (one simpler and sweeter, the other more complex), green, yellow, a dark, gravylike one called *chichilo* and the popular fruit-filled, mild red *manchamanteles.*

Elsewhere, the list goes on to include a chile-red soup called *mole de olla, moles* made of lamb *barbacoa,* and others thickened with ground seeds from the leguminous *guaje* trees (*gausmole*). There are all sorts of surviving stews/sauces they call *mole* in one form or another, but there are none that surpass the rich, dark-skinned Mexican beauty *mole poblano.* None that bring to the thick earthenware *cazuelas* more of the New World complexity and ingenuity or offer more of the native festal delight.

I've spelled out how to make that famous *mole* in the pages that follow. Most of you won't need to be convinced that the involved preparations for the Mexican National Dish are more than worth the effort. In addition, I've included recipes for a representative variety of other *moles,* all of which are simpler and equally delicious in their own ways.

For *mole* recipes in other chapters, see "*Mole*" in the Index.

Keys to Perfect Nut- and Seed-Thickened Sauces

Pureeing Nut- or Seed-Thickened Sauces: For centuries cooks have crushed nuts, spices and chiles on a three-legged stone *metate;* the effect is the same as stone grinding through a mill, though few of us have that option either. So we're left with the blender, which really chops rather than crushes. These hints will help get the smoothest texture. (1) Don't puree more than half a blenderful at a time. (2) Don't add any more liquid than is necessary to keep the mixture moving through the blades; if too thin, the entire mixture won't be drawn through the blades. (3) Stir the ingredients, blend on low until everything is uniformly chopped, then blend on high until smooth when rubbed between your fingers. (4) Always strain the mixture. (5) If the sauce looks coarse or gritty after simmering, reblend it, lightly covered, until smooth (a step not generally done in Mexico).

Serving Nut- or Seed-Thickened Sauces: As these sauces cook (or when they're made ahead and refrigerated), they will thicken considerably. The consistency should always be adjusted with a little broth, if necessary, just before serving. Once spooned onto a serving platter, the surface of a nut- and seed-thickened sauce may lose its sheen; spooning on a new coating restores its full beauty.

Mixing and Matching Mexican Sauces and Meats

Most all the saucy Mexican stewed-meat dishes are very flexible when it comes to which sauces go with which meats. I've written most of the recipes to yield about 3 cups of sauce (enough for 4 or more servings) so you can easily interchange them with different meat preparations; simply prepare the sauces with whatever broth complements the meat. Sauces most commonly served with a variety of meats are: *Mole Poblano* (page 197), Red *Mole* (page 201), Orange-Red *Mole* (page 158), Green Pumpkinseed *Mole* (page 203), Pumpkinseed *Pipián* (page 225), *Veracruzana* Sauce (page 212), *Adobo* Sauce (page 254), Northern-Style Red-Chile Sauce (page 250), Quick-Cooked Tomato-Chile Sauce (page 41), and Quick-Cooked *Tomatillo* Sauce (page 42). The various meat preparation methods are: chicken (page 61, Steps 1–3), duck (page 227, Steps 1, 3 and 6), turkey (page 199, Steps 1, 9, 11–12), tongue (page 213), pork (page 249, Step 1, leaving the meat in large pieces) and beef (page 132, Step 1, leaving the meat in large pieces).

THE STORIES OF *MOLE POBLANO*

There continue to simmer some engaging debates—between the covers of cookery books, on paper place mats and in the little pamphlets they hand out in Puebla—about just when, where and why *mole poblano* came to be *mole poblano* (not to mention whether the responsible hands were pale or Indian-brown). This dish, after all, is *the most famous* Mexican dish—though consumed considerably less than tacos, my instinct tells me. Clearly, it's too special to eat day after day: What tongue wouldn't eventually fail to appreciate the breadth of chile flavors embroidered elaborately with textured nuts and seeds, with the varied bursts of herbs, spices and chocolate, with the depths and heights of flavorful fruits and vegetables? All of it from a deep, dark sauce that the uninitiated say looks un-approachable . . . until they're captivated by the aroma of a dish originally known as *mole de olor—mole* of fragrance.

The proselytizing paper place mat I found lying before me one morning in Puebla, with its picture of angels holding a pot of True *Mole* (with an enormous turkey leg sticking up through the sauce), describes Sor Andrea's cleverness in surprising her seventeenth-century bishop with her newly created *mole* at the city's Santa Rosa Convent. But the passionate cookbooklet given to me in the tourist office, detailing the stews of the nuns, lays forth with what can only be described as religious fervor how Bishop Fernández de Santa Cruz requested Sor Andrea to concoct the Best Dish for Don Tomás Antonio de la Cerda y Aragón, Viceroy of New Spain, on the third Sunday before Lent, one of the years between 1680 and 1688. And I, for one, feel obliged to read the hushed pages reverently, to listen to the debates carefully, to walk over the sacred tiles of the Santa Rosa kitchen with studious consideration. As amused as I might sometimes be about the seriousness that discussions of *mole poblano* can induce, I'm captivated by the pride and continuity that these discussions have engendered.

Paco Ignacio Taibo was captivated enough to write a book about it all a few years ago (keeping his tongue at least as much in his cheek as in the sauce). You see, Sr. Taibo believes, as I have for years, that Mexico has a strong affinity for baroque, and Sor Andrea, of course, was directing culinary operations at the height of the great baroque clamor. "*Mole*," he says, "wouldn't be under-stood outside a baroque world, and Mexican baroque in Puebla has its most excellent site." That's only the beginning for Taibo:

> . . . *in the beautiful kitchen, adorned with [Talavera] tiles . . . [and] fra-grant with spices and chocolate, Sor Andrea had to make very difficult decisions. [She] decided to go in by the terribly complex ways of gastronomic baroque and summed up in one dish all of the luxury of the American country; it was a great*

moment, above all a valiant moment, very valiant. To fry an egg is a serious thing, as anyone well knows who can fry one well, but to make a mole before anyone else is an imaginative thing and one that only fearless souls could bring to pass.

I can imagine the act of mixing so many products in that kitchen enlightened by the brilliance of Puebla de Los Angeles; [but] what I find difficult to imagine is how the dinner ever took place.

I can imagine the coming and going of the nuns, ladened with trays and pitchers, adorned with their professional smiles and a whispering wonder.

I find it more difficult to [imagine] that the mole arrived at the table without the anxious censure of the Mother Superior, who could have seen in that plate the absolute break with the Court in Madrid.

But what is impossible to imagine is the expression of the Viceroy . . . when he came face to face with this dark-colored, thick-looking flattery of uncertain fragrance.

What did that [Viceroy] say when he was confronted with mole?
—PACO IGNACIO TAIBO I, Breviario del
mole poblano *[author's translation]*

Well, I remember what *I* said, that afternoon in Ixmiquilpan, Hidalgo, when I was sixteen and my tongue was lured by some of the complex swarthy sauce and a bit of meat. "It's different," I think the words were. But as the first forkful led to the second and third and fourth, I was hooked, I was ready to order seconds. Alas, it doesn't happen for everyone, even someone as worldly as Kate Simon, the insightful explorer of foreign turf. "The visitor soon hears about the glories of *mole*," she writes in *Mexico: Places and Pleasures*. ". . . Obviously, it is a thing to respect, but no non-Mexican has been known to develop a passion for it . . ." I'm sorry I've never met her.

DARK AND SPICY *MOLE* WITH TURKEY

Mole Poblano de Guajolote

After comparing dozens of recipes for Pueblan *mole*, I've come up with this version, which re-creates the rich-tasting complexity of what you'll be served in Mexico's gastronomic capital. Even with all the huge mounds of prepared *mole* pastes avail-

COOK'S NOTES

Techniques
Pureeing and Serving Nut-Thickened Sauces: See page 195.
Fat and Mole: In many Mexican sauces, the dollop of fat is thought to be essential for

ble in the Puebla market, many of the *fonda* and restaurant cooks still insist on preparing their own from scratch. Which underscores Paco Ignacio Taibo's opinion: "Its recipe isn't a recipe, but recipes. . . . For *mole* there are as many recipes as there are imaginations." It's a remarkable dish. And it's worth the effort.

YIELD: 12 to 15 servings, with 3 quarts of sauce

The meat:

> a 10- to 12-pound turkey

The chiles:

> 16 medium (about 8 ounces total) dried *chiles mulatos*
>
> 5 medium (about 2½ ounces total) dried *chiles anchos*
>
> 6 (about 2 ounces total) dried *chiles pasillas*
>
> 1 canned *chile chipotle*, seeded (optional)

The nuts, seeds, flavorings and thickeners:

> ¼ cup sesame seeds, plus a little extra for garnish
>
> ½ teaspoon coriander seeds
>
> ½ cup lard or vegetable oil, plus a little more if needed
>
> A heaping ⅓ cup (2 ounces) unskinned almonds
>
> ⅓ cup (about 2 ounces) raisins
>
> ½ medium onion, sliced
>
> 2 cloves garlic, peeled
>
> 1 corn tortilla, stale or dried out
>
> 2 slices firm white bread, stale or dried out
>
> 1 ripe, large tomato, roasted or boiled (page 352), cored and peeled
>
> OR ¾ 15-ounce can tomatoes, well drained

The spices:

> ⅔ 3.3-ounce tablet (about 2 ounces) Mexican chocolate, roughly chopped
>
> 10 black peppercorns (or a scant ¼ teaspoon ground)
>
> 4 cloves (or about ⅛ teaspoon ground)
>
> ½ teaspoon aniseed (or a generous ½ teaspoon ground)
>
> 1 inch cinnamon stick (or about 1 teaspoon ground)

good flavor. But as Paula Wolfert has so elegantly pointed out in her *Cooking of South-West France*, the fat's flavor is water soluble: Let it cook with the "stew" to add its savor, then skim the stuff off.

Balancing the Flavor of Mole: The flavors of *mole* begin to fuse during cooking; a day later, maybe two, the fusion is complete and the flavor is truly *mole*. For that reason, I add an initial measurement of salt and sugar, then I fine-tune those seasonings just before serving. Each underscores and balances a different face of this complex sauce.

Ingredients

Chiles: To prepare an authentic *mole poblano*, you must have the revered triumvirate of *mulato, ancho* and *pasilla; chipotle* isn't critical, though it adds a dimension I like. Without the right chiles, it just won't work. If they're lacking, try the Red *Mole* with One Chile variation (page 201).

Mexican Chocolate: In my opinion, the style of chocolate isn't as critical as the variety of chiles; the Mexican kind can be replaced in this recipe with 2 tablespoons unsweetened cocoa.

Timing and Advance Preparation

From start to finish, *mole poblano* takes about 6 hours (if the broth is on hand), about 3 hours of which are relatively unattended simmering or baking. That approach, however, doesn't allow the *mole* to develop the best flavor (nor does it leave the cook in much of a mood for a party). It is easiest to spread the preparations over 4 days. Day 1—assemble the ingredients and complete the

To finish the dish:
    ¼ **cup lard or vegetable oil**
    About 2½ quarts poultry broth (page 61), preferably made from turkey
    Salt, about 2 teaspoons (depending on the saltiness of the broth)
    Sugar, about ¼ cup

1. *The turkey.* If your butcher won't cut up your turkey, do it yourself: Cut the leg-and-thigh quarters off the body of the turkey, then slice through the joint that connects the thigh to the leg. Cut the two wings free from the breast. Then set the turkey up on the neck end and, with a cleaver, cut down both sides of the backbone and remove it. Split the breast in half. Reserve the back, neck and innards (except the liver) to make the broth. Cover the turkey pieces and refrigerate.

2. *The setup.* As with any recipe calling for twenty-six different ingredients, half the battle is won by getting yourself properly set up. Organize the ingredients as follows: stem, seed and carefully devein the dried chiles, reserving 2 teaspoons of the seeds; tear the chiles into flat pieces. If using the *chipotle,* seed it and set aside. Make measured mounds of sesame seeds, coriander seeds, almonds, raisins and onion. Lay out the garlic, tortilla and bread. Place the tomato in a large bowl and break it up, then add the chopped chocolate to it. Pulverize the remaining spices, using a mortar or spice grinder, then add to the tomato and chocolate. Have the lard or oil and broth at ready access.

3. *Toasting the seeds.* In a medium-size skillet set over medium heat, dry-toast the chile, sesame and coriander seeds, one kind at a time, stirring each until it has lightly browned. Add to the tomato mixture.

4. *Frying and reconstituting the chiles.* Turn on the exhaust fan to suck up the pungent chile fumes. Measure ¼ cup of the lard or oil into the skillet and, when hot, fry the chile pieces a few at a time for several seconds per side, until they develop a nut-brown color. Remove them to a large bowl, draining as much fat as possible back into the skillet. Cover the chiles with boiling water, weight with a plate to keep them submerged, soak at least 1 hour, then drain and add the *chile chipotle.*

5. *Frying the almonds, raisins, onion and garlic.* Heat the remaining ¼ cup of lard or oil in the skillet, add the almonds and stir frequently until browned through, about 4 minutes. Remove, draining well, and add to the tomato mixture. Fry the raisins for a minute or so, stirring constantly as they puff and brown. Scoop out, draining well, and add to the tomato mix-

toasting/frying in Steps 3 through 6. BUT DO NOT SOAK THE CHILES. Day 2—cut up the turkey and make your broth. Day 3—soak the chiles and make the sauce; brown and bake the turkey. Cool the turkey and sauce separately, then cover and refrigerate. Day 4—skin and slice the turkey, heat with the sauce and serve.

MENU SUGGESTIONS
Mexico's twentieth-century gastro-historian Amando Farga describes the solemn vision of Sor Andrea with her wooden platter of chocolated sauce, forming a trinity with a bearer of *tamales* and one of *pulque* (the ages-old fermented maguey juice). That was fine for Sor Andrea, but the *pulque* is really impossible for us and I think *tamales* don't work well for sopping up the sauce. (Even though from one book to the next they'll tell you to serve *mole* with simple unfilled *tamales,* I've never seen it served that way myself.) Regardless of its accompaniments, *mole poblano* means fiesta, celebration: It should always be served as a special attraction. It makes a very nice buffet dish, or, for a more formal, traditional meal, start with Tortilla Soup (page 96), accompany your *mole* with Pueblan Rice (page 264) and hot tortillas, then end with a stunning Almond Flan (page 283). I'd offer three drinks: a hearty dry red wine like Zinfandel, malty Dos Equis beer and Sparkling Limeade (page 311).

ture. Cook the onion and garlic, stirring frequently, until well browned, 8 to 9 minutes. Press on them to rid them of fat, and remove to the mixing bowl with the tomato and other fried ingredients.

6. *Frying the tortilla and bread.* If needed, add a little more fat, then fry the tortilla until browned, break it up and add to the mixing bowl. Lay the bread in the pan, quickly flip it over to coat both sides with fat, then brown it on both sides. Tear into large pieces and add to the tomato mixture.

7. *Pureeing the mixture.* Stir the mixture thoroughly and scoop ¼ of it into a blender jar, along with ½ cup of the broth. Blend until very smooth, adding a *little* more liquid if the mixture won't move through the blades. Strain through a medium-mesh sieve. Puree the 3 remaining batches, adding ½ cup broth to each one; strain.

8. *Pureeing the chiles.* Puree the drained chiles in 3 batches, adding about ½ cup of broth (plus a little more if needed) to each one; strain through the same sieve into a separate bowl.

9. *Frying the turkey.* Heat ¼ cup of the lard or oil in a large (at least 8-quart) kettle over medium-high. Dry the turkey pieces with paper towels and brown them in the lard in several batches, 3 or 4 minutes per side. Remove to a roasting pan large enough to hold them comfortably. Set aside at room temperature until the sauce is ready.

10. *Frying and simmering the sauce.* Pour off the excess fat from the kettle, leaving a light coating on the bottom. Return to the heat for a minute, then add the chile puree and stir constantly until darkened and thick, about 5 minutes. Add the other bowlful of puree and stir several minutes longer, until the mixture thickens once again. Mix in 5 cups of broth, partially cover, reduce the heat to medium-low and simmer gently 45 minutes, stirring occasionally. Finally, season with salt and sugar and, if the sauce is thicker than heavy cream, thin it with a little broth.

11. *Baking the turkey.* Preheat the oven to 350°. Pour the sauce over the turkey, cover the pan and bake until the bird is tender, about 2 hours. Remove the turkey from the pan and spoon the fat off the sauce (or, if serving later, refrigerate so the fat will congeal and be easy to remove).

12. *Presentation.* Let the turkey cool, skin it and cut the meat from the bones in large pieces, slicing against the grain; lay out the meat in 2 or 3 large baking dishes.

Shortly before serving, pour the sauce over the turkey, cover and heat in a 350° oven for 15 to 20 minutes.

Immediately before you carry the *mole* to your guests, spoon some sauce from around the edges over the turkey to give it a glistening coat, then sprinkle with sesame seeds.

Evolution of a *Mole* Lover
My recommendation, especially for meat-and-potato palates, is to start with Pork *Enchiladas* with Orange-Red *Mole* (page 158), follow with Red *Mole* (page 201), then proceed to the famous sauce . . . preferably at one of the little *fondas* in Puebla's La Victoria market, where the stuff gurgles away in enormous, aromatic *cazuelas*.

Mexican wooden cooking spoons

RICH RED *MOLE* WITH CHICKEN

Mole Rojo con Pollo

As famous as the Mexican *moles* are (and even though most are called *mole poblano*), not all of them are the dark, deep, anise-scented sauce from Puebla. No, the *moles* that spell out celebration in Guadalajara, Morelia, Guanajuato and just about everywhere else are lighter and a little more easy-going. Over the years, I've pulled together recipes from Otomí Indians, Zapotecs, city dwellers, nuns and even pure-blood Mexican Spaniards, and I've come up with this deliciously compromising—almost addictive—*mole* . . . a *mole* that I think would appeal to anyone who wasn't weaned in Puebla.

Such a special dish needs to be featured in a traditional dinner that runs from *Tlalpeño* Soup (page 97), made without chicken, through Mexican Rice (page 263) and the *mole*, to Caramel Crepes (page 294).

YIELD: 4 servings, with 4½ to 5 cups of sauce

The chiles:

    4 medium (about 2 ounces total) dried *chiles anchos*, stemmed, seeded and deveined

    2 medium (about 1 ounce total) dried *chiles mulatos*, stemmed, seeded and deveined

    1 medium (about ⅓ ounce) dried *chile pasilla*, stemmed, seeded and deveined

The nuts, seeds, flavorings and thickeners:

    1½ tablespoons sesame seeds, plus a little more for garnish

    About ⅓ cup lard or vegetable oil, plus a little more if needed

    2 heaping tablespoons (about 1 ounce) unskinned peanuts

    2 tablespoons raisins

    ¼ medium onion, thickly sliced

    1 clove garlic, peeled

    ⅓ ripe, small plantain, peeled and diced (optional)

    ½ corn tortilla, stale or dried out

    1 slice firm white bread, stale or dried out

COOK'S NOTES

Techniques
Notes on pureeing and serving nut-thickened sauces are on page 195. For notes on the role of fat in *mole* making and balancing the flavors of *mole*, see page 198.

Ingredients
Chiles: If all 3 chiles aren't available, prepare the one-chile *mole* variation below.
Mexican Chocolate: If this chocolate is unavailable, substitute 1 tablespoon unsweetened cocoa.

Timing and Advance Preparation
This *mole* takes about 3½ hours to prepare, of which 45 minutes are unattended simmering. It may be finished up to 2 days ahead; store the chicken and sauce separately, covered and refrigerated. Reheat the chicken in the sauce, thinning if necessary.

1 ripe, medium-small tomato, roasted or boiled (page 352), cored, peeled, and roughly chopped
OR ½ 15-ounce can tomatoes, well drained and roughly chopped
4 ounces (about 3 medium) *tomatillos,* husked, washed and simmered until tender
OR ½ 13-ounce can *tomatillos,* drained

The herbs and spices:

¼ of a 3.3 ounce tablet (about ¾ ounce) Mexican chocolate, chopped
½ teaspoon dried oregano
¼ teaspoon dried thyme
1 bay leaf
8 peppercorns (or about ⅛ teaspoon ground)
3 cloves (or a scant ⅛ teaspoon ground)
1 inch cinnamon stick (or about 1 teaspoon ground)

The meat:

1 medium (3½-pound) chicken, quartered (page 225)

To finish the dish:

About 5 cups chicken broth (page 61)
Salt, about 1 teaspoon (depending on the saltiness of the broth)
Sugar, about 1 tablespoon

1. *The setup.* Following the same general procedure described in Step 2 on page 199, set up the ingredients, completing all initial preparations detailed in the list of ingredients. Combine the tomato, *tomatillos,* chocolate, oregano and thyme in a large bowl; pulverize the bay leaf and spices, and add to the bowl.

2. *Toasting the sesame seeds.* Scoop the sesame seeds into a medium-size skillet set over medium heat, and stir until they turn golden brown. Scrape in with the tomato.

3. *Frying and reconstituting the chiles.* As directed in Step 4 on page 199, fry the chiles in *3 tablespoons* lard or oil, then reconstitute in boiling water and drain.

4. *The frying continues.* Return the skillet to the heat. (If there isn't much fat—or if you run low in the following frying steps—add a little more, but drain everything well or the *mole* will be greasy.) As directed in Steps 5 and 6 on pages 199–200, fry the almonds, raisins, onion, garlic, tortilla and bread;

TRADITIONAL VARIATIONS

Red Mole with One Chile: Prepare the *mole* as directed, using only *chiles anchos* (8 medium—about 4 ounces), omitting the tomatoes and using ½ tablet (about 1¾ ounces) chocolate.

Kitchen Spanish

The word *mole,* the Spanish transliteration of the Aztec counterpart for *sauce,* is still generically used by some Mexican cooks to mean any of the native, complex, cooked sauces. Still, *mole . . .* when it's said with that special pause and emphasis, means, **the** *mole:* the queen of sauces, with its dark, dried chiles and all.

if using plantain, fry it until golden (4 or 5 minutes) after the onion and garlic have been removed from the skillet.

5. *Pureeing the mixture.* Stir the mixture well, then scoop *half* into a blender jar, add ½ cup of the broth and blend until smooth, adding a *little* more broth if the mixture won't move through the blades. Strain through a medium-mesh sieve. Puree the remainder with another ½ cup of broth and strain.

6. *Pureeing the chiles.* Puree the chiles in 2 batches in the blender, adding ¼ cup of broth to each one (plus a little extra if needed to keep the mixture moving through the blades); strain through the sieve into a separate bowl.

7. *Browning the chicken.* Heat 1½ tablespoons of the lard or oil in a large (8-quart) kettle over medium-high. Dry the chicken pieces, then brown them in the hot fat, about 3 minutes per side. Remove and set aside.

8. *Frying and simmering the sauce.* Following the directions in Step 10 on page 200, fry and simmer the sauce, stirring in 2½ cups of the broth (rather than the 5 cups called for).

9. *Simmering the chicken.* Just before serving, bring the sauce to a simmer over medium heat, add the dark-meat quarters and cook 10 minutes, partially covered. Add the breast pieces and cook about 14 minutes longer, until tender.

10. *Presentation.* Remove the meat from the sauce and arrange on a warm, deep serving platter. Skim off any fat that is floating on top, then pour the sauce over the chicken, sprinkle on some sesame seeds and serve.

a sampling of regional cazuelas

GREEN PUMPKINSEED *MOLE* WITH CHICKEN BREASTS

Mole Verde con Pechugas de Pollo

Practically everything red in the national *mole* is replaced by something green in *mole verde:* tomatoes with *tomatillos,* red

COOK'S NOTES

Techniques
Serving Nut-Thickened Sauces: See page 195. The fine chopping of a spice grinder and blender is not the crushing/grinding of a *metate,* so

chiles with fresh green ones, spices with leafy herbs. But where dried chiles make up the bulky thickness in the former, here pulverized pumpkinseeds give a nicely textured body and a definitively Mexican flavor.

Because so many of us like to serve chicken breasts, I've used them with this elegant pale-green sauce. Such a refined dish would be beautiful with Pueblan Rice (page 264); start with *Seviche* (page 83) or the traditional Shrimp-Ball Soup with Roasted Pepper (page 102), and finish with Creamy Fresh-Coconut Dessert (page 285). A spicy white wine like Gewürztraminer would be nice, but Sparkling Limeade (page 311) would be more traditional.

YIELD: 4 servings, with about 3 cups of sauce

For the chicken and broth:
- ½ teaspoon salt
- 1 small onion, diced
- 3 large (about 3¾ pounds total) chicken breasts, halved (and, if you wish, half-boned, page 225)

For the sauce:
- 1 scant cup (about 4 ounces) hulled, untoasted pumpkinseeds (*pepitas*)
- 12 ounces (about 8 medium) *tomatillos,* husked and washed
  OR 1½ 13-ounce cans *tomatillos,* drained
- Fresh hot green chiles to taste (roughly 3 *chiles serranos* or 2 small *chiles jalapeños*), stemmed and seeded
- 5 large romaine lettuce leaves
- ½ medium onion, roughly chopped
- 3 small cloves garlic, peeled and roughly chopped
- 3 large sprigs fresh coriander (*cilantro*)
- ⅛ teaspoon cumin seeds (or a generous ⅛ teaspoon ground)
- 6 black peppercorns (or a big pinch ground)
- ¾ inch cinnamon stick (or about ¾ teaspoon ground)
- 2 cloves (or a pinch ground)
- 1½ tablespoons lard or vegetable oil
- Salt, about ½ teaspoon

For the garnish:
- A few sprigs of fresh coriander (*cilantro*)
- 4 radish roses

modern *mole verde* in Mexico is frequently coarse-textured. That can all be remedied by a final smoothing of the cooked sauce in the blender. (That's my addition to *mole verde* making.)

Timing and Advance Preparation
Mole verde can be prepared in about 1½ hours, half of which is devoted to unattended simmering. It may be completed through Step 4 a day ahead; store the sauce and chicken separately, covered and refrigerated. If necessary, thin before completing Step 5.

TRADITIONAL VARIATIONS
Simple Chicken Breasts in Tomatillo Sauce: For a quick, traditional-tasting main course, poach the chicken (Step 1), then prepare 2½ cups (1 recipe) Quick-Cooked *Tomatillo* Sauce (page 42) using the chicken broth. Reheat the chicken in the sauce and serve garnished with onion rings and fresh coriander.

CONTEMPORARY IDEAS
Quick-Fried Calf's Liver with Green Mole: Prepare the sauce with a light poultry, veal or beef broth (Steps 2 through 4). Dredge 6 thin calf's liver steaks in seasoned flour, then quick-fry them in vegetable oil over medium to medium-high heat, until rosy inside. Arrange on warm plates, spoon on the warm sauce and garnish with crumbled, toasted pumpkinseeds and fresh coriander.

1. *Simmering the chicken.* Bring 6 cups water and the salt to a boil in a large saucepan with the diced onion. Add the chicken breasts, skim off any grayish foam that rises during the first minute of simmering, partially cover and simmer over medium heat for about 12 minutes, until the breasts are *barely* done. If there is time, let the chicken cool in the broth. Remove the chicken; strain the broth, then spoon off all the fat that rises to the top.

2. *The pumpkinseeds.* Heat a medium-size skillet over medium-low for several minutes, then pour in the pumpkinseeds in a single layer. When the first one pops, stir them constantly for 4 to 5 minutes, until all have toasted and popped. Cool completely. In batches, pulverize the seeds in a spice grinder (or in a blender fitted with a miniblend container). Sift through a medium-mesh sieve, then stir in 1 cup of the broth.

3. *The vegetables and spices.* If you have fresh *tomatillos,* simmer them with the whole chiles in salted water to cover until tender, 10 to 15 minutes; drain and place in a blender or food processor. Simply drain canned *tomatillos* and place in the blender or food processor with the raw chiles.

Tear the lettuce leaves into rough pieces and add to the *tomatillos* along with the onion, garlic and fresh coriander. Pulverize the spices in a mortar or spice grinder, add to the blender, then process until smooth.

4. *Frying and simmering the sauce.* Heat the lard or oil in a large saucepan over medium. When hot, add the pumpkinseed-broth mixture and stir constantly as it thickens and darkens, 4 to 5 minutes. Add the vegetable puree and stir a few minutes longer, until very thick.

Stir in 2 cups of the chicken broth, reduce the heat to medium-low and simmer, partially covered, for about 30 minutes. For a smooth sauce, scrape into a blender jar, cover *loosely* and blend until smooth, then return to the saucepan. Season with salt and, if necessary, thin to a light consistency with a little broth.

5. *Finishing the dish.* Just before serving, add the chicken to the simmering sauce. When heated through, remove the breasts to a warm serving platter, spoon the sauce over them and decorate with sprigs of coriander and radish roses.

Regional Explorations

In Guerrero, where *mole verde* is a regional specialty, the local supply of already powdered, unshelled pumpkinseeds is used to give the sauce quite a distinct taste and texture. If given a choice, I go more for the versions with shelled seeds and more herbs (such as fresh coriander and the tasty romaine leaves) . . . like the one I've included here, based on Mayo Antonio Sánchez's recipe from *Cocina mexicana.*

I've been told numerous times (and I finally believe) that *mole verde* and *pipián verde* are essentially the same: Both can include a variety of nuts and seeds, *tomatillos* and herbs and/or spices. It simply seems that cooks in Puebla call their product *pipián verde,* while those in the rest of Central Mexico and down toward Acapulco favor *mole verde.* And in Veracruz, they use the words *mole verde* to mean an herby *tomatillo* sauce without seeds or nuts at all. Whatever it's called and however it's prepared, the dish is enjoyed as a main course at inexpensive *comidas corridas,* in sophisticated clubby dining rooms and even in the market *fondas.*

SIMPLE RED *MOLE* WITH MEAT, FOWL AND FRUIT

Manchamanteles de Cerdo y Pollo

The Oaxacans claim it as one of their seven *moles*, and the books list it in chapters about Guadalajara. But the only place I've eaten it with regularity is Mexico City. Wherever it comes from, it's always very popular with my guests: light, mild chile sauce seasoned with black pepper, cloves and cinnamon, then simmered with fruit.

I've chosen this recipe, based on one from *Tradiciones gastronómicas oaxaqueñas,* because it is simple and delicious and it makes a very good buffet dish. If you're not planning to set the dish out as the main offering on a buffet, you could serve it with a salad, after appetizers of Deep-Fried *Masa* Turnovers (*Quesadillas,* page 143) and before Mexican Rice Pudding (page 286) or Flan (page 283).

YIELD: 4 servings

    6 medium (about 3 ounces) dried *chiles anchos,*
       stemmed, seeded and deveined
    ¼ cup lard or vegetable oil, plus a little more if
       needed
    ½ medium onion, chopped
    5 large cloves garlic, peeled and halved
    1 pound lean, boneless pork shoulder, cut into 2-
       inch squares
    1 large (1¼-pound), whole chicken breast, half-
       boned and halved (page 225)
    2 cloves (or a pinch ground)
    3 black peppercorns (or a big pinch ground)
    ½ inch cinnamon stick (or about ½ teaspoon
       ground)
    2 slices firm white bread, broken up
    1 teaspoon salt, plus a little more if necessary
    2 tablespoons cider vinegar
    ¼ small (about 1 cup) fresh pineapple, cored,
       peeled and cubed
    1 ripe, medium plantain (see Ingredients in Cook's
       Notes)
    Sugar, about 1½ tablespoons

COOK'S NOTES

Ingredients

Chiles Anchos: These sweet chiles are perfect for this dish, though some cooks make the sauce more complex by replacing a couple of *anchos* with *pasillas* and/or *mulatos.* Using 10 California chiles is an option, but the flavor will be light.

Plantain: If a ripe plantain is unavailable, replace it with 2 cubed, green bananas; skip the frying and add them several minutes before removing the pot from the heat.

Timing and Advance Preparation

Allow about 1½ hours to prepare the *manchamanteles,* plus an additional hour for simmering. The dish may be prepared entirely in advance; remove it from the fire immediately after adding the plantain. Cool it quickly, cover and store up to 4 days in the refrigerator; it improves with a little age. Reheat slowly, covered, on the stovetop or in a 350° oven; thin with a little broth if necessary.

1. *The chiles.* Tear the chiles into flat pieces and toast them a few at a time on a griddle or heavy skillet over medium heat, pressing them down for a few seconds with a metal spatula, then flipping and pressing again; when they send up their aroma and change color, they're ready. Cover with boiling water, weight with a plate to keep them submerged, and soak 30 minutes.

2. *Browning the vegetables with meat.* Fry the onion with *2 tablespoons* of the lard or oil in a medium-size skillet over medium heat until soft, 6 or 7 minutes. Add the garlic and fry until the onion is quite brown, some 4 minutes longer. Transfer the onions and garlic to a blender jar, leaving as much fat as possible in the pan.

Raise the heat to medium-high and add more fat, if needed, to coat the pan. Dry the pork on paper towels, then brown it in an *uncrowded* single layer, 2 to 3 minutes per face; remove, draining well. Dry the chicken pieces, then brown them for 2 to 3 minutes per side, add to the pork and set the skillet aside.

3. *The sauce.* Drain the chiles and add to the blender. Pulverize the spices in a mortar or spice grinder and add to the chiles, along with the bread and 1 cup water. Stir, blend to a smooth puree, then strain through a medium-mesh sieve.

If necessary, add a little lard or oil to coat the skillet, then set over medium-high heat. When quite hot, add the puree all at once and fry, stirring constantly, for 4 or 5 minutes, until darkened and thick, dislodging any bits that earlier may have stuck to the pan.

4. *Finishing the dish.* Scrape the chile mixture into a large saucepan, stir in 2 cups water, the salt, vinegar and pork. Partially cover and simmer over medium-low for 45 minutes to an hour, until the pork is tender. Add the chicken and pineapple, cover and simmer 13 minutes.

While the chicken is cooking, heat a tablespoon of lard or oil in a medium-small skillet over medium. Peel and cube the plantain, then fry it until browned, 3 or 4 minutes and add to the *manchamanteles*. Stir in the sugar, taste for salt and thin with a little water if the sauce has thickened past a medium consistency; the flavor should be slightly sweet and fruity. Remove from the heat immediately and serve on warm, deep dinner plates.

TRADITIONAL VARIATIONS

An Elaborate Manchamanteles for a Crowd: Prepare the recipe, using a *double* quantity of meat and sauce ingredients and adding ¼ cup *each* skinned toasted peanuts and blanched toasted almonds to the chiles before pureeing; along with the pineapple, add 1 large sweet potato, 1 apple and 1 pear (all peeled, cored, if appropriate, then cubed). For a different dimension, add 1 cup (8 ounces) fried *chorizo* sausage with the chicken. Serve garnished with pickled *jalapeños.*

Kitchen Spanish

The name *manchamanteles* isn't Aztec or Mayan: just a joined pair of Spanish words that means "tablecloth stainer."

FISH AND SHELLFISH
❖
Pescados y Mariscos

Fish stall, Veracruz market

Veracruz is the perfect seafood town. A good rendition of the classic red snapper *a la veracruzana* is on the menu everywhere, and you're never far from a bowl of deliciously *picante* crab soup (*chilpachole*) or seafood cocktails and salads, or the *paella*-like *arroz a la tumbada,* or those delicious Gulf shrimp in browned garlic or *chipotle* pepper sauce.

And could there be a more perfect seafood market than the one in Veracruz? The tiled fish stalls are heaped with the brightest red snappers, large river prawns called *langostinos,* squirming crabs, fresh shrimp and at least two dozen more piscine delicacies that smell of nothing but fresh, saline seawater.

The whole market is alive with buyers and sellers all through the morning hours. Do they stop to survey the design of the colorful seaside produce, I always wonder, or the unique displays of the fat chickens and hanging beef? Do they move so quickly past the steam tables of taco fillings that they don't catch the scent of smoky *chipotle* peppers and aromatic herbs? Can they pass by my favorite seafood-cocktail bartenders and not want to watch them dash and dollop the olive oil and spicy vinegar into the tomatoey concoctions of oysters and shrimp?

By midafternoon, the beautiful assortment is nearly gone. Only the vendors with the ice-packed carts outside the market door continue to hawk their mullet, pompano, sierra and other small pan fish to those on their way home from work. As the sky darkens, the fluorescent beams in the restaurants show the eateries to be as full as they were earlier in the afternoon. Tables are crammed with expensive dishes no one would think of ordering were they not on vacation: platters of boiled shrimp for peeling; pompano baked with butter and herbs in a foil wrapper; whole baked snappers stuffed with shrimp and slathered with mayonnaise.

The beaches of Veracruz aren't especially memorable, nor is the spot where Cortés landed much to see. But I could spend weeks in the area, roaming all the eating places, before I'd get my fill of the simple, fresh seafood.

When Deann and I started our most recent expedition through Mexico—what turned into a six-month fifteen-thousand-mile culinary circuit—we crossed the border at Tijuana, then took the smooth, well-traveled highway toward Ensenada. It was my first real taste of the northwest and its remarkably fertile waters. We bought the hot-smoked bonito, yellowfin and bluefin tuna; we ate the seaside tacos full of battered fish fingers. We moved down the barren Baja peninsula, enjoying succulent, tender abalone under a crust of browned crumbs. We stayed for days in La Paz, getting to know the local stews, slow-roasts and steaks cut from sea turtle, and the rich stuffed turtle fin. There was shredded ray *machaca* in every little place, plus seafood cocktails, *seviches* and salads. On the streets, carts were laden with the *pata de mula* clams (with their dark-red meat) and the restaurants all served a delicious plate of quick-simmered or fried clams called *catarinas* (clams most everyone here would have called scallops: sweet white morsels with a little roe attached). The little eating places were filled with customers who had come to the sea to lie at its edges, play in its shallows, eat its yield; they wanted the salads of the larger, whelklike *caracol burro* or smaller *caracol chino*, and they ate the baked brown clams called *chocolatas*.

I began to sense that the Mexican seashore—all six thousand miles of it—offers those who live nearby a much more varied diet than is possible in the rest of the country. It's not that the cooks prepare all their choices in a notably wide variety of ways; in most cases all the stewing and saucing could do nothing but obscure the distinctive freshness. Broiled, lime-cured (*seviche*), fried with garlic (*al mojo de ajo*), simmered in chunky tomato-olive sauce (*a la veracruzana*) or sprinkled with hot sauce—that's all fresh seafood really needs.

We caught the ferry to the northwest mainland, to Topolobampo, Sinaloa, and found shrimp-rich waters and local specialties like shredded shrimp *machaca* for tacos and *chiles rellenos*, and fresh shrimp-ball soup. As we continued south (and even as far inland as Tepic, Nayarit) there was an increasing number of signs for *pescado zarandeado*, slashed fish smeared with garlic and turned over the coals. Down in Acapulco, everyone raves over the famous lime-cured *seviche* made from the mackerel they call sierra. As the shore curves east and becomes part of the state of Oaxaca, the markets are filled with huge mounds of stiff dried fish to soak and stew with tomatoes. They're stacked high, beside baskets of dried shrimp destined for simmering in a *picante* chile broth with potatoes and carrots (*caldo de camarón seco*) or pulverize and make into cakes (*tortitas de camarón*) and serve with cactus pieces in light-chile sauce.

The overland haul through dense, tropical Yucatán brought us to the Caribbean waters, to the spiny lobsters and delicious, tender octopus, oysters and fish in richly spiced, vinegary *escabeche*. Most restaurant menus listed the full range of typical Mexican seafood, then added *achiote*-seasoned *postas* ("fish steaks"), grilled for a dish called in Mayan *tikín-xik* or baked for *nac cum*.

Following the westward curve of the Gulf, we discovered the delicious pieces of roasted small shark (*cazón*) in the Campeche market; we tasted the rich meat in a dish with tomato sauce (*a la campechana*) and again in a sauced stacking of tortillas and black beans (*pan de cazón*).

The Grijalva and Usumacinta rivers that cut up the thick verdancy of Tabasco teem with a meaty, needle-nosed garlike fish called *pejelagarto*. It is sold smoked in the market in Villahermosa, and made into salads and scrambled with eggs. The rivers are home to a variety of small turtles that are featured in a regional green stew with exotic herbs or a dish made with their blood. There is little that is tastier than the large river prawns (called *piguas*) fried with garlic.

The Spanish heritage is felt all through the Gulf in popular dishes like squid and octopus in their swarthy ink. Little fish-stuffed fried turnovers are favorite snacks. Plentiful small blue crabs are stuffed or served in soup. And in the oil-rich port town of Tampico, the cooks make a subtly delicious red-chile sauce for fresh shrimp (*camarones en escabeche rojo*).

Mexicans who live inland seem much more atuned to fish and shellfish than landlocked Americans; scarcely any good-size market would be without a fish-frying eatery or seafood-cocktail vendor. Michoacán, a state whose name means "land of fish" in Tarascan, specializes in unimaginably delicate white fish from Lake Pátzcuaro and vicinity. And the state's frogs' legs and tiny *charales* (like whitebait) fill in when whitefish is too expensive. Nearly every region has some fresh-water trout, carp, bass and catfish. But in the Central states, they're wrapped in cornhusks like *tamales,* just as they have been for centuries, and baked on the griddle.

Like the rest of the nonaffluent world, Mexico has taken full advantage of its nutritive resources, especially those of the water. I've included a sampling of Mexico's tastiest seafood recipes in the following pages.

For seafood recipes from other chapters, see "Seafood" in the Index.

Keys to Perfect Fish Cooking

Filleting and Skinning a Round Fish: This is the method used for all fish except flat ones like flounder and halibut. Lay your gutted fish crosswise in front of you, its dorsal fin (the one at the top of the back) away from you. With a sharp, thin-bladed knife, slice across the width of the body just behind the gill and small pectoral fin, cutting down to the central backbone. With the knife held parallel to the counter, cut along the dorsal fin, from your first crosscut to the end of the tail; make certain your cut goes in all the way to the central backbone. At the point where the visceral (innards) cavity ends, slide your knife through to the other side of the fish, going over the backbone (illustration 2). With the blade angled slightly downward, cut all the way to the end of the tail; the tail portion of the fillet should now be free. Gently fold back the fillet freed from along the dorsal fin, then cut the meat free from the rib cage, which encloses the visceral cavity (illustration 3). The fillet will now be free, and, if the knife was always

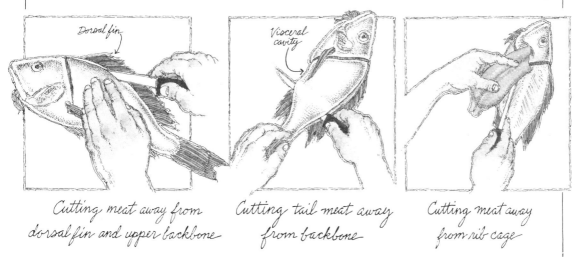

Cutting meat away from dorsal fin and upper backbone

Cutting tail meat away from backbone

Cutting meat away from rib cage

angled toward the bones, there will be little meat left on this side of the carcass. Flip the fish over and remove the fillet from the other side in the same manner.

Skinning Fish Fillets: Grasp the tail end of a fillet firmly, then make a crosswise incision near where you're holding, cutting down to *but not through* the skin. Angling the knife away from you, slide and slice it between the skin and flesh: Pull gently on the fish you're holding (it's still connected to the skin you're removing) while you push gently on the knife, always angling it down toward the skin (illustration 4).

Washing Fish with Lime: According to A. J. McClane's *Encyclopedia of Fish Cookery,* acids like vinegar and lime or lemon juice neutralize the ammonia that can be a problem in certain fish, especially the shark so popular in Mexico. Most traditional Mexican cooks recommend a short lime marinade before cooking any fish; marinating the fish too long will "cook" it, however, as it does for *seviche.*

Determining Doneness: Preferences are changing: Today, most people like their fish moist and just *barely* done. Rather than cook the fish until it easily flakes and/or separates from the bone (it will have lost considerable moisture by then), cook until it flakes under gentle but *firm* pressure.

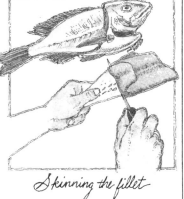

Skinning the fillet

FISH FILLETS WITH FRESH TOMATOES, CAPERS AND OLIVES

Pescado a la Veracruzana

To most aficionados, the mention of Mexican seafood brings to mind chunky, brothy tomato sauce with olives, herbs and chiles: *pescado a la veracruzana.* It is both classic and nationally ubiquitous, which means all cooks think they can and should make it—whether or not they've visited Veracruz. It's only in the seaside home, though, that I've tasted the beautifully light, distinctively *veracruzana* sauce with its special lilt of herbs and spices.

What follows is a recipe based on the version served at the Pescador restaurant in Veracruz. I'd offer it with the customary molded White Rice (page 261), and, for an all-Gulf meal, I'd start with Spicy Crab Soup (page 100) and have Butter-Fried Plantains (page 295) for dessert. Here's the place some might enjoy a fruity, dry white wine like a Chenin Blanc, or Sparkling Limeade (page 311).

COOK'S NOTES

Techniques
Filleting and Skinning Fish, Washing It with Lime and Determining Doneness: See page 211.
Poaching vs. Baking: Some cooks find the oven's indirect heat and slower cooking more comfortable than stove-top poaching. If doubling the recipe, use the baking method.

Ingredients
Fish: Róbalo (snook) is more common in Mexico (and much less expensive) than red snapper; its meat is firm and mild, like a grouper (sea bass) or one of the cods. Practically any rather mild, nonoily fish will work—striped bass, halibut, fluke, large rock cod, monkfish or the like. Fine-textured fish

YIELD: 4 servings

For the fish:

1½ pounds boneless, skinless meaty fish fillets like red snapper or halibut, preferably in 4 pieces each ½ inch thick
Freshly squeezed lime juice and a little salt

For the sauce:

3 tablespoons vegetable oil, preferably part olive oil
1 medium onion, thinly sliced
2 pounds (4 medium-large) ripe tomatoes, roasted or boiled (page 352), peeled and cored OR three 15-ounce cans *good-quality* tomatoes, lightly drained
2 cloves garlic, peeled and minced
20 meaty green olives (preferably *manzanillo*), pitted and roughly chopped
2 tablespoons large Spanish capers
2 medium pickled *chiles jalapeños,* store-bought or homemade (page 48), stemmed, seeded and sliced into strips
1 tablespoon pickling juices from the chiles
1½ teaspoons mixed dried herbs (such as marjoram and thyme)
2 tablespoons finely chopped flat-leaf parsley, plus a few sprigs for garnish
3 bay leaves
1 inch cinnamon stick
2 cloves
¼ teaspoon black peppercorns, very coarsely ground
1 cup light-flavored fish broth (page 62), bottled clam juice or water
Salt, if necessary

1. *The fish.* Rinse the fillets, lay them in a noncorrosive dish and sprinkle them with lime juice and salt. Cover and refrigerate about 1 hour.

2. *The sauce.* In a large skillet, heat the oil over medium, add the onion and cook, stirring frequently, until golden, 7 or 8 minutes.

While the onion is cooking, cut the peeled fresh tomatoes in half crosswise and squeeze out the seeds into a strainer set over a small bowl. Cut the tomatoes into 1-inch pieces and

don't jibe with the sauce and tend to fall apart.

Timing and Advance Preparation

If the broth is on hand, this superb dish takes an hour or less to prepare (plus the hour for marinating the fish). The sauce may be made up to 3 days ahead and stored in the refrigerator, covered; warm it to room temperature before completing Step 3.

TRADITIONAL VARIATIONS

Whole Fish a la Veracruzana: The dish is often made with two 1½-pound or four ¾-pound whole or pan-dressed fish; choose farm-raised trout, coho or catfish, whitefish, black bass, sea trout, perch, snapper or the like. Make 2 diagonal slices on each side, marinate them (Step 1), then use the baking method to finish the dish. Cooking time will be a few minutes longer.

Tongue a la Veracruzana: Soak a medium-to-small (2½-pound) beef tongue in salted water for several hours, then simmer in salted water (with a little onion, garlic and herbs), skimming at first, for about 2½ hours, until tender. Strain and *thoroughly* degrease the broth. Strip off the tongue's skin. Pull out the bones from the butt end and slice off ¾ inch where they were; discard. Trim off the fatty section along the bottom. Cut the trimmed tongue into ¼-inch slices and lay, overlapping, in several rows in a baking dish. Prepare the sauce as directed in Step 2, replacing fish broth with tongue broth. Pour over the meat, cover and bake 20 minutes at 350°, then garnish as directed.

place in a mixing bowl. Collect all the juices on the cutting board and add to the tomatoes, along with those strained from the seeds. Canned tomatoes need only be lightly drained, then cut into 1-inch pieces, collecting the juices as you go.

Add the garlic to the lightly browned onion and stir for a minute or so, then add the tomatoes and their juice. Simmer for 5 minutes to reduce some of the liquid.

Divide the olives and capers between two small bowls, and set one aside to use as garnish. To the other bowl, add the *jalapeño* strips, pickling juice, mixed herbs and chopped parsley. If you don't wish to have the whole bay leaves, cinnamon, cloves or cracked pepper in the finished sauce, wrap them in cheesecloth and tie with a string; otherwise, add them directly to the bowl containing the herbs.

When the tomatoes are ready, add the mixture of pickled things, herbs and spices, along with the fish broth (or clam juice or water). Cover and simmer 10 minutes, then taste for salt (and remove the cheesecloth-wrapped spices).

3. *Finishing the dish.* Fifteen minutes before serving, remove the fillets from the refrigerator and rinse them again. Either poach them in the sauce on top of the stove or bake in the sauce, as follows:

The stove-top method: Nestle the fish fillets in the sauce so they are well covered. Set the lid on the pan and place over a medium heat. After 4 minutes, turn the fillets over, re-cover and cook 2 or 3 minutes longer, until a fillet will flake under firm pressure.

The baking method: Preheat the oven to 350°. Place the fillets in a single layer in a lightly greased baking dish. Spoon the sauce over them, cover with aluminum foil and bake for 8 to 10 minutes, until the fish just flakes when pressed firmly with a fork at the thickest part.

Serve the poached or baked fillets on warm dinner plates with lots of the sauce, garnished with a sprinkling of the reserved capers and olives and a sprig of parsley.

Fish a la veracruzana

CONTEMPORARY IDEAS

Charcoal-Grilled Veal Chops a la Veracruzana: Prepare the sauce (Step 2), using veal or other meat broth, adding 1 large red bell or *poblano* pepper (roasted, peeled, seeded and sliced), and replacing the pickling juices with 1 tablespoon balsamic vinegar. Rub 4 thick veal chops with ground black pepper, ground bay leaves, mixed herbs and olive oil. Charcoal-grill over a medium-hot fire, then serve with the warm sauce spooned on top.

Salmon "Seviche" a la Veracruzana: Slice 1 pound salmon into thin fillets. Lay in a non-corrosive dish, cover with fresh lime juice (making sure the juice penetrates every layer), cover and refrigerate several hours or overnight, until the fish turns opaque. Prepare the sauce (Step 2); cool. Drain the salmon, then mix with the sauce. Serve cold with a sprinkling of capers, olives and parsley.

Regional Explorations

The Spaniards have migrated to Mexico in numerous waves through the centuries, the last major one, I'm told, having transpired during the homeland's civil war of the thirties. Many settled into farming and cattle raising in Veracruz, and it's my guess that this dish has really come into its own under their tutelage. It's a typical Mediterranean composite of those originally New World tomatoes and typically Old World condiments . . . including capers, which are listed in every *veracruzana* recipe but are rarely put in the dish (and rarely found in Veracruz groceries).

QUICK-FRIED FISH WITH TOASTED GARLIC

Pescado al Mojo de Ajo

"**No!**" I can hear them say. "You'll ruin the dish! You can't let garlic brown." I've heard it for years; I may have said it myself at one point, until I learned that slowly browned chunks of garlic, taken off before they get dark and bitter, have a superbly nutty flavor and a special sweetness.

Along with breaded, fried and *a la veracruzana*, *al mojo de ajo* is a standard preparation anywhere in the Republic that they cook fish. Luckily, it is delicious and very easy to do at home. The following method, based on one in Dueñas's *Cocina básica: pescados*, is one I especially like because the fish is quick-fried in garlic-flavored oil and butter, then a little lime juice is added to give it sparkle.

This dish welcomes a flavorful vegetable like Swiss Chard with Tomatoes and Potatoes (page 275). To dress up the meal, start with Fresh-Corn *Tamales* (page 185) or a soup and end with Flan (page 283) or Spicy Poached Guavas (page 297). Beer and Sparkling Limeade (page 311) go well with these flavors.

YIELD: 4 servings

> Four 10- to 12-ounce fish like bass, catfish or perch, whole or pan-dressed
> Freshly squeezed lime juice and a little salt
> 3 tablespoons unsalted butter
> 3 tablespoons vegetable oil
> 10 large cloves garlic, peeled and thinly sliced
> About ½ cup flour
> A scant teaspoon salt, plus a little more to season the pan sauce, if necessary
> 1 tablespoon freshly squeezed lime juice
> 2 tablespoons chopped flat-leaf parsley, plus a few sprigs for garnish

1. *The fish.* Rinse the fish. With a sharp knife, make 2 diagonal slashes on both sides of each one. Sprinkle them lightly, inside and out, with the lime juice and salt, lay in a noncorrosive dish, cover with plastic wrap and refrigerate about 1 hour.

COOK'S NOTES

Techniques
Washing Fish with Lime and Determining Doneness: All these techniques are discussed on page 212.
Slashing Fish: This is done when frying and charcoal-grilling whole fish to allow the heat to penetrate evenly.
Browning the Garlic: If the garlic darkens past golden, it will be bitter. The more oil and butter in the pan and the slower it cooks, the sweeter the garlic will be.

Ingredients
The Fish: Any small fish works nicely: pompano or snapper if available, farm-raised catfish, trout or coho, little bass (black or otherwise), pickerel, whitefish, rock cod, sea trout . . .

Timing and Advance Preparation
From scratch, this dish only requires ½ hour, plus an hour for marinating the fish.

TRADITIONAL VARIATIONS
Fish Fillets with Toasted Garlic: Replace the whole fish with four 6- to 8-ounce fillets, each ½ inch thick. Prepare as directed, omitting the slashing, and cooking the fillets for only about 3 minutes per side.

CONTEMPORARY IDEAS
Shrimp with Toasted Garlic and Avocado: Prepare the recipe using 2 pounds shrimp (peeled and deveined) in place of fish, and olive oil in place of butter; fry the shrimp (there is

2. *The garlic.* Heat the butter and oil in a large (12-inch) skillet over medium-low, add the garlic and very slowly cook, stirring frequently, until the garlic has turned golden, 3 or 4 minutes. Scrape into a small strainer set over a bowl and let the fat drain through, then return it to the pan and set the garlic aside.

3. *Frying the fish.* Spread the flour on a plate and mix in the salt. Rinse the fish, then pat dry with paper towels. Return the skillet to medium heat and, when hot, dredge the fish in the flour, shake off the excess and lay in the pan. Fry until golden and done, 4 to 5 minutes on each side. (Make a small, deep cut down to the backbone of one fish to determine if it is cooked through.) Remove the fish to a large serving platter and keep warm in a low oven.

4. *Finishing the dish.* With the skillet off the fire, add the reserved garlic, lime juice and chopped parsley. Return the pan to medium heat and stir constantly for about 1 minute, until the lime juice has mostly evaporated and the parsley has wilted. Taste for salt. Spoon the sauce over the fish and serve, decorated with parsley.

QUICK-FRIED FISH WITH ROASTED PEPPERS AND THICK CREAM

Pescado con Rajas y Crema

This is not a regional specialty but a family one, and I'm sold on the way a fresh, good-textured piece of fish combines with roasted peppers and thick, half-soured cream. My inspiration for this elegant, versatile dish comes from the occasional recipes for this sort of thing you find in cookbooks from Mexico; once or twice, I've tasted something similar in fancier restaurants.

Serve it with a Cress and *Jícama* Salad (page 89) for a special dinner, with some tasty filled *Masa* Boats (*Sopes,* page 168) or a bowl of *Tlalpeño* Soup (page 97) to start, and a fresh fruit ice (page 300) for dessert. The fish is good with a full-bodied white wine like a Chardonnay.

YIELD: 4 servings

no need for dredging in flour) in two batches. This makes a great appetizer for 8 people, served warm or cool, surrounding a bowl of Chunky Guacamole (page 44) for dipping. Or, marinate 2 pounds large prawns (peeled and deveined) overnight in the oil-garlic mixture from Step 2, charcoal-grill them over low coals, then serve them with this avocado mayonnaise: Peel and pit 1 avocado, place in a blender with ⅓ cup fresh lime juice, 1 egg, ½ cup chopped parsley, ½ cup beer and ½ small onion (roughly chopped); blend until smooth, then *slowly* add 1½ cups olive oil while the machine is running; season with salt.

COOK'S NOTES

Techniques
Filleting and Skinning Fish, Washing It with Lime and Determining Doneness: See page 212.

Ingredients
Fish: The flavors of this sauce won't overwhelm a good piece of fish like red snapper, salmon, halibut or striped bass. Shark done this way makes a deliciously rich dish.
Chile Poblano: Rather than replace an unavailable *poblano* with the blander long green chiles, I'd change the dish a bit and use a *serrano* (seeded and chopped) plus a red bell pepper (roasted, peeled, seeded and sliced).

1½ pounds boneless, skinless fish fillets like hali-
    but or bass, about ½ inch thick
Freshly squeezed lime juice and a little salt
2 tablespoons vegetable oil
½ medium onion, sliced ⅛ inch thick
2 cloves garlic, peeled and minced
1 large fresh *chile poblano,* roasted and peeled (page
    337), seeded and sliced into thin strips
1¼ cups Thick Cream (page 51) or whipping
    cream
Salt, about ½ teaspoon *each* for the sauce and for
    the dredging flour
About ⅓ cup flour
1 tablespoon unsalted butter
Thinly sliced tops of green onions, for garnish

1. *The fish.* Rinse the fillets, place in a noncorrosive dish
and sprinkle the lime juice and a little salt; cover and refrigerate
about an hour.

2. *The roasted-pepper cream.* Heat *half* the vegetable oil in a
medium-size saucepan over medium. Add the onion and cook,
stirring frequently, until lightly browned, 7 or 8 minutes. Add
the garlic and chile and cook 2 minutes longer, then stir in the
cream and simmer until the sauce coats a spoon rather thickly.
Season with salt.

3. *Finishing the dish.* About 10 minutes before serving, spread
the flour on a plate and mix in a little salt. Dry the fillets with
paper towels. Heat the butter and remaining tablespoon of oil
in a medium-large skillet over medium-high. When the butter
just begins to brown, quickly dredge the fillets in the flour,
shake off the excess and lay in the hot pan. Fry until lightly
browned, about 1½ minutes per side, then add the sauce, reduce the heat to medium and simmer for 2 or 3 minutes more,
until the fillets flake under firm pressure. Remove the fillets to
a warm serving platter, spoon the sauce over them, garnish with
the green-onion slivers and serve.

Fresh poblano chiles

Cream: The ripeness of thick
cream (page 51) adds real
depth here, so use it if at all
possible. Sour cream will curdle if heated here.

**Timing and Advance
Preparation**
Once the fish is marinated, this
dish can be ready in 30 minutes. If you're planning ahead,
make the thick cream, roast the
chile and, if you wish, complete Step 2. Finish Step 3 just
before serving.

**OTHER
CONTEMPORARY
IDEAS**
*Chicken with Rajas and
Cream:* Prepare the sauce as
directed in Step 2. Dredge 2
large boneless, skinless chicken
breasts (sliced in ½-inch strips)
in the seasoned flour, fry in the
butter and oil over medium-
high heat for about 5 minutes,
then complete as directed.
*Fish with Cream, Epazote and
Fresh Cheese:* Prepare the recipe as directed, adding 2 tablespoons finely chopped *epazote*
to the cream as it is simmering.
Along with the green onions,
sprinkle ½ cup crumbled goat
cheese or Mexican *queso fresco*
(page 327) over the fillets just
before serving.

CHILE-BATHED FISH GRILLED IN CORNHUSKS

Pescado Adobado en Hojas de Maíz

I've seen them in the frenetic Friday Toluca market every time I've been there: pieces of catfish, carp or little, minnowlike *charales*, bathed with a sharp red-chile sauce, packed into several layers of husk, and turned on a griddle until charred. The *picante* flavors of the fish and the smoky overtones from the blackened husks are delicious.

For the recipe that follows, I've taken this humble fish snack (found predominantly in Central Mexico and Michoacán) and turned it into a dish to serve at the table. It is quite an attractive presentation and a delicious blend of uncommon flavors. I call for the traditional taco garnishes—fresh coriander (*cilantro*) and onion—because I serve the dish with hot corn tortillas and encourage each person to make tacos with the tasty strips of fish. Accompany it with Pueblan Rice (page 264) and set out a big Mixed Vegetable Salad (page 87) to start, if you want. Pecan Pie with Raw Sugar (page 289) is good for dessert; beer, Mexican Sangria (page 322) or Sparkling Limeade (page 311) are my choices for beverage.

YIELD: 6 servings for a light meal with substantial accompaniments

> ½ **8-ounce package cornhusks**
> 1½ **pounds boneless, skinless meaty fish fillets like cod or catfish**
> ⅔ **cup (⅔ recipe) Red-Chile Marinade (*Adobo*, page 64)**
> **Salt as desired**
> ¾ **cup medium to finely chopped onion**
> 3 **tablespoons roughly chopped fresh coriander (*cilantro*), plus 6 sprigs for garnish**
> 2 **large limes, quartered**

1. *Soaking the husks and marinating the fish.* Put the cornhusks to soak in boiling water as directed on page 177. Cut the fish into 3-inch sticks that are ½ inch wide. Place in a noncorrosive bowl, measure in 6 tablespoons of the *adobo* paste and mix gently but thoroughly. Cover and refrigerate at least 2 hours.

COOK'S NOTES

Techniques
Filleting and Skinning Fish, and Determining Doneness: See page 211 for the details.
Wrapping and Cooking the Strips of Fish: Strips are used to duplicate the smeltlike *charales* and to allow the chile to penetrate the fish. The triple wrapping is quickly mastered; simply try to keep the package tight, since any tiny openings will let the flavorful juices leak out.

Ingredients
Cornhusks: See page 344.
Fish: Practically any nonoily fish tastes good here, though I'd choose a moderate-to-inexpensive one with a firm texture and large flake, like grouper/sea bass, cod, catfish, tilefish or monkfish. The carp and other strong fish that are used for this recipe in Mexico may be too aggressive for some palates.

Timing and Advance Preparation
Preparation time is roughly an hour (if the *adobo* is on hand), plus 2 hours for marinating the fish and soaking the husks. The fish may marinate for up to 24 hours, or the packages may be put together the evening before. The fish is best cooked just before serving; if slightly undercooked, it will hold in a *very low* oven for 15 or 20 minutes.

2. *The fish-filled cornhusk packages.* Choose the 18 largest cornhusks: They should be 6 inches across on their widest end; if any fall short, two may be laid together, overlapping at least 2 inches. From the extra cornhusks, tear off twenty-four ¼-inch-wide strips and tie them together in pairs, making 12 long ones. Divide the fish into 6 equal portions.

To form the packages, spread 1 teaspoon of *adobo* paste over a 2 × 3-inch area on the wide end of a husk. Lay half of one portion of fish in a single layer over the *adobo*-covered part of the husk. Lightly sprinkle with salt and top with the remaining half-portion of fish. Lightly salt again, then spread with a tea-spoon of *adobo* paste. Bring the uncovered sides of the husk up around the fish, tucking one under the other. Fold the unfilled, narrow end of the husk up over the filled portion, then flip the package over onto the wide end of another husk (open-end toward the center). Wrap the long sides of the new husk up around the package, overlapping them. Fold the narrow, un-filled portion of the husk up over the filled part, then flip the package over onto the wide end of yet another husk and wrap the package again. Lay the finished package flap-side down and tie it twice around its width with 2 of the cornhusk strips. Form the rest of the fish-filled packages in the same manner.

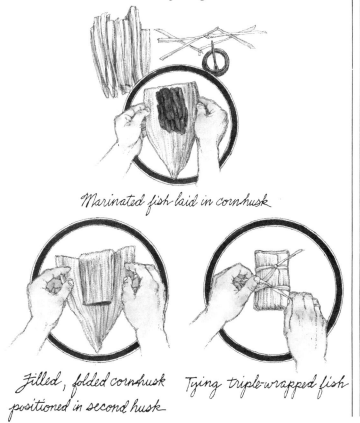

Marinated fish laid in cornhusk

Filled, folded cornhusk positioned in second husk

Tying triple-wrapped fish

TRADITIONAL VARIATIONS

Shrimp Adobados: Peel 1 pound medium-to-large shrimp, leaving the last shell segments and tails in place; devein them. Mix the shrimp with ⅓ cup *adobo* paste, cover and refrigerate for several hours. Just before serving, stir in ½ teaspoon salt and 3 table-spoons vegetable oil. Place in a single layer on an oiled baking sheet. Slide under a preheated broiler for a couple of minutes, turn the shrimp and broil sev-eral minutes longer.

3. *Cooking the packages.* About 20 minutes before serving, heat a large griddle over medium-high or turn on your broiler and position the rack 4 inches below the heat.

For griddle cooking: Lay the packages on the griddle. Cook 6 or 7 minutes on each side, plus an additional minute on each long edge.

For broiler cooking: Lay the packages on a baking sheet and slide them under the broiler. Flip after about 7 minutes (the cornhusks should have blackened), then cook 5 or 6 minutes longer.

Open one package and test for doneness (being careful to contain the juices).

4. *Presenting the dish.* Remove the strings from each package, then carefully pull away the two outer layers of husk, being careful not to lose any of the juices. Set each package on a warm plate, open up the remaining husk and gently push the fish into the center. Mix together the chopped onion and fresh coriander; sprinkle 2 tablespoons over each portion. Top each one with a sprig of coriander and lay a couple of lime wedges to the side. Serve immediately.

Fresh coriander (cilantro)

OYSTERS POACHED WITH MILD VINEGAR AND AROMATIC SPICES, TABASCO-STYLE

Ostiones en Escabeche

In Tabasco, the silky fresh-shucked oysters are frequently seasoned with a packet of coarse-ground *escabeche* spices (including the locally grown allspice) and poached in sweet banana vinegar. Even with the obvious hurdles, it's an easy dish to do well in the United States.

The following recipe is based on the version served at the Mariposa restaurant in Villahermosa (though I have reduced the vinegar a little—ours is stronger—and used fish broth rather than water; also, I sprinkle mine with fresh coriander (*cilantro*)

COOK'S NOTES

Techniques
Cooking Oysters: While the most judicious cooking of the oysters might be none at all, a *very gentle heat* and a *short* tour over the fire is a good alternative. They are ready when they turn white and their edges curl.

Ingredients
Chiles Güeros: These yellow-skinned chiles (often called *chiles picosos* in Tabasco) are similar to medium-hot banana or Hungarian wax peppers; I've also used 4 long green chiles as a substitute.

to add a special lift). Served cool with crusty bread, it makes a nice first course, though in Tabasco I've only had it warm. You can dress up the dinner with a starter of Deep-Fried *Masa* Turnovers (*Quesadillas,* page 143), then end with rich Mexican Rice Pudding (page 286).

YIELD: about 5 cups, serving 4 as a light main dish, 4 to 6 as an appetizer

⅓ teaspoon cumin seeds

6 cloves

¼ teaspoon allspice berries

¼ teaspoon black peppercorns

3 bay leaves

1 scant teaspoon dried oregano

¾ inch cinnamon stick

⅓ cup vegetable or olive oil (or a mixture of the two)

1 large onion, thinly sliced

3 small carrots, peeled and diced

6 cloves garlic, peeled and minced

6 long (4-inch) fresh *chiles güeros* or banana peppers, roasted and peeled (page 337), seeded and cut into ½-inch dice

3 tablespoons cider vinegar, plus a little more if necessary

1 generous cup mild fish broth (page 62), clam juice or water

1½ pounds shucked oysters, undrained (about 36 medium-to-small with a generous cup liquid)

Salt, about ¾ teaspoon (depending on the saltiness of the oysters)

About 3 tablespoons chopped fresh coriander (*cilantro*), for garnish

1. *The spices and herbs.* Measure the cumin, cloves, allspice and black pepper into a mortar or spice grinder and crush or process until *cracked* but not pulverized. Transfer to a small dish and measure in the bay leaves, oregano and cinnamon.

2. *The vegetables and flavorings.* Heat the oil in a large (12-inch) skillet over medium, add the onions and carrots and stir occasionally until the onion is soft, about 5 minutes. Mix in the garlic and chile and cook 2 minutes longer. Add the vinegar, broth (or clam juice or water) and spices to the skillet, cover and simmer over medium-low heat for 10 minutes. If

Oysters: Make sure already-shucked oysters are very fresh. If you shuck your own, plan on 26 to 36.

Timing and Advance Preparation
With the broth made, this simple dish takes 30 to 40 minutes. If possible, complete Steps 1 and 2 several hours (or days) in advance, cover and refrigerate. Or prepare the entire dish in advance and serve it at a cool room temperature.

TRADITIONAL VARIATIONS
Fish Fillets in Escabeche: Complete Steps 1 and 2, decreasing the oil to 2 tablespoons. Dredge 1½ pounds boneless, skinless fish fillets in seasoned flour, then brown in a little olive oil over medium-high heat. When the fish is nearly done, add the vegetable-broth mixture and simmer for a few minutes. Lift out the fillets, lay on deep plates and serve with the vegetables and broth spooned over them. Or let cool in the broth, cover and marinate overnight, refrigerated; serve at room temperature. Mackerel is frequently used for this dish, but my preference is red snapper, striped bass, halibut and the like.

Regional Explorations
In Tabasco, the air hangs like a soft moist blanket. The land flows around the Gulf: damp, low ground covered with jungle and chocolate trees and banana plantations. It is the home of Mexico's first known civilization, the Olmecs, and a number of unusual regional specialties: venison steaks, smoked *pejelagarto* fish, turtle in an herby *masa*-thickened sauce, armadillo in *adobo,* the

there's time, let stand off the fire (in a noncorrosive container) for several hours; the flavors will greatly improve.

3. *Finishing the dish.* Just before serving, add the oysters and their liquid to the vegetables, bring to a very gentle simmer over medium-low heat, and cook until the oysters are *just* firm, about 3 minutes. Remove from the heat, season with salt (and more vinegar, if necessary); take out the bay leaves and cinnamon, if you wish. Serve in deep plates, sprinkled with the fresh coriander.

braised capybaralike *tepescuintle,* and oysters in *escabeche.* Similar *escabeches* are made with octopus, whelk and squid all through the Yucatan; also, oysters in *escabeche* is a regional specialty of Guaymas, Sonora, a coastal town some two thousand miles diagonally across the country.

Earthenware pot and cups for café de olla

POULTRY
❖
Aves

Fonda, Guadalajara market

Poultry is without any doubt the most frequently chosen meat in Mexico—usually a good-size chicken with enough texture to remind you that it has toured the yard, and more than enough flavor to stand up to the *mole* or *tomatillo* sauce. That creature, however, wasn't the original Mexican fowl: Before they'd seen a chicken, the Aztecs had domesticated turkeys and Muscovy ducks and they were hunting a great variety of wild feathered creatures. One source tells us that a market outside the center of the old Aztec capital went through eight thousand birds every five days. The emperor was offered all kinds of fowl at his legendary meals; turkeys were even fed to the animals at the royal zoo.

Turkeys weren't the big-breasted, self-basting ones we think of today. No, they were a smaller, native variety closely related to our wild turkeys, and they are still the most commonly raised breed in Mexico. In Yucatán, the hunters took another species, the colorful oscillating turkey (*pavo del monte*); it is occasionally still offered in restaurants in the peninsula, but has yet to be domesticated.

Chicken came with the Spaniards and, from all indications, caught on immediately. Today (with the exception of the stray turkey or duck), it is *the* fowl of the Mexican market—fresh-killed and plucked, head and feet intact for the buyer to inspect (and use in the broth), spread out immodestly or hung up with a certain air of finality. They are nearly always fresh and flavorful.

Mexican chickens are generally simmered, steamed or braised until tender, simply because many are too tough for dry-heat roasting or frying. The whole boiled birds sit out in market *fondas* with the visibility of planned ornamentation, sometimes decorated with radish roses and spears of romaine, sometimes indiscreetly plunked down. As the hours pass, they lose their members, the joints going into the *mole, pipianes,* tomato or *tomatillo* sauce, or the meat shredded to fill or adorn the simple fare.

The turkey is the traditional bird for the celebratory *mole poblano* (though restaurants usually serve the *mole* with chicken). In Yucatán, the turkey is the focus of the baroque *pavo en relleno blanco* (with its pork stuffing, caper-and-olive-studded white sauce and chunky tomato sauce) as well as the *pavo en relleno negro* or *chirmole* (a sort of "blackened" version of the more comfortable first dish). You can make the aromatic Yucatecan *escabeche* with turkey, though most commonly it's spice-coated chicken that you find in the flavorful broth with pickled red onions. And chicken gets flavored with the Yucatecan *achiote* seasoning paste, wrapped in banana leaves and steamed (or baked in a pit) for the justifiably famous *pollo pibil.*

In restaurants, *cafeterías* and market eateries, chicken is offered fried or stewed in local sauces. In West-Central Mexico, most notably Morelia, the poached fowl is dipped in red-chile sauce before it's slipped into the hot oil, for the delicious *pollo a la plaza.* And the one spot I know of where chickens are never precooked is Sinaloa, where the slow-roasted *pollo a las brasas* is done over smoky coals. It is a simple specialty at its best in the outdoor grilling setups that dot the byways.

Wild-fowl specialties are not common public food in Mexico. Ducks, though usually not wild ones, are put on the tables of nicer restaurants in the large cities, along with an occasional quail. But in Guerrero, around Taxco, Iguala and Chilpancingo, roadside eating places have become famous for squab (*pichón*), iguana and rabbit, either with a dressing of garlic (*al mojo de ajo*) or in a light chile sauce called *chileajo*.

The recipes I've pulled together in this chapter take advantage of the varied approaches to Mexican poultry preparations; when you add in the *moles* made with chicken, the possibilities are broad indeed. As you'll discover while perusing the recipes, I've employed the traditional sauces with different birds in various stages of jointing and boning, to make them the most attractive and easiest to eat at the table.

For poultry recipes from other chapters, see "Poultry" in the Index.

Keys to Essential Poultry Preparations

Quartering a Chicken and Half-Boning the Breast: Bend back a leg-thigh portion, breaking the joint loose, then use a thin-bladed knife to cut it free, first cutting around the nugget of meat on the backbone just above the joint, then cutting through the joint and down the backbone to the tail; cut free the other leg-thigh portion in the same manner. With a large knife or poultry shears, cut along both sides of the backbone, through the ribs and collar bone, to the neck opening; remove the backbone and reserve for broth. Open out the breast, cavity-side down, then press firmly (or pound gently) on the center to loosen the breastbone (the breast should now lie flat); flip the breast over and pull out the large, dark-red breastbone and the white piece of cartilage that trails off from it. Cut down through the middle of the half-boned breast (you'll cut through the wishbone at the top) to separate into halves.

Boning Chicken Thighs: Lay a thigh skin-side down and slice through the flesh in a line from one joint to the other (down to the bone that connects them). Use the point of your knife to cut around and free the bone and joint cartilage at one end, then, grasping the freed end, cut and scrape the flesh from the bone all the way to the other end. Cut the flesh away from the joint and cartilage.

DUCK IN SMOOTH PUMPKINSEED SAUCE

Pato en Pipián Rojo

The sauce is wonderfully savory—nutty-tasting and colored with sweet red chile. It is beautifully served with duck at the small, European-style Fonda el Pato off Paseo de la Reforma in Mex-

COOK'S NOTES

Techniques
Half-Boning Duck: Many cooks like to partially bone the duck halves to make them easier to eat. Use a thin, pointed knife to free the rib cage on the

ico City, though I've never considered their version of the sauce quite as distinctive as the one made by market cooks in Puebla. So I've combined the delicious market sauce with the dressier duck of Mexico City. It looks elegant set on a plate beside a molded serving of Pueblan Rice (page 264). For an all-Pueblan dinner, you could start with Tortilla Soup (page 96) and serve a Creamy Fresh-Coconut Dessert (page 285). To drink, choose Mexican Sangria (page 322), *Jamaica* "Flower" Cooler (page 307) or even a soft, fruity red wine like Merlot or Beaujolais.

YIELD: 4 large servings, with about 3 cups of sauce

For the duck and broth:
- 2 medium ducks (5 pounds each), preferably fresh
- ½ medium onion, diced
- A generous ½ teaspoon salt
- 1 teaspoon mixed dried herbs (like marjoram and thyme)
- 3 bay leaves
- 2 tablespoons vegetable oil

For the sauce:
- 2 medium (about 1 ounce total) dried *chiles anchos,* stemmed, seeded and deveined
- 3 tablespoons lard or vegetable oil
- ½ medium onion, sliced
- 2 cloves garlic, peeled
- ⅓ cup (abut 1½ ounces) hulled, untoasted pumpkinseeds (*pepitas*), plus a few extra for garnish
- A scant ¼ teaspoon black peppercorns (or about ⅓ teaspoon ground)
- ⅓ teaspoon allspice berries (or about ½ teaspoon ground)
- ½ inch cinnamon stick (or about ½ teaspoon ground)
- 4 cloves (or about ⅛ teaspoon ground)
- ¼ teaspoon dried thyme
- 1 slice firm white bread, crusts removed and diced
- ⅓ cup (about 1½ ounces) skinned and roasted peanuts
- 1 canned *chile chipotle,* seeded and roughly chopped
- Sugar, about 1 teaspoon
- Salt, about ¼ teaspoon

For the garnish:
- 1 slice of onion, broken into rings

underside of each half, pull off any of the breastbone that is still attached, and cut off the collarbone up near the neck. Your goal is to remove all the bones in the breast half that are near or at the surface of the underside, leaving only the wing bone. Bone the thighs as you would chicken thighs (page 225).
Pricking and Frying the Duck: To help rid the duck skin of fat, it is pricked (allowing rendering fat to flow out), then fried on the skin-side only. If you still find the skin objectionable, remove it before saucing and baking.
Pureeing and Serving Nut-Thickened Sauces: See page 195.

Ingredients
Chiles Anchos: Because the sauce has only a small proportion of dried chiles, 3 or 4 New Mexico or California chiles could substitute for *anchos.*
Chiles Chipotles: Frequently, Mexican cooks omit this smoky-tasting fillip.

Timing and Advance Preparation
From scratch, allow 4 hours to prepare the dish, half of which won't require your active involvement. Steps 1 through 5 can be completed a day in advance; refrigerate the duck and sauce separately, covered. Bring the duck to room temperature, reheat the sauce, thin it (if necessary), then complete Steps 6 and 7.

CONTEMPORARY IDEAS
Charcoal-Grilled Duck in Cashew Pipián with Crispy Bacon: Slowly fry 4 slices bacon until crisp, reserve the fat

1. *Duck preliminaries*. Use a large knife or kitchen shears to split each duck: Cut through the ribs down both sides of the backbone (set the backbone aside to use in preparing the broth); open the duck out, cavity-side down, press down firmly on the breastbone to loosen it, then split the duck down the breastbone. Split the second duck in the same fashion. Finally, prick the skin sides of each half with a fork at 1-inch intervals, pushing the tines in only about 1/8 inch.

2. *Preparing the broth*. In a medium-size saucepan, combine the duck backs, necks, gizzards and hearts (but *not* the livers), plus 5 cups water, the onion and salt. Bring to a simmer, skim off any grayish foam that rises during the first few minutes of simmering, add the herbs and bay leaves, partially cover and simmer over medium-low for at least 1 hour, preferably 2 or 3. Strain through a fine-mesh sieve, then skim off all the fat that rises to the top.

3. *Frying the duck*. Heat the 2 tablespoons oil in a large (12-inch) skillet over medium. Dry 2 duck halves with paper towels, lay skin-side down in the hot oil, and fry for about 15 minutes without turning, until the duck skin is *well* browned; drain on paper towels. Pour off all but a thin coat of fat and fry the remaining duck halves in the same manner.

4. *Sauce preliminaries*. Tear the chiles into large flat pieces. Heat *2 tablespoons* of the lard or oil in a medium-size skillet over medium. When hot, quick-fry the chiles to toast them lightly, a few seconds on each side. Transfer to a small bowl, draining off as much oil as possible, cover with boiling water, weight down with a small plate, and soak about 30 minutes.

Cook the onion and garlic in the same skillet over medium heat until they have browned nicely, about 10 minutes. Remove them from the pan, draining well, and place in a large bowl.

Heat another medium-size skillet over medium-low for several minutes. Add the pumpkinseeds; when the first one pops, stir them constantly for 4 to 5 minutes, until all have toasted and popped. Crumble a few and reserve for garnish, then scoop the rest into the bowl with the onions.

Grind the spices in a mortar or spice grinder and add to the bowl, along with the thyme, bread, peanuts, *chipotle* and 1½ cups of the duck broth. Drain the chiles and add to the bowl.

5. *Pureeing, frying and simmering the sauce*. Scoop half of the mixture into a blender jar and blend to a smooth puree, adding *a little more* broth if the mixture won't move through the blades; strain through a medium-mesh sieve. Puree and strain the other half.

Heat the remaining tablespoon of lard or oil in a large

and coarsely crumble the bacon. Prepare the duck and broth (Steps 1 through 3); make the sauce (Steps 4 and 5), substituting cashews for the peanuts and doing all the frying in the rendered bacon fat. Prepare a medium-low charcoal fire and grill the duck for 20 to 25 minutes, turning frequently; keep a spray bottle on hand to squelch any flare-ups. Ladle the sauce over the grilled duck and garnish with cashews and the crumbled bacon.

Regional Explorations
Pepián (as Jaliscans call it) is a popular West-Central dish, served every day at the Libertad market in Guadalajara. I've read recipes for a rustic Northern version made from toasted corn, seeds, chiles and flavorings, but I haven't found it in the public domain. In Tamiahua, Veracruz, and in Tampico, a coarse, simple green *pipián* is made from pumpkinseeds and little else; I've had it straight on enchiladas and mixed with cream for fish. Down in Puebla, *pipián* comes in a pair: red with dried chile or green with *tomatillo*, green chiles and herbs; the latter is, for all intents and purposes, the Pueblan equivalent of the *mole verde* made in other parts of the country. With pumpkinseeds figuring into so many regional dishes in Yucatán, it's not surprising that they have a *pipián*, too; it's made with tomato, *epazote* and a host of spices, then thickened with *masa*.

Kitchen Spanish and History
When you taste a bite of *pipián*, it is a bit of Mexico's oldest tradition, for *pipián* was

saucepan over medium-high. When quite hot, add the puree and stir constantly for about 5 minutes, as it concentrates and darkens. Stir in 2 cups of the broth, cover and simmer over medium-low heat for about 45 minutes, stirring occasionally. When the sauce is ready, adjust the consistency, if necessary, by adding enough broth to make it the consistency of heavy cream. Season with sugar and salt.

6. *Baking the duck.* About 45 minutes before serving, pre-heat the oven to 350°. Lay the duck halves, skin-side up, in a large roasting pan. Pour the hot sauce over them, cover and bake for 25 to 30 minutes, until the duck is done (tender when pricked with a fork).

7. *Garnishing and presentation.* Remove the duck halves to a warm serving platter or individual plates. Tip the sauce to one end of the pan and spoon off the fat that has accumulated on top. Ladle the sauce over the ducks, garnish with the onion rings and crumbled pumpkinseeds and serve immediately.

Dried ancho chiles

CHARCOAL-GRILLED CHICKEN, SINALOA-STYLE

Pollo a las Brasas, Estilo Sinaloense

The smoky places are set up at crossroads or scattered around Sinaloan towns, with their bricked-in troughs for embers and their split chickens, searing and charring two feet above the fire. If there's a place to sit, it's usually folding chairs and tables; but what more is necessary for a wonderful picnic of *pollo a las brasas* (literally "chicken over the embers"), Charcoal-Grilled Baby Onions (page 277), *Salsa Mexicana* (page 35) and steaming corn tortillas?

You might want to add *Charro* Beans (page 270), Grill-Roasted Corn (page 272) or Zucchini with Roasted Peppers, Corn and Cream (page 273). *Picadillo* Turnovers (page 150)

among the earliest-recorded preparations. The Friar Saha-gún (1550s): "Here are told the foods that the lords ate. . . . Turkey with red chiles; . . . sauces of ordinary tomatoes and small tomatoes and yellow chili, or of toma-toes and green chili; . . . grey fish with red chile, tomatoes and ground squash seeds; . . ." In Central Mexico, these ingre-dients still form the backbone of the cooking, including *pi-pián*, one of the cuisine's most refined dishes. Like *mole verde*, its thickness, texture and satis-fying flavor come primarily from seeds (pumpkinseeds, ses-ame seeds or peanuts), and that is apparently why the Spaniards christened this In-dian standard with a name so closely resembling *pepita*, their word for seed.

COOK'S NOTES

Timing and Advance Preparation
Spend ½ hour preparing the chicken and marinade at least 4 hours ahead; it will take 1¼ hours to finish the dish, a good part of it spent waiting on the fire and then the chicken. The chicken may marinate for a couple of days, but its texture will be best when grilled just before serving.

TRADITIONAL VARIATIONS
Grilled Chicken with Another Flavor: Prepare the recipe as directed, using the following

would be a good informal appetizer, and Mexican Chocolate Ice Cream (page 300) with a drizzle of Kahlúa could be dessert. To drink: Mexican Sangria (page 322) or beer. This recipe, with its mild, garlicky marinade, is based on one that appeared in *Gastrotur* magazine.

YIELD: 6 to 8 servings

2 medium, whole chickens (3½ pounds each)

For the marinade:
1 small onion, roughly chopped
8 cloves garlic, peeled and roughly chopped
1⅓ cups freshly squeezed orange juice
½ teaspoon *each* dried thyme, marjoram and oregano
4 bay leaves, broken
A generous teaspoon salt
½ teaspoon freshly ground black pepper

1. *Splitting the chickens for grilling.* Using a large knife or kitchen shears, cut down both sides of the backbone of 1 chicken, through the joints where the legs attach, then on through the ribs; remove the backbone. Open the chicken out flat on your cutting board, skin-side up, and press on the breastbone to loosen it so the chicken will lie flat. For the nicest presentation, make a small incision through the skin toward the bottom of each thigh and press the end of the nearest drumstick through it; this will hold the leg in place as the chicken is grilled. Repeat with the second chicken, then lay them in a noncorrosive bowl.

2. *Marinating the chickens.* Puree all the marinade ingredients in a blender or food processor. Pour the mixture over the chickens and rub them to coat thoroughly. Cover and refrigerate at least 4 hours (or, preferably, overnight), turning the chickens several times.

3. *Grilling and serving the chickens.* About 1¼ hours before serving, light your charcoal fire, let it burn until the coals are only medium-hot, then position the grill about 8 inches above the coals and lightly oil it. Lay the chickens on the grill, skin-side up, and grill for 35 to 45 minutes, turning every 10 minutes and basting with any leftover marinade. They are ready when tender, and when a fork pricked deep into the thigh brings up clear (not pink) juices. (During the final 10 minutes of cooking, grill the onions, as described on page 277—Charcoal-Grilled Baby Onions—if you are using them.) Cut the chickens into quarters, lay them on a warm platter and serve.

marinade: pulverize ¼ teaspoon coriander seeds, ¼ teaspoon black peppercorns, ½ inch cinnamon stick, ⅛ teaspoon whole cloves and 1 bay leaf, then mix with 1 teaspoon salt, 1 teaspoon mixed herbs, 2 teaspoons paprika, ½ cup vinegar and 4 roasted cloves of garlic (peeled and mashed to a paste).

CONTEMPORARY IDEAS
Cornish Game Hens a las Brasas: Substitute 3 or 4 game hens for the chickens: Split and marinate them as directed, then grill them for 25 to 30 minutes.

a few Mexican beers

CHICKEN THIGHS WITH VINEGAR, OIL AND AROMATIC SPICES

Pollo en Escabeche

This is one of the most popular specialties of Yucatán: The bird—be it turkey or hen—is stewed, smeared with the robust *escabeche* spices, fried (or occasionally char-broiled), then served in its own savory broth with a beautiful crown of pickley-tasting onions and·roasted peppers.

Since the dish is historically associated with Valladolid (it can be called *escabeche de Valladolid, escabeche oriental* or just plain *escabeche*), I am offering this simple, savory recipe based on the best version I tasted there. I've called for thighs rather than whole chicken, because they stand up well to the cooking.

This informal dish goes well with crusty bread and Mixed Vegetable Salad (page 87). *Masa* Boats (*Sopes*, page 168) would be a tasty start to the meal, homemade ice cream (page 298) a nice finish. For drinks: beer or Tamarind Cooler (page 308).

YIELD: 4 servings

For simmering the chicken:

    8 (about 2½ pounds total) chicken thighs, boned if you wish (page 225)

    ¼ teaspoon black peppercorns, very coarsely ground

    ½ teaspoon cumin seeds

    ½ teaspoon dried oregano

    2 bay leaves

    1 teaspoon salt

    6 cloves garlic, peeled and halved

For finishing the dish:

    1½ tablespoons (½ recipe) Mixed-Spice Paste (page 67)

    1 tablespoon flour

    1 medium onion, sliced ⅛ inch thick

    4 long (4-inch) fresh *chiles xcatiques* or banana peppers, roasted and peeled (page 336), seeded, deveined and cut into long strips

COOK'S NOTES

Techniques
Coating and Frying the Chicken: If the seasoning paste is too firm to spread, knead it with the back of a spoon and, if necessary, work in a few drops of water. It will go on a little irregularly; after the coated chicken has stood un-covered, the coating will ad-here better. The flour dusting keeps the chicken from sticking to the pan; *medium* heat keeps the spices from burning. Using a well-seasoned cast-iron skillet is by far the best.

Ingredients
Chiles Xcatiques: These are like the *güeros* of the rest of Mexico: a yellow-skinned chile similar to our medium-hot ba-nana or Hungarian wax pep-per. I've also used 4 small, long green chiles and been satisfied.

Timing and Advance Preparation
Start at least 1¾ hours before serving (1 hour won't require your active involvement). The dish may be prepared through Step 2, cover and refrigerated. Let the chicken stand at room temperature, uncovered, for 45 minutes before completing Step 3.

TRADITIONAL VARIATIONS
Shredded Chicken in Esca-beche: Complete the recipe as directed, boiling the final vine-gar-broth-onion mixture until reduced by half; taste for salt. Add the chicken to the brothy mixture, skin-side down, and cool to room temperature.

¼ **cup lard or vegetable (or olive) oil**
¼ **cup cider vinegar**
Salt, if necessary

1. *Simmering the chicken.* Bring 7 cups of water to a boil in a large saucepan, add the chicken (plus a little more water if there isn't enough to cover it), then skim off any grayish foam that rises during the first few minutes of simmering. Add the black pepper, cumin, oregano, bay leaves, salt and garlic. Partially cover and simmer gently for 23 minutes, until the meat is tender (boned thighs will be done in about 20 minutes). Remove from the fire, and, if time permits, cool the chicken in the broth. Fish out the thighs and set them skin-side up on a plate. Strain the broth, skim off the fat that rises to the top and reserve 2½ cups broth.

2. *Coating the chicken.* When the chicken skin has dried, rub *1 tablespoon* of the seasoning paste over the skin side of the thighs; let stand 1 hour, uncovered.

3. *Finishing the dish.* About 25 minutes before serving, lightly dust the spice-covered side of the chicken with flour; pat gently to evenly distribute the flour and remove any excess. Rinse the onion, drain thoroughly and set aside with the strips of chile.

Set a large (12-inch) skillet over medium heat and add the lard or oil. When hot, lay in the chicken pieces, skin-side down, and fry until crispy, about 4 minutes per side. Drain on paper towels and keep warm in a low oven.

Return the pan to the heat and add the onion and chile. Cook for 4 to 5 minutes, stirring occasionally, until the onion softens. Add the vinegar, reserved broth and remaining ½ tablespoon seasoning paste, stirring to dissolve the paste. Simmer several minutes to blend the flavors. Taste for salt.

Place 2 thighs in each of 4 warm, deep plates. Top with a portion of the onion mixture and broth, and serve.

Skin, bone and coarsely shred the chicken; return the meat to the broth. Rewarm or serve cool.

CONTEMPORARY IDEAS

Charcoal-Grilled Fresh Tuna or Swordfish Steaks in Escabeche: Spread ⅔ of the spice paste on four 7- to 8-ounce fresh tuna or swordfish steaks. Cover and refrigerate for 8 hours. Prepare 2½ cups fish broth (page 62). Fry red (not white) onion and the chiles as directed in Step 3, using ¼ cup olive oil. Add the vinegar, fish broth and remaining spice paste, and boil until reduced by half. Brush the fish with olive oil, grill over a medium-low charcoal fire and serve with a ladle of the onion-chile-spice broth.

Kitchen History
In 1538, just 17 years after the fall of the great Aztec kingdom, it was recorded that the Spanish conquerors sat down to a festive New World table set with little birds in pickling sauce (*escabeche*)—a preparation they'd known in their homeland and one that has survived surprisingly unaltered in Yucatán, through 450 years of turmoil and mestizo evolution.

Olive oil, Baja California

YUCATECAN PIT BARBECUE

Eduardo Azcorra's narrow eyes sparkled when he found out I loved Yucatecan food. It was the first time I'd sat on a stool at his canopied stall in front of one of the Mérida markets, watching him serve his breakfast of *tamales colados* and carry on with all the other vendors as he kept a sharp eye on everyone's every movement—like a man who'd done with little all his life. His hair was graying and thin, but his enthusiasm belied a lively spirit. And when the subject was food or politics, in Mayan, Spanish or English, he never had to think up things to say.

He knew how to dig pits they call *pibes,* line them with rocks and build fires on top. He knew how to marinate little pigs or chickens in *achiote* seasoning and choose the right fragrant leaves—fig, guava, wild basil—to go over the coals. He understood how to wrap the meat in banana leaves, lay it on grates in the pit, and cover it with henequen bags and earth so it slowly cooked and steamed.

There is little difference between the pit cooking he spelled out and that of the lamb *barbacoa* so famous in Central Mexico. Of course, in Yucatán the seasonings are different, and the meat is wrapped in more flexible, more sealable banana leaves, rather than maguey. And in recent years, the cooks have translated the leaf-wrapped pit cooking into indoor steaming and baking; it doesn't give the food any taste of the fire, but it is certainly easier for most North Americans (many of whom, like me, don't even have a yard to dig in).

I've never tasted the pit-cooked versions of chicken or pork *pibil,* but several recipes suggest re-creating the pit-cooked flavor by heating the cooked meat over smoky charcoal. Perhaps—but I love the flavors as they are: aromatic with red *achiote* and spices, tart with bitter orange juice and herby with banana leaves. The following recipe, based on the one from Sr. Azcorra, show those flavors at their best.

Kitchen Spanish

Pib in Mayan, according to the authoritative *Diccionario de mejicanismos,* refers as much to the procedure of roasting—underground or in the modern oven—as it does to the hot pit; it can even refer to roasted food in general. To most Yucatecans, though, it still seems to conjure up scenes of earthy holes, *achiote*-marinated meat and banana leaves.

RED-SEASONED CHICKEN STEAMED IN BANANA LEAVES

Pollo Pibil

With the earthy, spicy marinade, the roasted peppers and fresh tomatoes, the fragrant banana-leaf wrapper and the crown of crunchy, pink pickled onions, this dish is one of the glories of Mexican cooking. I like to serve it by itself, with only steaming corn tortillas as an accompaniment. For a first course, creamy Fresh Corn Chowder (page 99) would be delicious, as would be a dessert of Spicy Poached Guavas (page 297) or fresh berries.

YIELD: 4 servings

> 2 large (about 2½ pounds total), whole chicken breasts, skinned and boned or half-boned (page 225)
> 4 (about 1¼ pounds) chicken thighs, skinned and boned if you wish (page 225)
> ¼ cup (1 recipe) *Achiote* Seasoning Paste (page 66)
> 6 tablespoons bitter orange juice (page 340)
> ½ teaspoon salt
> Four 12 × 18-inch rectangles of banana leaves
> 3 tablespoons lard or vegetable oil
> 1 medium onion, sliced ⅛ inch thick
> 4 long (4-inch) fresh *chiles xcatiques* or banana peppers, roasted and peeled (page 336), seeded, deveined and cut into long strips
> About 2 tablespoons vegetable oil for coating the banana leaves
> 1 ripe, medium-large tomato, cored and sliced in 8 rounds
> About ⅔ cup (½ recipe) Pickled Red Onions (page 50)

1. *Marinating the chicken.* Halve the chicken breasts and place in a noncorrosive bowl with the thighs. Mix together the seasoning paste, *4 tablespoons* of the bitter orange juice and the salt; if your homemade seasoning paste looks gritty, blend the mixture for a minute or so to smooth it out. Pour it

COOK'S NOTES

Techniques
Cooking in Banana Leaves: They will contain and flavor the cooking juices of the chicken; if they develop leaks, make foil "boats" to set them in.
A Single-Package Alternative: When I'm in a hurry, I make a single package of *Pollo Pibil* in an 11-inch metal tart pan that fits in my big steamer with ¾ inch all around for letting the steam rise: Line the pan with a single leaf (shiny-side up), then lay on 2 more leaves to meet in the center and overhang the edges. Brush with oil and arrange the chicken on top in a single layer; finish the layering as described. Fold in the leaves on the edges, then cover it all snugly with another leaf and a tight lid of foil.

Ingredients
Banana Leaves: Notes on locating, choosing, storing and preparing can be found on page 325. If unavailable, make the chicken packages with aluminum foil or parchment paper, though the effect isn't quite the same.
Chiles Xcatiques: These are like the *güeros* of the rest of Mexico: a yellow-skinned chile similar to our medium-hot banana or Hungarian wax peppers. I have also used 4 small long green chiles and been satisfied with the results.

Timing and Advance Preparation
Prepare the pickled red onions the day before. Once the chicken has marinated, you'll need 1 hour to prepare the

over the chicken, mix thoroughly, cover and refrigerate at least 4 hours or, preferably, overnight. Refrigerate the remaining bitter orange juice for use in Step 3.

2. *Other preliminaries.* Prepare the banana leaves as described on page 177 and cut eight 18-inch lengths of kitchen string for tying the packages.

Heat the lard or oil in a medium-size skillet over medium, add the onion and cook, stirring frequently, until well browned, about 10 minutes. Scoop the onion and *all* the lard or oil into a small dish, then mix in the chile strips.

3. *Preparing the packages.* Lay out the banana leaves shiny-side up and brush lightly with oil. Place a breast half and thigh in the center of each one, top with a portion of onion-chile mixture and 2 rounds of tomato. Sprinkle each with ½ tablespoon of the reserved bitter orange juice, a quarter of any fat remaining from the onion-chile mixture, and a quarter of the remaining marinade.

Chicken and condiments on banana leaf

Fold each of the packages: Pick up the two short sides of the leaf and bring them to meet (face-to-face, *not* overlapping), then fold over twice, to make a tight (French) seam; fold in the top and bottom, overlapping them in the center, then use 2 strings to tie the package snugly in both directions.

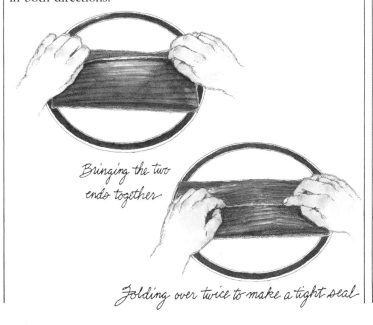

Bringing the two ends together

Folding over twice to make a tight seal

packages and ½ hour for steaming. The chicken may be kept in the marinade several days and the packages may be made early in the day you're serving; the chicken is best when steamed just before serving.

TRADITIONAL VARIATIONS

Cochinita (Pork) Pibil: Prepare the recipe through Step 2, substituting 2 pounds boneless pork shoulder (cut into 2-inch slabs) for the chicken. Line a large Dutch oven with 2 leaves (shiny-side up) and brush with oil. Layer as directed in Step 3, cover with the two remaining leaves (lightly oiled, shiny-side down), tucking them snugly around the meat. Cover and bake at 350° for about 2½ hours, until the meat is tender.

Fish in Banana leaves (Nac Cum): Prepare the recipe through Step 3, substituting 1½ pounds boneless, skinless fish fillets (choose halibut, bass, grouper, cod or the like) for the chicken and sprinkling a little chopped flat-leaf parsley over the fish before closing the packages. Steam over simmering water for 20 minutes, until the fish flakes.

Folded and tied chicken pibil package

4. *Steaming the chicken.* About 40 minutes before serving, set up a large steamer (see page 177) with an inch of water in the bottom. Place the packages on the steamer rack, cover and steam over medium to medium-low heat for 30 to 35 minutes. Retrieve a package, untie it and check that the thigh is cooked through and tender.

5. *Serving.* Remove the packages to warm dinner plates. Cut the strings and open up each package, being careful to contain the juices. Fold the edges of the banana leaves underneath for an attractive presentation, top with a little of the pickled red onions and serve.

Chicken pibil

CHILIED CHICKEN STEAMED WITH AVOCADO LEAVES

Barbacoa de Pollo, Estilo Guerrerense

In Southern Mexico, the preparation of *barbacoa* frequently changes from the maguey-wrapped, pit-cooked chunks of lamb (typical in Central states), to an aromatic dish of chile-mari-

COOK'S NOTES

Techniques
Cooking with Chile Veins: The veins contain the highest concentration of the chile's burning capsaicin; they're occasionally used, in small quantities, to spice up a dish.
Steaming the Chile-Coated Chicken: The chile paste will

nated goat that has been slowly steamed over a bed of anisey avocado leaves; it's sold in the markets to roll up into special tacos. On weekends in Guerrero, some cooks make a delicious version with chicken—which is certainly a simple alternative for us average North Americans.

My original recipe, from a market vendor in Tixtla, Guerrero, called for whole chicken; but I've given directions for half-boned breasts and boned thighs so you can serve your *barbacoa* easily as a main dish. It is simple, good fare for backyard parties, with a Mixed Vegetable Salad (page 87), Mexican Rice (page 263), plus hot corn tortillas, Fresh Green *Tomatillo* Sauce (page 36) and chopped red onions. I'd served *Jamaica* "Flower" Cooler (page 307) or beer to drink and Pecan Pie with Raw Sugar (page 289) for dessert.

YIELD: 4 servings

- 8 medium (about 2 ounces total) dried *chiles guajillos*
- 2½ tablespoons sesame seeds
- ½ inch cinnamon stick (or about ½ teaspoon ground)
- 3 cloves (or a big pinch ground)
- ½ teaspoon black peppercorns (or about ¾ teaspoon ground)
- ½ medium onion, roughly chopped
- 4 cloves garlic, peeled and roughly chopped
- 2 tablespoons cider vinegar
- 1½ tablespoons lard or vegetable oil
- Salt, about 1 teaspoon, divided between the marinade and the steaming liquid
- 2 large (about 2½ pounds total), whole chicken breasts, boned or half-boned (page 225)
- 4 (about 1¼ pounds) chicken thighs, boned if you wish (page 225)
- 15 avocado leaves (see **Ingredients** in Cook's Notes)

1. *The chile paste.* Stem the chiles, break them open, discard the seeds and carefully remove the veins, reserving them for later. Tear the chiles into flat pieces. Heat a griddle or heavy skillet over medium, then toast the chiles a few pieces at a time, pressing them firmly against the hot surface with a metal spatula until they crackle and change color, then flipping them over and pressing down to toast the other side. Cover them with boiling water, weight with a plate to keep them submerged, and soak for 30 minutes.

set up into a rather unattractive, dull coating as the chicken steams. For that reason, the meat is quickly simmered with the liquid to dissolve some of the coating and add richness to the broth.

Cooking the Chicken Breast: If you're like me and want your chicken breast really moist and barely done, add it to the steamer 10 minutes after you've started steaming the thighs.

Ingredients

Chiles Guajillos: When these are not available, 6 or 7 California or New Mexico chiles can be substituted.

Chicken: My recipe calls for breasts and thighs simply for ease of eating. A quartered chicken may be substituted if refinement isn't what you're looking for or if you're going to shred the meat for tacos.

Avocado Leaves: If you don't live in the Southwest or Florida, where avocado trees grow, line the steamer with lettuce leaves, then replace the avocado leaves with 20 bay leaves; add ½ teaspoon cracked aniseed to the steaming water. Strain the seeds out of the broth before serving.

Timing and Advance Preparation

Allow at least 4 hours to prepare and marinate the meat, then 45 minutes to complete the dish; total active involvement is about 1¼ hours. The chicken may marinate for 2 days; finish Steps 3 and 4 shortly before serving.

Toast the sesame seeds on the griddle or skillet, stirring for several minutes until golden; scrape into a blender jar. Toast the chile veins for a few seconds only and add them to the sesame seeds. Pulverize the spices in a mortar or spice grinder and add to the blender along with the onion, garlic, vinegar and ½ cup water.

Drain the chiles and stir into the blender. Blend until smooth, stirring and scraping down the mixture several times; add additional water only if absolutely necessary. Strain the thick mixture through a medium-mesh sieve.

Heat the lard or oil in a medium-size saucepan over medium-high. When quite hot, add the chile puree all at once and stir constantly, for 4 or 5 minutes, until very thick and dark. Season with about ½ teaspoon salt and cool.

2. *Marinating the chicken.* Halve the chicken breasts and place in a noncorrosive bowl with the chicken thighs. Scrape in the chile paste and mix thoroughly. Cover and refrigerate several hours or, preferably, overnight.

3. *Steaming the chicken.* About 45 minutes before serving, set up a large steamer (see page 177): Measure 3 cups water into the bottom and cover the steamer rack with a single layer of avocado leaves. Lay the chicken over the leaves, daub any remaining marinade on top, then lay on the remaining leaves. Cover and steam over medium to medium-low heat for 25 minutes.

4. *Finishing the barbacoa.* Remove the chicken and leaves, take out the steamer rack, then add the leaves to the simmering liquid. Boil over high heat until reduced to 2 cups, remove from the fire, skim off any fat and *lightly* season with salt.

Return the chicken to the broth, cover and simmer for 3 or 4 minutes; turn the pieces over and simmer a minute or so longer, until much of the marinade has dissolved into the broth. Serve the chicken in deep, warm plates with several spoonfuls of broth.

Avocado leaves (hojas de aguacate)

TRADITIONAL VARIATIONS
Shredded Chicken Barbacoa for Taco Fillings: Complete the recipe as directed, reducing the liquid to 1 cup. Remove the chicken from the simmering broth, skin, bone and shred it, then return it to the broth. Serve with Fresh Green *Tomatillo* Sauce (page 36) and chopped red onion.

Goat or Lamb Barbacoa: Prepare the recipe as directed, replacing the chicken with a 5-pound goat hindquarter or a 3-pound lamb shoulder. Allow about 3 hours for steaming—and watch that the liquid doesn't boil away. Bone the cooked meat, leaving it in large pieces. Heat it in the broth as directed in Step 4, then serve.

MEAT
❖
Carnes

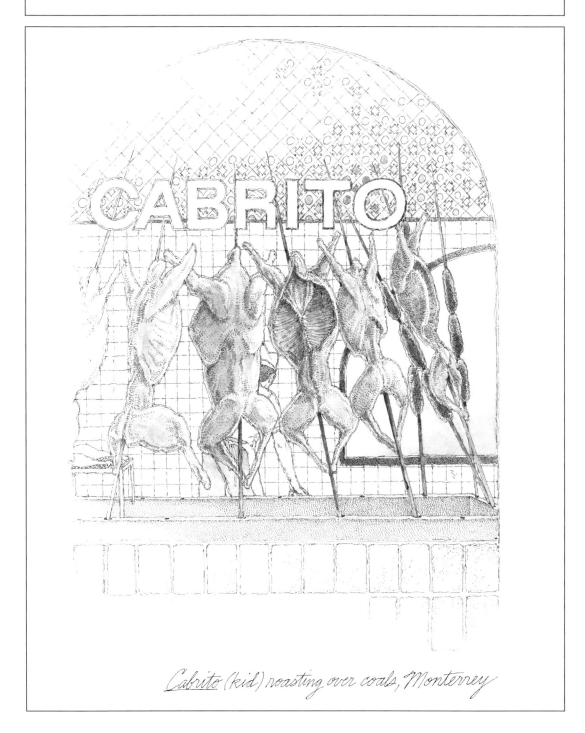

Cabrito (kid) roasting over coals, Monterrey

We stepped through the yellow metal door in the pink-painted, plastered *adobe,* into María Lara de García's home and twice-a-week *pozole* parlor. It was 6:45 in the morning in Almolonga, Guerrero, but there was every indication of midday: Everyone was up, dressed and finished with the morning chores; the huge caldron of *pozole* that had been simmering over the smoldering, smoky-gray fire was ready; the first customers had arrived as the eight-foot table was pulled into place; and the first quart-size earthenware *cazuelas* were being pulled off the wall for servings of the rich pork and hominy soup.

Deann and I had arrived in town the Sunday before, driving from Chilpancingo, where the air was warm, up over the first ridge of mountains, then climbing and winding our way on up to the dirt-road turn-off to the small village. It lay farther in, around a bend in the green valley, where the houses stumbled out over a little, steeply graded niche, split up by a few cobbled streets and rugged paths. We made the climb up to the land just above the church, where our friends Cliff and Sue Small live.

They smoothed our way into the culinary activity of the community, and after a few weeks, I arose at 4:00 A.M. and shined my flashlight on the path back to the Garcías'. María's husband, Beto, must have been up for some time, judging from the washtub of near-boiling water set over a hot, attractive fire. Three other men came into the utility yard made up of horse stalls, cisterns and a butchering table. They set about roping a pig, and within half an hour the animal had been slaughtered, bled and cleaned.

Routinely and swiftly, each part of the most common Mexican red-meat source was dispatched: the head for tomorrow's *pozole;* the trotters for María's dinner; the tripe, stomach and intestines put to soak in one of the shallow concrete sinks; the heart, liver, kidneys and portion of lower intestine set aside to be sold immediately.

It was 6:30 by this time, and the town's loudspeaker came on for the first of the day's announcements: Señora María Lara has pork and innards for sale; later there will be *chicharrones* and blood sausage. There arrived an almost immediate stream of ladies, wrapped tightly in shawls pulled high to guard their faces from the dawn chill. Each set her white dish, holding its well-counted pesos, in a line on the table. They would return, they all said, as soon as the innards were divided up.

Then María began cutting the innards into inch-size pieces and portioning them out for the ladies to take home and fry for midmorning *almuerzo.* Out in the yard, the soft fat from around the internal organs was collected for rendering into lard. The skin was cut from the carcass and hung on the line to dry before frying into *chicharrones.* Finally, the four quarters of the pig were hung on meat hooks above a table near the door to the patio.

The remainder of the morning was spent making *morcilla* (their delicious, mint-and-*cilantro*-flavored blood sausage), *pozole* and *chicharrones*. María and her assistants cooked in the open-air kitchen over wood fires, which were nestled into U-shaped supports that rose from the massive plastered mudbank that was the stove. It was the right setup for María's 25- to 40-gallon pots and, as María said, *pozole* that's not cooked in big batches all night over a smoldering fire lacks a certain special flavor.

Mexican pork is legendary for its succulence: It makes rich *chorizo* sausage, meatballs and ground-meat stuffings for *chiles rellenos* and turnovers; everywhere, it's slowly browned in its own fat for the delectably textured *carnitas*. In Chiapas, it's slow-roasted with chile-spice marinade (*cochito*); in Yucatán, the slow-cooking takes place in banana leaves with *achiote* seasoning (*cochinita pibil*). Nearly all Mexican cooks know how to do pork in a red chile–rich *adobo* marinade or sauce. Pueblans make the meat into a stew with tomatoes and *chipotle* peppers (*tinga*). And Northerners simmer it for their ubiquitous *carne con chile colorado;* a few of them also make a chile-flavored braise/roast called *asado*.

Cattle did well in Mexico after the Spanish brought in their starter herds in 1521, first in Veracruz and the Central highlands, then spreading extensively through the Northern reaches. Over the years, the North gained a reputation as the land of good beef—beef cut the North American way, nowadays. But the rest of the country usually puts up with lower quality: Their beef is either cut with the grain into thin sheets for salt preserving (*cecina*) or drying (*carne seca*), or it's slowly simmered to render it tender. Now and again, you'll encounter a nice steak in non-Northern spots, frequently a piece of tenderloin that has been thin-sliced like *cecina* and seared on a hot griddle. The fully dried beef, interestingly, also became a Northern specialty (perhaps because the area produced more beef than it could consume); so today, dishes made from jerky (like *machaca* or *machacado*) are associated with the North.

Without pigs or cows, pre-Columbian Mexico relied on the high-quality protein of beans, corn and tiny amaranth seeds, plus an abundance of wild game. In Yucatán and Sonora, there is still a predilection for deer. It is mild and delicious when pit-roasted in the Yucatecan manner, and cooks in other areas prepare it as steaks or dry it into jerky. Tabasco is a haven for wild things; the local specialties include the capybaralike *tepescuintle* and armadillo in all kinds of braises and red-chile stews. Iguana is a regional offering of Guerrero.

Kid slow-roasted over the embers (*cabrito al pastor*) is abundant in the northeast; in the same area and on down toward the Central highlands, the kid is simply roasted or stewed in *adobo* or in its own blood (*fritada*). And kid plays a role as well in *barbacoa,* pit-cooked meat that has been wrapped in aromatic leaves and set on a rack over simmering broth. In Central Mexico, large openair restaurants still cook maguey-wrapped lamb in brick pits and serve it with a *salsa borracha* of *pasilla* peppers and *pulque* (fermented maguey juice). But in most areas, the method has evolved away from the pit: In the West-Central states, lamb or kid is chile-marinated and slow-roasted on a rack in a sealed container (*birria*, they call it); in Southern Mexico, kid or chicken is chile-marinated and steamed in avocado leaves (*barbacoa*); and in Yucatán, it is the banana leaf–wrapped pork or chicken *pibil* that has moved out of the earth pit and into the oven or steamer.

And, of course, Mexicans never waste the innards. The tripe is the beloved stewed *pancita* of Central Mexico and the *menudo* soup of the rest of the country, especially the North. A mixture of the internal organs makes up a brothy *chocolomo* in Campeche and Yucatán, and a saucy *chanfaina* in many other places. I, for one, wouldn't want to go for charcoal-roasted *cabrito* without ordering the *machitos,* the tender liver wrapped in chitlings; they are among my most memorable gastronomical experiences.

As you can tell from this tour of Mexican preparations, meat is prized. Poultry and seafood are certainly well loved (and prepared in a good variety of ways), but special meat dishes really abound. I know that for our everyday meals many of us are leaning toward fish and chicken. But for those special occasions when you want to feature meat on the menu, you'll find some wonderful traditional Mexican recipes in this chapter.

For meat recipes from other chapters, see "Meat" in the Index.

QUICK-FRIED BEEF TIPS WITH MEXICAN FLAVORS

Puntas de Filete a la Mexicana

Any dish *a la mexicana* means a dish of what Mexicans have absorbed as a normal part of life . . . like the union of tomatoes, onions and chiles. When the tomatoes are fresh, ripe and chunky and the chiles are roasted *poblanos,* this dish of browned beef *a la mexicana* makes a simple and inviting statement in forthright flavors.

North of the border, we think of "tips" as cubes of meat from the sirloin tip or better, but Mexican butchery is less exacting. Someone with quality in mind will serve cubes of *filete* ("tenderloin"), but when cost is a concern, the pounded slices of beef (usually called *bisteces*) are in order.

Beef tips *a la mexicana* (or some variation) is a common

COOK'S NOTES

Techniques
Choosing the Best Ingredients and Treating Them Right: I have eaten this dish when it was simple perfection . . . as well as when it was less than inviting, when the meat was sweated in a half-hot pan and then simmered with harsh onions, mealy tomatoes and a dozen *serranos.* The trick is to choose the best ingredients and to brown the meat well.

restaurant and *cafetería* dish throughout the country, but it's most popular in the North. This version, patterned after the one served at Fonda el Refugio in Mexico City, is simple, but done with finesse. Serve it after a hearty first course of Melted Cheese with Peppers and *Chorizo* (page 82) with flour tortillas, accompany it with a salad and have ice cream with Goat-Milk Caramel (page 293) for dessert.

YIELD: 4 small servings

- 1 pound tender, lean, boneless beef like rib eye, tenderloin, short loin (New York), sirloin or even sirloin tip
- 2 medium fresh *chiles poblanos,* roasted, peeled and seeded (page 337)
- 1½ pounds (3 medium-large) ripe tomatoes, roasted or boiled (page 352), cored and peeled OR one 28-ounce can tomatoes, drained
- 2 tablespoons lard or vegetable (or olive) oil, plus a little more if needed
- 1 small onion, diced
- 1 clove garlic, peeled and minced
- ½ teaspoon mixed dried herbs (such as marjoram and thyme)
- 2 bay leaves
- ⅔ cup beef broth
- Salt, about ½ teaspoon (depending on the saltiness of the broth)

1. *Preliminaries.* Trim the meat of excess fat and cut into ¾-inch cubes; dry on paper towels. Dice the chiles into ½-inch pieces. Seed the peeled tomatoes, if you wish, by cutting across their width and gently squeezing out the seeds, then chop the tomatoes into ½-inch pieces.

2. *Browning the meat.* In a large skillet, heat the lard or oil over medium-high. When sizzlingly hot, add the cubes of meat in an *uncrowded single layer.* Brown them, turning frequently, for about 4 minutes (to about medium-rare). Remove the meat and reduce the heat to medium.

3. *Finishing the dish.* Scoop the onion into the skillet and fry until soft and beginning to brown, about 7 minutes. Add the garlic and stir for a minute or so longer, then add the chiles, tomatoes, herbs and bay leaves. Simmer, stirring frequently, until the tomatoes soften and the mixture becomes somewhat homogeneous, about 4 minutes; add the broth and simmer 5

Ingredients

Meat: Any piece of meat that you would fry, broil or grill works well. A less tender cut from the round could be used, if you return the meat to the pan when the tomatoes go in, cover the pan after adding the broth and increase the simmering time to 15 to 30 minutes (until the meat is tender).

Chiles Poblanos: As they do around Chihuahua, you can use 4 long green chiles (roasted, peeled and seeded), or even 4 *chiles serranos* (seeded only and *thinly* sliced).

Tomatoes: Good-quality, canned pear-shaped tomatoes are much better here than less-than-ripe mealy fresh ones.

Timing and Advance Preparation

Preparation time is about 45 minutes. The dish can be completed through Step 2 in advance; finish Step 3 in the 20 minutes before serving.

TRADITIONAL VARIATIONS

Beef Tips a la Ranchera: Prepare 2 cups Quick-Cooked Tomato-Chile Sauce (page 41). Cube and brown the meat as directed in Steps 1 and 2 above. Brown ½ small onion (sliced), then add 2 or 3 long green chiles (roasted, peeled, seeded and sliced), the tomato sauce and the broth. Simmer 10 minutes, then add the meat, heat and serve.

Pork a la Ranchera: Prepare the preceding variation recipe using 1 pound boneless pork shoulder, *but with one modification:* Add the pork with the tomato sauce, cover and simmer until tender.

minutes longer. Last, add the browned meat (and any juices that have collected around it). When the meat has heated through, remove the bay leaves, season with salt and the dish is ready for the table.

Fresh poblano chiles

BROILED BEEF WITH CLASSIC ACCOMPANIMENTS, TAMPICO-STYLE

Carne Asada a la Tampiqueña

There could scarcely be a restaurant dish more common, more distinctly Mexican, than this "combination" plate: a tender strip of quick-seared beef, a bowl of tasty beans, guacamole, a saucy enchilada and perhaps some lightly browned *rajas* of chile and onion.

The plate has nothing really to do with the port town of Tampico, but rather, was named by the *tampiqueño* José Luis Loredo. When the famous waiter moved from oil-rich Tampico to Mexico City in 1939 to open the Tampico Club, his *carne asada a la tampiqueña* became a signature dish. Though variations abound, I've presented the traditional version offered at such Loredo restaurants as Colonial Loredo and Caballo Bayo; I've left off the grilled square of cheese, simply because the necessary nonmelting, *panela*-style cheese is uncommon here. Flour or corn tortillas and a sauce like Red-Chile Sauce (page 37), *Chile Chipotle* Sauce (page 39), or *Salsa Mexicana* (page 35) are all you need to make this dish a meal. Beer, *Jamaica* "Flower" Cooler (page 307) or Mexican Sangria (page 322)

CONTEMPORARY IDEAS

Lamb Tips with Mexican Flavors: Cut 1 pound well-trimmed, boneless lamb loin into ¾-inch cubes. Sear the meat over a hot charcoal fire or brown it as described in Step 2. Follow the directions for Step 3, with the following modification: When the garlic has cooked 2 minutes, add 2 tablespoons tequila and let reduce to a glaze. Continue as directed, replacing the mixed herbs and bay leaves with 2 tablespoons chopped fresh coriander (*cilantro*).

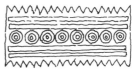

COOK'S NOTES

Techniques
Pan-Frying Meat: For the meat to have good browned flavor, dry it, heat the pan thoroughly and use a large pan (crowded meat sweats and stews).

Ingredients
Steak for Carne Asada: Tenderloin or short loin (where New York steaks come from) makes the best *carne asada.* The meat is traditionally cut with the grain into ¼- to ⅜-inch-thick "sheets" as for *Cecina* (page 57); or a 3-inch piece may be "roll-cut": Holding the knife parallel to the work surface, cut across the tenderloin ¼ to ⅜ inch below the surface; stop ¼ inch from the edge. Roll the meat over so the sliced sheet is hanging down on the right side. Starting where the last cut ended,

would be my drink choices; and I'd want a Sweet Fresh-Cheese Pie (page 288) for dessert.

YIELD: 4 servings

> 4 **(about 1½ pounds total) thin steaks cut from the tenderloin or short loin, or trimmed skirt steaks (see Ingredients in** Cook's Notes**)**
> **About 2 tablespoons freshly squeezed lime juice**
> **2½ to 3 cups (½ recipe) Brothy Beans (page 267)**
> **About 2 cups (⅔ recipe) Quick-Cooked** *Tomatillo* **Sauce (page 42)**
> **About ¾ cup (½ recipe) Roasted Pepper** *Rajas* **(page 278), made with whipping cream or broth**
> **About 1½ cups (½ recipe) Chunky Guacamole (page 44)**
> 4 **romaine lettuce leaves, for garnish**
> 4 **radish roses or a few radish slices, for garnish**
> 8 **corn tortillas, preferably store-bought**
> ¼ **cup vegetable oil, plus a little more if necessary**
> ½ **cup (about 2 ounces) crumbled Mexican** *queso fresco* **(page 327) or other fresh cheese like feta or farmer's cheese**
> **Several tablespoons finely chopped onion**
> **Salt and freshly ground black pepper, as desired**

1. *Seasoning the meat.* Lay the steaks in a noncorrosive dish and sprinkle both sides with the lime juice. Cover and refrigerate 1 to 4 hours.

2. *Other prepare-ahead preliminaries.* Scrape the cooked beans into one small saucepan and the *tomatillo* sauce into another; cover them and set aside. Scoop the *rajas* into a small, oven-proof dish, cover with foil and set aside.

3. *Last-minute preliminaries.* About an hour before serving, put together the guacamole. Lay the romaine leaves on a plate and mound a portion of guacamole on each one; decorate with radish roses or slices. Cover lightly with plastic wrap and refrigerate.

If the tortillas are moist, lay them in a single layer to dry until leathery. Heat the oil in a large, heavy skillet over medium-high. When hot enough to make the edge of a tortilla really sizzle, quick-fry the tortillas one at a time, about 3 seconds per side, to soften them. Drain well on paper towels, stack them up, wrap in foil, place in the oven and turn it on to 200°. Set the skillet aside to use for frying the meat.

cut across what is now the top, ¼ to ⅜ inch below the surface, stop ¼ inch from the edge, roll, cut, roll, cut . . . until you've "unrolled" the meat into a single sheet.

On the other hand, the butchers I surveyed in Chicago's four best Mexican groceries all said they'd choose a good skirt steak for *carne asada.* For directions on using it, see page 138.
Tortillas: See page 353.

Timing and Advance Preparation

Because this dish is a sampler of 5 distinct preparations, it takes some forethought and a couple of hours to make (if the beans are on hand). The *rajas* and *tomatillo* sauce can be made 2 or 3 days ahead, covered and refrigerated. The meat may be seasoned up to 4 hours in advance; Steps 3 through 5 should be completed just before serving.

TRADITIONAL VARIATIONS
Charcoal-Broiled Carne Asada: Simply prepare a hot charcoal fire and grill the seasoned meat over it; otherwise prepare the recipe as directed.
Carne Asada with Other Accompaniments: Frijoles Refritos (page 269) may replace the brothy ones; the enchiladas may be made with Red *Mole* (page 201) rather than *tomatillo* sauce.

CONTEMPORARY IDEAS
Marinated Steaks for Carne Asada: Heat 4 tablespoons vegetable or olive oil with ¼ teaspoon *each* ground allspice and black pepper plus 2 broken bay leaves. Let cool, then blend with 1 tablespoon lime

Set out the cheese and onion. Place the *rajas* and 4 large heatproof dinner plates in the oven. Set the beans and the *tomatillo* sauce over low heat to reheat.

4. *Frying the meat.* Dry the steaks on paper towels, then sprinkle with salt and pepper. Heat the skillet from Step 3 over medium-high; if there isn't enough oil left to lightly coat the bottom, add a little more. *When the pan is quite hot,* lay in the steaks. Fry rare or medium-rare, 1½ to 2 minutes per side; don't overcook. Remove to a wire rack set over a plate and keep warm in the oven. (As the meat "rests," it will reabsorb juices that would otherwise leak out when cut.)

5. *Assembling the dish.* Lay out the plates and assemble 2 enchiladas on each one: Remove a tortilla from the foil, lay it on the side of one plate, ladle a little sauce in the center, fold in half, then ladle sauce over the top; repeat with a second tortilla, letting it overlap the first one a little, then sprinkle them with the cheese and onion. Lay a steak on each plate, top with a portion of the *rajas,* then slide a "romaine boat" of guacamole in beside it. Serve immediately with bowls of steaming beans set to the side of each plate.

Carne asada a la tampiqueña

PORK-STUFFED CHILES IN SAVORY TOMATO SAUCE

Chiles Rellenos de Picadillo

*C*hiles *rellenos* are slid onto hundreds of plates in restaurants and market *fondas* throughout the Republic every day, and they

juice; pour over the steaks. Refrigerate overnight, turning several times. Prepare recipe as directed, omitting Step 1.

Regional Explorations
Guadalajarans are crazy about char-grilled *carne asada* steaks served on earthenware plates with Griddle-Baked Cheese *Quesadillas* (page 144), Charcoal-Grilled Baby Onions (page 277), Brothy Beans (page 267), *Salsa Picante* (page 40), Cactus-Paddle Salad (page 47) and Guacamole with *Tomatillos* (page 46). Variations on the theme are made throughout West-Central Mexico.

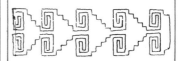

COOK'S NOTES

Techniques
Dipping and Frying the Chiles: Two points to remember in coating the chiles: Dipping them completely in the batter keeps oil from soaking

can be as different as the Northern long green variety stuffed with Chihuahua cheese, or the Veracruz meat-stuffed *jalapeños* wrapped in a tortilla to eat "taco-style" in the market. They might come filled with shredded crab or shrimp (as on the upper east and west coasts); they might be simple and unsauced, or made from reconstituted *chiles anchos,* or even stuffed with warm fried beans and set out unbattered.

I've encountered a great number of people smitten with a taste for these, which is unfortunate for them, because they do take a little time to prepare; I've set up a workable schedule under **Timing.** Saucy *chiles rellenos* need little to accompany them, only some Mexican Rice (page 263), perhaps a romaine salad, and Flan (page 283) for dessert. A lightly sauced, cheese-filled *chile relleno* makes an elegant first course.

YIELD: 8 stuffed chiles, 4 servings

> **8 large fresh *chiles poblanos***
> **About 2 cups (1 recipe) Quick-Cooked Tomato-**
> **Chile Sauce (page 41)**
> **1½ cups beef or pork broth**
> **Oil to a depth of ¾ inch, for frying**
> **About ¼ cup flour, plus another tablespoon for**
> **the eggs**
> **About 3 cups (1 recipe) Minced-Pork *Picadillo***
> **(page 132) or Northern-Style Shredded Beef**
> **(page 131), at room temperature**
> **4 large eggs, at room temperature**
> **½ teaspoon salt**
> **4 sprigs flat-leaf parsley, for garnish**

1. *Cleaning the chiles.* Roast and peel the chiles as directed on page 336, being careful not to overcook them or break off their stems. Seed them: Make a slit in the side of each one, from the shoulder down nearly to the point; with an index finger, scrape the seeds loose from the seed pods (just underneath the stem); under a gentle stream of water, flush the chiles clean of all their seeds, then drain. If you want milder chiles, *carefully* cut out the veins that run down the inside flesh of each one. Dry the chiles inside and out with paper towels.

2. *Other preliminaries.* In a small saucepan, mix the prepared tomato sauce with the broth (you may want to add ¼ teaspoon *each* ground cinnamon and black pepper, if you're using Oaxacan Minced-Pork *Picadillo*). Cover and place over very low heat. Heat the frying oil over medium-low.

3. *Stuffing the chiles.* Stuff the chiles with room-temperature

the insides, and quickly pulling them from the batter ensures a light, even coating. If the batter seems overly thick, whisk in a teaspoon of water. The batter is light and porous, so make sure the oil is 375°, or it will soak right in.

Ingredients

Chiles Poblanos: Though these are the most popular chiles for stuffing (because of their thick flesh, large size and rich flavor), different local varieties are used all across the Republic. Stateside, many choose the common, long green chiles. Substitute 12 medium ones in this recipe; the canned ones are soft and difficult to stuff.

Timing and Advance Preparation

When the filling and sauce are made ahead, the *chiles rellenos* take about 45 minutes to finish; refrigerated filling should come to room temperature before you use it. You may stuff the chiles a day in advance; cover and refrigerate until 1 hour before frying. Steps 3 and 4 must be completed just before serving. If you're forced to fry your *chiles rellenos* in advance (do it no more than 2 hours ahead), thoroughly drain them on paper towels, turning them over once; when you're ready to serve, set them 6 inches below a heated broiler for 4 or 5 minutes.

TRADITIONAL VARIATIONS

Cheese Chiles Rellenos: Prepare the recipe as directed, replacing the filling with 4 cups (1 pound) grated melting cheese (page 328) like Monterey Jack or mild cheddar; form the grated cheese into 8 ovals, then slip them into the seeded filling, leaving room to reclose the opening. If a chile won't re-form around the filling or if it is torn, "sew" it together with toothpicks; any that can be gently picked up by the stem without losing their filling are fine as is.

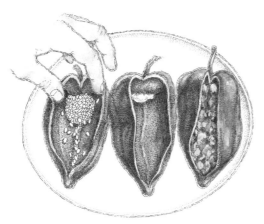

Peeled, cleaned and stuffed chiles

4. *Battering and frying the chiles.* Spread about ¼ cup flour onto a plate, then roll the chiles in it and shake off the excess.

Separate the eggs: whites into a clean mixing bowl, yolks into a small dish. Add the salt to the egg whites, then beat with a whisk or electric mixer set at medium speed until they are just stiff enough to hold a peak. Gently beat in the yolks one at a time, followed by 1 tablespoon of flour; stop beating when the flour is incorporated.

Bring the oil to 375°. Holding a chile by its stem, dip it completely into the egg batter, draw it out quickly, then lay it into the hot oil; batter 2 or 3 more chiles and lay them in the oil. (If a chile doesn't have a stem, set it on a fork, dip it in the batter, then roll it off into the oil; any uncovered spot can be dabbed with a little batter.) When the chiles are brown underneath, gently roll them over and brown the other side. Drain on paper towels and keep warm in a low oven. Batter and fry the remaining chiles, then drain with the others.

5. *Garnish and presentation.* Ladle about ¾ cup of brothy tomato sauce into each of 4 warm, deep plates, top with 2 chiles, then spoon a dribble of the sauce across the middle of each chile for decoration. Lay a sprig of parsley between the chiles and carry them to the table.

chiles and re-form. Though not usually to North American taste, many Mexicans prefer *queso fresco* (page 327) to the melting cheese.

Pan-Fried Chiles Rellenos, with Sauce and Without: Complete the recipe through Step 2, ignoring references to frying oil. Prepare 1½ times the batter (Step 3). Heat a little vegetable oil in a large, well-seasoned skillet over medium. Spoon out the batter into 3 or 4 rounds, lay a stuffed chile onto each one, then spoon a little batter over the top. When browned underneath, flip them over and brown on the other side. This method works well with the narrower, long green chiles. Serve with Quick-Cooked Tomato-Chile Sauce (no broth added), or serve without any sauce at all.

Black-Bean Chiles Rellenos: As a special side dish or vegetarian main course, prepare the chiles for stuffing (Step 1), fill them with 3 cups *Frijoles Refritos* made with black beans (page 269). Lay in a baking dish, pour 1½ to 2 cups Thick Cream (page 51) over them, sprinkle on a little salt and bake at 350° until lightly brown around the edges.

PORK WITH SMOKY TOMATO SAUCE, POTATOES AND AVOCADO

Tinga Poblana

Rich in roasted tomatoes, browned meat and smoky *chipotle* chiles—this is one of my favorite dishes and one my North American friends take to readily. In colonial Puebla, on the other side of the volcanos from mile-high Mexico City, *tinga* is offered as a stew in the restaurants, a filling for *tortas* in the snack shops and a stuffing for the *masa* turnovers available from street griddles.

The recipe that follows is based on the version served at Puebla's Fonda Santa Clara restaurant. It is a good warming stew with a spicy edge, and it makes a beautiful, simple meal with crusty rolls, a salad and Almond Flan (page 283). Beer, Tamarind Cooler (page 308), or even a robust red wine like Chianti or Zinfandel would go well here.

YIELD: 4 servings

- 1 pound lean, boneless pork shoulder, trimmed and cut in 1½-inch cubes
- ½ teaspoon mixed dried herbs (such as marjoram and thyme)
- 3 bay leaves
- 2 medium (about 10 ounces total) boiling potatoes like the red-skinned ones, quartered
- 1½ pounds (about 3 medium-large) ripe tomatoes, roasted or boiled (page 352), peeled and cored
  OR one 28-ounce can tomatoes, drained
- 4 ounces (½ cup) *chorizo* sausage, store-bought or homemade (page 55), removed from its casing
- 1 tablespoon vegetable oil
- 1 medium onion, diced
- 1 clove garlic, peeled and minced
- ½ teaspoon dried oregano
- 2 canned *chiles chipotles* in *adobo,* seeded and thinly sliced

COOK'S NOTES

Techniques
Browning the Ingredients: A good part of the depth and richness of this dish comes from a thorough browning in Step 3. And roasted (rather than canned or boiled) tomatoes underscore the browned flavors.

Ingredients
Chiles Chipotles: Without these peppers, the dish is no longer *tinga.* If you find the *chipotles* packed in vinegar, use them but don't stir in any vinegar from the can. If only dried ones are available, toast them lightly on a hot griddle, soak until soft, then stem, seed, slice and add.

Timing and Advance Preparation
Tinga can be made in 1½ hours. It improves with age: Prepare it through Step 4, cover and refrigerate for up to 3 days. Reheat slowly, then garnish as described in Step 5.

4 teaspoons of the *adobo* sauce from the can of chiles

Salt, about ½ teaspoon

Sugar, about ½ teaspoon

For the garnish:

1 ripe, medium avocado, peeled, pitted and sliced

4 ounces Mexican *queso fresco* (page 327) or other fresh cheese like mild goat or farmer's cheese (or even Muenster), cut into 8 fingers

A ¼-inch slice of onion, broken into rings

1. *The meat.* Bring about 1 quart salted water to a boil in a medium-size saucepan, add the pork, skim the grayish foam that rises to the top during the first few minutes of simmering, then add the herbs and bay leaves. Partially cover and simmer over medium heat until the meat is tender, about 50 minutes. (If there is time, let the meat cool in the broth.) Remove the meat, then strain the broth and spoon off all the fat that rises to the top; reserve 1 cup. When the meat is cool enough to handle, dry it on paper towels and break it into ¾-inch pieces.

2. *The potatoes, tomatoes and chorizo.* Boil the potatoes in salted water to cover until *just* tender, 12 to 15 minutes; drain, peel (if you want), then chop into ½-inch dice. Seed the tomatoes, if you wish, by cutting them in half crosswise and gently squeezing out the seeds; then chop into ½-inch pieces. Fry the *chorizo* in the oil in a large, heavy skillet over medium-low heat until done, about 10 minutes, stirring occasionally to break up any clumps. Remove, leaving as much fat as possible in the skillet.

3. *Browning the main ingredients.* Raise the heat to medium and add the onion and pork. Fry, stirring frequently, until *well browned,* about 10 minutes. Stir in the garlic and cook 2 minutes.

4. *Finishing the stew.* Add the chopped tomatoes, oregano and *chorizo,* mix well and simmer 5 minutes. Stir in the potatoes, the reserved cup of broth, *chipotle* peppers and *adobo* sauce from the can. Simmer gently for 10 minutes to blend the flavors, then season with salt and sugar.

5. *Garnish and presentation.* When you're ready to serve, scoop the simmering *tinga* into a warm serving dish and decorate with alternating slices of avocado and fingers of cheese. Strew the top with onion rings and serve.

TRADITIONAL VARIATIONS

Shredded Pork Tinga for Filling: Complete Step 1, using 1½ pounds pork and shredding the cooked meat rather than breaking it into pieces. Prepare the tomatoes (Step 2), then brown the onion and pork thoroughly in 2 tablespoons vegetable oil over medium heat. Add the garlic and cook 2 minutes. Add the tomatoes and oregano, simmer 5 minutes, then add the broth, *chipotle* peppers and *adobo* from the can, and simmer until thick. Season with salt and sugar.

CONTEMPORARY VARIATIONS

Charcoal-Grilled Chicken Tinga: Prepare the recipe as directed in Steps 2 through 4, ignoring references to pork and substituting poultry broth for pork broth. Bone 8 chicken thighs (page 225), then charcoal-grill them, basting with olive oil, until done, 20 to 25 minutes. Spoon the coarse, smoky sauce over them and garnish with diced avocado, diced fresh cheese and onion rings.

MEAT IN RED-CHILE SAUCE

Carne con Chile Colorado

> **CHILE CON CARNE:** *Detestable food that under the false Mexican title is sold in the United States [of America], from Texas to New York.*
> ——**DICCIONARIO DE MEJICANISMOS**
> *[author's translation]*

When it's made on Mexican soil and the name *chile con carne* is flipped around, I doubt the venerable Mexican dictionary writers describe the dish as "detestable" in the least. No, the Northern Mexican *carne con chile colorado* is a good, simple dish— mild, dried chiles mellowed with garlic and sparked with cumin —and it's so routinely served up on Northern plates and in Northern tacos and burritos that the rest of Mexico wonders if the cooks there know anything else. I once asked a Yucatecan woman, working in a Los Angeles tortilla factory with a bunch of Northern Mexicans, about the filling in the factory's *tamales*. She whispered, "With these folks, you can have *carne con chile* or *chile con carne*. Take your pick."

I've always smiled at the Texan claim of *inventing* "chili." I won't argue that it's their regional specialty, but the practice of cooking dried chiles with meat was in full gear when the Spaniards met the first American Indians. Of course, the Northern Mexican versions may seem simplistic to the Texans, who use *chile anchos,* occasionally tomatoes or beans, and almost always a gaggle of spices and a good draw of beer.

This recipe is one I learned from a restaurant cook in Chihuahua, and it can be featured as an informal main course, accompanied by flour tortillas and *Frijoles Refritos* (page 269) or a salad. To drink, beer or *Jamaica* "Flower" Cooler (page 307); and for dessert, Custard Ice Cream (page 299).

YIELD: about 3½ cups, 4 servings

- 8 medium (about 2½ ounces total) dried *chiles de la tierra* or New Mexico/California chiles, stemmed seeded and deveined
- 3 cloves garlic, peeled and roughly chopped
- ½ medium onion, roughly chopped
- 1 teaspoon dried oregano

COOK'S NOTES

Techniques
Using Chile-Soaking Liquid: The soaking liquid of most chiles is discarded to eliminate excess astringency from the dish. Here it is not so astringent, and some of it is used to underscore the forthright flavors of light-colored chiles, cumin and garlic.

Ingredients
Chiles de la Tierra: Though the similar, light-skinned *colorín* seems to be the most-used chile in Chihuahua, all the recipes I've collected call for the richer *chile de la tierra*. The New Mexico chile pods grown a few hundred miles away are similar and may be substituted one for one.

Timing and Advance Preparation
Allow 2 hours to complete the dish; your active involvement will be only about 30 minutes. The dish may be completed 3 or 4 days ahead, covered and refrigerated; it improves with a little age. Reheat slowly in a covered pan.

TRADITIONAL VARIATIONS
Northern-Style Red-Chile Sauce Without Meat: Complete Steps 1 and 2, then fry the sauce base in 1½ tablespoons lard or oil over medium-high heat, until thick. Stir in 2 cups beef broth, partially cover and simmer for 30 to 45 minutes. Season with salt. For a thicker sauce, add 2 tablespoons *masa harina* with the broth.

½ teaspoon cumin seeds (or a generous ½ teaspoon ground)
1½ tablespoons lard or vegetable oil
1½ pounds lean, boneless pork shoulder, cut into 1-inch cubes
Salt, about ½ teaspoon

1. *The chiles.* Heat a griddle or heavy skillet over medium and tear the chiles into flat pieces. Toast them on the hot surface a few at a time, pressing them down firmly with a metal spatula for a few seconds, until they crackle and change color, then flipping them over and pressing down for a few seconds more. Cover the chiles with boiling water, weight down with a plate to keep them submerged, soak 30 minutes, then drain and reserve 1 cup of the soaking liquid.

2. *The sauce base.* Transfer the chiles and reserved liquid to a blender jar. Add the garlic, onion and oregano. Pulverize the cumin seeds in a mortar or spice grinder, and add to the chile mixture. Blend until smooth, then strain through a medium-mesh sieve.

3. *Frying the meat.* Heat the lard or oil in a large skillet over medium-high. Dry the pork on paper towels, then lay it in the hot skillet *in an uncrowded single layer.* Fry until the meat is nicely browned, about 10 minutes, turning it and scraping the pan frequently.

4. *Simmering.* Add the chile puree to the pan. Continue to fry for 4 or 5 minutes, stirring and scraping the bottom frequently, until the puree is very thick and noticeably darker.

Scrape the mixture into a medium-size saucepan, stir in the salt and 2 cups of water. Bring to a boil, partially cover and simmer over medium-low heat, stirring occasionally, for 45 minutes to 1 hour, until the meat is very tender; if the sauce thickens beyond the consistency of heavy cream, add a little more water. Taste for salt, and the simple stew is ready to serve.

Hand-blown goblets, Tlaquepaque

Carne con Chile Colorado for Fillings: Prepare the recipe as directed, cutting the meat into smaller pieces. Simmer uncovered until fairly thick, then whisk in two tablespoons *masa harina.*

A Sonoran Chile Colorado with Powdered Chile: Toast 6 New Mexico/California chiles (they're similar to the *chile colorado* in Sonora) and pulverize in a spice grinder (or substitute 4 or 5 tablespoons store-bought powdered New Mexico chile without spices). Fry the meat as directed in Step 3, reduce the heat to medium, add 1 tablespoon flour and 3 cloves garlic (peeled and minced), and stir 2 minutes. Add 3 cups water and stir until it reaches a boil. Stir in the powdered chile, 1 teaspoon oregano, 1½ tablespoons vinegar and ½ teaspoon salt; simmer 45 minutes.

A NEARLY TRADITIONAL VARIATION

Chile con Carne with a Nod Toward Texas: Complete Steps 1 and 2, substituting 5 *chiles anchos* for the other pods, omitting the onion and increasing the cumin to 1½ teaspoons. Coarse-grind or chop 2 pounds of beef chuck, brown it in several batches in rendered beef suet or oil over medium-high heat. Return all the meat to the pan, add the sauce base and stir for several minutes, then scrape into a saucepan, add the salt, and 2 cups water (or 1½ cups beef broth and ½ cup beer). Simmer, partially covered, until the meat is tender. Just before serving, thin with a little water or broth, stir in 2 tablespoons *masa harina* and let simmer until nicely thickened.

SAVORY GOLDEN COUNTRY RIBS WITH AVOCADO RELISH

Carnitas con Guacamole

> **CARNITAS:** *Fried and seasoned meats in tacos and snacks that are commonly sold in streetside fry stands, and that constitute a true menace to health, though they are absolutely delicious.*
>
> ——DICCIONARIO DE MEJICANISMOS
> *[author's translation]*

In Mexico City's suburb of Tlalpan, there is a row of purveyors along Avenida Insurgentes, where you can see clearly how pork becomes delicious *carnitas*. Every part of the pig emerges from wide copper caldrons, half-boiled and half-fried, with a golden appeal. The flesh is soft and moist, the exterior has a savory browned chewiness. On warm Sunday afternoons, these *carnitas* places capture the spirit of outdoor, hearty, informal eating.

What you find commercially crisped into *carnitas* are huge chunks of pork, ones that can be sliced like a roast; at home, small pieces fit the pan better, but I don't like serving the small ones for a main course. So I've developed this country ribs *carnitas* dinner that does very nicely when you can't visit the rustic Mexican *carnitas* stands. Add some *Frijoles Refritos* (page 269), a big salad and plenty of *Salsa Mexicana* (page 35), hot tortillas, beer, tea or soda pop. This is the perfect spot for hot fudge sundaes, or at least warm Goat-Milk Caramel (page 293) over ice cream.

YIELD: about 1½ pounds *carnitas*, 4 servings

2½ pounds thick, meaty, pork country ribs

For the slow-fry method:
 2 pounds lard (or enough to cover the meat)
 ¼ cup water
 The zest (green rind only) of 1 lime, removed with
  a vegetable peeler in wide strips
 Coarse salt, about ½ teaspoon

COOK'S NOTES

Techniques
Slow-Frying Technique: Don't be alarmed by adding water to the melted lard: It ensures that the lard stays at a low temperature long enough for the pork to become tender. When it evaporates, the temperature gradually rises and the meat browns. This method produces the best-textured, most delicious *carnitas*.

Boil-Then-Fry Technique: This simple, less-involved alternative is really just well-browned, tender-simmered pork. If there is virtually no rendered fat when the liquid has evaporated, add enough lard to coat the pan nicely.

Judging the Doneness: For both techniques, simmer the meat slowly at first, *just* until tender; then move quickly on to browning. If you overcook the meat at either stage, you can wind up with dryish, tough ribs.

Ingredients
Lard: Use a good brand, preferably one that is open-kettle rendered. This method of cooking is hard on lard, but it can be strained and used for 3 or 4 future batches of *carnitas* before it must be discarded; store it very tightly covered in the refrigerator.

Timing and Advance Preparation
Allow about 1½ hours to prepare the *carnitas* (a little longer for the boil-then-fry method); there is little active involve-

For the boil-then-fry method:
> **Water to cover the meat**
> **½ teaspoon salt, plus a little coarse salt for sprinkling on before serving**

For serving:
> **About 2 cups (⅔ recipe) Chunky Guacamole (page 44) with all of its garnishes**

1. *The meat.* Trim off all but a thin layer of fat from the pork.

2. *The slow-fry method.* Melt the lard in a large (4-quart), heavy saucepan over medium-low heat. When it has melted but is not yet very hot, add the pork, water and lime zest. Cook with the lard at a *gentle* simmer, turning the pork occasionally, for about 40 minutes, until it is barely tender. Raise the heat to medium-high. If all of the water hasn't yet evaporated, the lard will come to a rolling boil, which will eventually diminish into small bubbles as the water evaporates. After the change occurs, the *carnitas* will need about 10 minutes to brown. Watch them carefully and remove when they are a *light* golden brown. Drain on paper towels and sprinkle with salt.

The boil-then-fry method. Place the meat in a single layer in a wide, heavy saucepan, add enough water to cover the meat by ½ inch, measure in the salt and set over medium heat. Simmer, partially covered, turning the pork occasionally, until the meat is barely tender, about 40 minutes. Uncover, raise the heat to medium-high and quickly boil away the liquid.

When you hear the meat begin to fry in its own rendered lard (once the water is gone), turn the heat down to between medium and medium-low. Let the pork fry, turning frequently, until evenly browned, about 30 minutes. Remove the ribs from the pan, drain on paper towels and sprinkle with a little salt.

3. *Serving.* While the meat is cooking, prepare the guacamole, scoop it into a serving bowl and garnish. Serve the crispy ribs on a warm serving platter and pass the guacamole to eat along with them. Or cut the meat off the bones and roll with the guacamole into tacos.

ment. The meat can be prepared several days in advance, then heated uncovered in a 350° oven until hot and crispy.

Regional Explorations
I've taken tortilla-wrapped bites of *carnitas* in every region of the country (though they're perhaps most famous in West-Central Mexico, especially Michoacán), and always, it seems, it's happened in memorable roadside stands, market stalls or open-air eateries with beautifully spotlighted displays of golden meat and *chicharrones*.

Carnitas

CHARCOAL-GRILLED PORK LOIN WITH RICH RED-CHILE SAUCE

Lomo de Puerco en Adobo

During part of the time I was cooking at Lopez y Gonzalez restaurant in Cleveland, I worked with a woman from Mexico City whose ways with an orange-flavored baked pork loin *adobado* met up with our charcoal grill to bring about this dish—one of our consistently popular offerings.

Unlike the homier stewed-meat version (see variation recipe) or my co-worker's pot-roasted loin with only a little sauce, the meat in this recipe is marinated in rich, red-chile *adobo*, then charcoal-grilled and sauced with more *adobo* that has been simmered separately with orange juice.

Serve a first course of Shrimp-Ball Soup with Roasted Peppers (page 102), then warm tortillas and a Cress and *Jícama* Salad (page 89) with the pork, and Almond Flan (page 283) for dessert: There could be no better eating. Personally, I'd like to drink a rich, soft red wine like Merlot or a fruity Zinfandel with the pork; the nonalcoholic Sparkling Limeade (page 311) is also good.

YIELD: 6 servings, with about 3 cups of sauce

For the sauce:

> 8 medium (about 4 ounces total) dried *chiles anchos*, stemmed, seeded and deveined
> 3 tablespoons lard or vegetable oil
> ½ medium onion, diced
> 3 cloves garlic, peeled
> 1⅔ cups broth (preferably pork), plus a little more for thinning the sauce
> A scant ½ teaspoon cumin seeds (about ½ teaspoon ground)
> 1 bay leaf
> ½ teaspoon dried oregano
> ¼ teaspoon dried thyme
> 6 tablespoons cider vinegar
> 1 cup freshly squeezed orange juice
> Sugar, about 1 tablespoon
> Salt, about ½ teaspoon

COOK'S NOTES

Techniques
Long-Soaking the Chiles: The longer soaking removes the harshness and bitterness that can plague pure-chile sauces. *Charcoal-Grilling the Pork, Judging Doneness and Letting It Rest:* Fires can vary widely in their heat, so timing here is difficult to estimate; but remember that slow-cooking produces the juiciest pork. A thermometer is by far the most reliable judge of doneness; if none is available, feel the resiliency of the meat—it should be firm but not stiff or hard. Letting the cooked pork rest for a few minutes allows time for the juices to be reabsorbed into the meat, so they don't run out when the meat is cut. *Correcting the Consistency of the Sauce:* Chiles don't bind like starchy nuts or flour. If the sauce is simmered until too thick, liquid will separate from the solids. Blending a slice of bread with the chiles will give the sauce a little more body.

Ingredients
Chiles Anchos: I have tasted *adobos* made with *guajillos* and their cousins, but they lack the richness of *anchos*.

Timing and Advance Preparation
All told, the dish takes about 2 hours to prepare, though soaking and marinating requires that you start at least a day ahead. The meat may marinate for several days, and the sauce keeps well for 4 or 5 days, covered and refrigerated.

For the meat:
>   2 to 3 pounds lean, boneless pork loin, with only
>   a thin cap of fat on one side

For the garnish:
>   ½ cup meaty green olives, preferably *manzanillos*
>   Several pickled *chiles jalapeños,* store-bought or
>   homemade (page 337)
>   1 slice of onion, broken into rings
>   Several slices of orange

1. *The chiles.* Tear the *chiles anchos* into flat pieces. Heat 2 tablespoons of the lard or oil in a medium-size skillet over medium, then quick-fry the chiles a couple of pieces at a time, toasting them for a few seconds on each side. Drain well, cover with boiling water, weight with a plate to keep them submerged and let soak for *several hours or overnight* to rid them of any harshness.

2. *The onions and garlic.* In the same skillet, fry the onion and garlic over medium heat, stirring occasionally, until well browned, about 8 minutes. Scoop out, draining as much fat as possible back in the pan, and place in a blender.

3. *Pureeing, frying and simmering the adobo sauce.* Drain the chiles, squeezing them gently to remove all the soaking liquid. Add to the onions along with ⅔ cup of the broth. Grind the cumin and bay leaf in a mortar or spice grinder and add them to the blender along with the oregano, thyme and *2 tablespoons* of the vinegar. Blend until smooth, then strain through a medium-mesh sieve.

Heat the remaining tablespoon of lard or oil in a large saucepan over medium-high. When quite hot, add the chile puree and stir nearly constantly for 5 to 7 minutes, until it is a thick, deep-burgundy mass.

Stir in 1 cup of the broth and the orange juice, partially cover, reduce the heat to medium-low and simmer for about 45 minutes. Season with sugar and salt, then cool.

4. *Marinating the pork loin.* Mix together ¼ cup of the cooled *adobo* sauce and the remaining 4 tablespoons of vinegar; cover and refrigerate the rest of the *adobo* sauce. If your pork loin consists of 2 pieces tied into a double thickness for roasting, untie them, then place in a noncorrosive container, pour on the sauce-vinegar mixture and coat well. Cover and refrigerate at least 12 hours, turning the meat in the marinade several times.

5. *Grilling the meat.* About 2 hours before serving, remove the meat from the marinade and set out to warm to room temperature. Build a charcoal fire and let it burn until only me-

TRADITIONAL VARIATIONS

Adobo as a Stew: This shows up all around Mexico (save Yucatán), containing everything from rabbit and chicken to kid, beef and armadillo. *For rabbit:* Brown a 3-pound rabbit (cut into serving pieces) in oil, then simmer in salted water with mixed herbs and bay leaves until tender (30 to 45 minutes). Prepare the sauce as described in Steps 1 through 3, using rabbit broth where broth and juice are called for; optionally, add 1 canned *chile chipotle* to the drained chiles. Simmer the rabbit in the finished sauce 15 minutes before serving. Garnish with onion rings, diced avocado and radish roses.

CONTEMPORARY IDEAS

Charcoal-Grilled Game Hens in Adobo: Prepare 3 medium (1¾-pound) game hens for grilling, as described for chicken on page 228. Complete the recipe as directed, substituting the hens for the pork and poultry broth for pork broth. Charcoal-grill the hens over a medium-low fire until tender, 20 to 25 minutes, basting frequently with olive oil. Split them in half and serve each half with a ladle of warm sauce and a sprinkling of the garnishes.

A Showstopper Buffet

Because I think char-grilled pork is such a beautiful, easy-to-serve dish, I've developed a buffet around it. Start with *Masa* Boats (*Sopes,* page 168), and *Jamaica* Sangria (page 307) or Margaritas (page 320); then serve small cups of Fresh Corn Chowder (page 99) to your guests as an ambulatory appetizer. Set the buf-

dium-hot. Position the grill about 6 inches above the coals and brush it with a little oil.

When the fire is right, remove the pork from the marinade and lay it on the grill, fat-side down. Turn it periodically until it feels firm and reaches an internal temperature of about 150°; the cooking will take roughly 50 minutes to 1 hour.

Set the cooked meat on a wire rack over a plate and let it rest in a low oven while you heat the sauce.

6. *Garnish and presentation.* Warm the *adobo* sauce in a small saucepan, thinning it with a little broth, if necessary, to achieve a *light* consistency (like moderately thin barbecue sauce). Taste for salt and sugar. Thinly slice the meat, then lay the slices overlapping on a warm platter. Spoon the sauce over the top and garnish with the olives, chiles, onion rings and orange slices. Serve immediately.

Dried ancho chiles

SLOW-STEAMED GOAT OR LAMB WITH MILD CHILE SEASONING

Birria de Chivo o de Carnero

Birria is the West-Central cousin of the Central *barbacoa*—the special-occasion, pit-cooked lamb in maguey "leaves." And for the most flavorful version of *birria*, lamb or goat is spread with chile paste and baked tightly covered to roast and steam in its juices. *Birria* vendors have come up with special pots and ovens to replicate the earth pits their forefathers made, and many (especially in Guadalajara) have done away with the maguey wrappers—relying exclusively on the chiles for added flavor.

This typical recipe, from one of the Guadalajara *birria* vendors, uses the slow-cooking juices for a delectable, brothy sauce flavored with oregano and tomato. Where the vendor used a

fet with Shrimp in Toasted Garlic (page 215), your pork loin, unsauced Cheese *Chiles Rellenos* (page 245) and a Mixed Vegetable Salad (page 87). Serve good crusty bread, lots of tortillas and plenty of beer (or even a dry, fruity red wine like Zinfandel and a full-flavored, fruity white wine like Chenin Blanc). For dessert: Pineapple Flan (page 284), Creamy-Fresh Coconut Dessert (page 285) and/or fresh fruit.

COOK'S NOTES

Techniques
Moist-Roasting in a Sealed Pot: This method approximates the techniques of the Mexican pit barbecues by having steaming liquid below the meat and a slight pressure from the sealed pot. The pressure and moisture help tenderize the meat of tough animals without drying it out. Some *birria* makers don't bother with sealing the pot, but I like the effects and the burst of aroma when the top is removed.

Chilaquiles—Quick-Simmered Tortilla Casserole (page 172)

Fresh-Corn *Tamales* with *Picadillo* (page 185)

Simple Red *Mole* with Meat, Fowl and Fruit (page 206)

Chile-Bathed Fish Grilled in Cornhusks (page 218)

Chicken *Pibil* Steamed in Banana Leaves (page 233)

Charcoal-Grilled Corn with Cream, Cheese and Chile (page 272)

Buttered Crepes with *Cajeta* Caramel and Pecans (page 294)

Fresh Prickly-Pear Ice (page 300)

special oven, I've called for a Dutch oven sealed with *masa*, as recommended in Velázquez de León's *Viajando por las cocinas de las provincias de la República Mexicana*. Like pot roast, *birria* needs to be featured at a special, informal dinner: serve it with hot tortillas, preceded by Chunky Guacamole (page 44); ice cream with warm Goat-Milk Caramel (page 293) would be a nice dessert. To drink: beer, perhaps a red wine like Zinfandel, or Tamarind Cooler (page 308).

YIELD: about 6 servings

One 5-pound piece young goat, perferably a hind-quarter
  OR one 3-pound bone-in lamb roast from the shoulder or butt-end of the leg
12 large (about 3 ounces total) dried *chiles guajillos*, stemmed, seeded and deveined
6 cloves garlic, unpeeled
3 tablespoons cider vinegar
A scant ¼ teaspoon cumin seeds (or a generous ¼ teaspoon ground)
A scant ½ teaspoon black peppercorns (or about ¾ teaspoon ground)
1 teaspoon salt
2 teaspoons sugar
1 pound fresh *masa*
  OR 1¾ cups *masa harina* mixed with 1 cup plus 2 tablespoons hot tap water
1 ripe, large tomato, roasted or boiled (page 352), cored and peeled
  OR ¾ 15-ounce can tomatoes, drained
1 teaspoon oregano
Salt, about ½ teaspoon
1 small onion, chopped into ⅛-inch dice
2 to 3 tablespoons fresh coriander (*cilantro*), coarsely chopped
2 small limes, quartered

1. *The meat.* Trim most of the fat from the meat (it is strong-tasting); if it is a goat hindquarter, cut into 2 pieces with a cleaver, severing it through the joint at the top of the leg. Place in a large noncorrosive dish.

2. *The chile marinade.* Heat a griddle or heavy skillet over medium. Tear the chiles into flat pieces and toast them a few at a time, pressing them against the hot surface with a metal spatula until they crackle and blister, then flipping them over

Ingredients
Meat: Birria is made with the stronger-flavored, tougher cuts or varieties of meat. Goat is available in many Greek, Middle Eastern and Latin American markets and lamb can be purchased nearly everywhere.
Chiles: The large *guajillo*-like *chilacates* frequently used for *birria* in Guadalajara are similar to our New Mexico variety; you may substitute 9 of the latter for the *guajillos*. Or use 6 *anchos* as they would in the version from Zacatecas.

Timing and Advance Preparation
Start marinating the *birria* at least 8 hours ahead; roasting takes about 3 hours and final preparations require 45 minutes. Your active involvement will be less than 1½ hours. The dish may be completed 2 or 3 days ahead through Step 4: Cover and refrigerate the meat and broth separately. Shortly before serving, wrap the meat in foil, heat it in the oven and heat the broth in a covered pan on the stove top. Complete Step 5 as directed.

and pressing them again. Cover with boiling water, weight with a plate to keep them submerged and soak 30 minutes. Roast the garlic on the hot griddle or skillet, turning frequently, until soft inside and blackened outside, about 15 minutes. Cool and peel.

Drain the chiles and place in a blender jar with the garlic and vinegar. Pulverize the cumin and peppercorns in a mortar or spice grinder, and add to the blender along with the salt and ¾ cup water. Blend until smooth, then strain through a medium-mesh sieve. Remove ½ cup, stir in the sugar, cover and set aside for the final glazing. Spread the rest of the chile paste over the meat, cover and refrigerate for at least 4 hours or, preferably, overnight.

3. *Slow-steaming.* Preheat the oven to 325°. Set a roasting rack into a deep, wide kettle or stockpot; if it doesn't sit at least 1 inch above the bottom of the pot, prop it up on custard cups, tin cans or the like. Measure in 3 cups of water, then lay the marinated meat on the rack and spread any remaining marinade over it.

Add water to the *masa* (or *masa harina* mixture) to make a soft dough. Roll tennis ball–size pieces between your palms to make ¾-inch ropes, then press them gently all around the top edge of your pot. Set the lid in place and press it into the *masa* to seal. Bake for 3 hours.

4. *Finishing the broth.* Break the seal by tapping the hardened *masa* with the back of a cleaver or mallet, and take off the lid; then carefully remove the tender meat. Take out the rack, spoon the fat off the broth, then measure it. You need at least 1 quart—if necessary, add water to bring it to that level. Pour the broth into a small saucepan.

Puree the tomato in a blender or food processor, add it to the broth along with the oregano, cover and simmer over medium-low heat for 20 minutes. Season with salt.

5. *Glazing and serving the birria.* Shortly before serving, remove the bones, large pieces of gristle and excess fat from the meat, keeping the pieces of meat as large as possible. Set the meat on a baking sheet, brush lightly with the reserved chile-paste glaze, then bake for 10 minutes to set the glaze.

Either present the meat on a large platter and pass the warm broth separately, or slice the meat across the grain and serve it in deep plates, awash in the broth. Mix the onion and fresh coriander, and pass it with the lime at the table.

CONTEMPORARY IDEAS

Lamb Shank Birria with Chipotle and Tomatillo: Prepare the recipe as directed, substituting 3 pounds of 1-inch-thick lamb shanks for the shoulder, adding 2 canned *chiles chipotles* (seeded) to the *guajillos* when you puree them, and replacing the tomato with 8 ounces cooked *tomatillos.* Simmer the broth in Step 4, uncovered, until reduced to the consistency of a light sauce. Serve the glazed shanks with a ladle of sauce, a sprinkling of onion and fresh coriander and a little crumbled toasted *guajillo* chile.

Dried guajillo chiles

RICE, BEANS AND VEGETABLES

❖

Arroz, Frijoles y Verduras

Rice cooking on open fire, Juchitán

Sometime about seven thousand years ago, when the early Mexicans had harvested their runner beans, they tucked away some in a cave in Tamaulipas. As things turned out, they never returned, and we were left a record of their earliest domesticates. When the Spaniards arrived in Mexico, the great masses were sustaining themselves on beans, simple boiled beans, from the large *ayocotes* to the tiniest black ones. Together with the rich lard from the pigs the Spaniards brought, those legumes became the definitively Mexican *frijoles refritos*—savory, thick and sprinkled with salty cheese. Still today, beans are essential to the Mexican table: Fried ones are the automatic accompaniment to (or ingredient in) most of the *masa*-based *antojitos,* plain soupy beans hold an old-time place in the afternoon *comida,* and bean preparations turn up as regional specialties everywhere.

Rice—as in "it comes with beans and rice"—is thought by the outside world to be on the combination plates all Mexicans have for dinner. Rice is not native, though, nor does it necessarily come on every plate. The grain made its way first to Spain, in the hands of the ruling Arabs. Later, it came to the New World, but not in the first shiploads of edibles—the Spaniards were more reliant on their wheat, cattle, olives and grapes. But when rice finally arrived, it found an agreeable home; it is one of the most venerable dishes on the modern Mexican table. Served as the second course in a midday *comida,* beautifully molded to accompany seafood, heaped onto a plate in a market *fonda,* or, yes, mounded next to the beans on plates in some Northern *cafeterías* or snack shops. The latter, I defend, only seldom occurs; combination plates really are scarce.

Vegetables, greens, squash, tomatoes and mushrooms were an important part of pre-Columbian eating—not as accompaniments to go alongside meat or something else, but rather, as the focus of dishes themselves. It's the same today: Purslane with pork, mushrooms with beef in *chile pasilla* sauce, cactus or *romeritos* with shrimp cakes, zucchini squash with cream and cheese—they're all filled with fresh, simmered vegetables and they're all main courses. Practically the only go-with vegetables Mexico knows (besides the little raw vegetable salad on lots of snack plates) are the green-chile *rajas* that flank grilled meat or chicken, the grilled green onions in Northern-style eateries and the common mound of fried potatoes.

In spite of what may seem a second-class status, vegetables in beautifully fresh piles and baskets fill up Mexican markets. Some are for sauces, like the *tomatillos,* tomatoes, onions, garlic and little chiles; others are eaten raw—more as salads—like cucumbers, avocados, *jícama,* lettuce, cabbage and radishes. Our focus here, though, are those that figure in cooked dishes: the round, light-green zucchinilike squash, green beans and peas, waxy boiling potatoes and sweet potatoes, cauliflower, cactus paddles, purslane, spinach, Swiss chard and squash blossoms.

Most all regions have the same general variety, though each uses them in different quantities and preparations. In Yucatán, the squash look like large, dark-green pattypans; there is bitter melon to roast, little fresh black-skinned beans called *espelones* and white-skinned *ibes*. High up in San Cristóbal de las Casas, Chiapas, the market is alive with Indian colors and full of exotic vegetables: green-skinned *pepinos,* hearts of palm, watermelonlike squash, squash runners, wild mushrooms and Chinese-like broccoli. Toluca offers more greens and wild mushrooms than most minds can fathom. And San Luis Potosí has the most delicious, earthy little wild potatoes called *papitas del monte.*

From the ways Mexican cooks translate all these goods into substantial stews and such, one would hardly expect a Mexican cookbook to have chapters of accompaniments, as this one has. No, in traditional cookbooks from Mexico, the bean recipes are in with the *antojitos* or in a chapter called *verduras*—a collection of vegetable-meat stews, plus *chiles rellenos,* stuffed squash and hefty vegetable puddings. Rice recipes, on the other hand, are found with the soups. Here, I've pulled together in a single chapter recipes from all three areas, because that's how they'll be most useful in North American menu planning. I've even adapted a few of the stew recipes to use as vegetable go-withs.

For vegetable recipes from other chapters, see "Vegetables" in the Index.

Keys to Perfect Rice
Techniques

Choosing a Pan: A heavy, nonreactive 7- to 8-inch diameter 1½- to 2-quart pan with a tight-fitting lid is ideal for even cooking.

To Soak or Not to Soak: In Mexico, I wash off all the powdery residue and miscellaneous debris from the market-variety rice, then soak it (to rid it of excess starch) and dry it. In the United States, I omit that step because the rice is cleaner, it's sprayed with a water-soluble coating of vitamins and I don't think soaking adds perceptibly to the texture.

Frying Rice: Mexican rice is made pilaf-style, that is, raw rice that is fried, then simmered in broth. The frying cooks the kernels' outer coating, which means they won't stick together. Rice that is browned has a distinctive flavor, which is critical to authentic Mexican red rice.

Cooking Temperatures and Times: If, after 15 minutes simmering and a few minutes steaming off the fire, the rice isn't done, return it to medium-low heat, covered, for a few minutes. If the liquid has been absorbed, sprinkle on a tablespoon of water; if the rice is damp, cook it for a couple of minutes covered, then uncover and let some of the moisture evaporate. (Some cooks find the even heat of an oven more comfortable for rice cooking: After adding the liquid, bake in a 325° oven for 15 minutes, then steam out of the oven for about 5 minutes.) The age and type of rice will affect the cooking. Overcooked rice will have splayed ends and taste mealy.

Holding and Reheating Rice: When the rice is done, I cool it immediately rather than keep it warm (which risks overcooking it). Cooled rice (even if cooled only to lukewarm) can be successfully reheated slowly in a hot-water bath. Or spread it into a 1-inch layer in a baking pan, cover with foil and heat in a 325° oven for about 15 minutes.

Molding Rice: It is common in the Gulf and Yucatán for a little dome of molded white rice to come on plates of seafood. It is easy to do: Pack a custard cup full of warm, cooked rice, quickly invert it over a warm dinner plate and slowly lift it off. A rice ring may be made in a similar fashion: Pack 1 recipe of any warm rice into a 4-cup ring mold, top with an up-turned serving platter, invert, then lift off the mold. Garnish, if you wish, with the typical parsley and slivers of pimento.

Ingredients

Rice: Though most Mexican cookbooks printed in the United States call for long-grain rice, what I've found in Mexico is closer to medium-size grains. Either one works, though I like the meaty texture of medium-grain rice.

Keys to Perfect Beans
Techniques

Discarding Floaters: Beans that float in the water generally have air pockets that harbor dirt or mold.

Soaking: Though not common in Mexico, soaking improves the beans' texture and digestibility. The latter is true only if you discard the soaking liquid, says the Bean Advisory Board, because the offending oligosaccharides have been leached from the beans into the water. Little protein, nutrition or flavor is lost in the liquid.

Tenderizing and Toughening Additives: Adding a pinch of baking soda to the water helps to soften the beans more quickly. Too much not only tastes bad, but "affects the nutritional value adversely," say the researchers. Salt, however, like all acids (tomatoes, vinegar, chiles and so forth), keeps the beans from softening, so add salt and acids *after* the beans are tender.

Cooking Times and Temperatures: If you start the beans off slowly and keep them at a *very gentle* simmer, they will be beautifully whole with good texture. Soaked beans will cook in less time than dry ones—sometimes up to half the time.

Quick Beans: If you're short on time, dry pintos can be ready to eat in about 1½ hours by giving them the 1-hour quick-soak described in Step 1 on page 268, then cooking them in 3 cups fresh water (along with the onions and fat) in a pressure cooker for 30 minutes. Release the pressure and check the beans: If they're not done, simmer them until tender (either under pressure or not). Soaked black and other hard beans require at least 45 minutes to cook in the pressure cooker.

Ingredients

Beans: Each variety has its own vivid color and subtly different flavor and texture. For more details on which varieties are cooked in each Mexican region, see page 268; in the United States, use what you like and can get (go out of your way for the delicious black beans if you haven't tried them). Prebagged beans are generally cleaner than ones in bulk; stored at room temperature and well sealed, they keep a year.

a sampling of regional <u>*cazuelas*</u>

MEXICAN TOMATO-COLORED RICE (WITH FRESH VEGETABLES)

Arroz a la Mexicana (con Verduras)

The flavors here are of nutty browned rice, tomato and good broth—classic, familiar Mexican flavors. It's not surprising, then, that this red rice is found in every settlement, nor that it finds regional transformations into main courses with meat and fish.

This traditional recipe comes from Sra. Villalobos of Juchitán, Oaxaca—with a few modifications from open *cazuelas* and wood fires to closed pans and gas. It is a good accompaniment to most any main course or can be served *comida corrida*–style as a second course, after the soup and before the poultry, meat or what have you; it works fine on a buffet or, if your reflexes are so trained, can go on the plate with beans and enchiladas, *a la norteamericana*.

YIELD: about 3½ cups, 4 servings

> 1½ tablespoons vegetable oil
> 1 cup long- or medium-grain rice
> 1 small onion, finely chopped
> 1 large clove garlic, peeled and finely diced
> 1 ripe, medium-small tomato, roasted or boiled
>   (page 352), cored and peeled
>   OR ½ 15-ounce can tomatoes, drained
> 1½ cups broth (preferably poultry) or water
> Salt, about ½ teaspoon if using salted broth, 1
>   teaspoon if using unsalted broth or water
> 1 cup fresh or (defrosted) frozen peas (optional)
> 1 large carrot, peeled and chopped into ¼-inch
>   dice (optional)
> Several sprigs of fresh coriander (*cilantro*) or flat-
>   leaf parsley, for garnish

1. *Frying the rice.* About 40 minutes before serving, measure the oil into a 1½- to 2-quart saucepan set over medium heat. Add the rice and onion, and cook, stirring regularly, until both are lightly browned, 7 to 10 minutes. Mix in the garlic and cook a minute longer.

Techniques
Notes about cooking rice are on page 261.

Ingredients
Rice: See page 262.

Timing and Advance Preparation
The active preparation time is about 15 minutes (add a little more if using the vegetables), plus 25 minutes for simmering and steaming. The rice may be made a day or two ahead, quickly cooled, covered and refrigerated. Reheat as directed above.

TRADITIONAL VARIATIONS
Mexican Red Rice with a Variety of Flavors: One large *poblano* or 2 long green chiles (roasted, peeled and chopped) can be added with the tomatoes. Or 1 large fresh tomato (peeled and chopped) and 2 or 3 tablespoons of chopped fresh coriander can be added when the heat under the rice is turned off.

Juchitecan Rice with Pork and Green Chile: Simmer ¾ pound boneless pork shoulder (cubed) in salted water until tender; drain, degrease the broth and reserve. Complete the recipe through Step 3, adding 2 or 3 *chiles jalapeños* (seeded and sliced) when you add the garlic, using the pork broth for liquid, and adding the cooked pork with the broth. Fluff and serve as a simple main course.

2. *The liquid ingredients.* While the rice is frying, prepare the tomato: Seed it, if you like, by cutting it in half width-wise and squeezing out the seeds, then puree it in a blender or food processor. Pour the broth or water into a small pan, add the salt and bring just to a simmer.

3. *Simmering and steaming the rice.* Add the pureed tomato to the browned rice and cook for a minute, stirring several times. Add the simmering broth, stir the rice, scrape down the sides of the pot, cover and reduce the heat to medium-low. Cook 15 minutes, then turn off the heat and let the rice stand 5 to 10 minutes, covered, until the grains are tender (but not splayed).

4. *The optional vegetables.* While the rice is cooking, simmer the fresh peas until tender (4 to 20 minutes, depending on their size and freshness), then drain and set aside; frozen peas only need to be defrosted. Separately, simmer the carrot 5 to 8 minutes, drain and add to the fresh or defrosted peas.

5. *Finishing the rice.* When the rice is tender, add the optional vegetables and fluff with a fork to separate the grains and stop the cooking. Scoop the rice into a warm serving dish, decorate it with fresh coriander or parsley, and it is ready to serve.

WHITE-RICE PILAF WITH CORN, ROASTED CHILES AND FRESH CHEESE

Arroz a la Poblana

In Puebla, there has grown up a traditional juxtaposition of fresh corn, roasted *chiles poblanos* and the sharp fresh cheese they call *queso ranchero* (literally "ranch cheese"). A number of restaurants offer the inspired combination in a white-rice dish that is not only an interesting melding of flavors, but useful in

COOK'S NOTES

Techniques
Notes about cooking rice are on page 261.

Ingredients
Rice: See page 262.
Chiles Poblanos: These are the only chiles used in Puebla, but if necessary, substitute 4 or 5 large long green chiles (roasted, peeled, seeded and sliced).

planning menus. *Arroz a la poblana* is beautiful as a ring or molded into mounds to serve with saucy dishes like Duck in Pumpkinseed *Pipián* (page 225).

YIELD: about 5 cups, 4 to 6 servings

> 1½ tablespoons vegetable oil
> 1 cup long- or medium-grain rice
> 1 small onion, finely diced
> 1¾ cups broth, preferably poultry
> Salt, about ½ teaspoon if using salted broth, 1 teaspoon if using unsalted broth
> 3 medium, fresh *chiles poblanos*, roasted and peeled (page 337), seeded and sliced into short, thin strips
> The kernels cut from 1 large ear fresh sweet corn (about 1 cup)
>   OR 1 cup frozen corn, defrosted
> ½ to ¾ cup (2 to 3 ounces) crumbled Mexican *queso fresco* (page 327) or other fresh cheese like feta or farmer's cheese
> Several sprigs of watercress or parsley, for garnish

1. *The white rice.* About 40 minutes before serving, combine the oil, rice and onion in a 1½- to 2-quart saucepan over medium heat. Stir frequently for about 7 minutes, until the onion is translucent but not browned. Meanwhile, add the salt to the broth and bring to a simmer.

Add the broth to the rice mixture along with the chiles and corn, stir well, scrape down the sides of the pan, cover and simmer over medium-low heat for 15 minutes.

2. *Finishing the dish.* When the rice has cooked 15 minutes, let stand off the fire, covered, 5 to 10 minutes, until the grains are tender (but not splayed). Add the crumbled cheese and toss the whole assemblage with a fork to mix the ingredients and stop the cooking. Scoop into a serving bowl, decorate with watercress or parsley and serve.

Aged and fresh Mexican cheese (queso fresco and queso añejo)

Timing and Advance Preparation

The rice takes about 40 minutes, half of which won't actively involve you. It may be completed up to 2 days ahead, quickly cooled, covered and refrigerated. Reheat as directed on page 261.

TRADITIONAL VARIATIONS

White Rice with Fried Plantain: Prepare the white rice according to Step 1, then let steam off the fire for 5 to 10 minutes. Peel and cube 2 very ripe plantains and fry them in a little vegetable oil over medium heat until browned and sweet. Toss with the finished rice.

HERB-GREEN RICE WITH PEAS

Arroz Verde

A number of years ago, when I was cooking with Don Ricardo and María Merrill in their cooking school in León, Guanajuato, Mrs. Merrill laid out the rice rules: White rice is for christenings and weddings, red rice gets made every day and green rice is holiday rice—traditions I've heard given voice numerous times since. (The one exception I'm aware of is that white rice is served at most meals on the Gulf.)

Though all the cooks say they know about making green rice, it's only rarely offered in Mexican eating places. This recipe is based on Mrs. Merrill's version, and its herby, green-chile flavor is especially delicious alongside Fish with Toasted Garlic (page 215) or Charcoal-Grilled Chicken (page 228).

YIELD: about 4 cups, 4 to 6 servings

- ½ medium onion, roughly chopped
- 1 rib celery, roughly chopped
- 6 sprigs fresh coriander (*cilantro*), plus a few sprigs for garnish
- 6 sprigs flat-leaf parsley, plus a few sprigs for garnish
- 2 fresh *chiles poblanos,* roasted and peeled (page 337), seeded and roughly chopped
- 1 large clove garlic, peeled and sliced
- ⅔ cup broth (preferably poultry) or water
- Salt, about ½ teaspoon if using salted broth, 1 teaspoon if using unsalted broth or water
- 1 cup fresh or (defrosted) frozen peas
- 1½ tablespoons vegetable oil
- 1 cup long- or medium-grain rice

1. *Preparing the green-herb mixture and peas.* Place the onion, celery, fresh coriander, parsley, *chiles poblanos* and garlic in a small saucepan, add 1¼ cups water, cover and bring to a simmer over medium heat. Cook until the celery and onion are tender, about 10 minutes, then remove from the heat and let cool a few minutes until lukewarm, covered. Puree the mixture (including liquid) in a blender or food processor, return to the pan and add the broth or water and the salt.

Simmer the fresh peas, if using them, in salted water to cover until tender, 4 to 20 minutes, depending on their maturity and freshness. Drain thoroughly and set aside; frozen peas only need to be defrosted.

2. *Frying the rice.* About 40 minutes before serving, combine the vegetable oil and rice in a 1½- to 2-quart saucepan over medium heat. Stir frequently until the rice turns opaque but not brown, about 7 minutes. Meanwhile, heat the broth mixture to a simmer.

3. *Simmering, steaming and finishing the rice.* Add the hot liquid to the rice, stir, scrape down the sides of the pan, cover and simmer 15 minutes over medium-low heat. Let the covered pan stand 5 to 10 minutes off the fire until the grains are tender (but not splayed). Add the peas to the pan and fluff the rice with a fork, mixing thoroughly. Scoop into a warm serving bowl, garnish with the fresh coriander and/or parsley and serve.

BROTHY BEANS

Frijoles de la Olla

*O*lla: the pot, an orange-brown earthenware cooking pot. And those who've tasted the beans that come from it know that the *olla* and contents share an earthy exchange of flavors. Today, it is less common that the *ollas* do their cooking nestled in live coals; so, sadly, one rarely finds beans that blend a slight smokiness with the clay and elementally bland starch. Instead, the cooking is over a gas burner and, more often than not, the clay has been replaced by enameled metal or plain aluminum.

Thousands eat these brothy beans every day in simple market *fondas,* with a stack of hot tortillas, a little coarse salt and some hot green chiles. And they're on hand in many Mexican kitchens, to be doled out at a moment's notice if hunger persists after the meal's main course. Even a few midday *comidas corridas* in old-style eateries still offer them that way—after the stew is finished, before the pudding arrives. But because today's progressive portions are no doubt larger than in earlier, leaner times, the beans come to the table less and less.

YIELD: 5 to 6 cups (or possibly more), serving 4 as a main dish, 6 as a side dish

Flat-leaf parsley (perejil)

COOK'S NOTES

Techniques
Notes about bean cooking are on page 262.

Timing and Advance Preparation
Start the beans at least 6 hours ahead (3 hours ahead if quick-soaking them). Beans have a better texture when they're cooled in the broth, then reheated; all bean dishes improve in flavor with at least a day's age. Covered and refrigerated, beans keep beautifully for 4 days or longer. Reheat them slowly, stirring occasionally to avoid scorching.

TRADITIONAL VARIATIONS
Yucatecan "Strained" Beans:
In a blender, puree ½ recipe cooked black beans, with some

    2 cups (about 13 ounces total) dry beans: pink, pinto, black or another variety

    2 tablespoons lard, bacon drippings or fat rendered from *chorizo* sausage

    1 small onion, diced

    1 large sprig *epazote* for black beans (optional)

    Salt, about 1 teaspoon

1. *Rinsing and soaking the beans.* Measure the beans into a colander, pick out any tiny dirt clods or pebbles, rinse and place in a 4-quart pan. Add 6 cups water, remove any beans that float, and let soak 4 to 8 hours, until you see no dry core when you break one open. Or quick-soak the beans by boiling them for a minute or 2, then letting them stand off the fire for 1 hour. Drain the beans completely.

2. *Cooking the beans.* Cover the beans with 6 cups fresh water, add the lard or other fat, onion and optional *epazote,* and bring slowly to a simmer. Partially cover and simmer over medium-low heat, stirring occasionally, until they are *fully* tender, 1 to 2 hours. If you see the beans peeking up through the liquid, add hot water to cover them by ½ inch; without enough water, the beans may cook unevenly and tend to stick on the bottom.

Season with salt, remove the *epazote,* and the beans are ready to serve.

of the bean broth or water; strain through a medium-mesh sieve. Fry ½ medium onion (chopped) and a *chile habanero* or other hot green chile (left whole but slit down the side) in a tablespoon of lard or other fat until soft. Add a sprig of *epazote* (if available) and the beans, bring to a boil over medium heat, stir in enough bean broth to make a medium, bean-soup consistency, then let simmer for a few minutes to blend the flavors. Taste for salt. This Yucatecan variation is served as a simple bean accompaniment to other dishes.

Black Bean Soup: Though not very commonly served in Mexico, the preceding variation makes a nice soup, adding, perhaps, a dollop of sour cream or sherry, a handful of chopped green onion or chives and some fried tortilla strips.

Regional Explorations

The color of the beans changes distinctly as you cross the country: In the northwest, the most common bean is a yellowish, tan-skinned one called *piruano;* in north-central and northeastern Mexico, the beans are pintos (*cabras*); the variety in Central and West-Central Mexico is large, but the purplish *flor de mayo* and tan *bayo* are most popular (they are popular elsewhere as well); and in Southern, Gulf Coastal and Yucatecan Mexico, the bean of choice is black, and nearly always stewed with a sprig of *epazote.* Small white beans are available everywhere, but are usually used in special dishes.

Earthenware bean pots (ollas)

FRIED BEANS

Frijoles Refritos

Brothy beans are undeniably humble when set next to a dollop of rich, well-fried *frijoles refritos*. The two share the same beginnings, though, and fried or not, beans do remain part of Mexico's ages-old nutritive foothold. That partly explains, I suppose, why fried beans usually share the plate with the typical Mexican snacks, everywhere from market stalls to respectable dining rooms. The other part of the explanation, of course, is that they simply taste good: when their texture is thick and coarse, when the pork lard is full of meaty flavor, and when they're dressed out with salty *queso añejo* and tortilla chips.

My method of making *frijoles refritos* calls for less fat than many Mexican recipes. There are two drawbacks to this approach, however: There's not enough lard to keep them moist and shiny for long, and they can have less flavor *unless* a really good-tasting fat is used. So, please read the note on keeping fried beans warm, and use the most flavorful fat you can lay your hands on.

YIELD: about 2¼ cups, 4 to 6 servings

> 2 tablespoons rich-flavored pork lard, bacon drippings or fat rendered from *chorizo* sausage
> ½ to 1 small onion, finely chopped (optional)
> 1 large clove garlic, peeled and minced (optional)
> 2½ to 3 cups (½ recipe) Brothy Beans (page 267), undrained
> Salt, if necessary
> 3 to 4 tablespoons crumbled Mexican *queso añejo* or *queso fresco* (page 327), or cheese like mild Parmesan, feta or farmer's cheese, for garnish
> Several tortilla chips, for garnish

1. *Browning the onion and garlic.* If using the onion and/or garlic, heat the fat in a medium-size skillet over medium. Fry the onion until browned, 8 minutes; add the garlic and cook 2 minutes. Raise the heat to medium-high. (If not using onion or garlic, heat the fat in the skillet over medium-high.)

2. *Mashing and frying the beans.* Add one third of the beans and their broth to the skillet. Mash them with the back of a

COOK'S NOTES

Ingredients
Lard or Other Fat: If, for dietary reasons, you're not using lard or bacon or *chorizo* renderings, use vegetable oil and the full amount of onion and garlic.

Timing and Advance Preparation
With cooked beans on hand, fried beans take about 20 minutes. They may be made up to 4 days ahead, covered and refrigerated. Reheat them *slowly* in a covered pan; stir in a little broth or water to achieve a soft consistency that holds its shape in a spoon.

A NOTE ON KEEPING FRIED BEANS WARM: Fried beans can be kept warm and in good condition for an hour or more if you scrape them into a heatproof bowl when they're still a little soft, cover and set in a pan of hot water over very low heat. If they thicken too much, stir in a little broth or water just before serving.

A MODERN VARIATION
Fried Beans from Canned Beans: Well-rinsed canned beans can be made into quite decent fried beans when the cook is short on time. Prepare the recipe as directed, using a 16-ounce can of beans, 1½ tablespoons fat, ½ small onion (optional), 1 clove garlic (optional) and water or broth for the bean broth. Makes 1⅓ cups.

wooden spoon, a blunt-bottomed wooden "potato" masher (which in Mexico is a bean masher) or a potato masher with holes in it. When the beans are coarsely pureed, add the next third, mash, then add and mash the final third. Let the beans simmer, stirring nearly constantly, until they are thick but a little softer than you want to serve them. (They will continue to thicken after you take them off the fire.) The entire mashing and cooking process should take about 8 minutes. Season with salt.

3. *Finishing and garnishing the beans.* Just before serving, heat the beans over a brisk fire, stirring in a little broth or water if they have thickened more than you'd like. Serve on a warm platter, sprinkled with the crumbled cheese and decorated with the tortilla chips.

Mexican bean masher

BEANS WITH BACON, ROASTED CHILE AND FRESH CORIANDER

Frijoles Charros

After days scouring Monterrey's charcoal-grilling establishments that specialize in *arracherra* ("skirt steak") and *cabrito* ("kid"), we came across a little open-air setup with a vertical spit of pork layered for *tacos al pastor* (called *tacos de trompo* there) and an earthenware *olla* simmering over radiant coals. It wasn't until then that I realized how tasty the town's ubiquitous *frijoles charros* ("cowboy beans") could be.

Here is the recipe for those typically brothy beans, with their smoky bacon flavor, green chiles and fresh coriander. (Many printed recipes call for pickled pork rinds and the like, but I've never found them served that way.) The beans are a perfect match for most meats off the grill, like chicken (page 228) or skirt steak (page 138).

YIELD: about 8 to 10 cups, serving 6 as a main course, 8 to 10 as a side dish

- 1 pound (about 2½ cups) pinto or other light-colored beans
- 4 ounces fatty pork shoulder, cut into ½-inch cubes
- 8 thick slices bacon, cut into ½-inch pieces
- 1 medium onion, diced
- 2 large fresh *chiles poblanos,* roasted and peeled (page 337), seeded and chopped
- 2 ripe, medium-small tomatoes, roasted or boiled (page 352), cored, peeled and chopped OR one 15-ounce can tomatoes, drained and chopped

Salt, about 1 teaspoon
½ cup roughly chopped fresh coriander (*cilantro*)

1. *Soaking the beans.* Pick over the beans for any foreign pieces, then rinse and place in a 4-quart pot. Add 2 quarts water, remove any beans that float, and soak for 4 to 8 hours, until water has penetrated to the core of the beans. Or quick-soak by boiling the beans for about 2 minutes, then letting them stand 1 hour. Drain the soaked beans.

2. *Preliminary cooking.* Measure 2 quarts of fresh water into the pot of beans, add the pork, bring slowly to a boil, partially cover and simmer over medium-low heat, stirring occasionally, until the beans are tender, 1 to 2 hours.

3. *Flavorings.* Fry the bacon in a medium-size skillet over medium-low heat, until crisp, about 10 minutes. Remove the bacon, pour off all but 2 tablespoons of fat and raise the heat to medium. Add the onion and chiles and fry until the onion is a deep golden brown, about 8 minutes. Stir in the tomato and cook until all the liquid has evaporated.

4. *Final simmering.* Add the tomato mixture, bacon and salt to the cooked beans. Simmer, stirring occasionally, for 20 to 30 minutes, to blend the flavors. If the beans are very soupy, uncover, raise the heat and simmer away the excess liquid. For a thicker broth, puree 2 cups of the beans (with their liquid) and return to the pot.

Just before serving, taste for salt and stir in the chopped fresh coriander. Serve in warm bowls.

be made several days ahead, covered and refrigerated. Reheat slowly, then add the fresh coriander.

TRADITIONAL VARIATIONS

Frijoles Borrachos: My favorite *frijoles charros* are made with the *borracho* ("drunken") addition of 1 cup beer, used in place of 1 cup water in Step 2.
Frijoles Fronterizos: Prepare the recipe as directed, replacing the pork with 2 tablespoons lard or bacon drippings, and the bacon with 8 ounces (1 cup) *chorizo* sausage.

CHARCOAL-GRILLED CORN WITH CREAM, CHEESE AND CHILE

Elote Asado

Out on a walk in practically any Mexican town, who can pass up the always-present fresh ears of chewy field corn, turning and crisping over the coals? Who isn't attracted to the smoky-smelling, pit-roasted ears (*pibinales*) when they're poured from gunnysacks in Yucatán? And who doesn't like the fried corn kernels with *epazote* and chiles in Toluca (*esquites*), or the ones served from big boiling *cazuelas* in the capital's Alameda Park, or the ones topped with cream, powdered chile and cheese in the northeastern states?

Our sweet corn isn't the same to me, boiled and buttered and served as a summertime vegetable. It lacks a little backbone. So when I'm having it, I usually give it the taste of an open fire, a squeeze of lime and a sprinkling of hot powdered chile . . . or the lavish spread of butter, cream and cheese of this recipe. Serve it anytime you're grilling, and you'll please practically everyone.

YIELD: 6 servings

> 6 ears fresh sweet corn, in their husks
> 3 tablespoons unsalted butter, melted
> About ½ cup Thick Cream (page 51) or commercial sour cream mixed with a little milk or cream
> ⅓ cup crumbled Mexican *queso añejo* or *queso fresco* (page 327), or cheese like Parmesan, feta or farmer's cheese
> About 1 tablespoon hot powdered chile (see Ingredients in Cook's Notes)

1. *Preliminaries.* About an hour before serving, place the ears of corn in a deep bowl, cover with cold water and weight with a plate to keep them submerged. Light your charcoal fire and let it burn until the bed of coals is medium-hot; adjust the grill 4 inches above the fire.

2. *Grilling the corn.* Lay the corn on the grill and roast for 15 to 20 minutes, turning frequently, until the outer leaves are blackened. Remove, let cool several minutes, then remove the

COOK'S NOTES

Techniques
Soaking in Water, Roasting in the Husk: The preliminary soaking keeps the outside from burning right off the bat and the inside damp enough to steam. First roasting in the husk penetrates the corn with leafy flavor, but the step is often omitted—especially with sweet corn.

Ingredients
Corn: The meaty, nonsweet field corn used in Mexico can be prepared as directed; those who like no-nonsense eating will love the texture.
Powdered Chile: Powdered *chile de árbol* is the cayenne of Mexico. My favorite choices, though, are powdered *guajillo* and New Mexico chile— they're less hot, so I can put more on.

Timing and Advance Preparation
Start soaking and fire building an hour before serving. There is little else to do in advance; if you plan to have your charcoal fire going for a long time, you may complete the in-husk steaming well ahead of the final grilling.

TRADITIONAL VARIATIONS
Fresh Corn, Fried (Esquites): In Toluca and Mexico City the corn is occasionally prepared as follows: Cut the kernels from 6 cobs, then fry in 3 tablespoons lard or vegetable oil (or butter)

husks and silk. About 10 minutes before serving, brush the corn with melted butter, return to the grill and turn frequently until nicely browned. Serve right away, passing the cream, cheese and powdered chile for your guests to use to their own liking.

ZUCCHINI WITH ROASTED PEPPERS, CORN AND CREAM

Calabacitas con Crema

It is well known to most North Americans who've traveled in Mexico that vegetables as a side dish are rarely to be found. The country seems to be filled with exceptionally carnivorous public eaters, though in the privacy of their homes most of them are used to whole meals of vegetables stewed with chiles and other traditional flavors, with only a scrap of meat thrown in, perhaps. (Mexican cookbook writers often include recipes for these homey vegetable dishes, frequently exaggerating the size of the meat scraps, I think.)

This recipe comes from the *cafetería* that we lived above in Mexico City, where it was served as a main dish—without any meat whatsoever. In addition to featuring it as a light main course with tortillas and a salad, I use it as a side dish for the one-pot Juchitecan Rice with Pork (page 263) or with any of the sauceless grilled meats (pages 136, 138 or 228).

YIELD: about 2 cups, 4 servings

> 1 **pound (4 small) zucchini, ends trimmed and cut into ½-inch cubes**
> 1 **scant teaspoon salt, plus a little more to season the sauce, if necessary**
> 1 **tablespoon unsalted butter**
> 1 **tablespoon vegetable oil**
> **The kernels cut from 1 large ear fresh sweet corn (about 1 cup)**
>   **OR 1 cup frozen corn, defrosted**
> 1 **fresh *chile poblano*, roasted and peeled (page 337), seeded and sliced into thin strips**
> ½ **medium onion, thinly sliced**
> ⅔ **cup Thick Cream (page 51) or whipping cream**

with hot green chile to taste (seeded and sliced) and 2 or 3 tablespoons chopped *epazote*. Season with salt.

COOK'S NOTES

Techniques
"Sweating" the Zucchini: Because our zucchini is more watery and bitter than the tennis ball–size, light-green squash common in Mexico, I usually salt and "sweat" zucchini (to draw out the bitter liquid) before cooking.

Ingredients
Chiles Poblanos: When you cannot find any, use long green chiles (roasted, peeled, seeded and sliced).

Timing and Advance Preparation
After the ½ hour "sweating," the dish takes 25 to 30 minutes to complete. Steps 1 and 2 may be done early in the day you're serving; when cool, mix all the vegetables together, cover and refrigerate until 1 hour before serving.

CONTEMPORARY IDEAS
Zucchini with Cream and Chicken or Cheese: For a light main course, quick-fry 2 small, boneless, skinless chicken breasts (dredged in flour) in a little vegetable oil until just cooked through; remove and cut into 1-inch cubes. Or cube 6 to 8 ounces fresh or melting cheese (page 328) like Monterey Jack or mild cheddar. Pre-

1. *"Sweating" the zucchini.* In a colander, toss the zucchini with the salt; let stand over a plate or in the sink for ½ hour. Rinse the zucchini, then dry on paper towels.

2. *Cooking the vegetables.* Heat the butter and oil over medium-high in a skillet large enough to hold the zucchini in a single layer. When quite hot, add the zucchini and fry for 8 to 10 minutes, stirring frequently, until the zucchini is browned and just tender. Remove the zucchini, draining as much butter and oil as possible back into the pan. Reduce the heat to medium.

Add the corn kernels, chile and onion. Stir regularly until the onion is lightly browned, 8 to 10 minutes.

3. *Finishing the dish.* A few minutes before serving, stir in the cream and the zucchini and simmer for a few minutes, until the cream is reduced to a thick glaze. Add a little salt, if necessary, scoop into a warm dish and serve.

QUICK-FRIED ZUCCHINI WITH TOASTED GARLIC AND LIME

Calabacitas al Mojo de Ajo

Though not traditional, I've combined the typical toasted garlic preparation *mojo de ajo* with quick-fried zucchini. For those who crave vegetables and want a sauceless, typically Mexican-tasting preparation to serve with their Mexican dinners, this is my recommendation. It goes well with most of the saucier main dishes like smoky Pork *Tinga* (page 248) or Green Pumpkinseed *Mole* (page 203).

YIELD: 4 servings

    1 pound (about 4 small) zucchini, ends trimmed
        and cut into ½-inch cubes
    1 scant teaspoon salt, plus a little more to season
        the finished dish, if necessary
    1 tablespoon unsalted butter
    1 tablespoon vegetable oil
    5 cloves garlic, peeled and very thinly sliced

pare the recipe as directed, adding the chicken or cheese at the last minute, giving it time to heat through or soften slightly. Serve with Pueblan Rice (page 264) or Green Rice (page 266).

COOK'S NOTES

Techniques
"Sweating" the Zucchini: See page 275.
Browning the Garlic: See page 275.

Timing and Advance Preparation
When the zucchini has sweated for ½ hour, Steps 2 and 3 can be completed in 20 minutes. The sweating may be done early in the day you are serving, but finish Step 3 just before serving.

1 tablespoon freshly squeezed lime juice
A generous ¼ teaspoon freshly ground black pepper
½ teaspoon dried oregano
2 tablespoons chopped flat-leaf parsley

1. *Sweating the zucchini.* In a colander, toss the zucchini with the salt; let stand ½ hour over a plate or in the sink. Rinse the zucchini, then dry on paper towels.

2. *Browning the garlic and frying the zucchini.* About 15 minutes before serving, heat the butter and oil over a medium-low heat in a skillet large enough to hold the zucchini in a single layer. Add the garlic and stir frequently until light brown, about 3 minutes. *Do not burn.* Scoop the garlic into a fine-mesh sieve set over a small bowl, then scrape the strained butter mixture back into the pan; set the garlic aside. Raise the heat to medium-high.

Add the zucchini to the pan and fry, stirring frequently, for 8 to 10 minutes, until browned and tender but still a little crunchy. Remove from the heat.

3. *Finishing the dish.* Add the lime and toasted garlic; toss thoroughly. Sprinkle with the pepper, oregano and parsley, then mix, taste for salt and serve in a warm dish.

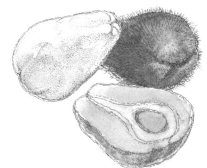

Spiny and smooth chayote squash

SWISS CHARD WITH TOMATOES AND POTATOES

Acelgas Guisadas

Here is another of the typical vegetable dishes that are often cooked with a little pork or chicken. This tasty, homey prepa-

CONTEMPORARY IDEAS

Chayotes al Mojo de Ajo: The squashlike *chayote* that in Mexico is often stuffed or put in stews is great with garlic: Peel, pit and slice 2 large (1½ pounds total) *chayotes* and use in place of the zucchini. In fact, steamed green beans, carrots, broccoli and asparagus are all good *al mojo de ajo:* Simply prepare the garlic, add the cooked vegetable and flavorings to the pan and toss until warm.

COOK'S NOTES

Timing and Advance Preparation
The dish takes ½ hour to make. Steps 1 and 2 can be done a day ahead, covered and refrigerated. Reheat just before serving, then finish Step 3.

ration, based on one from Rodriguez' *La comida en el México antiguo y moderno,* can serve as anything from a light main dish (with cubes of fresh cheese stirred in at the last moment), to a vegetarian taco filling or an accompaniment to simple broiled or charcoal-grilled meat, poultry or fish. Swiss chard, one of the most common greens in Mexico, has a good texture and a flavor that's a little fuller than spinach, so it works beautifully in this kind of preparation. Though frequently stewed for a long time, it seems to have the best texture when just wilted, as I've directed.

YIELD: about 2½ cups, 4 servings

- 1 tablespoon lard, vegetable oil or butter
- 1 small onion, thinly sliced
- Fresh hot green chiles to taste (about 1 *chile serrano* or ½ *chile jalapeño*), stemmed, seeded, deveined and thinly sliced
- 1 ripe, medium-small tomato, roasted or boiled (page 352), cored and peeled
  OR ½ 15-ounce can tomatoes, drained
- 2 medium-small (about 8 ounces total) boiling potatoes like the red-skinned ones, cut in ¾-inch dice
- ½ cup any poultry or meat broth or water, plus a couple tablespoons more if necessary
- 4 leaves *epazote* (optional)
- Salt, about ½ teaspoon
- ½ bunch (about 4 ounces) small Swiss chard, stems cut off and leaves sliced crosswise in 1-inch strips

1. *The flavorings.* In a medium-size saucepan, heat the lard, oil or butter over medium. Add the onion and chile, and cook, stirring frequently, until the onion is lightly browned, 7 or 8 minutes. Roughly chop the tomato, add it to the pan and cook for 3 or 4 minutes longer, to reduce the liquid a little.

2. *The potatoes.* Stir in the potatoes, broth, optional *epazote* and salt. Cover and cook over medium-low heat until the potatoes are tender, about 10 minutes. Check the amount of liquid: If most has been consumed, add a little more broth; or, if it is very soupy, quickly boil it down, uncovered, until only ¼ cup is left.

3. *Steam-cooking the chard.* Mix in the chard, cover and cook over medium heat until the greens are tender, about 3 minutes. Uncover and taste for salt. There should be enough tomatoey broth to coat the vegetables. Serve right away.

TRADITIONAL VARIATIONS

Pork with Swiss Chard: Boil ⅓ to ½ pound cubed pork in salted water until tender, about 45 minutes. Prepare the recipe as directed, using the pork broth in Step 2 and adding the meat with the chard.

CHARCOAL-GRILLED BABY ONIONS WITH LIME

Cebollitas Asadas

I can't imagine eating slivers of charcoal-grilled meat wrapped in tortillas and dashed with hot sauce (*Tacos al Carbón*, page 137), without also wanting the requisite plate of grilled over-grown green onions. They're so simple, so sweet and smoky that I can't understand why we didn't have them with our summertime steaks when I was growing up. We do now.

YIELD: 6 to 8 servings

> 3 **bunches large green onions (see Ingredients in** Cook's Notes)
> 2 **tablespoons vegetable oil**
> 2 **large limes, cut into wedges**
> **Salt, as desired**

1. *Preliminaries.* About 45 minutes before serving, light your charcoal fire and let it burn until medium-hot. Cut the roots off the onions, trim ½ inch off the tops, and pull off any withered outer layers.

2. *Grilling the onions.* Position the grill 4 to 6 inches above the coals; fold a square of aluminum foil in half and lay it on one side of the grill. Lightly brush the onions with oil, then lay them on the grill, bulb-side over the coals and green-side over the aluminum foil. Grill, turning frequently, for 7 to 12

Fresh-dug white onions (cebollas)

COOK'S NOTES

Techniques
Grilling over Foil: Laying the green tops over foil on the grill protects them from burning while the bulbs roast and sweeten directly over the coals.

Ingredients
Green Onions: Our small green onions aren't as common in Mexico as a larger variety with a bulb about 1 inch across—perfect for grilling without softening too quickly. In Chicago, they are often called knob onions. Everyday green onions (a.k.a. scallions in the East) work OK, but choose the largest ones so there is a sizable chunk of white bulb to bite into.

Timing and Advance Preparation
There is little to do: Just build your fire and grill the onions. They can be held for a few minutes in a low oven.

TRADITIONAL VARIATIONS
Griddle-Fried Onions: Green onions are delicious browned over medium heat in a little vegetable oil (or, for extra flavor, in bacon drippings). Thick slices of white or red onion can be done the same way, but they're best brushed with oil and done over hot coals.

minutes (depending on the size of your onions), until the bulbs are browned and the green tops soft. Remove to a warm serving platter, squeeze a couple of lime wedges over them and sprinkle with salt. Serve with the remaining lime wedges to the side, for those who want more.

ROASTED PEPPERS WITH ONIONS AND HERBS

Rajas de Chile Poblano

When the chiles have been charred over glowing charcoal, gently fried with browned onions, then simmered with garlic, herbs and cream—there isn't a Mexican who wouldn't call it simple, traditional perfection. I've called for these *rajas* (they're substantial enough to be called a vegetable) numerous times throughout the book: on a plate of Steak *a la Tampiqueña* (page 243), with grilled meat for *Tacos al Carbón* (page 137), to stuff Central Mexican–Style *Tamales* (page 181) and in many of the variation recipes. The single word *rajas*, by the way, simply means "strips," though Mexican cooks always seem to understand it to mean "strips of green chile." What other kind could there be?

YIELD: about 1½ cups

    4 medium, fresh *chiles poblanos*, roasted and peeled
        (page 337)
    1½ tablespoons vegetable oil
    1 medium onion, sliced ¼ inch thick
    2 cloves garlic, peeled and minced
    ⅔ cup Thick Cream (page 51), whipping cream
        or broth
    ½ teaspoon mixed dried herbs (such as thyme,
        oregano and marjoram)
    2 bay leaves
    Salt, about ½ teaspoon (depending on the salti-
        ness of the broth)

1. *The chiles.* Stem and seed the chiles; for milder *rajas*, cut out the veins. Slice the chiles crosswise into ¼-inch strips.

COOK'S NOTES

Ingredients
Chiles Poblanos: *Rajas* can be (and are) made from most any locally available fresh chiles: frequently it's 6 of the common long green ones or 7 of the occasionally available *chilacas* (roasted and peeled). When adventure dashes all concerns for authenticity, any big meaty pepper (fresh pimentos, red or green bells, cubanelles) will work. They can all be delicious.

Timing and Advance Preparation
Rajas can be ready in 25 minutes or less. They keep well, covered and refrigerated, for several days. Reheat them slowly in a covered pan.

TRADITIONAL VARIATIONS
Rajas as a Vegetable: Prepare the recipe as directed, adding the kernels cut from 1 ear of corn (1 cup) or ½ pound steamed green beans (ends snipped) along with the cream or broth.
Rajas with Tomatoes, for Filling Tamales: Prepare the recipe as directed, omitting the herbs and replacing the cream

2. *Frying the vegetables.* Heat the vegetable oil in a medium-size skillet over medium. Fry the onion, stirring frequently, until it begins to brown, 7 or 8 minutes. Stir in the garlic and chile strips and cook 2 minutes.

3. *The simmering.* Add the cream or broth, the herbs and bay leaves, and simmer until the liquid has reduced to a light coating for the vegetables; the simmering should go quickly enough that the chiles don't get too soft before the liquid has reduced. Remove the bay leaves and season with salt.

Fresh poblano chiles

or broth with one 15-ounce can tomatoes (drained and pureed). Season with salt and cool before using.

CONTEMPORARY IDEAS

My Favorite Rajas: Roast, peel, seed and slice 2 *poblanos* and 2 small red bell peppers. Fry the onions (Step 2), using olive oil. Stir in the pepper strips, 4 cloves of *roasted* garlic (minced), 3 tablespoons *each* cream, beef broth and white wine, and 2 bay leaves; simmer until the liquid is nearly consumed. Add the salt, a little fresh thyme and a good sprinkling of black pepper.

DESSERTS

❖
Postres

Ice cream stand, Oaxaca market

The scope and sphere of Mexican sweet things is still a puzzle to me. "Order a flan," I hear the tourists whisper. "It'll be safe." Safe, as opposed to the potential spoonful of something thick and gooey and called *cajeta,* or a chunk of pumpkin cooked in dark, spicy syrup.

Still, I find myself looking forward to the dessert tables at dressier traditional restaurants, to exploring the thick, sweet spoonfuls of almost macaroonlike *cocada,* the soft custard of *natillas,* the syrupy curds of *chongos,* or the thick-textured, jellied guava paste (*ate*) with fresh cheese. It *is* an exploration in a way, for the desserts are difficult for North American eyes to categorize. None seem to have that familiar crust or the cakey layers; or, if they do, there's no chocolate or nicely cooked apples or rich buttercream. The ever-present flan comes the closest to home, its comforting baked custard bathed with light caramel; the well-known rice pudding is generally there, too, though few make that choice in a nice restaurant. So the non-Mexicans pass over the Mexican desserts, they tell me, and go right on to their coffee or an after-dinner brandy, Kahlúa or anisette.

All the differences aside, Mexican desserts really *are* a deliciously varied lot. Nearly all of them trace their heritage to Spain—whether puddings, custards, candies or some seemingly improbable combination of all three. In fact, the entire concept of desserts—the post-dinner segregation of tangential sweet things—is a European one that apparently had no pre-Columbian equivalent. For the ruling Indian empire, sweet and savory were tastes to be intermingled, as they once were in medieval Europe; and just as the European ways of thinking were modified, so were the Mexican.

The greatest credit for this sweetening of Mexico goes to the Spanish nuns, whose custom was to prepare and sell sweetmeats to generate money for their orders. They brought to Mexico not only their milk, egg yolks, sugar and almonds, but the knowledge of how to turn them into the custards, puddings and candies that still remain the national favorites. And adding all the New World fruits and nuts to their list of dessert-making ingredients certainly increased their already-large repertory.

Every region of Mexico knows the handful of classics that are nearly always served at table: the custards (be they flan, *jericalla* and *queso napolitano*), the rice pudding, the syrup-poached fruit and the occasional cheesecakelike *pay de queso.* All are familiar with fruit ices and ice creams, too, but only in Oaxaca or the Gulf do they create a special interest; even there, the frozen treats are more for a snack than a respectable "dessert." The same is true of fried plantains: While they're popular, they're usually viewed as snacks in the coffee shops—as are the pies.

When it comes to the candied sweets, however, they are the source of great regional pride. They're carried onto buses and into cars by departing visitors. They're enjoyed with everyday regularity, set on tables for dessert after a big midday *comida* or for something to go with *café con leche* in the evening. Everywhere, some regional version of the national sweets are a favorite street food: milk fudge, coconut candies, nut brittles and chunks of candied sweet potato, pumpkin or bisnaga cactus.

Though Puebla is recognized as the candy capital of Mexico—from its *camotes de Santa Clara* (mashed, sweetened, flavored sweet potato) to its *pepita* milk fudge and fragile nut shortbread (*polvorones sevillanos*)—four other areas certainly stand out: Morelia, Michoacán, for its tender fruit "jellies" (*ates*) and chewy little sheets of caramel (*morelianas*); San Cristóbal de las Casas, Chiapas, for its sweet shops with a seemingly infinite variety of coconut candies, cookies, tiny turnovers, egg-yolk candies, boxed fruit pastes (*cajetas*) and the preserved fruits in alcohol; Oaxaca, for its cakey sweets made with light-textured *manón*, and meringues, puff-pastry turnovers with custard (*empanadas de lechecilla*) and coconut–raw sugar bars (*jamoncillo de coco*); and Mérida, Yucatán, for its pumpkinseed marzipan.

Sweet snacks are special holiday snacks, too. Where there are Spaniards, there will be the delicious *turrones* at Christmas, usually imported from Spain. I've been fascinated by the fanciful molded sugar skulls, coffins and miniature plates of enchiladas, fruit and the like that fill the markets during the Day of the Dead celebrations in early November; they're set on the home altars in memory of the deceased and his or her earthly likings. Special breads are made for that day, too: Some are round shapes with dough modeled into drooping crossbones on top, others are pointed, oblong shapes meant to represent the spirits. Near the time of Three Kings Day, when the children receive presents, most of the bakeries are overflowing with rings of egg bread with candied fruit and a little doll somewhere inside; tradition has it that the one who gets the doll gives a party February 2. Oaxaca at Christmas is without doubt one of life's greatest pleasures, from the elaborate radish-carving festival and Christmas Eve parade to the paper-thin fritters (*buñuelos*) that are served every night on the square. Of course, every town has its festival, every town has the sweets it enjoys.

In deciding on recipes for this chapter, I trained one eye on the regional Mexican sweet things and another on my dinner table. I looked everywhere, from the street stalls to the fanciest traditional eateries, to come up with this mixture of classics, local specialties and a couple of personal adaptations of Mexican originals—all of them sweets that make good desserts on my table, offering a pleasant resolve after a full-flavored Mexican meal. And most of them are light as well; all of them are welcome.

VANILLA-FLAVORED CARAMEL CUSTARD

Flan

COOK'S NOTES

The traditional recipe I've outlined below is based on the standard from Veláquez de León's *Mexican Cook Book Devoted to American Homes:* creamy-smooth and rich, with a good amount of vanilla and lots of caramel. Many cooks nowadays use sweetened condensed milk for their flan and their results are not unlike the reduced-milk version of this older recipe. When I want a really light dessert—which I often do after a spicy meal—I make the variation with unreduced milk and all whole eggs; for special occasions, there is almond, pineapple or spirited flan. Besides being a sure winner, any flan is an easy and nice-looking dessert.

YIELD: 10 servings, in 10 individual molds or 1 large one

For the milk reduction:
  2 quarts milk
  1 cup sugar

For the caramel:
  1 cup sugar (⅔ cup for a large flan)
  ⅓ cup water (¼ cup for a large flan)

For finishing the custard:
  6 large eggs
  6 large egg yolks
  1 teaspoon vanilla extract

  1. *Reducing the milk.* Bring the milk and 1 cup sugar to a boil in a *large* saucepan. Regulate the heat so the mixture simmers briskly without boiling over; stirring regularly, let reduce to 1 quart, about 45 minutes.
  2. *The mold(s) and hot-water bath.* Set 10 custard cups or a large mold (see Equipment in **Cook's Notes**) in a baking pan deep enough to hold 2 inches of water. Put a teakettle of water on to heat, preheat the oven to 350° and position the rack in the middle.
  3. *The caramel.* Measure the appropriate amount of sugar into a small, heavy saucepan, dribble in the corresponding amount of water (first around the sides, then over the sugar),

Techniques
Baking: Overbaking, the most common pitfall, results in a Swiss cheese–looking exterior and curdy, watery custard.
Unmolding: It is not tricky: The caramelized sugar melts into a liquid lining for the mold, allowing the custard to slip right out.

Equipment
Molds: For the custard to bake evenly and look nicest, choose an 8-inch, 2½-quart soufflé dish. The most common mold in Mexico, however, is a 5- to 6-ounce custard cup.

Ingredients
Vanilla: See page 353.

Timing and Advance Preparation
For best results, start a large flan the day before serving, small ones at least 6 hours ahead. Preparation time is about 1 hour, plus 30 to 50 minutes of baking. Flan can be baked several days ahead, covered and refrigerated.

TRADITIONAL VARIATIONS
Almond Flan: For a rich, nutty-tasting, cheesecakelike texture, add 6 ounces (1⅓ cups) *finely* ground blanched almonds to the reduced milk (Step 1) and simmer 2 or 3 minutes until thickened. For the smoothest texture, blend (lightly covered) for several minutes. Complete and pour into small molds; bake about 40 minutes, leaving uncovered for the first 20 minutes. If you

and stir several times. Bring to a boil, wash down the sides of the pan with a brush dipped in water, then simmer over medium heat, without stirring, until the syrup begins to color. Swirl the pan continually over the fire until the syrup is an even *deep* amber. Immediately pour the caramel into the mold or divide it among the custard cups, then tilt the mold or cups to distribute it over the bottom and sides.

Lining flan mold with caramel

4. *The custard.* Beat the eggs, yolks and vanilla in a large bowl until liquidy. Slowly beat in the hot reduced milk, strain through a fine-mesh sieve (to remove any membranes or milk "skins"), then pour into the mold(s).

5. *Baking the flan.* Fill the baking pan containing the custard(s) with 2 inches of simmering water, cover lightly with foil and bake until the custard has just set (a knife inserted near the center will come out clean), about 30 minutes for the individual molds, 40 to 50 minutes for a large one. Remove from the oven and let cool in the water bath (the custard will set completely as it cools).

6. *Unmolding the flan.* For the best results, thoroughly chill the cooled custard(s). Run a non-serrated knife around the edge, penetrating to the bottom, then twist the dish back and forth to ensure that the custard is free from the mold. Invert a deep serving plate over the top, reverse the two and listen for the flan to drop. Individual custards may need a gentle shake from side to side to release any suction holding them in. If there still is caramel on the bottom of the mold, either scrape it out onto the flan, or set the mold in very hot water (or over a low fire) until it softens enough to pour out.

Traditional flan

like, add 1 teaspoon almond extract to the custard.
Pineapple Flan: Caramel and pineapple are a very good match. Replace the milk with 1 quart unsweetened pineapple juice (or strained fresh pineapple puree); heat with the sugar (Step 1) but don't reduce. Complete and bake as directed, flavoring the custard with ½ teaspoon ground cinnamon and a pinch of ground cloves.
A Very Light-Textured Flan: Prepare as directed, using 1 quart milk and 8 whole eggs. Simply warm the milk with the sugar, rather than reducing it.
Flan with Condensed Milk: Dilute one 14-ounce can sweetened condensed milk with 2¼ cups milk, then warm it and use in place of the reduced milk in Step 1; canned milk gives a distinct taste, however.

CONTEMPORARY IDEAS

My Favorite Flan: Prepare as directed, simmering the milk (Step 1) with a 2-inch cinnamon stick and adding 2 teaspoons *each* Kahlúa and dark Jamaican rum along with the vanilla (Step 4). After unmolding, splash the flan with a little Kahlúa or rum.

Regional Explorations

Most regions have their own custard specialties: In Guadalajara, the custard is soft, yellow with yolks and baked in a cup until the top browns (*jericalla*). In the Gulf, the flavor moves past the common vanilla and cinnamon to add orange, coconut or almond. In Yucatán and vicinity, a dense, rich, almost cheesy-tasting flan is the choice (*queso napolitano*). And here and there some fresh cream cheese goes in to give substance to the light custard.

CREAMY FRESH-COCONUT DESSERT

Postre de Cocada

Sitting on the dessert table at the famous Fonda el Refugio restaurant in Mexico City, amidst the brilliantly colored paper flowers, there's nearly always a green-glazed, Michoacán-style leaf-shaped serving bowl that's filled with golden *cocada*. Its lightly browned top gives way to dense, fresh coconut held together with just a little rich custard. "Pudding" is really the wrong word to describe this dessert; "macaroon in pudding form" may be closer.

Since coconuts are readily available throughout Mexico, many places commonly serve a preparation similar to this one, especially restaurants in Central Mexico. The following recipe is based on one from María A. de Carbia's *México en la cocina de Marichu*, though I've made it a little creamier to duplicate the version at Fonda el Refugio. It is very good and rather elegant in small portions after a big meal, but is equally at home on a picnic.

YIELD: 6 to 8 servings

 1 medium (1¾-pound) fresh coconut with lots of liquid inside
 1 cup sugar
 1½ tablespoons good-quality sweet or dry sherry
 6 large egg yolks
 3 tablespoons milk or whipping cream
 ½ cup (about 2 ounces) sliced almonds
 1½ tablespoons unsalted butter, cut into small bits

1. *The coconut.* Hull and peel the coconut as directed on page 341, reserving and straining the liquid. Grate the meat (it should be medium-fine).

2. *Cooking the coconut.* Measure the coconut liquid and add enough tap water to bring the total quantity to 1 cup. Place the grated coconut in a medium-size, heavy saucepan, stir in the liquid and sugar and set over medium heat. Cook, stirring frequently, until the coconut becomes transparent (it will look almost candied) and the liquid has reduced to a glaze, 20 to 30 minutes. Stir in the sherry and cook for 3 or 4 minutes longer, to evaporate its liquid, then remove from the fire.

COOK'S NOTES

Techniques
Thickening the Cocada: After the egg-yolk mixture goes into the hot coconut, make sure the heat under your pan isn't too high, or the yolks can curdle. In no case should the coconut mixture come near a boil.

Ingredients
Coconut: See page 341 for information on choosing and working with fresh coconuts. Desiccated coconut is inappropriate here.

Timing and Advance Preparation
If you work quickly, the coconut can be prepared in 45 minutes (including the initial 15 minutes in the oven); 45 minutes more and the *cocada* will be ready. It may be completed through Step 3, covered and refrigerated for 2 or 3 days. Let it warm to room temperature, then brown shortly before serving.

3. *Thickening the cocada.* Beat the yolks with the milk or cream, stir in several tablespoons of the hot coconut, then carefully stir the warm yolk mixture into the coconut remaining in the pan. Return to medium-low heat and stir constantly until lightly thickened, about 5 minutes. Scrape the *cocada* into an ovenproof serving dish.

4. *Browning the finished cocada.* Spread the almonds onto a baking sheet and toast in a 325° oven until lightly browned, about 10 minutes.

Shortly before serving, heat the broiler. Dot the *cocada* with butter, run under the heat and let brown for a minute or so. Watch carefully: The sugar in the *cocada* will caramelize very quickly. Strew with the toasted almond slices and the dessert is ready to serve.

MEXICAN RICE PUDDING

Arroz con Leche

This dessert is softer and more cinnamony than our baked rice pudding. The flavors are simple and close to home, but it's easy to develop a thoroughgoing love for it, spoonful after spoonful. . . . Mexican people everywhere serve it as regularly as they do flan; it's creamy and, in its own way, light and soothing.

This is an especially pretty and tasty recipe, based on one from Zelayarán's *Las 500 mejores recetas de la cocina mexicana.* It would be welcome after a hearty soup like *Menudo* (page 109) or Shrimp-Ball Soup (page 102); it travels well to potlucks. Leftovers, thinned with milk and warmed, are very good for breakfast.

YIELD: 8 to 10 servings

2 inches cinnamon stick

A 2-inch strip of lime zest (colored rind only), ¾ inch wide

1 cup rice

1 quart milk

¾ cup sugar

¼ teaspoon salt

4 large egg yolks

½ teaspoon vanilla extract

¼ cup raisins

1 tablespoon unsalted butter, cut into bits

Ground cinnamon, for garnish

1. *The rice.* Bring 2 cups water to a boil in a medium-size saucepan, add the cinnamon stick and lime zest, then cover and simmer over medium heat for 5 minutes. Pour in the rice, let the mixture return to a boil, stir once, then cover and cook over medium-low heat for 20 minutes, until all the liquid is absorbed and the rice is tender.

2. *The pudding.* Stir in the milk, sugar and salt, and simmer over medium to medium-low heat, stirring frequently, until the liquid shows the *first* signs of thickening, 20 to 25 minutes. Take from the heat and remove the cinnamon stick and zest. Beat the egg yolks until runny, stir in the vanilla and a few tablespoons of the hot rice, then stir the yolk concoction back into the rice mixture. Mix in *half* the raisins, then spoon the rice pudding into a decorative 8-inch-square baking dish.

3. *Browning and finishing the pudding.* Preheat the broiler and dot the rice pudding with butter. Set the dish under the heat long enough to brown the top, 3 or 4 minutes. Sprinkle with the remaining raisins and the ground cinnamon, and serve warm or at room temperature.

Cinnamon sticks (canela)

won't involve your direct participation. It may be prepared through Step 2 a day or two ahead, then buttered and broiled shortly before serving.

TRADITIONAL VARIATIONS

Coconut-Rice Pudding: Prepare the rice as directed in Step 1. Hull, peel and grate a fresh coconut (page 341), reserving the coconut liquid. Add enough milk to the coconut liquid to bring the volume to 1 quart. Complete Steps 2 and 3, using the milk-coconut mixture where milk is called for and stirring *half* the grated coconut into the rice pudding when you add the yolks. Sprinkle a little coconut over the pudding before browning.

Regional Explorations

Rice pudding brings to my mind the volatile, chancy crowd of Mexico City's Garibaldi Square, where this dessert, only one of the attractions, sits in huge, milky masses stuck with a raisin or two for decoration. Or sometimes I'm reminded of the well-used walkways around the Oaxacan market, where ladies sell it in paper cups at sundown. Or I picture any of a dozen other typical scenes: from rude, makeshift street stands to well-appointed traditional restaurants—where *arroz con leche* is the thing you have.

SWEET FRESH-CHEESE PIE

Pay de Queso

Anywhere a cheesecake is welcome, you can serve this *pay de queso*. It's rich with fresh cream cheese, but light, sweet and often studded with raisins. In fact, it's even lighter and more elegant than most of our cheesecakes, and I think it goes particularly well with an untraditional spoonful of pureed fresh fruit.

This recipe for *pay de queso*—a dessert known in nearly every *cafetería* in the country—is based on one given to me in Tabasco, where loaves of dense, delicious cream cheese are a specialty. After more than a dozen experiments, I came up with proportions that utilize our "natural" cream cheese and still retain that wonderful texture of my favorite version of this pie—the one at Mexico City's famous sweets shop Dulcería de Celaya. My only regret is that our cream cheese doesn't taste as cheesy.

YIELD: one 9-inch pie, 6 to 8 servings

For the crust:

     5 slices (4 ounces) firm white bread, untrimmed
     2 tablespoons sugar
     2 tablespoons unsalted butter
     2 tablespoons solid vegetable shortening

For the filling:

     1 pound "natural" (no gum additives) cream cheese, at room temperature (see Ingredients in Cook's Notes)
     ¾ cup sugar
     ¼ teaspoon salt, plus a little more for the egg whites
     ¼ teaspoon ground cinnamon
     1 tablespoon flour
     ½ teaspoon vanilla extract
     3 large egg yolks, at room temperature
     2 large egg whites, at room temperature

1. *The crust.* Pulverize the bread in a blender or food processor; there should be about 1⅔ cups. Combine the crumbs

COOK'S NOTES

Ingredients

Cheese: "Natural" cream cheese—without locust-bean (or other) gum—is similar to the Mexican *queso crema;* I've found Fleur de Lait brand distributed nationally. Our common cream cheese makes a much heavier pie. A very mild domestic goat cheese or the German *quark* (or what's often called baker's cheese) will also work here.

Vanilla: See page 353.

Timing and Advance Preparation

The pie takes about 40 minutes to put together, 40 minutes to bake and an hour to cool. It can be baked a day ahead, covered *lightly* (plastic wrap has a tendency to stick) and refrigerated. Bring to room temperature before serving; it doesn't cut well when cold.

CONTEMPORARY IDEAS

Sweet Fresh-Cheese Pie with Pine Nuts and Raisins: Toast 2 tablespoons pine nuts for 10 minutes at 325°; cool them, then toss with 3 tablespoons raisins and 1 teaspoon flour. Fold into the batter with the last addition of egg whites and bake as directed.

Regional Explorations

The old shop opened in 1874 on Fifth of May Street in Mexico City, down by the Cathedral, and it's still filled with muted lights, etched windowpanes, an old oak case with

and sugar in a bowl. Melt the butter with the shortening, then pour over the crumbs and mix well. Pat into an even layer in a 9-inch pie pan. Chill 20 to 30 minutes.

2. *The filling.* Preheat the oven to 375° and position the rack in the upper third. Place the cheese in a food processor or electric mixer, add ½ *cup* of the sugar, ¼ teaspoon salt, the cinnamon, flour, vanilla and egg yolks, and process or beat until very smooth. If using a food processor, scrape the mixture into a large mixing bowl.

Using a large wire whisk or an electric mixer at medium speed, beat the egg whites with a pinch of salt until they hold a firm peak, then beat in the remaining ¼ cup of sugar at half-minute intervals, 1 tablespoon at a time. Continue beating until they hold a stiff, shiny peak again. Stir ⅓ of the egg whites into the cheese batter, then gently fold in the remainder in 2 additions. Scoop into the crust.

3. *Baking.* Immediately set the pie in the oven. Bake 5 minutes, then lower the heat to 325° and bake 25 minutes; turn off the oven and let the pie cool for 15 minutes with the door closed. Remove from the oven and cool completely before serving. It will have puffed and browned during baking, but will settle to its original height as it cools.

PECAN PIE WITH RAW SUGAR AND SPICES

Pay de Nuez

Though you'll find them in nearly every little *cafetería* and in many restaurants, pies (or the homophonous, Spanish-spelled *pay*) are a recent addition to the Mexican dessert repertory. The choice seems always the same: lime meringue, apple, sweet fresh-cheese and pecan—the latter being one of my favorites, in spite of the fact that (or perhaps because) it tastes a lot like those north of the border.

Since pecan pie is so popular in Mexico (and since pecans are native to the New World), I developed this special version that features Mexican raw sugar and typical Mexican spicing. I

curved glass and a stunning arrangement of exquisite crystallized fruit and old-style candies: Each piece is a jewel. Half of one shelf of Dulcería de Celaya is devoted to sweets to eat on a plate rather than out of hand—what we'd call desserts. It's there you can taste the really good *chongos* (tender curds in sweet whey), flan and old-fashioned cakelike egg-yolk squares called *huevos reales* ("royal eggs"). And at the Dulcería fresh-cheese pie reaches its pinnacle.

COOK'S NOTES

Techniques
Pastry Making: For a tender, flaky crust, follow these guidelines: Have *everything* cool (even refrigerate the flour if the kitchen is hot); work the fat into the flour quickly and evenly, but stop while you can still see tiny bits; once you've added the liquids, don't overwork the dough (pressing the tines of a fork through the flour will be sufficient); don't add too much water (a wet dough will turn out tough);

think you'll really like the result . . . though I'm sure less traditional Mexicans would consider my project of Mexicanizing pecan pie rather unprogressive.

YIELD: one 9-inch pie, 6 to 8 servings

For the crust:
- 1 cup (4½ ounces) all-purpose flour
- 2 tablespoons lard, well chilled and cut into ½-inch bits
- 3 tablespoons unsalted butter, well chilled and cut into ½-inch bits
- 2 large egg yolks
- 1 tablespoon ice water, plus a little more if necessary
- ⅛ teaspoon salt
- ½ teaspoon sugar

For the filling:
- 4½ ounces *piloncillo*, chopped
  OR ⅔ cup packed dark-brown sugar plus 1½ tablespoons molasses
- ½ cup clear corn syrup
- 1 inch cinnamon stick
- 4 cloves
- 8 peppercorns, very coarsely ground
- 6 tablespoons unsalted butter, diced
- 3 tablespoons Thick Cream (page 51) or commercial sour cream
- 1½ cups (about 5¼ ounces) pecan halves or pieces
- 1 large egg
- 2 large egg yolks
- ¼ teaspoon salt
- ½ teaspoon vanilla extract
- 1 tablespoon flour

1. *The dough.* Measure the flour, lard and butter into a bowl. With a pastry blender, quickly work in the fat until the flour looks a little damp (rather than powdery) but *small* bits of fat are still visible.

Mix together *1* of the egg yolks, the ice water, salt and sugar; reserve the remaining egg yolk for Step 3. Little by little, work the ice-water mixture into the flour mixture with a fork. The dough will be in rough, rather stiff clumps; if there is unincorporated flour in the bottom of the bowl, use the fork to work a little more ice water into it. Press the clumps of dough to-

always use a light touch; and don't omit the chilling (the dough will be hard to work with if you do).
Prebaking the Crust: The crust is prebaked to avoid any sogginess. If my unweighted prebaking isn't your style, butter a piece of lightweight aluminum foil, lay it (buttered-side down) directly on the crust, fill with raw rice, beans or the like, then prebake the crust without worry of sliding or puffing. Remove the foil and weights after 10 minutes, then bake several minutes to dry out. Omit the glazing; cool.

Ingredients
Lard and Butter: I've developed this recipe using both: Lard gives imcomparable tenderness; butter gives incomparable flavor. Don't substitute one for the other or vegetable shortening for both; it won't work in these proportions.
Piloncillo: If using large (9-ounce) cones of this raw sugar, you'll need ½ of a cone; if using small (¾-ounce) cones, you'll need 6 of them.
Vanilla: See page 353.

Timing and Advance Preparation
Allow 20 minutes to prepare the pastry and 1 hour (or up to 3 days) to let it rest. In 45 minutes the pie can be in the oven; allow ½ hour for baking and 1 hour for cooling. It is best eaten within half a day of baking, rewarmed.

gether into a single mass, wrap in plastic and refrigerate at least 1 hour.

On a lightly floured surface, roll the dough into a 12-inch circle. Transfer to an 8-inch pie pan or 9-inch tart pan (¾ inch deep, with removable bottom), finish the edge (crimp for a pie pan, pinch up and press to secure on the vertical edge of the tart tin), then trim off the excess dough. Cover and refrigerate while you prepare the filling.

2. *The filling.* Place the *piloncillo* (or brown sugar and molasses), corn syrup, cinnamon stick, cloves and peppercorns into a small saucepan. Measure in ⅓ cup water, cover and place over medium-low heat. After the mixture has come to a simmer, uncover and stir until the *piloncillo* has dissolved. Simmer over medium heat until reduced to 1 cup, about 10 minutes. Strain through a fine-mesh sieve, add the diced butter and cream, and stir until the butter is melted. Let cool, stirring occasionally.

Heat the oven to 325° and position the rack in the middle. Spread the pecans over a baking sheet and bake until toasted through, 10 to 15 minutes. Remove and cool.

Whisk together the egg, 2 egg yolks, salt, vanilla and flour. Stir into the cooled sugar-spice mixture.

3. *Prebaking the crust.* Heat the oven to 425°. Prick the bottom of the crust at 1-inch intervals, then bake until set and *very lightly* browned, about 10 minutes. Check the crust every couple of minutes: If it slips down in any spot, press it back into place with the back of a spoon; if it bubbles up, prick it with a fork to release the steam. Beat the remaining egg yolk to break it up, then brush it over the crust, carefully sealing up all the holes. Cool the crust to lukewarm. Reduce the oven temperature to 325°.

4. *Finishing the pie.* Spread the pecans over the crust, then pour on the filling mixture, coating all the nuts. Bake about 35 minutes, until the filling is slightly puffed and no longer jiggles about when the pie is gently shaken. Cool to completely set the filling, then serve.

Unrefined sugar (piloncillo)

CONTEMPORARY IDEAS

Walnut Pie with Honey: Prepare the pie as directed, decreasing the corn syrup to 7 tablespoons, adding 1 tablespoon honey with the corn syrup and replacing pecans with walnuts.

MEXICO'S GOLDEN, CARAMELY *CAJETA*

The heavy-set son ushered us down a narrow hallway toward a 15-gallon, hammered copper pot (the traditional *cazo* used for candy making) filled to the brim with today's goat milk. As we moved past it, the passage opened onto a narrow room with a 2-foot-high, bricked-in stove along one side. There, four more huge *cazos* boiled over strong gas jets. A barrel of sugar stood nearby with a wooden paddle propped up beside it; in the small bottling room at the end was a shelf that held baking soda, cinnamon, vanilla and alcohol, plus glass bottling jars in sizes from a cup to a quart.

The family's task was to transform the rich-tasting goat milk into a fudgey-consistency, sweet, golden syrup known as *cajeta,* the specialty of their hometown, Celaya, Guanajuato. The baking soda, I learned, was what helped it to brown, the cinnamon, vanilla and alcohol gave it the different flavors the customers wanted. To my taste, theirs was the best I've had: soft and rich without all the glassy glucose of the industrialized variants; full with the taste of goat milk and browned milk solids without the strength of added caramelized sugar. At the small Cajeta Vencedora factory and shop in Celaya, the family would even mold the *cajeta* into flimsy wooden *cajas* ("boxes"), the old-fashioned way to sell the sticky stuff and what gave it its name.

The bottled *cajeta* that is sold nationwide (even in the United States) is a far cry from the original *cajetas* of fruits and nuts that were cooked with sugar to a thick, preservable consistency, packed into boxes and kept for special occasions. Only in the abundant candy shops of San Cristóbal de las Casas, Chiapas, have I still seen them selling little oval boxes filled with a dark, sticky *cajeta* made of peach or quince, or of sugar and egg yolks.

Hammered copper cooking vessel (cazo)

GOAT-MILK CARAMEL WITH SPIRITS

Cajeta de Leche Envinada

One Mexico City restaurant makes a rich, warm pudding of caramely *cajeta* and serves it in a bowl; the more typical variety (like this recipe adapted from Cajeta Vencedora) is a little too sweet to put out like that. Many Mexicans I know eat it spread on waferlike María cookies, and the chain ice cream places swirl it into the frozen confections. (I even enjoy it warm over ice cream, like hot fudge.) But the dressiest way to serve *cajeta* is with crepes, as they do in many of the fancier traditional restaurants: The buttery crepes and toasted nuts are a perfect foil for the wonderful caramel. The crepe recipe that follows the one for *cajeta* is based on the version served at the comfortably elegant San Ángel Inn in Mexico City.

YIELD: about 1½ cups

    1 **quart goat milk**
    1 **cup sugar**
    1 **tablespoon corn syrup**
    ½ **inch cinnamon stick**
    ¼ **teaspoon baking soda**
    1 **tablespoon grain alcohol**
        OR 1 tablespoon sweet sherry, rum or brandy

1. *The initial mixture.* In a large (at least 4-quart), heavy-bottomed saucepan or kettle, combine the milk, sugar, corn syrup and cinnamon, and bring to a simmer, stirring. Dissolve the baking soda in 1 tablespoon water, *remove the pan from the heat,* then stir in the soda mixture; it will bubble up, so have a spoon ready to stir it down.

2. *Boiling the caramel.* Return the pan to the fire and adjust the heat so the liquid simmers at a steady roll. Stir regularly as the mixture reduces. When the bubbles start changing from small, quick-bursting ones to larger, glassier ones—in 25 to 40 minutes—*reduce the heat* to medium-low. Stir frequently and thoroughly, washing the spoon each time, until it thickens into a caramel-brown syrup that's a little thinner than corn syrup.

3. *Finishing the cajeta.* Strain the *cajeta* through a fine-mesh sieve into a small bowl or wide-mouthed jar. Let cool a few minutes, then stir in the alcohol. Cool completely before covering.

COOK'S NOTES

Techniques
Cooking the Cajeta: There's little danger of scorching during the initial reduction. You must, however, stand beside the pot for the final few minutes of cooking.

Testing the Cajeta for Doneness: The syrup should have a little body when hot and be very thick—almost unpourable—*at room temperature.* To double-check the consistency, simmer the mixture until thick enough that you can see the bottom of the pan when you stir quickly through it, then remove it from the fire, put a couple of *drops* on a cold plate and let cool a moment. Should these drops turn out stiff when cool, reheat the *cajeta* and stir in a little water; if runny, continue simmering.

Ingredients
Goat Milk: Look for it in many grocery stores and most health-food stores. You can use cow's milk, but the taste is noticeably different.

Equipment
Cajeta-Cooking Pans: The larger and heavier, the better. Enameled cast iron works nearly as well as the traditional copper pot.

Timing and Advance Preparation
You'll need about an hour to prepare the *cajeta,* some of it for unattended simmering. It keeps for months, covered and refrigerated.

BUTTERED CREPES WITH CARAMEL AND PECANS

Crepas con Cajeta

YIELD: 4 servings

For the crepes:
- ½ inch cinnamon stick (or about ½ teaspoon ground)
- 3 cloves (or a big pinch ground)
- 1 cup milk
- 2 large eggs
- ¼ teaspoon salt
- 1 teaspoon sugar
- ½ teaspoon vanilla extract
- ⅔ cup all-purpose flour
- 1 tablespoon melted unsalted butter

For finishing the dish:
- 8 tablespoons (4 ounces) unsalted butter
- 1 cup (about 3½ ounces) pecans, roughly chopped
- About 1½ cups (1 recipe) Goat Milk Caramel (page 293), at room temperature

1. *The crepe batter.* Pulverize the cinnamon and cloves in a mortar or spice grinder, then place in a blender jar or food processor with all the remaining crepe ingredients *except* the butter. Process until smooth, stopping the machine once to scrape down the sides. With the machine running, pour in the 1 tablespoon melted butter. Set aside to rest for 2 hours. Before using, thin with a little water, if necessary, to the consistency of heavy cream.

2. *Making the crepes.* Set a 7-inch skillet or crepe pan (see Equipment in **Cook's Notes**) over medium to medium-high heat and brush *very lightly* with oil. When quite hot, pour in about ¼ cup of the batter, quickly swirl it around to coat the bottom, then immediately pour the excess (what hasn't stuck) back into the blender jar.

Cook until the edges begin to dry, 45 seconds to 1 minute. Loosen the edges with a knife and trim off the irregular part (where you poured off the excess batter). Using your fingers or a narrow spatula, flip the crepe (it should be golden brown).

COOK'S NOTES

Techniques
Crepe Making: Letting the batter stand produces better-textured crepes; if it is too thick, the crepes won't be delicate. The pan should be hot enough to make a thin (but not tissue-thin), even layer stick when the batter is swished over it. A pan that's too heavily oiled won't let anything stick. Should some of the crepes turn out crisp, they will soften after being stacked with the others and covered with plastic.

Ingredients
Vanilla: See page 353.

Equipment
Crepe Pans: I've used steel ones, Teflon, the back of my aluminum omelet pan: They all work. But my favorite is a well-seasoned, 7-inch cast-iron skillet. It has remarkably steady heat and requires almost no oil.

Timing and Advance Preparation
Start the batter 2 hours ahead; it takes an hour to make and fill the crepes. The dish may be completed through Step 3 a day ahead, wrapped and refrigerated. Rewarm to room temperature, then complete Step 4. If the crepes are layered with waxed paper and covered with plastic, they may be refrigerated for 3 or 4 days.

Cook about a minute longer, until golden brown underneath, then remove to a plate. Continue making crepes in the same manner, greasing the pan from time to time and stacking the finished crepes (there should be at least 12) on top of one another; cover with plastic wrap.

3. *Toasting the pecans and filling the crepes.* Melt the 8 tablespoons butter in a medium-size skillet over medium-low heat. Add the pecans and stir frequently for about 10 minutes, until the nuts are toasted and the butter is browned. Remove the nuts with a slotted spoon and set the skillet of browned butter to one side of your work space.

Lay out a crepe, prettiest-side down, brush with the browned butter and spoon a scant tablespoon of *cajeta* on one side. Fold in half and press gently to spread out the filling. Brush the top with butter, fold in half to form a wedge and brush with butter again. Lay in a buttered, decorative baking dish. Repeat the buttering and filling with 11 more crepes, arranging them, slightly overlapping, in two rows in the baking dish. Cover with foil and scrape the remaining *cajeta* into a small saucepan.

4. *Finishing the dish.* About 20 minutes before serving, preheat the oven to 325°. Bake the crepes for 10 minutes to warm them through. Heat the remaining *cajeta* over medium-low. Drizzle it over the warm crepes, strew with the nuts and serve at once.

BUTTER-FRIED PLANTAINS WITH THICK CREAM

Plátanos Machos Fritos con Crema

Through the lushly tropical, banana-growing land of Tabasco, the *cafeterías* write *plátanos fritos* on their menus (add a few cents if you want them fried in butter) and they serve them with thick, soured cream. Outside our Oaxacan apartment most afternoons, a young man came around with his wood-heated cart that was loaded with tender plantains warmed over pineapple rinds. And all the country's fairs have at least one stand that fries *churros*, potato chips and these whole, golden cooking bananas.

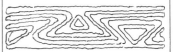

COOK'S NOTES

Ingredients
Plantains: The plantains must be soft and blackening; otherwise, they will be bland rather than sweet. They're usually sold green, so buy them well in advance.

Timing and Advance Preparation
From scratch, the dessert takes 15 to 20 minutes. Plantains will not oxidize like bananas, so they may be sliced several

Plantains are a favorite everywhere: They are astringent when raw, but if they're soft—nearly black-ripe—when they go on the fire, they're delicious and sweet as they come off. I like to serve them for brunch or a Sunday evening snack, simply fried in butter and topped with cream. With the cinnamon, rum and nuts called for below, they make a special, simple dessert for an informal dinner.

YIELD: 4 servings

> 1½ cups Thick Cream (page 51)
> OR 1¼ cups commercial sour cream thinned with about ⅓ cup cream
> ¾ cup nuts (pecans, slivered blanched almonds, walnuts or pine nuts)
> 3 medium, very ripe plantains (see Ingredients in Cook's Notes)
> 4 tablespoons unsalted butter
> ⅓ cup dark rum
> ½ teaspoon ground cinnamon
> 3 tablespoons sugar

1. *The cream and nuts.* Stir the thick cream gently to smooth it out; if you're using commercial sour cream, mix it with the cream. Refrigerate until ready to serve.

Preheat the oven to 325°. Spread the nuts onto a baking sheet and toast until golden, 10 to 15 minutes.

2. *Frying the plantains.* Peel the plantains and slice on a diagonal into ¼-inch-thick ovals. Just before serving, melt the butter in a very large (12-inch) skillet over medium to medium-low heat, then arrange the plantains in a single layer. Fry until deep golden, 3 to 5 minutes per side. (If necessary, fry them in 2 batches, keeping the first batch warm in a low oven.) Transfer to a warm serving platter.

3. *Finishing the dish.* Return the skillet to the heat, add the rum, cinnamon and sugar, and stir until a glaze is formed (ignite the mixture with a match, if you wish, to burn off the alcohol). Pour over the plantains. Sprinkle on the toasted nuts and serve immediately, passing the cream separately.

hours in advance of frying; little more can be readied prior to cooking.

TRADITIONAL VARIATIONS

Fried Plantains with Cajeta and Cream: Some of the street vendors fry the plantains as directed above, then spoon on the cream and drizzle on about ½ cup of Goat-Milk Caramel (page 293).

Strawberries (or Other Fruit) with Cream: Around Irapuato, Guanajuato, roadside stands sell crimson strawberries in rich, ripe cream. Two pints berries and 1 cup sweetened Thick Cream (page 51) or commercial sour cream (thinned with a little cream) are enough for 4 to 6 servings. Papaya, mango, peaches and nectarines are all very nice served this way.

POACHED GUAVAS IN SPICY SYRUP

Guayabas en Almíbar

When I brought home my first kilo of ripe guavas one winter and piled them in a bowl on the table, I found it difficult to walk by without stopping to inhale their spicy aroma. I'd planned to cook them into the thick jellied paste they call *ate,* but I wound up poaching them in a cinnamon-flavored syrup as they do in traditional restaurants across Mexico. The gentle, short cooking captures their aroma, develops their flavor and enhances their delicate texture; in short, it shows off the fruit at its best. I heartily recommend poaching guavas when you can lay your hands on some (they're mostly available during fall and winter months). And if they're the pink ones, the dish will be particularly beautiful.

YIELD: 4 generous servings

> 3 pounds ripe guavas (page 344)
> 1⅓ cups sugar
> 4 inches cinnamon stick
> 6 cloves
> 2 strips of lime zest (green rind only), 2 inches
>   long and ¾ inch wide
> 2 teaspoons freshly squeezed lime juice
> ¼ teaspoon vanilla extract

1. *Preparing the fruit.* Peel the guavas, cut in half and scoop out the seedy centers with a teaspoon, leaving only the shells. Set the prepared fruit aside.

2. *Poaching the fruit.* In a large saucepan, combine the sugar, cinnamon stick, cloves, lime zest, juice and 2½ cups water, and bring to a simmer, stirring. Cover and simmer over medium-low heat for 20 minutes.

Uncover, strain, return the syrup to the pan and set over medium heat. When the syrup returns to a simmer, add the prepared fruit and partially cover. Poach until tender but firm, 5 to 10 minutes, depending on the ripeness. Uncover and let the fruit cool in the syrup.

3. *Reducing the syrup.* With a slotted spoon, remove the fruit. Boil the syrup over medium-high heat until reduced to 1 cup, about 15 minutes. Remove from the heat, stir in the vanilla and pour over the fruit; cool and serve.

COOK'S NOTES

Techniques

Preparing the Fruit: Guavas, like avocados, react with low-carbon knives and turn dark. Guavas are easy to work with, the only drawback being the small quantity of clean, seedless flesh that each fruit gives.

Ingredients

Vanilla: See page 353.

Timing and Advance Preparation

Preparing the guavas for poaching takes about ½ hour; poaching and cooling takes 1½ to 2 hours, almost all of it unattended. The dish may be completed 2 or 3 days ahead, covered and refrigerated. Let the guavas warm to room temperature before serving.

TRADITIONAL VARIATIONS

Other Cinnamon-Poached Fruit: When guavas are unavailable, substitute 2 pounds quinces, pears or apples: Peel, core and cut into large pieces, placing the cut fruit in a bowl of water into which you've squeezed ½ lemon or lime. Drain, add to the syrup and simmer slowly for about 25 minutes for quinces, about 15 minutes for apples or pears. Complete the recipe as directed.

A Note for Guava Aficionados:

I was never keen on raw guavas until I had some whirled in the blender with milk and sugar to make a *licuado:* The flavor and perfume were there, without the mealiness of the fresh fruit.

TROPICAL FRUIT ICES AND EXOTIC ICE CREAMS

There is a general rule that the farther you come down from the cool temperate regions that make up the bulk of Mexico, the more you'll see the little store-fronts outfitted with cold cases stocked with ices and ice creams, bright-colored Popsicles and fruit drinks. The rule has at least one major exception, however: Temperate-climate Oaxaca City has Mexico's most talked-about tradition of ices and ice cream.

For generations, the *neveros,* as the vendors call themselves, had set up cano-pied tables, chairs and ice buckets on one side of Alameda Park in Oaxaca City; but when the city decided to beautify things, the *neveros* found themselves dis-placed to the year-round market (a bonus for the customers) and a few spots out by one of the churches. Theirs has always been a simple craft: Mix the sweet, ripe bounty of the warm earth with a little sugar, pour it into tin canis-ters that are packed in ice and salt, then spin them by hand, scraping and mix-ing from time to time, until the insides hold forth in coarse, slushy coldness.

What's most unpredictable about the whole affair is, first, the enthusiasm with which the country reveres these vendors (at Chagüita, the most renowned stand, there are pictures of different celebrities' pilgrimages to eat the fruit-flavored cupfuls). And second, there are the flavors: They move quickly past the predictable mango, coconut and peach to such unimaginable (occasionally rather unpalatable) ingredients as avocado, cheese, corn, *burned* milk, even pork rind, and one made of roses and almonds.

The Oaxacan specialties come in three styles: fruit with water, fruit with milk, and a smooth alternative with milk and egg yolks, called *nieve de sorbete.* For the recipes here, I've combined what I learned hanging around the stands with notes given in Guzmán's *Tradiciones gastronómicas oaxaqueñas.* And if you want the honest-to-goodness, coarse, *granita*-like texture of the market ices, use the "still-set" freezer method I've outlined in the notes.

Kitchen Spanish

Nieve (literally "snow") and *helado* (literally "frozen") both refer to ice cream in Mexico. The new chains generally call their offerings *helados,* while some of the older shops label the ices *nieves* and ice creams *helados.* But it's not always that cut-and-dried. In Oaxaca, most everything is a *nieve,* even if it is made with custard.

Keys to Perfect Ices and Ice Creams
Techniques

Adding Alcohol: Besides adding flavor, a little rum, Triple Sec or what have you will make the mixture freeze more slowly, give it a finer consistency and keep it from freezing solid.

Flavoring Fruit-Based Concoctions: The mixture should be fairly sweet (the sugar's potency is diminished a little by freezing); lime, as well as sugar, can brighten dull (or underripe) fruit flavors; and alcohols can add richness.

Freezing Without an Ice Cream Freezer: For a coarser, *granita*-type (and, truthfully, more authentic) texture, make the ice or ice cream base with alcohol, place in a stainless-steel bowl in your freezer and beat every 45 minutes for several hours, until it holds its shape in a spoon. About 30 minutes before serving, beat it once more; if frozen solid, break it up and beat it quickly, in batches, in a food processor, to give it a light consistency.

Ripening and Storing: An ice cream freezer will only take the mixture to a soft-frozen state; to firm it, "ripen" in the freezer or in a new packing of salt and ice for several hours. Ices and ice creams without emulsifiers and stabilizers will become more crystalline the longer they're frozen, so plan to eat them a few hours (at most a day) after freezing. Store tightly covered.

Ingredients

Fruit: Ripe, strong-flavored, perfumey fruit is what you're after. Scout the bruised and over-ripe bargains: They'll have a riper flavor (texture is of no concern), and you can simply cut out the bad spots.

Equipment

Ice Cream Freezers: All of these ices were tested in a Waring 2-quart ice cream maker that uses ice cubes and table salt. Any freezer will work and they all have their peculiarities, so read the directions.

CUSTARD ICE CREAM WITH CINNAMON AND VANILLA

Nieve de Sorbete

Generally, this beautifully light ice cream is made with milk (some cooks make it even less creamy by omitting the cooking); on occasion, though, I want a really rich, smooth frozen dessert, so I'll replace the milk with half-and-half. Two tablespoons brandy or dark rum are a delicious, though nontraditional, addition.

COOK'S NOTES

Techniques
See page 298.

Ingredients
Vanilla: See page 353.

Timing and Advance Preparation
Preparing the custard takes about 30 minutes, cooling 40 minutes. The base can be finished a day or two ahead, cov-

YIELD: about 1½ quarts, 8 servings

    1 quart milk
    1½ cups sugar
    2 inches cinnamon stick
    10 large egg yolks
    1 teaspoon vanilla extract

1. *The cinnamon-flavored milk.* Combine the milk, sugar and cinnamon stick in a large, heavy, noncorrosive saucepan (preferably enameled cast iron). Bring to a boil, stirring frequently, then simmer, covered, over medium-low heat for 10 minutes. Remove from the fire.

2. *The custard.* Beat the egg yolks until runny. Slowly whisk in 1 cup of the hot milk mixture, then whisk the yolk mixture into the milk remaining in the saucepan. Return the pan to medium-low heat and cook, stirring almost constantly, until the custard has thickened enough to coat a wooden spoon (it should be 185–190°), 7 to 10 minutes. Do not let the mixture come near a boil or the egg yolks will curdle. Immediately strain through a fine-mesh sieve, then stir in the vanilla and cool to room temperature, stirring occasionally. If there is time, cover and chill before freezing.

3. *The ice cream.* Scrape the custard into the canister of your ice cream freezer and freeze according to the manufacturer's directions. For a firmer ice cream, "ripen" for several hours by placing in your freezer or by repacking the ice cream freezer with a new round of ice and salt.

FRESH PRICKLY-PEAR ICE

Nieve de Tuna

I've written the main fruit-ice recipe using prickly pears simply because preparing the fruit requires a little more explanation. Ices made of more common fruit follow the same general procedure, as detailed in the variations. Prickly pear ice is delicious with the nontraditional addition of 1½ tablespoons Cointreau.

ered and refrigerated. Once the ice cream is frozen, plan 2 or 3 hours for it to "ripen."

TRADITIONAL VARIATIONS

Mexican Chocolate Ice Cream: Prepare the recipe as directed, adding a 3.3-ounce tablet of Mexican chocolate (pulverized) to the ice cream just before it finishes freezing.

Custard Ice Cream with Fruit Flavors: Complete the recipe as outlined, adding 1 to 1½ cups prepared fruit from the following list just before the ice cream finishes freezing (optional accompanying spirits, to be added to the ice cream base, are listed in parentheses):

Nectarines, peaches or mangos: peeled, pitted and chopped (2 tablespoons brandy or golden rum)

Blackberries: lightly crushed (2 tablespoons blackberry liqueur, brandy or Triple Sec)

Strawberries: hulled and crushed (2 tablespoons Triple Sec, Cointreau, Grand Marnier or framboise).

COOK'S NOTES

Techniques
See page 298.

Timing and Advance Preparation
It takes about ½ hour to prepare the ice base; it can be done a day ahead, covered and refrigerated. Plan 20 to 30

YIELD: 5 to 6 cups, 6 to 8 servings

3½ pounds (about 18 medium) fresh prickly pears
  (*tunas*) (page 349)
1 cup sugar, plus a little more if necessary
About 3 tablespoons freshly squeezed lime juice

1. *Preparing the prickly pears.* Cut a ½-inch slice off both ends of the prickly pears, then make a ½-inch-deep incision down one side, end to end. Carefully (remember, there are little stickers) peel off the rind, starting from your incision: The rind is thick and, if ripe, will easily peel away from the central core of fruit. Roughly chop the peeled prickly pears.

2. *The ice base.* Place the fruit in a blender or food processor, add 1 cup water, the sugar and lime juice, and blend for several minutes, until the sugar is dissolved. Strain through a medium-mesh sieve; taste for sweetness and tartness, adding more sugar or lime juice as necessary. If time permits, chill thoroughly.

3. *Freezing the ice.* Pour the mixture into the canister of your ice cream freezer and freeze according to the manufacturer's directions. When the ice comes from the machine, it may be rather soft; for a firmer texture, let it "ripen" in your freezer for a couple of hours before serving.

Prickly pear cactus fruit (tuna)

minutes to freeze the ice and at least 2 hours to "ripen" it.

TRADITIONAL CONTEMPORARY VARIATIONS

Mango, Peach, Nectarine or Cantaloupe Ice: Peel, pit and/or seed about 2 pounds (slightly more for cantaloupe) fruit, to yield 2 cups of fruit pulp. Puree with 1½ cups water, ¾ to 1 cup sugar, and lime juice to taste. Freeze according to the manufacturer's directions. A tablespoon or so of dark rum is a delicious addition.

Strawberry, Blackberry, Boysenberry or Kiwi Ice: Puree 2½ cups of packed-down fruit (hulled and halved strawberries, peeled and diced kiwi) with 1 cup water, ¾ to 1 cup sugar and about 2½ tablespoons fresh lime juice. Freeze according to the manufacturer's directions. A tablespoon or so of Triple Sec or Cointreau are good additions.

Nieve de Limón: Prepare the Lime-Zest Cooler on page 310, reducing the water to 3 cups. Freeze the mixture according to the manufacturer's directions. Optionally, add 1 tablespoon each tequila and Triple Sec for a mock margarita ice.

DRINKS
❖
Bebidas

Drink stand, Oaxaca market

There is but a single drink that comes to most North American minds when Mexican food is on the menu: margaritas, the sweet-and-sour, pale-green cocktail that is linked to Mexico by its shot of tequila. In reality, it's just the tequila that's Mexican, not so much the cocktail itself; for rarely does tequila get mixed up with anything in Mexican tradition, save a lick of salt and a squirt of lime.

Though the first Mexicans didn't do any distilling, it didn't take the Spaniards many years to get the country going with stills. The first spirits were called simply *aguardiente* ("firewater") *de mezcal,* referring to the local maguey from which the liquor was made. Still today, all but the most famous firewater (the one made from the thin-spiked blue maguey in the vicinity of Tequila, Jalisco) retains the name *mezcal.* Famous or not, they are all poured into shot glasses (some might say a little too frequently), then drunk according to a set of well-respected traditions.

The first ritual drink in Mexico was *pulque,* the fermented sap of a large, gray-green maguey. Though it is low in alcohol and high in nutrients, the simple ferment was strictly controlled during pre-Columbian times, and drunkeness was not tolerated. Nowadays, it is much less a part of everyone's libationary custom than, say, the good light and dark Mexican beers that have become so popular in the United States.

The native drink we should probably accord the most reverence is chocolate, simply because of the passionate stir it has created in our country. And, of course, its botanical name, *Theobroma,* does mean "food of the gods." It, too, served as a ritual drink for priests and nobles in pre-Columbian Mexico; but centuries of greater democracy brought it into the morning and evening routines of the less powerful, less aristocratic. In Oaxaca, the smells of fresh-ground chocolate permeate busy streets around the market. And inside at the market *fondas,* the dark chocolate gets whipped into a frothy hot brew and set out with rich egg bread (*pan de yema*), or it's used in a foamy cold drink (*tejate*) made with mamey seeds, cocoa flowers and corn *masa.* Through chocolate-growing Tabasco, a wine is made from the sweet-sour pulp surrounding the beans in the pod; and in the markets there, they grind the beans with *masa,* dilute the mixture and serve it cool (*pozol*). In Chiapas, the beans are ground with toasted corn and *achiote* seasoning for a cool drink called *tescalate.*

Wherever chocolate comes to the lips, it's nearly always coarse-ground and in liquid form—something of a disappointment, I know, for anyone whose vision of chocolate has a designer label or a dense, fudgey consistency. Personally, I've never found a cup of cinnamon-and-almond flavored Mexican hot chocolate to be anything but sheer joy.

More frequently consumed than a foamy sweet cup of the somewhat expensive chocolate, is the milky *café con leche.* Some very good coffee is grown in Mexico, though most of it destined for export. Much of what remains, luckily, gets filtered in espresso machines or pot-brewed and sweetened with dark sugar and spices (*café de olla*).

Anyone who has visited Mexico knows that one's consumption of liquid increases—because of the high altitudes or the warm temperatures. But even if we were to drink as much here in this country, I don't think it would be as enjoyable: Pop cans simply aren't as pretty to look at as the glass barrels full of colorful Mexican drinks. Though most of these "natural" soft drinks are made from fruit, they're always accompanied by an unchanging trio: brewed, bright-red *jamaica* "flowers"; a tart, sweet cooler flavored with the insides of the tamarind pod; and a version of the Spanish *horchata*, here made of steeped, finely ground rice and cinnamon. All these drinks are set out everywhere—though most famous in Oaxaca—and their fruity flavors are sweet and uncomplicated to match the unpretentious, spicy snacks they're frequently paired with.

Mexico's soil received its first vineyards only three years after the Spanish conquest, but production was slight and of little gastronomical interest until this century. Nowadays, varietal wines are filling grocery-store shelves and playing a greater role in middle-class Mexican drinking—perhaps even more than the sangria of coarse red wine and sparkling limeade that has been popular in cities for some time.

No Mexican from the highlands would forgive me for failing to mention the wintery *ponche* they love to serve at the Christmastime *posadas*. Warm and fruit-filled, the stuff can pack a real punch, with its liberal lacing of cane alcohol (*aguardiente de caña*). While *ponche* is for special occasions, *atole*—the warm, light, *masa*-thickened porridge—has been consumed daily since before the Spaniards came, and it is more nutritionally sound and comforting than any other Mexican libation. Even when *atole* is made with milk, fruit, nuts or chocolate, Mexico thinks it's a little old-fashioned. Nonetheless, it is *the* drink to have with *tamales;* it is the bearer of tradition in a country where *pulque* is almost gone, a country up to its gills in pop bottles.

While many cuisines offer little in the way of beverages, Mexican food is inseparable from the drinks that accompany it. They're delicious and unusual, and they'll give your Mexican meals an authentic flavor. So don't overlook all the refreshing and satisfying variety I've included in this chapter.

Hand-blown goblets, Tlaquepaque

MORE ON MEXICAN SPIRITS

The original Mexican alcoholic drink, **Pulque,** has retained a following through the years, especially in the cooler, higher, drier areas of northern Central and West-Central Mexico, where the large *pulque*-producing maguey is so abundant. At ten to twelve years of age, just before flowering, the heart of that maguey is "castrated," leaving a cavity for the sap, or *aguamiel* (literally "honey water"), to collect in; the liquid goes into a vat with a yeasty starter, then it's allowed to ferment for 1 to 2 weeks before selling. *Pulque* is slightly viscous and foamy, with interesting herbaceous overtones; some of it is *curado* ("cured") with fruits, sugar, nuts and the like. Unfortunately, *pulque* seems to be less and less common in Mexico with each passing year.

Beer, however, is not on the wane, and Mexico has some very good brews that are imported to the United States and go well with Mexican fare: Superior (a nice aroma and a full-bodied taste that is slightly sourish but attractive to many people); Bohemia (perfumey aroma and a bright taste with nice, lingering hops); Dos Equis (a slightly caramel aroma and a rich, malty taste that goes on and on); Negra Modelo (a sweet, heavy aroma and a rich, dark taste that hints at licorice and sassafras); Corona (a slightly sweet aroma and a light, crisp flavor); Tecate (a beer made popular by advertising that it should be drunk with lime and salt . . . which, in my opinion, help the beer a lot); Carta Blanca (more or less a Mexican Coors). There are others (some of them only available regionally), but these are the ones you'll likely find in the United States.

Though the first grape vines were planted shortly after the conquest, for political and cultural reasons the Mexican **Wine** industry really didn't get off the ground until the 1930s. Even though the industry is just coming of age, there is some good wine to be had—many of the better wines are varietals and readily available in large Mexican grocery stores; only a few have ever been imported into the United States. The best wines seem to come from northern Baja California and Querétaro; many grapes are also grown in Aguascalientes and in the Comarca Lagunera region, among others. Wines we've tasted and enjoyed are: Misión Santo Tomás Barbera (Baja California); Hidalgo Riesling-Traminer (Querétaro); Clos San José Merlot and Cabernet (Querétaro); Marqués del Valle Cabernet Reserve (Baja California); Santo Tomás Cabernet (Baja California); L.A. Cetto Petit Syrah (Baja California); Don Ángel Cabernet (Aguascalientes); and Domecq Zinfandel. The latter company, Domecq, including its labels Calafia, Los Reyes and Padre Kino, produces the most ubiquitous wines in the country; most of what's in the bottle is only passable, in my opinion. Two major problems that face Mexican wines, however, are that the restaurants aren't completely comfortable serving them (nor are all the customers comfortable drinking them), and matching wines with the frequently full-flavored Mexican fare is no mean feat. The first will probably be resolved with time, but the second will take constant evaluation. Here are my rules of thumb for serving wine with Mexican food: Rarely should the wine be subtle. Follow the accepted rules for what goes with red and white, but always lean toward a red if the dish is rich with herbs, spices and dried chiles; choose reds that are as earthy and straightforward as the dish. I favor Zinfandels, fruity Beaujolaises or Merlots, gutsy Chiantis, some young Cabernets and, for certain dishes, simply a good, red table wine; Lee Ellis of Seattle, Washington, recommended Côtes du Rhônes to me, and I agree that they work well. When white wines are in order, I recommend those that are dry (or just off-dry) and richly flavored, like Gewürztraminers, some Chenin Blancs and Rieslings, and even some full-flavored Sauvignon Blancs. A big, oaky Chardonnay can taste very good with some of the citrusy Yucatecan dishes.

Mescal, including the famous regional variety tequila, is another well-known Mexican libation. The major difference between mescal and tequila is the maguey you start with—tequila can be made only from the *Agave tequilana,* a small blue maguey from around Tequila, Jalisco. Both were originally called *aguardiente de mezcal, mezcal* referring to the heart (also known as the *piña*) of the maguey. The hearts of mature magueys are roasted and shredded, then the juice is squeezed out; sugar may be added, then it is fermented, distilled and aged. Most connoisseurs will say that the best Mexican distillates are well-aged tequilas; they can be very good, almost cognac quality, but some of the smoky-tasting local mescals from Southern Mexico and the northern Central states still linger in my mind. Sauza brand tequila comes in five grades: Tres Generaciones, Conmemorativo, Hornitos, Extra and the lowly Blanco; Cuervo goes from 1800, to Centenario, Especial and Blanco; Herradura has an Añejo, Reposado, Blanco Suave and Blanco. There are dozens and dozens of other labels of tequila, but those three are the most common. Gusano Rojo and Monte Albán are the most widely distributed mescals available in the United States; both are from Oaxaca (and include a maguey worm in the bottle), but neither compares to the good-quality mescal (a *siglo* or *pechuga*) available in Oaxaca City.

a few Mexican beers

COOLERS

Aguas Frescas

Two piercingly tart flavors from Asia found secure Mexican homes in a couple of revitalizing drinks that match well the capsicum, *tomatillos* and strong herbs important to so much of Mexican cooking. *Agua de jamaica* is gorgeous and crimson, and sugar brings its taste to a balanced sweet-sour perfection, like a thirst-quenching, herby cranberry juice. *Agua de tamarindo* is rich and coffee-brown with underlying flavors of molasses and lemon. And a third traditional drink, *horchata,* is milky with ground rice (and sometimes coconut), and shot through with pure cinnamon at its most refreshing.

    These are the triumvirate of Mexican everyday drinks, and for years they've meant total refreshment—long before soda pop. Whether ladled out of street-stand glass barrels or served in hand-blown glasses at the nicest tables, each has that homemade freshness I miss in frozen lemonade, Coke or Pepsi. For all the Mexican snacks (*antojitos*), they are the time-honored accompaniment.

JAMAICA "FLOWER" COOLER

Agua de Jamaica

I serve *jamaica* as a nonalcoholic drink before a big dinner, poured over ice in tall glasses or wine goblets. Though it goes nicely with Mexican snacks and appetizers, the flavor doesn't seem to do a lot for the nicer main dishes; mixed with red wine, however, it makes an interesting sangria. Whenever you serve it, *jamaica*'s color adds festivity.

YIELD: about 5 cups, 5 or 6 servings

    2 cups (2 ounces) *jamaica* "flowers" (page 345)
    ¾ cup sugar, plus a little more if necessary

    1. *Boiling and steeping.* Bring 6 cups water to a boil, add the "flowers" and sugar, and stir while the mixture boils for a

COOK'S NOTES

Timing and Advance Preparation
Start 2 hours before serving; *jamaica* keeps up to 5 days, covered and refrigerated.

TRADITIONAL VARIATIONS
Jamaica Sangria: Prepare ½ recipe *jamaica*, using ⅔ cup of sugar. Strain and stir in 2½ cups dry, fruity red wine and 2 or 3 tablespoons fresh lime juice. Taste for sweetness and tartness; serve over ice.

minute. Pour into a noncorrosive bowl (preferably one that won't stain) and steep 2 hours.

2. *Finishing the drink.* Strain through a sieve, pressing on the "flowers" to extract as much liquid as possible. Taste for strength and sweetness: If it is too pungent, add water; if too tart, add sugar. Cover and refrigerate, stored in a noncorrosive container, until time to serve.

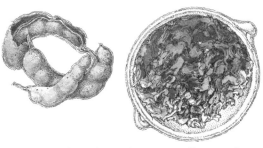

Tamarind pods and jamaica "flowers"

TAMARIND COOLER

Agua de Tamarindo

The tamarind pods mature on tall trees in warm, humid climates before they're picked and heaped in loose marketplace mounds, each pod looking like a fat, barky broad bean. The dark, sticky pulp underneath the rough exterior provides the flavor, and occasionally, you'll find the extracted pulp packed into small envelopes or jars: plain, sugared or flavored with chile for a snack. Soaking the pods, however, is an easy way to get at the essence, and the outcome is always fresher tasting. Ice-cold *tamarindo* is delicious served with charcoal-grilled foods, as well as enchiladas, tacos and such.

YIELD: about 3½ cups, 4 servings

> 8 ounces (about 8 large) fresh tamarind pods (see Ingredients in Cook's Notes)
> ½ cup sugar, plus a little more if necessary

1. *Cleaning the tamarind pods.* Hold a pod in one hand, loosen the stem with the other, then firmly pull out the stem, along with the runners that trail down between the shell and pulp. Peel off the shells.

2. *Boiling.* Bring 1 quart water to a boil, add the tamarind pods and sugar, then boil 1 minute. Pour into a noncorrosive container.

3. *Steeping.* Let stand 2 hours (really fresh pods will be completely soft in about 1 hour, old ones may require 2½ hours or more). Using your hand or the back of a wooden spoon, break up the softened pods to free the pulp and seeds; knead the fibrous material carefully to free all the pulp.

4. *Finishing the drink.* Strain the mixture through a fine-mesh sieve, pressing hard on the seeds and fibers to extract as much of their essence as possible. Adjust the sweetness to suit your taste, then cover and refrigerate until serving. Stir before pouring.

ALMOND-RICE COOLER

Horchata

This has the simplest and most familiar flavors of the three most common *aguas frescas:* a slightly chalky, thirst-quenching refreshment with a flavor reminiscent of rice pudding. This recipe is based on the version served at the nationally famous Casilda's *aguas frescas* stand in Oaxaca, where the crushed pulp of the tiny cactus fruit (*jiotilla*) is often stirred in to make the liquid pink. Their version relies in good part on the almonds to give it richness and body. I was forewarned that only hand-grinding on the *metate* would make it good; that's close to the truth, but I did finally come up with a blenderized version that works.

This drink is light but rich—exceptionally good hot-weather party fare, poured over ice.

YIELD: about 1½ quarts, 6 to 7 servings

    6 **tablespoons rice**
    6 **ounces (about 1¼ cups) blanched almonds**
    1 **inch cinnamon stick**
    Three 2-inch strips of lime zest (colored rind only),
        ¾ inch wide
    About 1 cup sugar

in ⅓ to ½ cup brandy and a little fresh lemon juice. Taste for sweetness, serve over ice.

Kitchen Spanish
Occasionally, *aguas frescas* (literally "fresh waters") will be referred to as *aguas preparadas* ("prepared waters"), to emphasize the fact that they're made, rather than store-bought like soda pop.

COOK'S NOTES

Techniques
Grinding/Blending: Be careful to pulverize the raw rice thoroughly (a miniblend container on a blender is second-best to a spice grinder) and to blend the soaked mixture until it loses most of its grittiness.
Straining: Unless you have a super-fine-mesh French *chinoise* strainer, use the 3 layers of dampened cheesecloth, or the drink will be gritty-tasting.

Timing and Advance Preparation
Start 7 hours (preferably a day) ahead; your active involvement will be about 20 minutes. It keeps 5 days or more, covered and refrigerated.

1. *Soaking the rice and almonds.* Thoroughly pulverize the rice in a blender or spice grinder. Transfer to a medium-size bowl and add the almonds, cinnamon stick and lime zest. Stir in 2¼ cups of hot tap water, cover and let stand at least 6 hours or, preferably, overnight.

2. *Blending and straining.* Scoop the mixture into the blender jar and blend for 3 or 4 minutes, until it no longer feels very gritty. Add 2 cups of water, then blend for a few seconds more. Set a large sieve over a mixing bowl and line with *3 layers* of dampened cheesecloth. Pour in the almond-rice mixture a little at a time, gently stirring to help the liquid pass through. When all has been strained, gather up the corners of the cheesecloth and twist them together to trap the dregs inside. Squeeze the package firmly to expel all the remaining liquid.

3. *Finishing the horchata.* Add 2 cups of water and stir in enough sugar to sweeten the drink to your taste. If the consistency is too thick, add additional water. Cover and refrigerate until you're ready to serve. Stir before pouring.

LIME-ZEST COOLER

Agua Preparada de Limón Rallado

> *The **agua** frescas deserve a separate chapter. There are many [of them] and many who make them, but the **aguas** of Casilda are a class apart. Whoever thinks of refreshment thinks of Casilda. . . . Standing or sitting on the modest benches in the interior of the old Oaxacan market, you can hear [the insistent requests] in front of the green* ollas *from Atzompa: two* **horchatas** *with cactus fruit, three* zapotes, *one plum, and so on . . . to all the points of a fruitful rosary, greedily repeated in dry throats.*
> ——ANA MARÍA GUZMÁN DE VÁSQUEZ COLMENARES,
> **Tradiciones gastronómicas oaxaqueñas**
> *[author's translation]*

I never met Oaxaca's famous Casilda, but I spent many afternoons at her renowned drink stand, in front of the glass pitchers of bright-colored fruit drinks and the earthenware pots. It's there I learned about *agua de limón rallado,* the fragrant green

drink made of the colored skin of underripe limes. Casilda's niece runs the stand now, with a conscientious pride and generous grace. And she freely shared many of the details of her trade, even to bringing me a sack of underripe limes and the rough clay mortar (*chirmolera*) to demonstrate the preparation of this Oaxacan specialty. It is such a distinctive, delicious liquid that I've used it in my Margarita (page 320) and I freeze it into an ice (page 301) as they do in Oaxaca.

YIELD: 1 quart, 4 to 5 servings

8 large *dark-green* limes
¾ to 1 cup sugar (or even a little more, if desired)

1. *Steeping the lime zest.* Using a very fine, rasplike grater—*not* a citrus zester—remove the limes' green zest (no white). Add 1 quart water, using a little of it to rinse into the bowl any zest that has clung to the grater. Let stand 1 hour. (Wrap and refrigerate the fruit for another use.)

2. *Finishing the drink.* Strain the zest mixture through a fine-mesh sieve, pressing firmly on the solids to extract as much liquid as possible. Add enough sugar to sweeten the drink to your taste, stirring until dissolved. Cover and refrigerate until serving time. Serve over ice.

*Lava rock and earthenware mortars
(molcajete and chirmolera)*

SPARKLING LIMEADE

Limonada

Since lime is one of Mexico's national flavors, it's not surprising that a glass of cold sweet-sour limeade is one of the national drinks. Unlike the simple drink from the street vendors' tables, the *limonada* of the coffee shops and restaurants is often mixed with sparkling mineral water, making it more refreshing yet.

We make *limonada* at home a lot because it nicely complements Mexican dishes—even some of the most refined ones, and it makes a very special nonalcoholic choice at any dinner party.

YIELD: about 5 cups, 5 to 6 servings

> ½ to ⅔ cup sugar
> 1⅓ cups freshly squeezed lime juice (roughly 8 to
>   10 limes)
> 1 quart sparkling water

Add the smaller amount of sugar to the lime juice and stir until the sugar is dissolved. Add the sparkling water, stir and taste for sweetness; add more sugar if desired. Pour over ice and serve immediately.

Mexican lime juicer

FRUIT AND MILK SMOOTHY

Licuado de Leche y Fruta

Mariano Dueñas' small pamphlet on the modern variety of Mexican refreshment praises the "delicious and nutritive *licuado*" as the salvation of Mexican health. Apparently he's not alone, for the entire country has enthusiastically adopted the blender-made concoctions and all the burnished-Formica juice bars that serve them. Life is the better for it, I think, because *licuados* offer an alternative to overripe fruit in the trash can and too much candy at the snack bar. Made from milk, they are filling (a complete breakfast, says Sr. Dueñas) and much less like soft drinks than the related *aguas frescas* and *licuados de agua* that are made with water.

YIELD: 1⅓ to 1½ cups, 1 large serving

1 **cup cold milk**
1 **to 1½ tablespoons sugar, plus more if necessary**
3 **to 5 ounces (½ to ¾ cup) fruit (banana, canta-loupe, mango, persimmon, papaya, straw-berry, watermelon or guava), peeled, hulled, seeded and/or cored, as necessary, and cut into small cubes**

1. *Blending.* Combine all the ingredients in a blender jar and blend until very smooth.

2. *Straining.* If there are seeds, skins or stringy fibers, strain through a medium-mesh sieve, taste for sweetness and serve in tall glasses.

TRADITIONAL VARIATIONS

Polla: Combine ¾ cup milk, ¼ cup *rompope* (egg liqueur), 1 tablespoon sweet sherry and 1 egg in a blender jar. Blend until frothy and serve.

Licuados with Water: The juice bars also make *licuados* with water instead of milk; some fruit (like watermelon and pineapple) tastes better that way. Made in large quantities with less fruit and more sugar, they are sold by the street vendors, alongside the *horchata* and such: In batches, blend 1½ pounds fruit with 1½ quarts water; strain and sweeten, then add a little chopped fruit to float about.

MAKING OAXACAN CHOCOLATE

Sometimes they brought [Montezuma] in cups of pure gold a drink made of the cocoa plant, which they said he took before visiting his wives.
——BERNAL DÍAZ CASTILLO, 1492–1580, chronicler of the conquest

The common walled dwellings that hug the walkways and streets of Mexican towns create a peculiarly strong sense of public versus unapproachable private . . . in a country that is so renowned for open festivity. I felt it acutely in Juchitán, Oaxaca, where day after day I heard inexplicable fire-fueled pops and cracks from behind the high wall across the alley from where I was staying.

Only after several careful and courteous inquiries was I hesitantly invited into the private patio of the *chocolatera.* Her cacao beans crackled as they roasted, her charcoal-heated *metate* coarsely ground the greasy beans back and forth with the cinnamon, almonds and sugar, and her hands patted the paste into fat cigar shapes. The result was then mixed up with water in a green-glazed Oax-acan chocolate mug and whipped frothy with a wooden *molinillo*. The rich flavor of the fresh, strong chocolate needed nothing more than that water to bring it to life.

For most of us nowadays, chocolate is thoroughly refined; it's spoken of and handled as other precious commodities. We moved long ago beyond the traditional, uncomplicated drink, beyond its original role as liquid sustenance, to all sorts of overcomplicated concoctions and prestigious labels. Until now. When we hear talk once again of the "discovery" of the "wonderful Mexican chocolate," with its satisfying savor.

> *If any man has drunk a little too deeply from the cup of physical pleasure; if he has spent too much time at his desk that should have been spent asleep; if his fine spirits have temporarily become dulled; . . . we say, let him be given a good pint of amber-flavored chocolate . . . and marvels will be performed.*
> —BRILLAT-SAVARIN, The Physiology of Taste, *1825*

Chocolate, from pod to frothy beaten drink

CINNAMON-FLAVORED HOT CHOCOLATE

Chocolate

Volumes have been filled with details of the engaging cocoa bean. Historians have debated the etymology of its New World name—from Nahuatl for "bitter water," from Mayan "hot water"

COOK'S NOTES

Techniques
Blending Warm Mixtures:
Warm mixtures expand when blended and will pop the top off a well-sealed blender jar, so cover without sealing.

or simply from the choco-choco sound of the ancient chocolate beater in the pot—and they've not come to any conclusion. Researchers have singled out the precious varieties that served as New World currency well after the Spanish conquest. They've described the elegant chocolate-drinking cups of Montezuma and the various flavors, from savory to sweet, that went in with the ground beans. They've followed it to Europe, to the courts and chocolate parlors and even into (and back out of) the churches; and finally, they've moved on to the smooth Swiss confections that made chocolate a candy (helping, I suppose, to spread the final covering over its "barbaric" New World roots). Chocolate has gone so far from home that today few realize what a vital role the rustic cup of hot chocolate plays in Mexican life.

YIELD: about 3 cups, 3 to 4 servings

    2½ cups milk (or water)
    A 3.3-ounce tablet Mexican chocolate, roughly
        chopped

  1. *Simmering.* In a medium-size saucepan, simmer the milk (or water) with the chocolate for a few minutes over medium-low heat, stirring constantly to dissolve the chocolate.
  2. *Beating.* Either pour into a pitcher and beat well with a Mexican *molinillo* (chocolate beater), whisk or electric mixer, or pour into a blender, *loosely* cover and whiz until thoroughly mixed. Either way, you should wind up with a nicely frothy drink. Serve at once.

POT-BREWED COFFEE WITH RAW SUGAR AND SPICES

Café de Olla

Today, Mexico's best coffee is ripened and dried along the roadways in the cloud-blanketed highlands of Chiapas and over through Veracruz and Oaxaca. The prime beans are usually roasted a little darker than ours—almost a Viennese roast—and

Ingredients
Mexican Chocolate: See page 339.

Timing and Advance Preparation
The French gastronomer Brillat-Savarin and his articulate translator M.F.K. Fisher both recount the benefits of letting chocolate set overnight, thus concentrating the flavor and turning it velvety-smooth. It works, though it's common in Mexico to just blend and serve.

CONTEMPORARY IDEAS
Spirited Mexican Chocolate: Prepare the Mexican hot chocolate, add ⅓ to ½ cup golden rum, brandy, Kahlúa or orange liqueur, beat or blend, then serve.
Mocha Mexican Chocolate, Hot or Iced: When the milk and chocolate have simmered, add 4 tablespoons ground dark-roasted coffee, stir, cover and set in a warm place for 4 or 5 minutes. Strain, beat and serve. It's also good over ice or with ⅓ to ½ cup Kahlúa stirred in.

COOK'S NOTES

Ingredients
Piloncillo: Use about ½ of one large (9-ounce) cone of the raw sugar; or use 6 or 7 of the small (¾-ounce) cones.

they brew a nice, medium-bodied liquid with some spunk. They tell me it's the second-class beans that get roasted darker, to a mahogany black with a shining sugar coat.

The steam-powdered espresso machines in the city *cafeterías* extract a trio of ethnic brews: *espresso,* straight, foamy and Italian; *café con leche,* mixed with hot milk, French-style (but so common one would mistake it for purely Mexican); or *americano,* simply diluted with water. The more rural brew leans toward the Spanish, the history books say, but it seems like a Mexican-flavored campfire version to me. *Café de olla* at its best is pot-boiled in earthenware with molassesy *piloncillo* sugar and spices like cinnamon, anise or cloves. These days, many traditional city restaurants offer the dark, delicious drink more regularly, served in old-fashioned earthenware mugs at the end of the meal.

YIELD: about 1 quart, 4 to 5 servings

> 4 to 5 ounces *piloncillo,* roughly chopped
>   OR ½ to ⅔ cup packed brown sugar, plus 1
>   teaspoon molasses
> 2 inches cinnamon stick
> A few aniseeds (optional)
> ⅔ cup (2 ounces) Viennese-roast coffee, medium
>   to coarse grind

1. *Boiling and steeping.* In a noncorrosive pan, combine 1 quart water, the sugar, cinnamon and optional aniseed. Bring slowly to a boil, stirring to melt the sugar. Stir in the coffee, remove from the fire, cover and steep for 5 minutes.

2. *Straining.* Strain the coffee through a fine-mesh sieve into cups or mugs and serve immediately.

Earthenware pot and cups for café de olla

Timing and Advance Preparation

Coffee is always best made just before serving; the longer the warm coffee sits with the grounds, the harsher it will become.

TRADITIONAL VARIATIONS

Café con Leche: To make the ubiquitous early-morning or late-night beverage, brew extra-strong coffee in a drip pot with ½ cup Viennese-roast coffee and 1½ cups water (or brew 1⅓ cups espresso in a stove-top pot). Heat 1⅓ to 2⅔ cups milk (depending on how strong you like your *Café con Leche*—Mexicans typically drink it weak), and stir in the coffee. Pass sugar separately.

CONTEMPORARY IDEAS

Pot-Brewed Coffee with Kahlúa: For a nice after-dinner coffee, add 1 to 2 tablespoons Kahlúa to each small cup.

Regional Explorations

Coffee comes most beckoningly into its own in the old Spanish colonial strongholds. Three in particular stand out: Mérida, Yucatán, where *greco* brings a tiny cup with grounds still in it (an influence of the Lebanese population); the great Parroquia restaurants in Veracruz, where waiters come to fill your cup dramatically from the kettles of strong coffee and steaming milk; and the market in Hermosillo, Sonora, with its coffee *fondas* serving a thick, unflavored black coffee strained through cloth bags.

MASA-THICKENED HOT CHOCOLATE

Champurrado (Atole de Chocolate)

I have friends who have worked in the high, remote corners of Mexico, where beans and tortillas make up the daily ration and special occasions find an earthenware pot bubbling with the simple *masa* porridge called *atole*. Sometimes it's sweet, other times it's flavored with pungent leaves of *epazote* and hot little chiles, like the Aztec *atolli* described by Friar Sahagún in the 1550s and the fresh-corn *chileatole* I've had from the huge clay *ollas* on the streets of Puebla at dusk.

In the present-day Mexican culinary order, *atole* goes with *tamales* like fries with burgers, though some people have begun to think the drink is old-fashioned and ask for a Squirt or Coke instead. The heart-warming drink can come in flavors from plain (*blanco,* they call it) to fruit, nut and chocolate, and in textures from smooth with a cornstarch thickening to coarsely flecked with fresh-ground *masa;* it can be rich with milk or thin with water. Being a North American, I predictably go first for the special Oaxacan *atole* called *champurrado,* since it's flavored with chocolate. Alongside the main recipe, there are variations for other flavors.

YIELD: 1 generous quart, about 5 servings

> ½ cup fresh *masa*
>> OR a scant ½ cup *masa harina* mixed with a generous ¼ cup hot tap water
> 2 cups milk
> A 3.3-ounce tablet of Mexican chocolate, chopped
> 2½ ounces *piloncillo,* chopped
>> OR ⅓ cup packed dark-brown sugar plus ½ tablespoon molasses
> A few aniseeds, crushed (optional)

1. *The base.* Measure 1¾ cups water into a blender jar or food processor, add the *masa* (or *masa harina* mixture), blend until smooth, then pour into a medium-size saucepan.

2. *The atole.* Add the milk, chocolate, *piloncillo* (or brown sugar and molasses) and optional crushed aniseed. Bring to a simmer, whisking constantly, then simmer over medium-low heat, whisking frequently, until the chocolate and *piloncillo* are completely dissolved, about 5 minutes. Strain, if you wish, then serve in cups or mugs.

COOK'S NOTES

Ingredients
Mexican Chocolate: See page 339.
Piloncillo: If you buy large (9-ounce) cones of the raw sugar, it takes a little less than ⅓ of one; if they're small (¾-ounce) cones, you'll need a little more than 3.

Timing and Advance Preparation
Any *atole* can be ready in 10 minutes or so; it may be kept warm over a pan of hot water for an hour (though you may need to thin it with a little milk before serving). It is not at its best when reheated.

TRADITIONAL VARIATIONS
Nut Atole: Replace the chocolate with ½ cup finely ground pecans, walnuts or blanched almonds, adding them with the *masa.* Add ¼ teaspoon ground cinnamon as the *atole* simmers, or ½ teaspoon vanilla when it comes off the fire. Increase the sugar, if desired.
Pineapple Atole: Prepare the recipe as directed, reducing the water to 1½ cups, blending 1½ cups cubed fresh pineapple (peeled and cored) with the *masa,* replacing the milk with 1½ cups water, and omitting the chocolate and aniseed. You may wish to increase the sugar.
Strawberry Atole: Prepare the recipe as directed, reducing the water to 1½ cups, blending 1½ cups strawberries (hulled) with the *masa,* reducing the milk to 1½ cups, and omitting the chocolate and aniseed. This is best made with ⅔ cup granulated sugar rather than *piloncillo.*

A PUBLIC PARTY,
MEXICO CITY–STYLE

The parking lot spreads out below Arroyo restaurant in southern Mexico City. On Sunday afternoon, you leave your car with the attendant, who somehow wedges it in with the hoard of others, you climb the rising walk—past lottery-ticket sellers, ladies offering rose bouquets and milk fudge, coconut candies and crystallized fruit—into an open room that smells of smoldering coals and frying pork. To one side, the men put maguey-wrapped lamb into specially built, wood-fired pits. Men across the way tend copper caldrons of browning pork called *carnitas* or plunge sheets of pork skin into hot fat for it to burst into the beloved crisp, honeycomb sheets of *chicharrón*. And completing the triangular arrangement of the room is the setup of drinks: the fruit-filled *aguas frescas* in stunning colors, *pulque,* tequila, mescal and the spicy chaser *sangrita.*

The place is huge; it must seat five hundred or more in its various rooms with open sides and rafters hung with bright-colored tissue-paper cutouts. The bands roam freely: An accordian carries from the *norteño* group in one room, regulated by an insistent snare and guitar; a white-clad harp player stands near the table with his *jarocho* band, waiting for someone to recommend one of the fast-paced *zapateados;* and *mariachis* blare trumpets, plunk *guitarrones* and sing forth with sweet, heartfelt violin refrains. The space is so charged with its own festivity, as to make memory of another reality seem distant at the very least.

The *pulque*—that slightly foamy, fermented juice of the maguey plant—tastes rich and thick with unusual herbaceous undertones. One group has ordered the *pulque curado* with red strawberries or pink guavas. Another is tearing the paper seals from their tiny individual bottles of tequila, pouring them into the narrow shot glasses, then taking them in a one-two punch with shots of the chile-heated tomato-orange concoction they call "little blood" (*sangrita*).

The afternoon passes slowly at Arroyo. First, a plate of thick *masa* cakes (*tlacoyos*) in green sauce; then tender lamb *barbacoa* with a light scent of wood and maguey and a splash of the dark *salsa borracha;* chewy, well-browned pork (*carnitas*) and guacamole; tortillas hot off the press. Three generations at every table, grandmothers buying soft-centered meringues for the children and fathers singing along with the tales of remorse, misguided love and pride for the home state. The Sunday afternoon passes as the crowds order their seconds, refills on the drinks and another round of songs. Luckily, it seems to pass slowly.

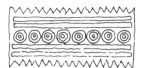

TEQUILA SHOOTERS WITH SPICY CHASER

Tequila con Sangrita

Really, how do you drink the fiery liquid—the tequila, the mescal? Straight from the little glasses? With lime? With salt? With *sangrita*? There are no definitive answers, as best I can tell. Carl Franz, clearly a neat sort of drinker, writes in *The People's Guide to Mexico* that a little salt licked off the back of the hand raises the saliva at the back of the throat and protects "sensitive tissues from the burning alcohol," which generally comes in strong shots. He adds: "The lime will also do this and when taken after the drink cleanses the mouth of the awful taste of the liquor." (*Awful* taste? What has Franz been drinking?) Virginia B. de Barrios, in her book *A Guide to Tequila, Mezcal and Pulque*, espouses a lime-tequila-salt routine (rather than Franz's reversal). And to add to the confusion, I'll report that I've frequently seen folks dip a wedge of lime in salt, take a belt then suck the salted lime.

Personally, I like the liquor with the popular, fresh-tasting, *picante* chaser for which I've given a recipe below—or simply with a bite on a lime wedge. And the better the tequila, the less necessary you'll find the flavorful accoutrements. I always put them out, though, to let each person suit his or her preference.

YIELD: about 1 cup *sangrita*, 4 to 8 shot-size servings

For the sangrita:
- ½ cup freshly squeezed orange juice
- 4 teaspoons grenadine syrup
- ¼ cup tomato juice
- ¼ cup freshly squeezed lime juice
- ½ teaspoon or more *Salsa Picante* (page 40) or bottled hot sauce
- ¼ teaspoon salt

For serving:
- ½ pint easy-drinking tequila (see Ingredients in Cook's Notes)
- 2 limes, cut into wedges (optional)
- A small dish of salt (optional)

COOK'S NOTES

Ingredients
Tequila: A really good bottle is expensive, but there is no comparison to its easy-drinking smoothness. Sauza's Tres Generaciones ("Three Generations"), Cuervo's 1800 and Herradura's Añejo ("Aged") are top of the line; Cuervo's or Sauza's gold varieties or Herradura's Reposado are good mid-priced alternatives. The inexpensive white (clear) tequilas are generally too harsh to serve this way.

Equipment
Shot Glasses: In Mexico, tequila is traditionally served in narrow glasses that are about 3 inches tall and hold 1½ ounces or so; I've also bought the tiny "mugs" called *copitas* (or *tequileros* or *mezcaleros*) made of earthenware and available in markets in Guerrero, Jalisco and perhaps other places, too. Any small glasses will work, however.

Timing and Advance Preparation
Mix together the *sangrita* at least an hour before serving; it will keep for about a week in the refrigerator, covered.

In a bottle or pitcher, mix together all the *sangrita* ingredients. Cover and refrigerate for at least an hour, allowing the flavors to meld.

When you're ready to serve, pour the *sangrita* into 4 to 8 tiny glasses (any 1½- to 3-ounce glass can serve the same function as a shot glass), then divide the tequila into 4 to 8 more small glasses. Serve a glass of each to your guests; pass the lime wedges and dish of salt for those who prefer to take their tequila the other way.

Tequila and tequileros (shot glasses)

TEQUILA-LIME COCKTAIL

Margarita

I admit to a stab of pain when I hear North American restaurant goers proclaim that their favorite part of a Mexican meal is the margaritas. Drunk before the meal . . . two or three of them. But then who can fault the diners when so many of our Mexican-American restaurants specialize in uneventful plates of beans and rice?

Now all this doesn't mean I don't enjoy a good margarita now and again. But I think the ones from the standard guides

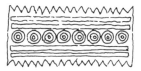

COOK'S NOTES

Techniques
Blending with Egg White:
This bartender's trick gives a rich foaminess.

Ingredients
Tequila: Within reason, the better the tequila, the better the margarita. However, the

(1½ ounces tequila, ½ ounce Triple Sec, ½ ounce lime juice and a little sugar, shaken with ice and strained) are simply too strong for those weaned on margaritas made mostly of commercial sweet-and-sour mix. So I've developed what I think is a very good, fresh-tasting margarita, frothy and not too strong. You have to start a little ahead, but it'll be one of the best you've had. If you're so inclined, rub the rims of the glasses with a lime wedge, then dip them in a dish of kosher salt.

YIELD: about 3½ cups, 4 servings

    1¼ **cups Lime-Zest Cooler (page 310)**
    ¼ **cup freshly squeezed lime juice**
    ⅛ **teaspoon salt**
    1 **cup decent-quality, drinkable tequila (see In-**
        gredients in Cook's Notes)
    ⅓ **cup Triple Sec**
    1 **cup ice cubes**
    1 **egg white (optional)**

  1. *Preparing the base.* Mix the prepared Lime-Zest Cooler with the lime juice, salt, tequila and Triple Sec, and let stand for ½ hour for the flavors to blend.

  2. *Finishing the margaritas.* Just before serving, pour the mixture into a blender jar and add the ice cubes and optional egg white. Blend for 30 to 45 seconds, until the ice is chopped (and the egg white is whipped to a froth). Serve immediately over cracked or crushed ice.

finest, cognac-quality variety won't be shown at its best when mixed with lime, salt and sugar, nor will the harsh, un-aged clear tequilas gain much smoothness from the additions. My rule is to use nothing less drinkable than Cuervo's gold Especial.

Timing and Advance Preparation
You must start at least 2 hours ahead to prepare the lime-zest cooler and steep the cooler with the alcohol. Neither preparation takes much time to make and the base may be completed several hours in advance. Blend the margaritas just before serving.

Maguey for tequila

RED-WINE COOLER WITH FRESH LIME

Sangria Mexicana

This Mexican cousin to the Spanish drink of red wine, fruit juice, liqueur and sugar is a simple, sparkling limeade-and-wine cooler. As one who enjoys red wine, I'm happy that they stir these up in restaurants all over Mexico; until recently, most of Mexico's wine production has been pretty coarse stuff, so the additions to the glass have been welcome. The bartenders in even the smallest establishments like to float the wine over a denser, lime-flavored layer made with a special syrup; but it's just as good simply stirred up.

YIELD: about 5½ cups, 6 servings

⅔ cup freshly squeezed lime juice
⅔ cup sugar
3 cups dry, fruity red wine, like Beaujolais, Zinfandel or many red table wines
1 cup sparkling water
4 to 6 wheels of lime, with a cut made on one
  side

1. *The lime-sugar syrup.* Mix together the lime juice, sugar and ¼ cup water, stirring until the sugar dissolves.
2. *The sangria.* Just before serving, pour the wine into a pitcher and stir in the sparkling water and lime syrup. Serve over ice in tall glasses, each garnished with a wheel of lime wedged onto the rim.

Hammered copper pitcher, Michoacán

COOK'S NOTES

Ingredients
Red Wine: It doesn't need to be expensive and shouldn't be subtle: Look for dry fruity and *drinkable;* a thin wine will benefit from this preparation, where a tannic one will still taste rather harsh.

Timing and Advance Preparation
The sangria takes 15 minutes. The lime-sugar syrup can be made ahead and refrigerated. Complete Step 2 just before serving.

CONTEMPORARY IDEAS
Sangria with Other Juices: Replace part of the lime juice in the preceding recipe with orange juice, or all of it with a combination of grapefruit and orange; adjust the sugar to suit your taste. Some drink makers like to stir in a little Triple Sec or flavored brandy.
White-Wine Sangria with Tequila: Prepare the preceding recipe with a medium-dry, fruity white wine (like a Chenin Blanc or Gewürztraminer), replacing ½ of the lime juice with orange juice and adding ¼ cup tequila.

GLOSSARY OF MEXICAN INGREDIENTS AND EQUIPMENT

❖

Vegetable stand, Aguascalientes market

ACHIOTE: The brick-red *achiote* seeds, collected from the pods of a small tree that grows throughout Yucatán, are widely available in the United States. They are often called *annatto* seeds, and are in many chain groceries and markets that cater to Mexicans and Caribbeans. In Mexico, a paste made from *achiote* seeds is more common than the seeds themselves; in Chiapas and Oaxaca, the paste is usually pure, while in Yucatán it contains herbs and spices. Occasionally the Yucatecan seasoning paste shows up in the United States, but you will usually have to make your own from the seeds (page 66); don't be tempted to buy the Puerto Rican *achiotina* (*achiote*-flavored fat). The very hard seeds are a powerful coloring agent; they last indefinitely in a closed jar at room temperature.

AVOCADO LEAVES (*hojas de aguacate*): These leathery, substantial leaves from the avocado tree (of the laurel family) are about 7 inches long and 3 inches wide. Only ones picked from large trees grown outdoors will have the characteristically anisey, herby aroma and flavor. In many recipes, the leaves are lightly toasted, then ground or cooked with other ingredients. Here, I've called for them in Chicken *Barbacoa* (page 235) only—used untoasted, to line a steamer. Substitutions are suggested in the recipe.

Avocado leaves

AVOCADOS (*aguacates*): Though different varieties of avocados show up in different regions, the one everyone prizes is the Hass, which is grown extensively in California and Mexico. It is a medium-size, oval fruit with a knobby skin that ranges from dark green to black-brown when ripe. The flesh is very

Hass avocado

flavorful (richly herby, with almost nutty overtones) and it has good keeping qualities. Second choice is the Fuerte variety: a medium-size, pear-shaped fruit with a thinner, almost smooth, greener skin. The flavor and keeping qualities are second to the Hass. Other green, thin-skinned, pear-shaped varieties include the Bacon, Zutano and Pinkerton. Reeds are round, and like most other Florida varieties (such as the Booths) are huge. All of these have rather poor keeping qualities and less flavorful (often stringy) flesh. More and more markets (especially Mexican ones) sell avocados that are ripe, meaning they yield to firm, gentle pressure. Never buy avocados with dark, soft spots or ones so ripe that the pit is loose inside. Firm/hard avocados can take 4 or 5 days to ripen in a warm spot. Keeping them in a closed paper bag traps the naturally emitted ethylene gas, which will cause them to ripen more quickly. Avocados that have just reached ripeness can be refrigerated for longer keeping: up to 10 days for Hass, but considerably shorter time for other varieties.

BANANA LEAVES (*hojas de plátano*): These large, fragrant green leaves are used in Southern, Yucatecan and Gulf Coastal Mexico for wrapping food before it's baked or steamed. Because they impart a distinct flavor, they're worth tracking down. Though Mexican groceries rarely carry them, I always find them in Filipino stores (and some large Oriental or Indian ones) and occasionally in Puerto Rican/Caribbean markets. They're usually sold frozen in 1-pound packages. Look for leaves that are intact—no obvious rips or shredding. If frozen, defrost them overnight in the refrigerator. They'll last for a month or more refrigerated; if they mold, just wipe them off. They are always steamed or passed over a flame to make them more pliable before using; the details are on page 177.

BEANS (*frijoles*): See page 268.

BITTER ORANGE: See Citrus Fruits

CACTUS PADDLES (*nopales* or *nopalitos*): These are the paddle-shaped stems (called *pencas* in Spanish, but often mistakenly referred to as "leaves" in English) from several varieties of prickly-pear cactus plants. They're used most frequently in the cooking of West-Central and Central Mexico. They are often available fresh in Mexican groceries (I've even seen them in some of the chain supermarkets, too). Most anywhere they carry Mexican goods,

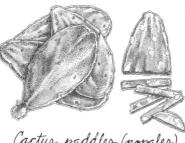

Cactus paddles (nopales)

you'll find canned ones that have been cleaned, cooked, sliced and packed with flavorings (they only need to be drained and rinsed before using). The texture and flavor of fresh paddles is considerably better than that of canned, and I choose the medium-size ones (roughly 4½ inches wide by 8 inches long, weighing 8 to 10 ounces) that are firm (never droopy). Loosely wrapped and refrigerated, they will keep for several weeks.

To Clean Fresh Cactus Paddles:

Holding a cactus paddle gingerly between the nodes of the prickly spines, trim off the edge that outlines the paddle, including the blunt end where the paddle was severed from the plant. Slice or scrape off the spiny nodes from both sides. If you are boiling the cactus, cut it into ¼-inch strips (or ½-inch dice as some cooks recommend).

To Cook Fresh Cactus Paddles:

Boiling is the most common method of cooking: For 4 medium paddles, bring 4 quarts water to a boil in a 6- to 8-quart pot, heavily salt it and optionally add ¼ teaspoon baking soda (to lessen the discoloration). Add the prepared cactus and boil uncovered over medium-high heat until quite tender, 15 to 20 minutes. (Failing to cook the cactus long enough will leave you with sticky cactus that continues to leak a mucilaginous substance—similar to what okra exudes, known as *baba* in Spanish; also, *baba* will make the water thick and foamy, so watch for boilovers.) Rinse the cooked cactus for several minutes under cold water, then drain thoroughly on paper towels.

My favorite way to cook cactus (because it involves no *baba*-leaching water) comes from West-Central Mexico, where whole charcoal-grilled or griddle-cooked cactus paddles sometimes accompany regional specialties: Leave the paddles whole after cleaning, simply scoring each side lengthwise 3 times with a knife. Brush each side with vegetable oil, then sprinkle with salt and a little lime juice. Roast them over a medium-low charcoal fire (which gives them a wonderful flavor) for 15 minutes, turning occasionally, or roast them on a griddle heated to slightly lower than medium, turning, for about 20 minutes. For the most even cooking, roast them in the oven at 350° for about 25 minutes. Cool, then cut it into strips or dice.

CAZUELA: See Cooking Equipment

CHAYOTE: This lesser-known relative of the squash is becoming widely available in U.S. supermarkets; most common is the pale-green, smooth-skinned variety, though the dark-green, spiny *chayote* occasionally shows up in Mexican groceries. I've rarely seen it labeled anything but *chayote*, though I've heard it is called "mirliton" in Louisiana and "vegetable pear" or "pear squash" in other parts. Unwrapped and refrigerated, *chayotes* keep for a month or more. They're usually peeled and halved, then the pit is cut out. They can be boiled, fried or stuffed, though boiling usually leaves them with a watery taste and texture, like a cross between zucchini and potato. An average *chayote* weighs 8 to 10 ounces.

Spiny and smooth chayote squash

CHEESE (*queso*): Mexico has never much been known for its cheese, though one type in particular plays a strong supporting role in the taste of Mexico's food. It's an easily made cake of fresh cheese (not unlike our farmer's or ricotta cheese) that goes directly from farmhouses and small factories to traditional tables. It gets crumbled on snacks, fried beans and rice, mixed with other flavorings to fill turnovers or chiles,

Aged and fresh cheese

cubed to put into soups and stews, and sliced to go in sandwiches or to eat with gelled fruit pastes as a dessert. And some of this crumbling cheese is sold drier, having been aged.

Of course, this garnishing fresh cheese isn't exclusive: A few good regional cheeses—made to melt like most of our cheeses—are used to stuff into turnovers and chiles, to crown special modern enchiladas, and to melt into *queso fundido*. Their use in traditional fare, however, is much less extensive than that of the fresh cheese.

Regional Explorations:

Because the regional variations in fresh and melting cheeses are so numerous, I have chosen only to mention the most famous ones. **West-Central Mexico:** Very good *queso fresco* (literally "fresh cheese") is available here, especially the smooth-textured ones from San Juan del Río, Querétaro; the dry, salty *queso añejo* (literally "old cheese") from Cotija, Michoacán, is the most famous *queso añejo* in the country (and is, as far as I know, the only Mexican cheese regularly imported into the United States); and the moist, porous, fresh *queso panela*, frequently sold in the little baskets in which it drains, is one of the region's glories. **Oaxaca:** There's the famous, tightly wound balls of string cheese (*quesillo*), which make delicious eating when they're aged a few weeks. **Tabasco and Chiapas:** Tabasco is famous for its dryish loaves of ripe-tasting, almost crumbly cream cheese (*queso crema* or *doble crema*); Chiapas has a similar cheese, but it's popularly made into balls and wrapped with string cheese (*queso de bola con corazón de mantequilla*). Chiapas, colonial stronghold that it is, also makes a tasty, Spanish-style *manchego*. **Toluca:** There they sell a dryish fresh cheese for making simple turnovers (called *queso asadero*, literally "grilling cheese," because it softens nicely when heated), flavored with *epazote* and *chile manzano*. **Chihuahua:** There's a type of mild cheddar called *queso menonita* because it is made by the large, German-speaking Mennonite population; elsewhere this cheese is called *queso Chihuahua*.

CHEESES CALLED FOR IN THIS BOOK

Fresh or Aged Crumbling Cheese: In Mexico, this white cheese is available in nearly all markets; it ranges in size from huge blocks to tiny cakes, and in texture from fine (almost smooth on the tongue) to coarse and spongy; all of it breaks apart or crumbles readily when pressed between the fingers (like the dry fresh farmer's cheese). Most of it softens when heated (often exuding whey), but it usually will not melt. Most is made from skimmed (usually unpasteurized) milk, is sold within a day or two of making (so it is often still draining whey), and has a high water content (so it may spoil if not stored properly). Some versions are specially made for aging (they seem to dehydrate more than ripen, perhaps because of the high salt content). Most Mexican fresh cheeses taste fresh and milky (rather than cheesy) and they have a good amount of acid and salt. An aged cheese retains some of that milkiness (though it's sharper) and it doesn't have the nutty, developed-cheese flavor of a Parmesan—a cheese you'd think it would resemble. Other names for *queso fresco* are simply *queso, queso ranchero* ("ranch cheese"), and, occasionally, *queso de metate* (if its curds have been smoothed on the *metate*); names for *queso añejo* include *queso Cotija, queso oreado* (literally "aired cheese"), and *queso seco* ("dry cheese"), plus the more distinct varieties like *sierra* and *morral,* which fill the same function.

In the United States, the *queso fresco* available from most of the cheese companies that specialize in Mexican cheese (Cacique and Supremo, among others) often tastes cheesy (like a Muenster) or bland; the only exception I can recommend is the 5-ounce round of "*queso fresco*/Mexican-style cheese" made by Supremo in Chicago. When that's not available, I usually use the creamier feta cheese to replace either *queso fresco* or *queso añejo*, though it is more strongly flavored. To tame its brininess, soak it in water for an hour or two; to give it a more authentic texture, let it dry out at room temperature, turning occasionally, for a day or two. Some other substitutes for *queso fresco* are: dry (pressed), fresh farmer's cheese, usually available in pear-shaped slabs (this doesn't have the acidity or saltiness of *queso fresco*; crumble and add salt); dry-curd cottage cheese (this has a high moisture content, so press it between paper towels, then crumble and add salt); a mild, domestic, fresh goat cheese, like the small rounds made in California, New York or New Jersey (these are tangier and creamier than *queso fresco*, but they have a similar fresh quality). In addition to feta, some other substitutes for *queso añejo* are: a mild Parmesan, Romano or Sardo (they all lack that milkiness and are more cheesy-flavored, though they can be crumbled/grated appropriately) or the *dry* ricotta (not the soft variety packed in tubs) available in some specialty cheese stores (look for salted ricotta/*ricotta salata* or aged ricotta).

Melting Cheese: In Mexico, this could be the mild, cheddar-like Chihuahua cheese, the Northern *asadero* (most commonly, it's like a creamy, whole-milk mozzarella), the stringy, rather rubbery Oaxacan *quesillo*, or any of the numerous mild, bricklike cheeses.

In the United States, I've not been happy with most of the imitation Chihuahua or *asadero* cheeses made here, so I usually choose a mild white cheddar, Jack or whole-milk mozzarella; brick and domestic Muenster are too bland for my taste, though not necessarily inauthentic. Most Mexican melting cheeses are uncolored; the real Chihuahua has a touch of yellow color added. In Mexico, a melted cheese that strings (*hace hebras*, as they say) is highly prized.

CHILES, IMPORTANT (THOUGH PERHAPS DISPUTABLE*) FACTS

What are they and why are they called that? Chiles are the fruit of a plant in the genus *Capsicum*, most of the species in Mexico being *annum* (though *chinense* and *frutescens* are also represented). The fruit (sometimes called a pod) can range from mild to extremely pungent (in English, we say "hot"; in Spanish, it's *picante*, **not** *caliente*), from sweet to astringent and from fresh to dry. Names vary from country to country and even within countries: The Spanish likened

---

*Upon stepping into the field of chile research, one is flooded with a jumble of information, much of it contradictory. I've tried to pull out the information that will be most useful to the cook, as well as to answer the basic questions most often asked in my classes.

the pod's pungency to that of black pepper (that is, *pimienta*) and so called them *pimientos,* hence our English label *pepper.* Spaniards who stayed on in Mexico called them *chiles* after the Aztec *chilli;* Americans heard that Spanish *chile* as "chili," and remnants of that Anglicized spelling and pronunciation still persist (needlessly, I think, except perhaps in the case of the Texas State Dish). In other parts of Latin America, the pod is called *ají* (and sometimes *uchú,* among other names). So what it boils down to is that "chile" means "pepper"— and not just "hot pepper" or the redundant "chili pepper"; many researchers also include the bell peppers in the group. In Spanish, an adjective follows the word *chile* to distinguish the variety (or cultivar, in botanical terms): *chile ancho* (literally "wide chile"), *chile poblano* ("Pueblan chile"), and so forth.

Heat vs. Flavor: Capsaicin is the incendiary culprit: Some varieties of peppers don't have it, others do . . . and in a range of dosages. You've probably heard the oft-repeated axiom "the smaller the pepper the hotter it is," but all the exceptions make it a rather useless saying to me. Peppers might not always deliver what you think they've promised: Supposedly mild peppers can turn out to be hot and vice-versa, and no one has developed a foolproof way to regulate them; weather conditions, among other things, seem to have quite an effect. Besides some degree of searing, there are flavors, too, and each variety has a distinctive one that changes noticeably from green to mature to red-ripe to dry. Mexicans generally seem to be as aware of flavor as they are of heat.

What's Hot and What's Not: The greatest proportion of capsaicin is concentrated in the internal white veins and the seed pod; seeds, apparently, are hot only by association. Carefully removing the seed pod and veins will make a chile less *picante.* If that isn't enough, I've had good luck soaking the chiles for several hours in heavily salted water. The upper third of the chile always seems hotter than the rest.

Why Can't I Figure Out Which Pepper Is Which, and Does It Really Matter? First, there are well over a hundred varieties of known chile cultivars; second, they cross-pollinate readily; third, different soils and climates produce different chiles from the same seeds (meaning that, a *chile poblano* grown in Texas won't be exactly the same as one grown in Aguascalientes); fourth, Mexico is a land rich in regional distinctions (including individual regional names for foodstuffs); and fifth, the United States has no national ruling committee telling us what chiles are to be called. In spite of those five demoralizing problems, there is hope for the North American lover of Mexican food: You can taste a good part of the breadth of Mexican cooking with only a handful of fresh and dried chiles— all of which show up in U.S. Mexican markets (and some chain groceries) with a relatively uniform, easily recognizable look (despite what they might be called). Throughout the book, I have employed the chile names most commonly used in Mexico and the United States (my apologies to those in California, where the names are sometimes different).

Cooking with and Eating Chiles: Most cooks with an instinct for self-preservation wear impermeable gloves when working with peppers: Capsaicin is not water soluble and will linger on your fingers for hours (even days), causing them (or any other body part they come in contact with) to burn. Jean Andrews writes in *Peppers: The Domesticated Capsicums* that a mild bleach solution apparently renders the capsaicin water soluble, and so can be used to rid your hands of the burning stuff; it has worked for me. Now, besides being a flavorful source of vitamins C and A, most chiles are enjoyed because they're hot, and each one has a different kind of heat: Some quickly take effect, then dissipate, while others set in slowly; some burn the front of your mouth, others the back (toward the throat). When you eat something beyond your chile tolerance (in Spanish, you've become *enchilado(a)*), you should drink something cold (soda pop, beer or the like); it will help sooth temporarily while you wait for the burn to abate. If you're in acute discomfort, try some sugar, or bread, or milk, or guacamole (but by the time you've gotten through all that, the sensation will no doubt be gone).

CHILES, CANNED OR BOTTLED *Canned Chipotles en Adobo:* Though there is a considerable flavor difference between a rehydrated dried *chipotle* and one that has been canned with tomato sauce, vinegar and spices, I've only included recipes in this book that I think work well with the canned chiles; dried *chipotles* are more difficult to find, while canned ones are in nearly every little Mexican grocery. Be careful of the brands, though: San Marcos packs the really smoky *chipotles mecos* with a minimum of added flavor; La Preferida packs *chipotles mecos,* but with lots of sugar in the sauce; Embasa packs the smaller *moras/chipotles colorados* that taste good but light, compared to *mecos;* and La Costeña makes an unhappy, chopped-up, "pickled" affair with *moras.* Stored in a noncorrosive container, covered and refrigerated, the canned *chipotles* should last for a couple of weeks or longer. In Mexico, you can also get straight pickled *chipotles;* they are not usually right for these recipes.
Pickled Fresh Chiles: Though for the best texture and taste, I heartily recommend that you make your own (page 48), some store-bought pickled chiles (called *chiles escabechados, chiles en escabeche* or *chiles encurtidos*) are quite good; *jalapeños* are the most popular, but you can also find *serranos, güeros* and any number of not-typically-Mexican varieties. Though batches of the same brand can vary, look for chiles that are firm and unbroken and in a good-flavored brine. Stored in a noncorrosive container, covered, refrigerated and with sufficient brine to cover the chiles, they will keep for several months.
Canned Peeled (Long) Green Chiles: Rather than resort to green pepper when fresh *poblanos* or the long greens (like Anaheims) are unavailable, I'd get a can of these. Unfortunately, most of what you can find on the grocery-store shelves is quite soft. Choose ones that are fire-roasted for the best flavor. There are 2 or 3 in each 4-ounce can.

CHILES, DRIED (*chiles secos*): The small hot ones are usually pureed into a sauce to pep it up, while the larger ones (most of which are much milder than the small ones) are used to provide the bulk of a sauce's substance and flavor. Little ones are less frequently toasted before using, it seems to me, and they're often bought powdered or crushed. The larger dried chiles are generally toasted, pureed and strained (removing those tough skins), then cooked with flavorings to make a sauce.

Regional Explorations

Some researchers have devoted their lives to identifying and cataloging the distribution and names of the hundred-plus chile varieties in Mexico. What follows here is obviously not exhaustive, but simply a sketch of Mexico's rich chile complexity, highlighted by the most well-known regional types. Yucatán uses few chiles, primarily just a locally grown, small, hot *chile seco*. On the other side of the coin, in Oaxaca I collected 22 different dried chiles. Among the most unusual were: the wide-shouldered, brittle, 4-inch-long, red, yellow and black *chilhuacles;* the brittle, narrowish, 4-inch-long, red and yellow *chilcostles;* the hot, brittle, finger-size red and yellow *chiles de onza;* and the smoky, near-burgundy, wrinkle-skinned 3- to 4-inch-long *chiles pasillas oaxaqueños.* Just about anywhere, you can find the sweet-tasting, wrinkle-skinned *ancho* and the brick-red, brittle-skinned *guajillo* or some relative; to those two you can add the *chile mulato* and *pasilla,* since most cooks demand their availability for use in their *moles. Chipotles* are a popular sauce flavoring in Puebla and Veracruz, and the cooks here and there throughout the country like to use the 1¼-inch spherical, brittle, dark brick-red *chiles cascabeles* for sauces, too. Everywhere, the cooks require the services of one of the orange-red hot peppers like the slender, small, fingerlike *chile de árbol,* the ½-inch oblong *chile piquín,* the ¼-inch spherical *chile tepín* and/or the narrow, stemless, 2-inch-long *chile japonés.*

Locating, Storing and Cleaning:

Small (1½-inch), narrow, hot dried chiles are available in most groceries and many chain stores carry a few of the larger ones (New Mexico/California or *ancho*). A wide variety will be available in such places if you live in Chicago or the Southwest. Many kinds are available at most Mexican groceries, and specialty food stores frequently carry some as well. If dried chiles look sandy or dirty (some are open-air dried), simply wipe them off with a cloth.

Seeding and Deveining:

Break off the stems, then tear (or, if necessary, cut) open the chiles; shake or pick out the seeds and pull (or cut) out the lines of light-colored veins. (Small hot chiles are frequently not broken open after stemming: If they're not too hard or brittle, simply roll them gently between your thumb and fingers to loosen the seeds, then shake them out through the opening at the top.)

Toasting:

Toasting brings out and enhances the flavor of nearly every chile, though not all cooks or traditional preparations will call for it. Directions for griddle-toasting are included in the recipes. You know the chiles are toasted when they've crackled, blistered, changed color slightly and released their chile aroma (if they smoke, the griddle is too hot or they've been left on too long). As the chiles cool, they will crisp some; only if you're making chile powder must the chiles be toasted so thoroughly that they are completely crisp when cool.

VARIETIES OF DRIED CHILES CALLED FOR IN THIS BOOK

Chile Ancho: Ancho (literally "wide") is the name for a dried *poblano.* The dried chile will be in the neighborhood of 3½ to 4 inches long, with broad shoulders (2 to 2½ inches wide) that taper to a point; the skin will be quite wrinkled, and in the package the chiles will look almost black (though holding one up to the light will show it to be a *very* dark burgundy). An average *ancho* weighs ½ ounce. Always look for untorn, clean, *soft,* aromatic chiles (they'll smell a little like prunes). A puree of soaked *chiles anchos* will be brownish red with a mild, rich, almost sweet taste (it reminds me a little of milk chocolate) and a bit of residual bitterness. Per ounce, *ancho* gives more pulp than most chiles. Regional names include: *chile pasilla* (Michoacán and vicinity, plus California); the generally descriptive *chile de guisar* or *chile de color/colorado* (Mazatlán, Tampico, Querétaro, among the smattering); and in the northwest and northern West-Central areas there is a small hot *ancho* they call *chino.*

Chile de Árbol: When you can find *chiles de árbol* in a fresh state, they generally go by that same name. This vibrant, orange-red dried chile is usually slightly curved and measures in at about 3 inches long and ½ inch wide, tapering to a sharp point; the skin is smooth, rather brittle and translucent. Forty-five mixed-size *chiles de árbol* weigh 1 ounce. Choose them as you would *guajillos.* A puree of soaked *chiles de árbol* will be a beautiful burnt orange with a *very* hot, sharp, straightforward dried-chile flavor. Regional names for this chile include: *parado* and *palillo* (San Cristóbal de las Casas, Chiapas), *cambray* (Monterrey), and *pico de pájaro* (northern west coast).

Chile Chipotle: Chipotle (from the Nahuatl for "smoked chile") is the name of a smoke-dried *jalapeño* (the chile doesn't air-dry well, so it must be force-dried, in this case with warm smoke). The dried chile is about 2½ inches long and 1 inch wide; it smells smoky (you should be able to smell it through the package), is brittle and wrinkle-skinned, and is the only chile I know with a woody tan color. An average *chipotle* weighs slightly over ⅛ ounce. Look for *chipotles* that are firm and unbroken. A puree of soaked *chiles chipotles* will be dark brown, with heat that comes on like a freight train and a flavor that is the essence of sweet smoke; it is not astringent, nor is the dried-chile flavor very pronounced. In Puebla and Veracruz, the name *chipotle (colorado)* is used for a slightly smaller, dark-burgundy, wrinkle-skinned, smoky-smelling chile; in those places, the *chipotles* described above are called *chipotles mecos* (the latter word meaning, literally and confusingly, "red with black stripes"). Those smaller, reddish *chipotles* (called *moras* in much of the rest of Mexico) aren't as sweet or smoky-tasting as the

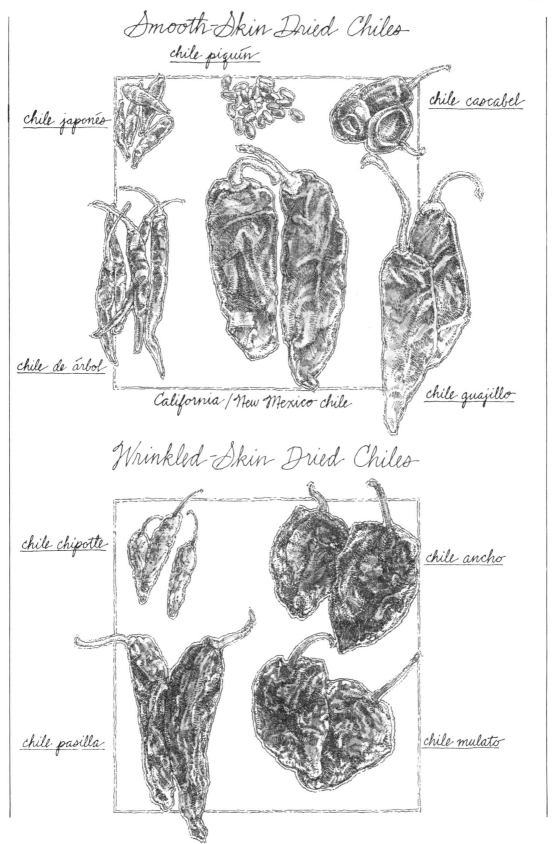

Smooth-Skin Dried Chiles

chile piquín

chile japonés

chile cascabel

chile de árbol

California / New Mexico chile

chile guajillo

Wrinkled-Skin Dried Chiles

chile chipotle

chile ancho

chile pasilla

chile mulato

chipotle meco, and they have a stronger dried-chile flavor; they're at least as hot as the *chipotles mecos* and very astringent. These are sometimes canned under the label *chipotles.*

Chile Guajillo: On the rare occasions you find *guajillos* (literally "little gourd") in a fresh state, they generally go by that same name. This burgundy-colored dried chile comes in a range of sizes (depending on the exact variety), but an average one is 4½ inches, slowly tapering from a 2-inch width to a blunt point; the skin is smooth with some large wrinkles or folds, rather brittle and translucent. An average *guajillo* weighs about ¼ ounce. Always look for unbroken *guajillos* that are not too brittle and that don't have any light-colored patches (which indicate that moth larvae have eaten away the flesh). A puree of soaked *chiles guajillos* will be an earthy, bright red with a medium-hot, nonsweet, strong, uncomplicated dried-chile flavor, a little tartness and just a hint of smokiness. Per ounce, *guajillos* gives much less pulp than *anchos;* their skin is very tough. Though this 4½-inch, not-too-hot *guajillo* (in parts of West-Central Mexico, it is called *mirasol*) is the most common variety, there is frequently available a much hotter, thinner, slightly smaller, more pointed *guajillo pulla* (literally "taunting *guajillo*"). And in parts of West-Central and Northern Mexico, a chile is available that looks like (and is described by many market vendors as) a large, completely mild *guajillo;* it is very similar to the New Mexico/California variety. Regional names for the latter are listed under New Mexico/California Chile.

Chile Mulato: A *mulato* (literally "dark-skinned") looks almost identical to an *ancho,* except when held up to the light: The *mulato* will then look darker. Though when fresh/green, this chile looks like a *poblano,* few are sold in that state in Mexico. Average weight and choosing considerations are the same as those for *ancho.* A puree of soaked *chiles mulatos* will be brown/black with a very full, rounded, medium-hot, nonsweet taste that is much less astringent than that of a *chile pasilla. Mulatos* yield a fair amount of pulp per ounce.

Chile Pasilla: Pasilla is the name for a dried *chile chilaca.* The long, evenly wide, blunt dried chile will range from 4 to 6 inches in length and 1 to 1½ inches in width; the skin is wrinkled like that of an *ancho,* and the color (both in the package and held up to the light) will be more or less black. An average *pasilla* weighs ⅓ ounce. Choose them as you would *anchos.* A puree of soaked *chiles pasillas* will be brown-black with reddish overtones, and it will be medium-hot to hot and have great depth and complexity of flavor that goes on and on—not at all sweet, and quite astringent. *Pasillas* yield a fair amount of pulp per ounce. Regional names include: *chile negro* (Michoacán and vicinity, plus California) and, variously, *chile pasilla negro* or *chile pasilla de México.*

New Mexico/California Chile: Some variety of this chile is available through most of West-Central and Northern Mexico under various names: *chilacate* (Guadalajara), *chilaca* (Monterrey), *de la tierra* or *colorín* (2 distinct varieties in Chihuahua), *colorado* (Sonora), *guajón* (Zacatecas), and *cascabel* (northern West-Central and Tampico—not to be confused with the small, round *cascabel*, a word meaning, literally, "jingling bells"). In its fresh state, the chile is similar to or the same as what we call a long green chile in the United States (simply *chile verde* in Mexico). This burgundy-colored dried chile is usually 6 inches long and 2 inches wide, slowly tapering to a blunt end; the skin is smooth, has less wrinkles than a *guajillo* but otherwise resembles it. An average New Mexico/California chile weighs about ⅓ ounce. Choose them as you would *guajillos*. A puree of soaked New Mexico/California chiles will be an earthy, bright red with a rather bland, uncomplicated red-chile flavor and a little tartness; most of those sold in Mexico are completely mild, though in the United States you can get some that range to quite hot. Per ounce, New Mexico/California chiles give much less pulp than *ancho;* their skin is very tough. Though some authorities say this chile is often labeled *guajillo* in the United States, I have not found it to be true.

CHILES, FRESH (*chiles frescos*): Fresh chiles, usually small hot ones, are added to a dish to give that unmistakable, sprightly, fresh capsicum character. Occasionally, the small ones are boiled or roasted on a griddle, softening them for pureeing with other cooked ingredients. Some varieties (like *jalapeños* and *güeros*) are customarily pickled. The chiles most commonly cooked before using, however, are the large ones: Their skins are blistered and removed (they are a little tougher than those of small chiles and would come off in annoying sheets in the finished dish). Then the chiles may be pureed with other ingredients to make a coarse, vegetabley sauce, but most frequently they're sliced into strips (*rajas*) to cook with meat or vegetables, or they're kept intact and stuffed through a slit in the side.

Regional Explorations:

Again, here is a selective chile tour of Mexico—at best, an evocative sketch of the fascinating complexity that remains to be explored. Mexico's favorite—at least most commonly known—fresh chiles are the large *poblano* and the small *serrano*. Of course, with only those two, Mexican food would lose a lot of its regional complexity: Most cooks know of the fat little *jalapeño* and those on the coasts (especially the Gulf) buy the tiny round, very hot, fresh *chiles piquines* (a.k.a. *amashitos* and *chiles de monte*). Small quantities of green bell peppers (*pimiento/chile morrón [verde]*) are in many markets, but to my knowledge they play no major role in traditional fare, save in the Yucatán (where they're very corrugated, quite small and called *chile dulce*). A rather narrow yellow chile is popular in Yucatán, and it (and a shorter cousin) shows up, often pickled, in markets around West-Central (and some in Central) Mexico. The Yucatán's favorite little boxy, lantern-shaped *chile habanero*, in shades from green to yellow to orange, are reported to be a thousand times hotter than *jalapeños*, but the heat dissipates rather quickly and the distinct, herbaceous flavor is remarkable. In the high elevations between Michoacán and Puebla, as well as in Chiapas, I've tasted lots of the larger, hot, boxy yellow-orange *manzano/perón* peppers. The long and slender (6 × ¾-inch) black-green, rough-looking *chile chilaca* is well utilized in parts of West-Central Mexico (as well as a few other locales). And in the Northern states, especially around Chihuahua, it's the rather flat, long, pale-green chile (like our Anaheim or California chile) that is the workhorse of the chile family.

Locating and Storing:

Almost all groceries carry *jalapeños* (and often *serranos*) nowadays, as well as the common banana peppers. *Poblanos* occasionally show up in chain supermarkets, but you'll likely have to go to a Mexican grocery to find them. Long green chiles are readily available in the Southwest. Store all fresh chiles in the refrigerator, lightly covered; most varieties will last several weeks.

Seeding and Deveining Small Uncooked Chiles:

Cut or break off the stems, cut the chiles in half lengthwise, then cut out the veins and scrape out the seeds.

Roasting Small Chiles:

Simply lay the chiles on an ungreased griddle or skillet set over medium heat, and turn until the chiles are soft (they will be blackened in places). Small chiles are occasionally roasted (or sometimes just boiled) to soften them for easy mashing or pureeing.

Roasting Large Chiles:

Though the primary purpose of roasting chiles is to loosen the skin for peeling, different methods produce different-tasting results. I can recommend three methods. (1) *To flame-roast,* hold a chile with a pair of tongs (or impale it on a fork) while you turn it very slowly over a high gas flame (some people do this over an electric burner), until the entire surface is blackened and blistered, about 1½ minutes, depending on size. (This is my favorite method because it produces the least-cooked, best-textured chile with a rustic taste; a very flavorful variation is to roast the chiles over a very hot charcoal fire, as Mexican cooks have for centuries.) (2) *To broiler-roast,* lay the chiles on a baking sheet and set them as close to a preheated broiler as possible; turn them as they blister and darken, until entirely blackened, 4 to 8 minutes, depending on the heat source and size of chiles. Because oil conducts heat so well, brushing the chiles with vegetable oil will help them blister more evenly. (3) *To oil-blister,* heat 1 inch of vegetable oil to 375°, then fry whole chiles in it, a few at a time, turning frequently until evenly blistered, 2 to 3 minutes. The chiles blister quickly but will not blacken or develop much flavor, so I recommend this method only for chiles that will be stuffed.

Peeling and Seeding Large Roasted Chiles:

Immediately place the roasted chiles in a plastic bag or damp towel to steam for a few minutes. (Steaming helps loosen the skin more fully, but it also continues to cook the chiles; don't leave the chiles in their steamy environment too long—you may even omit the steaming altogether—if you want the chiles to be quite firm.) Simply rub off the charred skin and rinse. To seed, cut off the stem, cut in half lengthwise, remove the seed pod, scrape out the seeds and cut out the white veins.

VARIETIES OF FRESH CHILES CALLED FOR IN THIS BOOK

Chile Güero: The pale-green to yellow *güero* (literally "light-skinned") chiles (a variety of which is known in the United States as banana/Hungarian wax peppers) will be about 4 to 5 inches long and 1¼ inches wide, eventually narrowing to a point; they have a squared-off shoulder with a scalloped calyx. An average *güero* weighs about 1¼ ounces. The medium-hot flesh is medium-thin and juicy, and it tastes light with a distinct floweriness. Regional names include: *xcatic* (Yucatán) and, occasionally, *chile largo.* A short, pointed *chile güero* is frequently available in the West-Central and North; it often goes by the name *caribe,* and looks like our Santa Fe chiles.

Chile Jalapeño: The medium- to dark-green *jalapeño* (literally "Jalapan") chiles will be about 2½ inches long and 1 inch wide, tapering gradually to a blunt point; they have an average shoulder and look fat. There are numerous different-size varieties, many of which have corky-looking, light-color striations covering much of the pepper (these are very evident in the dried *chipotles* and some of the pickled *jalapeños,* where the striations keep the skin from coming off). An average *jalapeño* weighs ½ ounce. The medium-hot to hot flesh is thick and juicy, and it tastes a *little* sweeter and more complex (though not necessarily better) than a *serrano.* Though they're *jalapeños* to us, most Mexican cooks know them as *cuaresmeños* or, in certain Central towns, *huachinangos* (both of which can also refer to specific subtypes); pickled ones, however, are always called *jalapeños.*

Chile Poblano: The dark-green *poblano* (literally "Pueblan") chiles will average 3½ to 4½ inches long and 3 to 3½ inches wide, tapering gradually to a point; besides their color, they are most easily recognizable by their high shoulders and sunken (technically lobate) tops, where the stem connects. An average *poblano* weighs 2½ to 3 ounces. The mild to medium-hot flesh is medium-thick and not juicy, with a rich and complex taste (especially when cooked). Choose unblemished ones that are not too twisted (which makes them difficult to roast and peel). Regional names include: *chile para rellenar* (literally "stuffing chile"— northern West-Central and northwest Mexico, among other places) and simply *chile verde* ("green chile"); in the United States I've heard them called *pasillas* (mostly California) and, occasionally, *anchos.*

Chile Serrano: The medium-green *serrano* (literally "mountain") chiles will be about 2½ inches long and ½ inch wide (though there are different-size varieties), eventually coming to a blunt point; they have virtually no shoulder and may curve toward the end. An average *serrano* weighs a little less than ⅙ ounce. The hot flesh is thin and not juicy, and it has a strong, almost grassy-tasting green-chile character that I love. It is often called simply *chile verde* in Mexico.

Long Green Chiles: These light-green, rather flat-looking chiles will measure about 6 inches long and 2 inches wide, gradually tapering to a blunt end; they may have squared-off or sloping shoulders, depending on the variety. An average

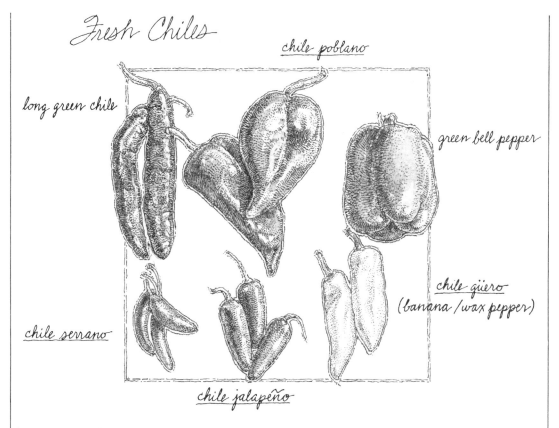

Fresh Chiles

chile poblano

long green chile

green bell pepper

chile güero
(banana/wax pepper)

chile serrano

chile jalapeño

long green chile weighs roughly 1½ to 2 ounces. The mild to medium-hot flesh is medium-thick and juicy, and its taste is rather bland but with considerably more flavor than a sweet, watery green pepper. In Northern Mexico, the only place I've ever seen them sold fresh, they're called simply *chile verde;* in the southwest part of the United States, they can be labeled Anaheim (after one of the original cultivars), California, New Mexico and mild chile pods, among other names.

CHILE, POWDERED (*chile en polvo*): For something hot, the choices are endless: There's the plain old cayenne pepper (which, apparently, is made from a variety of small hot peppers), but I don't think it has as much flavor as the powdered *chile de árbol* available in Mexican groceries. The ground *chile piquín* won't irritate the stomach, they say, but it's so hot I like to mix it with a little milder powdered *guajillo* or New Mexico/California chile. Most all of what's labeled "chile/chili powder" in the United States contains spices in addition to the powdered mild chile. Because it loses its flavor and color, buy it only in small quantities and store it in a sealed jar in a cool place.

CHICHARRONES: These are the porous, crackling-crisp, deep-fried sheets of pork rind that are available throughout Mexico—in the meat stalls in markets, from baskets on the streets and on appetizer plates in traditional restaurants.

They are one of Mexico's favorite snacks. The freshest, tenderest *chicharrones* are ones that have just been fried (you'll find them in huge golden sheets in many Mexican groceries on weekends). Most of our grocery stores carry small packages (labeled "pork rinds"), though they never seem to taste as good as the ones from Mexican stores.

CHOCOLATE: The somewhat dark, rather coarse-ground Mexican chocolate is whipped with milk or water for the classic Mexican warm beverage, and a little is ground with the spices for *mole poblano*. Mexican chocolate never completely melts as ours does. One brand or another is sold in all Mexican groceries and many chain supermarkets. I like the flavor of the commonly available Ibarra brand because it includes almonds and a good portion of cinnamon, both of which make it quite rich; the 3.3-ounce Ibarra tablets are what I've called for throughout the book. Other brands (Abuelita, Morelia, Presidencial and so forth) are fairly comparable, though the tablets of each brand are a different size. Wrapped in plastic and stored at room temperature, Mexican chocolate keeps for a year or more.

CHORIZO: This Mexican sausage is fresh pork sausage, flavored with a fair portion of dried chile, numerous spices and a good shot of vinegar. It must be cooked before eating and is generally used crumbled (it doesn't slice well after cooking). The Spanish *chorizo* occasionally available in the United States and Mexico is usually a cured sausage and doesn't really make a comparable substitute. Most Mexican groceries with butchers make their own *chorizo* (and it varies widely); other Mexican groceries often carry it frozen. Rarely is any of the North American–made *chorizo* as good as what you'll make following the recipe on page 55. Refrigerated, *chorizo* will keep for 1 week or more; frozen, it lasts several months.

CILANTRO: See Coriander, Fresh

CINNAMON (*canela*): According to a spice buyer at one of the largest packers of Mexican foodstuffs, the shaggy-looking, tightly packed, multilayered cinnamon sticks that are sold in U.S. Mexican groceries (they closely resemble those sold in Mexico) are from Ceylon, which all the authoritative spice books say produces the true cinnamon (*Cinnamomum zeylanicum*). These sticks are softer and much easier to grind than the prettier, more agressively scented, darker cinnamon sticks from the related cassia (*Cinnamomum*

Cinnamon sticks

cassia) tree. The latter are what show up in most grocery stores—ideal for use as swizzle sticks, but I don't like them much for cooking. Measurements in this book are for chunks of the shaggy-looking cinnamon stick (roughly ½ inch in diameter); it can be powdered in a mortar or with an electric spice grinder.

CITRUS FRUITS: Any peripatetic marketgoer in Mexico could write a book on the citrus varieties available: from the everyday limes, tangerines, oranges and grapefruits, to at least 3 other lime varieties, shaddocks, citrons, *china lima, naranja lima, mandarina reina,* bitter oranges and innumerable crosses. For cooking purposes, bitter oranges and limes are most important.

Bitter Oranges: Also called sour orange, Seville orange and, in Spanish, *naranja agria* (literally "sour orange"), small quantities of this large, rough-skinned fruit can be found sporadically throughout Mexico, while in Yucatán it is abundant. In most countries, these oranges are prized for their highly aromatic skin (to use in marmalade, liqueurs and the like), but in Mexico only the juice is used. To me, the juice has an unmistakable citrus flavor, a little like grapefruit with only a *hint* of orange flavor; it's nearly as tart as a lemon. Only once have I seen bitter oranges in a U.S. market, though some experts say they do show up occasionally during winter months. Without them, I make a similar-tasting substitute juice as follows:

MOCK BITTER ORANGE JUICE

YIELD: 1 generous cup

  6 tablespoons freshly squeezed lime juice
 12 tablespoons freshly squeezed grapefruit juice
 ½ teaspoon finely minced orange zest (colored part only)

Mix all the ingredients in a noncorrosive bowl and let stand 2 to 3 hours; strain to remove the zest. Use within 24 hours.

Limes: The most common variety in Mexico is the small Mexican or Key lime that turns yellow as it ripens; its juice is more tart than our darker-green Persian/Tahitian (seedless) limes. Mexican limes rarely show up in markets in the United States, except in some large Mexican communities and some parts of Florida. In Mexican Spanish, limes are called *limones,* which sounds like the English for *lemon*—but they are not lemons; there is a *limón dulce,* a sweet variety of lime, but it is not widely found. There are sweet and sour *limas,* too, distinguished by the pronounced nipple on the blossom end and very unusual taste. In the Guadalajara market, they serve the juice of the sweet *lima,* while in Yucatán, among other places, the sour *lima* is squeezed into broth to flavor it. I have found our yellow lemons sold commercially only in northwest Mexico, where they are called *limónes reales.*

COCONUTS (*cocos*): Fresh coconuts are available in grocery stores year round. Choose ones that contain lots of liquid and ones in which the 3 eyes are not soft or moldy. A good coconut will keep for several weeks in the refrigerator.

To Hull and Peel a Coconut:

Drive an ice pick (or twist a corkscrew) into 2 of the holes, then drain the liquid (what's often called "coconut water" or sometimes erroneously "coconut milk") into a cup. Place the coconut in a preheated 325° oven for 15 minutes (this loosens the flesh from the shell), crack it into large pieces with a hammer, then pry the meat from the shell. Using a small knife or a vegetable peeler, trim off the dark skin from the coconut meat; then grate or chop.

COMAL: See Cooking Equipment

COOKING EQUIPMENT: To do Mexican cooking well, there is really little out-of-the-ordinary equipment that is necessary: Most anyone who likes to cook will have the right collection of knives, pots, pans, skillets, bowls and so forth. Specifically, you'll find it useful to have an inexpensive medium-mesh sieve and, if possible, the following characteristically Mexican items.

A sampling of regional <u>cazuelas</u>

Earthenware bean pots (<u>ollas</u>)

Cooking Pots: The traditional pots are earthenware, low-fired and glazed on the inside only. Wider ones, shaped like flat-bottomed bowls, are *cazuelas* for cooking stews and such; taller ones that narrow toward the top are *ollas* for beans and soups. There are also special *ollas* for brewing coffee and beating chocolate. According to the experts, the glazes contain lead; I cook in them anyway, as the Mexicans have for centuries, but I heed the FDA's recommendation that nothing (*especially* anything acidic) should be stored in them. These even-cooking pots are made for use directly over a flame; you can "season" the pan by boiling water in it first (it's a good idea to do it every time if you use the pot infrequently), and some cooks recommend that you rub the unglazed outside with a clove of garlic to eliminate an overly earthy taste. That taste, however, is the reason most cooks like *ollas* and *cazuelas* made of *barro* ("clay"). On the other hand, they are slow to heat and quite breakable, so many cooks are switching to aluminum or enamelware (*peltre*).

And, if you're serious about equipment, take my recommendation and buy a 12-inch cast-iron skillet for frying, a large Dutch oven for braising and a large steamer for *tamales*. And keep your eye out for bright-colored serving platters and bowls; your Mexican food will look beautiful in them.

Griddles: The original griddles, called *comales* in Spanish, were made of clay; though clay griddles are still available in parts of Southern, Central and West-Central Mexico, they've mostly been replaced by flat pieces of steel—many of which remind me of well-seasoned French omelet and crepe pans. Cast-iron griddles are commonly available in the North, and that is my choice because they are easy to season and they heat so evenly.

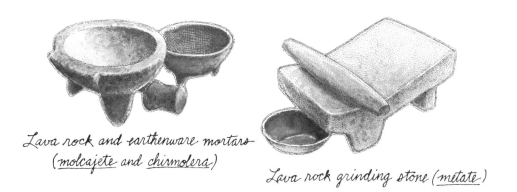

Lava rock and earthenware mortars (molcajete and chirmolera)

Lava rock grinding stone (metate)

Grinding Implements: For centuries, Mexican cooks have used the three-legged basalt mortars (*molcajetes*) and pestles (*tejolotes*) for grinding spices, tomatoes, *tomatillos* and the like; a medium-size one is about 8 inches across, 5 inches high, holds about 1 quart and is made from basalt (lava rock) that is very heavy and not too porous. Larger quantities or drier mixtures (such as corn for *masa*, reconstituted dried chiles, nuts and so on) have long been ground to a paste on a sloping, three-legged basalt *metate* (12 × 18 inches), using a basalt *mano* (resembling a slightly flattened rolling pin) to work the ingredients back and forth. The rather backbreaking grinding is done on a downward slope into a bowl that sits at the lower end. Though a blender actually chops more than grinds, it commonly replaces both the *molcajete* and the *metate* in Mexico and almost exclusively replaces them in the United States. The blades of a food processor are slower than those of a blender (they won't completely puree the harder substances like nuts, chile skins and so on), so the machine isn't terribly useful for Mexican cooking. I keep a *molcajete* out at all times, using it to pulverize small quantities of spices; an electric spice/coffee grinder works well for large quantities and for pulverizing nuts. For the adventurous cook who wants to make a sauce in the *molcajete,* first grind the hardest ingredients (like onion, garlic and fresh chile), then add the softer items (like tomatoes) and finish your work.

Tortilla Presses: Rather than improvise by pressing corn-tortilla dough between plates, I highly recommend spending the few dollars they ask for a tortilla press; the results will be in your favor. Most are cast iron or aluminum; I like the stable, heavier iron and I suggest you look for a press that shows about ⅛-inch clearance between the plates on the hinge side. In Mexico, presses made from mesquite wood are also available, especially around Guadalajara.

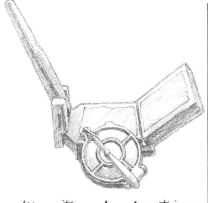

Mesquite-wood and cast-iron tortilla presses

CORIANDER, FRESH (*cilantro*): In the last half-decade, luckily, this pungently aromatic, sprightly flavored herb (not to be confused with the coriander *seeds* from the same plant) has found its way into groceries and markets nearly everywhere. It is an essential garnish for many tacos and is critical in sauces like *Salsa Mexicana* (page 35) and in *Seviche* (page 83). *Cilantro* is a fragile herb, so choose bunches that look healthy, not yellowing or wilted; the leaves should be full-grown, not feathery. All but the coarsest stems can be used. Stored in a glass of water, loosely covered with a plastic bag and refrigerated, fresh corian-

Fresh coriander (cilantro)

der will last for a week or more; bunches with roots attached will keep longer. Its aromatic flavor is diminished by cooking or drying. Pureed with vegetable oil, packed into jars, topped with a little oil and refrigerated, it can be kept for months, though a certain freshness will be lost.

CORN, DRIED FIELD (*maíz*): Though the only readily available dried corn kernels most of us know is popcorn, dried field corn (the white—occasionally yellow—nonsweet, starchy corn that is used to make the dough (*masa*) for corn tortillas or *tamales*) can be purchased in some Mexican groceries (where it is generally sold for *pozole* making). A more sure bet is to buy it from a tortilla factory (ask for *maíz seco en grano*); I've also bought dried field corn in feed stores, where it's sold for the chickens (make sure the kernels are good-looking, whole kernels and that they haven't been sprayed with anything you don't want to eat). For the prettiest, whole-kernel hominy and the best-textured *masa* for *tamales,* Mexican cooks like the large-kerneled, *maíz cacahuazincle;* unfortunately, I haven't seen it for sale in the United States. Whole dried blue corn, which can be purchased in parts of our Southwest (and in some specialty food shops), is another variety of starchy field corn and is sometimes used for tortilla dough. Stored tightly covered in a dry place, field corn will keep for at least 1 year.

CORNHUSKS (*hojas de maíz*): These dried husks from the large ears of field corn are used to wrap *tamales* (and occasionally other food) in Mexico. Some chain supermarkets and nearly all Mexican groceries carry them. Choose the longest ones and make sure they're not bug-eaten or ripped. Wrapped and stored in a dry place, they will keep at least 1 year.

Epazote

EPAZOTE: This is a pungent-smelling, jagged-leaf herb/weed, growing about 2½ feet high. You may very likely have pulled it out of your garden: Many gardeners call it pigweed; English-speaking herbalists call it wormseed, Jerusalem oak and pazote, among other names, and they use it as an anthelmintic. It is rarely used in Northern and West-Central cooking; elsewhere it is famous with black beans, in cheese *quesadillas* and in certain *moles* and to-mato or *tomatillo* sauces. Some say it is an ac-quired taste; in any case, many dishes lack a certain authenticity of flavor without it. In Yucatán, it is called *apazote*. Occasionally, *epazote* can be found along with other produce in large Mexican communities: in Los Angeles, I rarely saw it (though it grew as a weed in the flower bed outside my apartment); in Chicago, it shows up frequently in the larger Mexican groceries, and in Cleveland, it was overtaking a friend's garden. I have air-dried it with only minor loss of flavor, and now I've discovered a local spice company doing the same (roughly, a generous teaspoon of crumbled dried leaves equals 1 branch—7 leaves—*epazote*); dried works best in cooked dishes (that is, not *quesadillas*). When sold by the herbalists, it is mostly stems. They have the *epazote* flavor, but they should only be used in beans . . . per-haps a sauce.

GUAVAS (*guayabas*): When you find fresh guavas in a well-stocked grocery store or Latin American market, they'll be plum-sized with a thin, yellowish-green skin and a salmon-colored or off-white flesh; they're ripe when just soft-ening and very aromatic. Once ripe, they may be refrigerated for several days. I think of guavas as a late fall/winter crop, but I've seen them in the markets at other times as well. What is sold as pineapple guava (it is green-skinned) is really feijoa; it has a similar taste but is unrelated.

HOJA SANTA: This large, soft leaf (*Piper sanctum*) and its immediate relatives have a complex herby-spiciness with a strong, driving, anise flavor. It is popular in Oaxaca, Chiapas, Veracruz, Tabasco and a little in Yucatán, and it changes name more frequently than any other herb I know: I've personally heard *hierba santa, acuyo, mumu, momo,* and *hoja de Santa María;* one scholarly source lists 27 common names. Unfortunately, I've never seen this herb in the United States (or found a reference to it—hence no English name), so I've developed adequate substitutes for each recipe. Should you buy some in Mexico, air-dry the leaves, then crumble them and use 1 tablespoon or more where a leaf is called for.

JAMAICA: The rather small, dried *jamaica* "flowers" are not flowers at all, but the deep-red calyxes (what cover the blossoms before they open) from a plant that goes by a variety of names. In health-food stores, look for Jamaica flowers, hibiscus flowers, roselle and Jamaica sorrel (they're the red of Red Zinger tea). In Mexican groceries look for *jamaica* or *flores de jamaica.* To make a lively-tasting drink, choose deep-crimson "flowers"; older ones lose their color and flavor. Stored tightly covered in a dry place, they will last about 1 year.

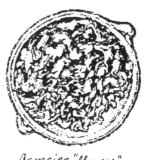

Jamaica "flowers"

JERKY (*carne seca*): In large Mexican communities, some of the butchers will make it, and in the western United States, it is not difficult to find. If you're looking for store-bought jerky for recipes in this book (instead of making your own, page 57), look for pieces with even color and no signs of frayed edges. Never buy the easily chewable "jerky" that has been chopped up and put back together like particle board. Lightly wrapped and kept in a dry place, jerky keeps for several months.

JÍCAMA: In Mexico, this brown-skinned roughly beet-shaped root vegetable is usually eaten raw, frequently with no more than a squirt of lime, a little salt and some hot powdered chile. It has a crisp texture and gentle sweetness reminiscent of fresh water chestnuts; it is more porous, though, and often sweeter, which explains its affinity with fruit. The *jícama* harvest begins in the fall in Mexico, but I've seen *jícama* in Mexican groceries and some chain supermarkets year round in the United States. The smaller ones are sweeter and won't be woody. Choose ones that are firm and show no sign of molding or shriveling.

Depending on its state when purchased, a *jícama* will keep for several weeks unwrapped in the refrigerator. An average *jícama* weighs 1 pound.

LARD AND OILS (*manteca y aceites*): In recent years, cheaper vegetable oil has begun to supplant the traditionally Mexican lard, so I have left the choice up to the cook in most recipes. Let me state perfectly plainly, though, for those of you who have developed that inexplicable squeemishness about lard, that according to the USDA, lard has *less than half* the cholesterol of ordinary, respectable butter. I use lard when I want its flavor (just as I use butter), but I always buy a rich-tasting, home-rendered one from the Mexican market. If a good lard is unavailable, render your own pork fat rather than choosing the flavorless, hydrogenated loaves of lard commonly available in grocery stores. Many kinds of vegetable oils are available in Mexico, most of them sunflower (*girasol*) or safflower (*cártamo*) oils; mixed vegetable and soy-bean oil are currently making inroads; corn oil (*aceite de maíz*) seems to be in abundant supply in western Mexico. Olive oil (*aceite de oliva*), most of which comes from northern Baja California, is rarely used in traditional public food. I've called for it in some recipes, where typical or used on occasion. Mexican olive oil is rather aggressive, in the Spanish style, so occasionally I mix it with vegetable oil.

LETTUCE (*lechuga*): Romaine (*lechuga orejona*) still seems to reign as the lettuce of preference in Mexico, though head (iceberg) lettuce (*lechuga romana* or *lechuga de bola*) is becoming more popular (especially in the North) and leaf lettuce is all you'll find in Yucatán.

LIME, SLAKED (*cal*): Not to be confused with the citrus fruit, this white powdery substance is calcium hydroxide, also known as builder's or mason's lime. The first Mexicans probably made it from burning seashells, and they used it both to set stucco and to treat dried corn, making the corn more digestible and more nutritious. North American cooks have used it to firm cucumbers before pickling (Mexicans use it in like fashion to firm fruit before candying). It is available here in builders' hardware stores (in large quantities) and in pharmacies (ask for slaked lime/calcium hydroxide powder), though I heartily recommend that you take a jar to a tortilla factory and ask them to fill it with *cal;* then you'll know you've got the right thing for making hominy and tortilla or *tamal* dough. Stored in a dry place and well sealed, it will keep indefinitely. Quicklime (calcium oxide) is also sold in markets in Mexico, in rocky-looking pieces. It must first be "slaked" by placing it in water (there will be a strong, immediate reaction and lots of bubbling) then allowing it to stand for a few minutes until all activity has stopped; this water is then used for cooking the corn.

LIMES: See Citrus Fruits

MASA: Though technically the word means "dough" in Spanish, in Mexico it is generally understood to be "corn dough," the ubiquitous dough of tortillas and *tamales*. Fresh *masa*—made from treated, soaked, ground field corn and water—can be purchased at tortilla factories in 2 ways: with a smooth consistency for making tortillas and, upon request (if you're lucky), with a coarser consistency for making *tamales*. (Be careful to differentiate between *masa para tamales* and *masa preparada para tamales*: The latter, available at some tortilla factories and large Mexican groceries, is the coarse-textured *masa* mixed with lard and flavorings.) If there is a choice, buy from a tortilla factory that makes the whitest *masa*, generally indicating that the bitter *cal* used to treat the corn has been washed off completely; the only time white doesn't equal pure is when the *masa* is made from yellow corn. For tortillas, the fresh dough should be wrapped, refrigerated and used within 1 day. If using within a few hours, there is no need to refrigerate. Even before the *masa* spoils (3 or 4 days), it will lose the plasticity crucial to making light tortillas. *Masa* for *tamales* can be frozen for a month or more, well wrapped. When fresh *masa* is called for in this book, the smooth-ground *masa* for tortillas should be used, unless otherwise indicated.

MASA HARINA: This powdery-looking meal, sold in many chain supermarkets and all Mexican groceries, is fresh corn *masa* that has been force-dried and then powdered. It is not at all the same as fine-ground corn meal, in either taste or application. It is certainly more readily available to the average cook than the quick-perishing fresh *masa*, but the flavor is a little different. The Quaker Oats brand is most common, though I have had better luck with the Maseca brand, occasionally available in Mexican groceries in the United States. Stored in a dry place and well wrapped, it will last a year or so.

METATE: See Cooking Equipment

MOLCAJETE: See Cooking Equipment

NOPAL CACTUS: See Cactus Paddles

NUTS AND SEEDS (*nueces y pepitas*): When the word *nuez* is used in Mexico, it usually refers to the native pecan. Walnuts are quite common, especially in Central Mexico, and they're called *nuez de Castilla* ("nut of Castille"). The rest of the world's nuts can show up, too, where you least expect to find them. Peanuts are a New World crop (though not truly a nut) and they're a popular street food (sprinkled with chile or entombed in caramel). In Campeche, there are cashews, though the fruit (*marañón*) seems to be more highly prized than the nut. Pumpkinseeds (that is, seeds from a great variety of green/tan pumpkins or other large squash) have been eaten by Mexicans since the dawn of history. In Mexico, they can be purchased shell-on, hulled, raw, toasted or ground, and each variety has its particularities of taste and texture. For the recipes in this book, I've called only for the hulled, untoasted, pointed, flat green pumpkinseeds that can be found in most health-food stores and nearly all Mexican groceries (they're often called simply *pepitas*). Stored in the freezer (like all nuts) and well wrapped, pumpkinseeds will last 6 months or more. They are commonly toasted before they're ground into a sauce or eaten out of hand.

OLIVE OIL: See Lard and Oils

OLLA: See Cooking Equipment

ONIONS (*cebollas*): By far, the most commonly used onion in Mexico is the white one, and you can frequently buy them just-dug, with their green tops still attached. Second most common is the red onion, but its role seems to be more as a garnish than a part of general cooking. Yellow onions seldom make an appearance . . . which I think is understandable when you taste them side by side with the white ones: The yellows have a muddy flavor compared to the clean, definitively oniony taste of the whites. As called for in this book, a small onion weighs about 4 ounces, a medium one is about 6 ounces and a large one about 8 ounces. A medium red onion weighs 8 to 10 ounces.

Fresh-dug white onions (cebollas)

OREGANO: As has happened with some other herbs and spices, the Spanish word *orégano* has become a blanket term to cover just about any herb that tastes vaguely like oregano. In the Monterrey market alone, I bought 3 different oreganos in one stall (labeled by place of origin: San Luis Potosí, Durango and Nuevo León), all of which had a very different leaf. As best I can tell, the most commonly sold variety, and the one imported to the United States as Mexican oregano, is in the verbena family: *Lippia Berlandieri* Shawer, *Lippia graveolens* H.B.K. or *Lippia Palmeria* wats; its aroma and taste are certainly distinct from the Mediterranean oregano (*Origanum vulgare* L.). Look for leaf Mexican oregano (usually including a few stems) in Mexican groceries and some health-food or specialty shops (Spice Islands even packs it); the leaves are deeply veined, ½ to ¾ inch long, with a rough, matte surface (they are a little fuzzy when fresh).

PARSLEY, FLAT-LEAF (*perejil*): In some parts of the country, it is difficult to find this very flavorful parsley, often called Italian parsley. Though the everyday curly parsley can be substituted, the flavor is much weaker.

PEPITAS: See Nuts and Seeds

Flat-leaf parsley (perejil)

PILONCILLO: This is the old-fashioned, hard, tawny-brown unrefined sugar that flavors certain traditional dishes; the name refers to the conical or truncated pyramidal shape. Other names include *panela* (used throughout the southern and southeastern states) and *panocha* (a less specific term that also covers some candies). Though all varieties taste like a particularly molassesy brown sugar, you occasionally have the choice between lighter (*blanco* or *claro*) or darker (*oscuro* or *prieto*). The most common shape for Mexican unrefined sugar (and the one most frequently imported to the United States) is a truncated cone, either small (roughly ¾ ounce) or large (about 9 ounces). The cones are very hard; I find it easiest to chop them up with a serrated knife, though chopping *piloncillo* is never easy. It is available at most Latin American groceries and occasionally it'll be mixed in with the Mexican goods in a well-stocked chain supermarket. Stored in a dry place and well wrapped, it lasts indefinitely.

Unrefined sugar (piloncillo)

PLANTAIN (*plátano macho*): This is the large, rather thickskinned cooking banana with a yellowish flesh; an average one is 9 to 11 inches long, weighing 10 to 12 ounces. It is used extensively in the Caribbean, often when green and not yet sweet (it's not unlike a potato). In Mexico, plantains are most frequently used fully ripe (soft, with an almost completely blackened skin), when they have developed their full sweetness. Most any Latin American or well-stocked grocery will carry them. They take several days to ripen, so plan ahead, but once ripe, they may be refrigerated for several days. Some will have a woody core that needs to be cut out.

PRICKLY-PEAR CACTUS FRUIT (*tuna*): This is the greenish-yellow oval fruit of the prickly pear (*nopal*) cactus; an average one is about 3 inches long and weighs about 3 ounces. It has almost imperceptibly tiny spines at nodes all over the outside, so handle it very carefully. The inner flesh is mildly sweet (with overtones of melon) and filled with tiny seeds. If you're lucky, the flesh will be a beautiful, deep-crimson/purple. They are most plentiful in the fall and in Mexican groceries. I've also seen them in run-of-the-mill supermarkets, Greek fruit stands, you

Prickly pear cactus fruit (tuna)

name it. Choose ones that are not blemished, then store them for up to a month, lightly wrapped, in the refrigerator. In a Mexican grocery, be careful not to get the *tuna agria* ("sour prickly pear," a.k.a. *xoconostle*) used in parts of Central and West-Central Mexico for flavoring soups.

PUMPKINSEEDS: See Nuts and Seeds

To Make Mexican-Style Radish Roses:

Holding a radish root-side up, use a small pointed knife to score it at ⅜-inch intervals, making each incision ⅛ inch deep and cutting from the pointed root down to the stem. Next, free a "petal" by cutting between 2 scores just below the surface (holding the blade almost parallel to the surface), starting at the root and stopping just before you reach the stem end; free the rest of the "petals" in the same way. Soak in ice water for at least ½ hour, so the "petals" will open out further and become firm.

Scoring the radish at intervals   *Slicing between the scores to release the "petals"*

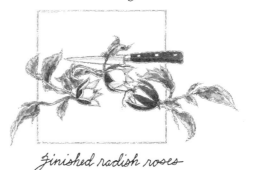

Finished radish roses

RADISHES (*rábanos*): The behemoth, long red radishes that are prized for figure carving during Oaxaca's Christmastime radish festival may be dazzling, but everyday radishes are used to decorate all kinds of Mexican food. They're often carved into roses, leaving the leafy part attached.

RICE (*arroz*): Though most Mexican cookbooks printed in the United States call for long-grain rice (and Mexico's cookbooks simply call for *arroz*), I've mostly found what looks like a medium-size grain used in Mexico. It has a meatier, less "puffy" texture when it is cooked. I like the medium grains, so that is what I recommend, and the Mexican groceries around Chicago carry at least as much medium-grain rice as they do long-grain, which says something, I think.

SEVILLE ORANGES: See Citrus Fruit

SQUASH BLOSSOMS (*flores de calabaza*): These are the long (about 5-inch) blossoms from the hard squash (like pumpkin, not zucchini) that are sold with a good-size piece of stem intact. They are not very common in the United States, except occasionally in specialty or Italian groceries; little zucchinis with blossoms still attached have lately become quite chic,

Squash blossoms (flores de calabaza)

but that's not the same. Though I've not grown them myself, one gardener tells me that you only pick the male pumpkin flowers (they won't bear fruit). When I buy them in Mexico, I use them the same day; they don't keep well.

TAMARIND PODS: These 4-inch, slightly curved, brown pods (they look like oversize bean pods) are from a tall, originally Asian tree. The very tart, rich-brown insides are used for a drink in Mexico. Look for them in many Latin American groceries and even some chain ones. When choosing tamarind pods, flex one between your hands: If it's fresh, the barklike shell will come free easily and the

Tamarind pods

pulp will be soft. If you wind up with some sticky-shelled ones, soak them in hot water for 5 minutes before peeling.

TOMATILLO: This small, plum-size, light-green, tart-tasting fruit in a papery husk comes to many fresh-produce counters (in large grocery stores as well as Mexican ones) nowadays; it is the foundation of the most common Mexican green sauces. It is closely related to the smaller, husk-wrapped ground cherry,

Tomatillos

the vines of which I've seen creeping through the wild numerous times in the United States. The husk resembles the related Chinese lantern plant "flowers." For regional names, see page 43. Always choose unblemished *tomatillos* that completely fill the husk. Loosely wrapped and refrigerated, they will last several weeks. The husks come free easily; though I've seen the fruit used raw in a sauce, it is usually simmered or dry-roasted (either inside the husk or out) until tender. An average *tomatillo* weighs 1½ ounces.

TOMATO (*jitomate* or *tomate*): This always-popular red fruit is generally sold throughout Mexico both in the round variety (*jitomate de bola*) and the pear-shaped (*jitomate guaje,* also called Roma, Italian or plum tomatoes in the United States). Through Northern Mexico and from Oaxaca over through Yucatán, the name is *tomate;* in the rest of the country, they use *jitomate.* Ripe, fresh tomatoes are essential to many Mexican dishes: pear-shaped tomatoes (to use in cooked sauces) are available year round in many of our markets (they ripen on the windowsill quite well). For a wintertime fresh *salsa mexicana,* pear-shaped are a little too pulpy, so I sometimes use ripe cherry tomatoes and squeeze out their seeds. When good, fresh tomatoes are unavailable, most cooked sauces can be made with a top-quality brand of canned tomatoes (preferably pear-shaped ones) that are packed in juice. In most public cooking, fresh tomatoes are used. For cooked stews and sauces, fresh tomatoes are usually cooked first, either by boiling (actually simmering) them until tender or by roasting them directly on a griddle; then they are peeled, cored and, for a refined dish, seeded. For garnishes and relishy *salsas,* fresh tomatoes are simply cored and chopped. As called for in this book, a medium-small tomato weighs 6 ounces, a medium-large is 8 ounces and a large weighs 10 ounces. An average pear-shaped tomato weighs 2½ ounces.

To Boil Tomatoes:

Simply place them in water to cover, bring to a boil and simmer over medium heat until tender, about 12 minutes, depending on size and ripeness. Remove with a slotted spoon, cool, gingerly peel off the skin, then cut out the core.

To Roast Tomatoes:

Roasting tomatoes directly on the griddle can make a mess (the skins stick and burn), so I usually place a sheet of foil on the griddle first, then lay on the tomatoes and turn them occasionally for about 15 minutes, depending on size and ripeness, until the flesh is soft and the skin blistered and blackened. Cool, peel away the skin and cut out the core. For a very easy, successful alternative, we owe thanks to Diana Kennedy: Lay the tomatoes on a foil-lined baking sheet, place as close to a preheated broiler as possible, and let them roast, turning once, until soft and blackened, 12 to 15 minutes, depending on size. Peel and core (and always use the tasty juice they exude during roasting). When possible, I always roast fresh tomatoes. This concentrates and enriches their flavor, while boiling just leaches it out.

TORTILLAS, CORN: Because store-bought, factory-made corn tortillas are available in many cities these days, and because they're not all created equal, here is a guide to which type of tortilla works best in the different preparations: *Chilaquiles, Other Baked/Simmered Tortilla Dishes and Soups:* Use the same kind of tortilla as for enchiladas (see below). Stale homemade ones will work here. *Crisp-Frying (Tostadas, Chips, Tacos):* Use thin tortillas made from rather coarse-ground *masa*, preferably ones that are unpuffed and somewhat dry. At a tortilla factory, you can often buy a special tortilla meeting the above description if you request tortillas for tostadas or chips. For the rolled Crispy-Fried *Tacos* (page 139), and even for tostadas and chips, thicker tortillas are frequently used in Mexico: Fried until just crisping, they make chewy, meaty tacos; crisp-fried for tostadas or chips, most North Americans would call them rather hard (and often greasy). My recommendation is never to use homemade tortillas for frying. A dozen very thin, 5½-inch tortillas weigh about 8 ounces. *Enchiladas:* Use thick and rather dry tortillas. Thick ones won't quickly disintegrate in the sauce, and dry ones won't absorb quite so much oil when they're quick-fried. Homemade ones will work here if they're flexible enough not to crack when rolled. A dozen rather thick, 5½-inch tortillas weigh about 11 ounces. *Quesadillas from Ready-Made Tortillas:* Use thick and preferably fresh tortillas: thick so they offer a substantial casing for the filling, and fresh so they taste good. Very flexible homemade tortillas will work here. *Tortillas to Serve at the Table:* Thick, fresh tortillas are best (see below for instructions concerning steam-reheating tortillas to eat out of hand); homemade ones are very good here.

To Steam-Heat Store-Bought or Homemade Corn Tortillas:
Wrap a stack of 12 tortillas in a clean, heavy towel, place in a steamer over ½ inch of water, cover and bring to a boil over medium-high heat. When steam comes puffing out from under the lid, time 1 minute, then remove from the fire and let stand 15 to 20 minutes. Held in a very low oven, the tortillas will stay warm and moist for an hour or more.

VANILLA (*vainilla*): Some would say that vanilla, the pod of a tropical orchid vine, is Mexico's most distinguished contribution to this planet's spices. The Spaniards learned of the precious stuff from the Aztecs, who had early on discovered how to repeatedly sweat and dry the pods to develop the white crystalline vanillin—a compound that isn't found in the uncured pod. Today, vines transplanted to Madagascar supply most of the vanilla in our markets, though the Mexican bean is still well respected. In Mexico, vanilla is used almost without exception in liquid form, and, I am sorry to report, little of it is pure extract. In fact, most of that famous/infamous inexpensive Mexican vanilla (like Molina and Paisa brands) gets its very distinctive "vanilla" scent from coumarin, a fragrant chemical substance that occurs in tonka beans; the FDA has banned the import of coumarin-laden vanilla to the United States because high doses of coumarin are harmful. In many Mexican resorts, *pure* vanilla extract is available for the tourists, but brands vary widely; in Papantla, Veracruz, at the heart of the chief vanilla-growing area, I've bought a good pure extract (Vai-Mex brand) as well as good vanilla beans. If you use the Mexican vanilla a la Molina, et al. (I've grown rather fond of the flavor), you'll probably want to use a little less than normal.

VEGETABLE OILS: See Lard and Oils

VINEGAR (*vinagre*): Probably the most common commercially made vinegar in Mexico (aside from distilled white) is made from pineapples; in the North, I've also seen quite a bit of apple vinegar. In the markets, however, it's not unusual to find a remarkably mild fruit vinegar made from whatever is in abundance: pineapples in Oaxaca, bananas in Tabasco and so forth from town to town. In translating recipes from cookbooks printed in Mexico, I've found that the quantities of vinegar called for frequently make an overly sharp dish; no doubt many of the recipes were written for the milder, weaker homemade stuff. I have adjusted all the recipes in this book for 5 percent acetic acid, "table strength" vinegar (all testing was done with Heinz apple-cider vinegar).

FINDING MEXICAN INGREDIENTS

Nowadays, Mexican communities dot the United States. There are little Mexican groceries, big *supermercados* and tortilla factories springing up in places that only a few years ago could offer nothing more adventurous than bottled taco sauce or a can of *jalapeños*. Many chain groceries now keep fresh coriander beside their parsley, stock several varieties of fresh peppers, and from time to time mix in fresh *tomatillos* or *jícama* or plantains with the Oriental cabbage and other new standards.

   In the notes that accompany the recipes, I've tried to reflect the current general availability of Mexican ingredients throughout much of the United States. Not all cooks, however, will find such ready access, so for them I recommend the following. First, really scour the national chain groceries (because they often carry much of the same produce and canned foods across the country, and they often have Mexican goods, even outside the Southwest). Second, look under "groceries" in the Yellow Pages and explore any that have Hispanic names (all the Mexican ones will have your basic supplies; Puerto Rican, Cuban or Central American ones will have some stock that will be of interest to you). Third, look under "tortilla factories" in the Yellow Pages (there might be one closer than you think, and it's not uncommon for them to carry groceries, too). As a last resort, order a stock of nonperishables by mail:

Casa Moneo
210 W. 14th Street
New York, NY 10011

La Preferida Inc.
3400 W. 35th Street
Chicago, IL 60632

Or order seeds for grow-your-own produce:

J. A. Mako Horticultural Enterprises
P.O. Box 34082
Dallas, TX 75234

Listing Mexican markets in cities across the United States seems superfluous to me; so many go in and out of business every week. However, several large markets that I never pass up the chance to visit are:

The Grand Central Market
317 S. Broadway
Los Angeles, CA 90013

Supermercado Cardenas
3922 N. Sheridan
Chicago, IL 60613

El Mercado
1st Avenue and Lorena
East Los Angeles, CA 90063

Casa del Pueblo
1810 Blue Island
Chicago, IL 60608

Taco shop, Mexico City

SELECTED
BIBLIOGRAPHY

Aguirre, María Ignacia. *Prontuario de cocina para un diario regular*. Mérida, Yucatán: Fonapas/Yucatán, [1832] 1980.

Andrews, Jean. *Peppers: The Domesticated Capsicums*. Austin, TX: University of Texas Press, 1984.

Arbingast, Stanley, et al. *Atlas of Mexico*. Austin, TX: Bureau of Business Research, 1975.

Barrios, Virginia B. de. *A Guide to Tequila, Mezcal and Pulque*. México, D.F.: Editorial Minutiae Mexicana, 1971.

Beltrán, Lourdes A., ed. *Doña Trini: la cocina jarocha*, 2nd ed. México, D.F.: Editorial Pax-México.

Benítez, Ana M. de. *Cocina prehispánica*. México, D.F.: Ediciones Euroamericanas, 1976.

Brillat-Savarin, Jean Anthelme. *The Physiology of Taste*. trans. M.F.K. Fisher. New York: Harcourt Brace Jovanovich, [1825] 1978.

Calderón Gómez, Sandia Marina. "Cocina regional del sureste: Campeche, Quintana Roo y Yucatán." Thesis, Escuela Superior de Administración de Instituciones, México, D.F., 1975.

Carbia, María A. de. *México en la cocina de Marichu*, 3rd ed. México, D.F.: Editorial Época, 1969.

La cocina poblana. Puebla: Editorial "Puebla," 1939.

Comida regional tabasqueña. Tabasco: Dirección de Turismo, 1984.

Cortés, Hernán. *Conquest: Dispatches of Cortés from the New World*, intro. and commentary by Irwin Blacker. New York: Grosset and Dunlap, 1962.

Crosby, Alfred W., Jr. *The Columbian Exchange: Biological and Cultural Consequences of 1492*. Westport, CT: Greenwood Press, 1972.

Díaz del Castillo, Bernal. *Historia verdadera de la conquista de la Nueva España*. Buenos Aires: Espasa-Calpe Argentina, 1955.

———. *The Conquest of New Spain*, trans. J. M. Cohen. Harmondsworth, Middlesex: Penguin Books, 1963.

Dueñas F., Mariano. *Cocina básica* (series). México, D.F.: Alfabeto Cía. Editorial.

Enciclopedia de México. México: Enciclopedia de México, 1966–1977.

Espejel, Carlos. *Mexican Folk Ceramics.* Barcelona: Editorial Blume, 1975.

Ewing, Russell C., ed. *Six Faces of Mexico.* Tucson, AZ: University of Arizona Press, 1966.

Farb, Peter and George Armelagos. *Consuming Passions: The Anthropology of Eating.* Boston: Houghton Mifflin, 1980.

Farga, Amando. *Historia de la comida en México,* 2nd ed., rev. by Robert Ayala. México, D.F., 1980.

Farga Font, José. *Cocina veracruzana y de Tabasco, Campeche y Yucatán.* México, D.F.: Editores Mexicanos Unidos, 1974.

Fernández, Beatriz L., María Yani and Margarita Zafiro. . . . *y la comida se hizo . . . ,* Vol. 1–4. México: ISSTE, 1984.

Flores de Vallado, Soledad. *Lo mejor de la cocina yucateca,* 3rd ed., Vol. 1 and 2. Mérida, Yucatán: Editorial Vallado.

Franz, Carl. *The People's Guide to Mexico.* Santa Fe, NM: John Muir Publishers, 1972.

Gastrotur. México, D.F.: Editorial Efectiva, Numbers 1–25, 28–32, March 1982– October 1984.

Guzmán de Vásquez Colmenares, Ana María. *Tradiciones gastronómicas oaxaqueñas.* Oaxaca, 1982.

Hernández F. de Rodríguez, Concepción. *Cocina y repostería práctica,* Vol. 1 and 2. Mérida, Yucatán.

Iglesias, Sonia. *Los nombres del pan en la Ciudad de México.* México, D.F.: Ediciones del Museo Nacional de Culturas Populares, 1983.

Kennedy, Diana. *The Cuisines of Mexico.* New York: Harper and Row, 1972.

———. *Recipes from the Regional Cooks of Mexico.* New York: Harper and Row, 1978.

Laborde Cancino, J. A. and P. Pozo Compodónico. *Presente y pasado del chile en México.* México, D.F.: Instituto Nacional de Investigaciones Agrícolas, 1982.

Landa, Diego de. *Yucatán Before and After the Conquest,* trans. with notes by William Gates. New York: Dover Publications, Inc., [1566] 1978.

Lawrence, D. H. *Mornings in Mexico,* intro. by Ross Parmenter. Salt Lake City, UT: Gibbs M. Smith, Inc., 1982.

El maíz, fundamento de la cultura popular mexicano. México, D.F.: Ediciones del Museo Nacional de Culturas Populares, 1982.

Mangelsdorf, Paul C. *Corn: Its Origin, Evolution and Improvement.* Cambridge, MA: Harvard University Press, 1974.

Martínez, Elviro and José A. Fidalgo. *Cocina mexicana.* México, D.F.: Editorial Everest Mexicana, 1983.

Martínez, Maximino. *Catálogo de nombres vulgares y científicos de plantas mexicanas.* México, D.F.: Fonda de Cultura Económica, 1979.

McClane, A. J. *The Encyclopedia of Fish Cookery.* New York: Holt, Rinehart and Winston, 1977.

Mena de Castro, Adela. *Cocina campechana.* Mérida, Yucatán: Editorial Zamna, 1960.

Molinar, Rita. *Antojitos y cocina mexicana.* México, D.F.: Editorial Pax-México, 1975.

———. *Dulces mexicanos.* México, D.F.: Editorial Pax-México, 1969.

Monroy, Salazar. *La típica cocina poblana y los guisos de sus religiosas,* 2nd ed. Puebla, 1945.

Morales, Ángel. *La cultura del vino en México.* Monterrey: Ediciones Castillo, 1980.

Murguía, M., ed. *Manual del cocinero, dedicado a las señoritas mexicanas.* México, D.F.: Joaquín Porrúa, [1856] 1983.

Nieto García, Blanca. *Cocina regional mexicana.* México, D.F.: Editorial Universo, 1980.

Novo, Salvador. *Cocina mexicana: o historia gastronómica de la Ciudad de México,* 3rd ed. México, D.F.: Editorial Porrúa, 1973.

Nuevo cocinero mejicano. Paris: Librería de Rosa y Bouret, 1872.

Parra, Mercedes de la. *Recetas prácticas de cocina jalisciense.* Guadalajara, Jalisco: Editorial Font, 1983.

El Patronato de Promotoras Voluntarias de la Casa Cuna del DIF/YUCATÁN. *Flor de guisos y postres tradicionales de Yucatán.* Mérida, Yucatán: Fonapas/Yucatán.

Paz, Octavio. *The Labyrinth of Solitude.* New York: Grove Press, 1961.

Portillo de Carballido, María Concepción. *Oaxaca y su cocina*. México, D.F.: Editorial Orión, 1981.

Ramos Espinosa, Alfredo. *Semblanza mexicana*. México, D.F.: Editorial Bolívar, 1948.

Ramos Espinosa, Virginia. *Los mejores platillos mexicanos*. México, D.F.: Editorial Diana, 1976.

Read, R. B. *Gastronomic Tour of Mexico*. New York: Dolphin Books, 1972.

Recetario mexicano del maíz. México, D.F.: Ediciones del Museo Nacional de Culturas Populares, 1983.

Robelo, Cecilio A. *Diccionario de aztequismos,* 3rd ed. México, D.F.: Ediciones Fuente Cultural.

Robertson, James D. *The Connoisseur's Guide to Beer*. Aurora, IL: Caroline House Publishers, Inc., 1982.

Rodríguez Rivera, Virginia. *La comida en el México antiguo y moderno*. México, D.F.: Editorial Pormaca, 1965.

Rosengarten, Frederic, Jr. *The Book of Spices*. New York: Pyramid Books, 1973.

Rozin, Elisabeth. *Ethnic Cuisine: The Flavor-Principle Cookbook*. Brattleboro, VT: The Stephen Greene Press, 1983.

Ruz Vda. de Baqueiro, Lucrecia. *Cocina yucateca,* 17th ed. Mérida, Yucatán, 1983.

Sahagún, Fray Bernardino de. *General History of the Things of New Spain,* Vol. 9, trans. and annotated by Arthur J. O. Anderson and Charles E. Dibble. Santa Fe, NM: The School of American Research, 1953.

Sánchez, Mayo Antonio. *Cocina mexicana*. México, D.F.: Editorial Diana, 1964.

Sánchez García, Alfonso. *Toluca de chorizo*. Toluca, Edo. de México: Serie de Arte Popular y Folklore, 1976.

Santamaría, Francisco J. *Diccionario de mejicanismos,* 3rd ed. México, D.F.: Editorial Porrúa, 1978.

Simon, Kate. *Mexico: Places and Pleasures*. Garden City, NY: Doubleday, 1965.

Stephens, John L. *Incidents of Travel in Yucatán,* Vol. 1 and 2. New York: Dover Publications, Inc., [1843] 1963.

Soustelle, Jacques. *Daily Life of the Aztecs on the Eve of the Spanish Conquest,* trans. Patrick O'Brian. Stanford, CA: Stanford University Press, 1961.

Taibo, Paco Ignacio, I. *Brevario del mole poblano*. México, D.F.: Editorial Terra Nova, 1981.

Velázquez de León, Josefina. *Antojitos mexicanos*. México, D.F.: Editorial Velázquez de León.

———. *Cocina de Chihuahua*. México, D.F.: Editorial Velázquez de León.

———. *Cocina de Nuevo León*. México, D.F.: Editorial Velázquez de León.

———. *Platillos regionales de la República Mexicana*. México, D.F.: Editorial Velázquez de León, 1946.

———. *Salchichonería casera*. México, D.F.: Editorial Velázquez de León, 1946.

———. *Mexican Cook Book Devoted to American Homes*. México, D.F.: Editorial Velázquez de León, 1947.

———. *Cocina de la Comarca Lagunera*. México, D.F.: Editorial Velázquez de León, 1957.

———. *Cocina de San Luis Potosí*. México, D.F.: Editorial Velázquez de León, 1957.

———. *Cocina de Sonora*. México, D.F.: Editorial Velázquez de León, 1958.

———. *Cocina de León*. México, D.F.: Editorial Velázquez de León, 1959.

———. *Viajando por las cocinas de las provincias de la República Mexicana*, 2nd ed. México, D.F.: Editorial Velázquez de León, 1972.

———. *Tamales y atoles*. México, D.F.: Editorial Velázquez de León, 1974.

———. *Cocina oaxaqueña*. México, D.F.: Editorial Universo, 1984.

Watt, Bernice K. and Annabel L. Merrill. *Composition of Foods*. Washington, DC: Consumer and Food Economics Institute, United States Department of Agriculture, 1975.

Wauchope, Robert, ed. *Handbook of Middle American Indians*, Vol. 1 and 6. Austin, TX: University of Texas Press, 1967.

Zelayarán Ramírez, Bertha. *Las 500 mejores recetas de la cocina mexicana*. México, D.F.: Gómez-Gómez Hnos. Editores.

100 recetas de pescado. Secretaria de Pesca.

INDEX